THE SEXUAL LIFE
OF SAVAGES

THE SEXUAL LIFE
OF SAVAGES

in North-Western Melanesia

An Ethnographic Account of Courtship, Marriage,
and Family Life among the Natives of the
Trobriand Islands, British New Guinea

BRONISLAW MALINOWSKI

Introduction by
ANNETTE B. WEINER

With a Preface by
HAVELOCK ELLIS

Beacon Press   Boston

Beacon Press
25 Beacon Street
Boston, Massachusetts 02108

Beacon Press books are published under the auspices
of the Unitarian Universalist Association
of Congregations in North America.

First Edition 1929
Second Edition 1931
Third Edition, with a Special Foreword, 1932
First, second, and third editions originally published by
Routledge & Kegan Paul Ltd., London
First published as a Beacon paperback in 1987
Introduction © 1987 by Beacon Press
All rights reserved
Printed in the United States of America

00 99 98 97 96   10 9 8 7 6 5

Library of Congress Cataloging-in-Publication Data

Malinowski, Bronislaw, 1884–1942.
The sexual life of savages in North-western Melanesia.

Reprint. Originally published: London: G. Routledge,
1929. With new introd.
Bibliography: p.
Includes index.
1. Ethnology—Papua New Guinea—Trobriand Islands.
2. Sex customs—Papua New Guinea—Trobriand Islands.
3. Family—Papua New Guinea—Trobriand Islands.
4. Trobriand Islands (Papua New Guinea)—Social life and
customs.   I. Title.
GN671.N5M347   1987   306.7′0995′3   86–47760
ISBN 0-8070-4607-8

To my friend
E. POWYS MATHERS

CONTENTS

Contents

Contents

LIST OF ILLUSTRATIONS

x

LIST OF ILLUSTRATIONS

Between pages

xi

LIST OF ILLUSTRATIONS

xii

INTRODUCTION
Annette B. Weiner

THE appearance of *The Sexual Life of Savages in North-Western Malanesia* was a publishing event. The *New Republic* called it "the most important single contribution in the field of primitive sexology" (Slaughter 1929, 130); *Nature* claimed that *The Sexual Life of Savages* has "an established place as a sociological classic, which in the future no serious student of culture in its broadest terms will be able to pass by" (Pitt-Rivers 1929:872). Ruth Benedict (1929, 4), writing for the *New York Herald Tribune,* said that in Malinowski's hands Trobrianders "are no wooden counters on an ethnographic diagram, but three-dimensional men and women whose ambitions and motivations we know how to understand"; the *New Statesman* called the book "unique in its character and quality . . . a classical and permanent work of reference in the general study of anthropology" (*New Statesman* 1929, x). True to the reviewers' claims, *The Sexual Life of Savages* became required reading for all serious students of anthropology. Malinowski's pioneering descriptions of Trobriand Islanders' social lives, loves, and desires were transformed into an essential part of the history of anthropological inquiry.

Malinowski, however, was not the only person at this time writing about "savages" and "sex." In the 1920s, these were sensational topics that led to speculative hypotheses about the evolution of mind and sexuality based on bits and pieces of ethnographic reports. The *New Republic*'s review of *The Sexual Life of Savages* was entitled "Savage Mentality and Sex" (Slaughter 1929), and Malinowski's book was discussed with two other new publications:

Introduction

The Mind of the Savages, by the French theologist Raoul Allier, and *Studies of Savages and Sex* by the British classical scholar Ernest Crawley. Malinowski, however, presented a radical departure. Unlike Allier and Crawley, whose work was based on scattered information collected by others, such as missionaries, travelers, and ethnographers who had spent only a few weeks or months in the field, Malinowski based his study on two years of ethnographic fieldwork during which he lived among Trobriand Islanders in their own villages.

For subsequent generations of anthropologists, Malinowski's accounts of his Trobriand fieldwork, along with his flamboyant personality and superb teaching, merged into a controversial and highly complicated legacy. Today, Malinowski's lasting influence on the field of anthropology can be measured more by the continuing controversies over every important aspect of his work. In 1957, fifteen years after his death, some of his former students, distinguished scholars in their own right, published a collection of personal and evaluative considerations of Malinowski's contributions to the scientific study of culture. These essays (Firth 1957a), overwhelmingly more critical than praising, marked only the beginning of what has become a saga in itself: the continual reassessment of Malinowski's theoretical and ethnographic shortcomings in an effort to lessen the hold that Malinowski's voice has had on generations of anthropologists. The publication of his field diaries in 1967 again ignited debate as many claimed that his personal field experiences did not match his carefully formulated directives on how an anthropologist should carry out fieldwork.[1]

Yet, despite all the disclaimers, his Trobriand ethnography continues to enthrall each generation of anthropologists through its intensity, rich detail, and penetrating revelations. The distinctive quality and tone of Malinowski's ethnographic writing remain potent, emphatically and personally instructing the reader how to enter into the lives of Trobrianders, cautioning them to beware of ethnocentric conclusions, and explaining how seemingly strange behaviors have pragmatic functions and must be understood on their own terms.

With the republication of *The Sexual Life of Savages*, this historic book introduces another generation of readers to the analytical controversies that have emerged from Malinowski's Trobriand ethnography. Is there a reason, however, aside from pedagogical value, in making *The Sexual Life of Savages* available once again? Can we learn something today from the ethnographic situation and from the historical climate in which the book was written?

By its title alone, *The Sexual Life of Savages* recalls the turbulent years in the early decades of this century when anthropologists struggled to disprove the nineteenth-century evolutionists' claims that put "savages" on a cultural level far below civilization. This was the major battle that Malinowski and others of his time, such as Franz Boas and Margaret Mead, fought and won. To read this book today is to be reminded that anthropology is inherently political because it is a discipline that makes people recognize much more than they thought they knew about human nature and its complexity. Malinowski (1922a) believed in the possibility of establishing a "New Humanism" based on the "scientific study" of the widest range of ethnographic facts, which in the course of time would give us a deeper grasp of human society and culture.[2] Such understanding would enhance and change our perceptions of the world and would have political consequences for the way individuals and nations dealt with each other. Malinowski never relinquished this vision of what anthropology as a scientific discipline should be. Of late, however, this perspective has become less clear as anthropologists recognize the growing complexity in the lives of the people they study while they face the dilemmas of how to make their research of consequence to those lives. Contemporary concerns with ethnographic methods have prompted some scholars to argue that, at best, the ethnographic enterprise can be described only as "fiction." [3] In this light, the reemergence of Malinowski's voice speaking about the social and sexual life of Trobrianders may serve once again to inspire confidence in what is most vital in ethnography.

Bronislaw Kasper Malinowski was born on 7 April 1884 in Kraków, Poland. His father, a prominent professor of Slavic philology, had a deep interest in Polish folklore and ethnology. As a graduate student, Malinowski entered the Jagellonian University at Kraków to pursue advanced studies in physics and mathematics, but he soon took up work in philosophy and psychology as well. In 1908, his doctorate was awarded with the highest honors in philosophy of science for his thesis entitled "On the Principle of the Economy of Thought." [4]

As a child, Malinowski suffered from poor health that continued to plague him periodically throughout his life.[5] After he finished his studies in Kraków, recurring health problems forced him to postpone further work. As a respite from his studies, he read Sir James Frazer's *The Golden Bough*, which awoke in him an abiding interest in anthropology.[6] He then enrolled in courses at the University of Leipzig with the eminent philosopher and psychologist Wilhelm Wundt and the historical economist Karl Bücher. Although he spent only three semesters at Leipzig, the interests of both scholars greatly influenced Malinowski's future direction in anthropology. Then in 1910 Malinowski went to London to work under the anthropologist Charles Seligman and the sociologist Edward Westermarck at the London School of Economics.

INTRODUCTION

To fulfill one part of his doctoral requirement, Malinowski, on the basis of published accounts, wrote *The Family among the Australian Aborigines* (1913). This study shows Westermarck's influence and foreshadows what would become the foundation for Malinowski's later work on Trobriand kinship. Spencer and Gillen's study (1904), which documented that Australian Aborigines did not recognize physiological paternity, had sparked extensive interest among anthropologists. If marriage was not based on the right to have sexual intercourse and, further, if men were thought not to play any role in biological reproduction, then how could one characterize marriage in this kind of society? Malinowski countered these arguments by showing that what some writers referred to as sexual "license" should by no means be interpreted as promiscuity. Following Westermarck, he claimed that the family was primary and even what appeared to be premarital promiscuous sexual behavior was always surrounded by social rules, such as incest taboos and kinship classifications, which prohibited such behavior with some categories of persons. Further, even if paternity was not recognized as a biological fact, the family was still a cohesive sociological unit because the nurturing role of the father was sociologically significant. Much later in Malinowski's Trobriand studies, these ideas would become central themes in *The Sexual Life of Savages*.

Malinowski's other mentor, C. G. Seligman, had done extensive survey-type field work in New Guinea, first in 1899 as a member of the famed Cambridge Expedition to Torres Straits, the first interdisciplinary study of "savage" peoples, and then in 1904 on an ethnographic tour of the Massim, i.e., the coastal areas and island populations along the eastern tip of the New Guinea mainland, including the Trobriands.[7] At the time, recording particular customs by questioning a few local informants and missionaries on board ship or at mission stations was fairly common practice, especially in this part of the world where the goal was to collect as much information as possible about unknown peoples before their traditional customs were obliterated under the impact of Western colonization.[8]

In 1914, Seligman arranged for funding so that Malinowski could pursue survey fieldwork in the southeast part of mainland British New Guinea, then under the colonial jurisdiction of Australia. Malinowski departed for Australia, but upon arriving his plans were complicated by the outbreak of World War I. As a Pole of Austrian nationality Malinowski was technically an enemy alien. Although the Australian authorities permitted him to proceed with his research, his immigration status was continually in review for the four years he remained in Australia and New Guinea.

On Seligman's advice, Malinowski embarked from Australia to undertake research among the Mailu speakers who live in coastal and island villages along the southeastern shore. He had to travel by boat from one area to another collecting ethnographic and linguistic information. From the first part of Malinowski's published diaries, we can judge how difficult this first fieldwork experience was, for his studies were delayed by problems with transport as well as by interruptions from missionaries who were actively involved in this area. Altogether, Malinowski spent a little under three months with the Mailu, the usual length of time that ethnographers then spent in the field. Upon his return to Australia, Malinowski wrote up an extensive report (1915) on Mailu customs, which, when published, fulfilled the second half of his doctoral requirement.

In Australia Malinowski again made plans to return to New Guinea and work with several other groups about whom little was known. He booked passage on a ship headed for some villages along the northeastern coast, but when the vessel made a stop at Kiriwina, the largest island of the Trobriand group, Malinowski stayed on, thereby altering the course of his work and the direction of social anthropology.[9] Malinowski spent a total of two years in residence between 1915 and 1918, returning once to Australia. In his field diaries, he wrote with a burst of bravado that he was accomplishing in the Trobriands what none of his well-known teachers and colleagues had done. He had recorded vast amounts of information and his observations were detailed over a long period of time. As he was well aware, no one in England had done this kind of in-depth fieldwork before.

When he returned for the last time from the Trobriands he lived in Melbourne, and in 1919 married Elsie Rosaline Masson, the woman he mentioned so often in his published Trobriand diaries. The couple left Australia the following year for England and then spent a year in Tenerife, in the Canary Islands, where Malinowski, with the editorial help of his wife, finished his first Trobriand monograph, *Argonauts of the Western Pacific* (1922b).[10] This book was a watershed in British social anthropology, and marked ethnology's coming of age as a scientific discipline. Malinowski s descriptions of *kula*, an overseas network of exchange relationships that link Trobrianders with people living on other islands in the Massim region, destroyed the earlier concepts of "primitive economic man" as engaging in unmotivated and simplistic economic pursuits, and illustrated that exchange and labor could be complexly organized. In the introduction, he set out the parameters of fieldwork methodology, illustrating the importance of field studies that lasted for a year or more, and cautioning that the ethnographer must learn to work in the local language and establish rapport with informants. Rules of behavior had to be situated within the practices of social and political events.

INTRODUCTION

An isolated outrigger canoe had no meaning without an understanding of who built it, who had the right to sail it, and who performed the necessary magical spells employed during its use. The cardinal rule of fieldwork, therefore, should be to see reality from "the natives' point of view."

In 1921 Malinowski began giving lectures at the London School of Economics, and in 1924 he was appointed to a readership in anthropology at the University of London (tenable at the London School of Economics). Three years later he was named to the chair in anthropology and his eminent leadership within British anthropology was assured. A brilliant teacher, Malinowski conducted renowned seminars that attracted students from many disciplines and trained a generation of distinguished British social anthropologists. He remained in London for almost twenty years, although during that time he traveled widely.

Altogether, Malinowski wrote three major monographs on the Trobriands, in addition to the publication of many essays and shorter theoretical works.[11] In addition to *The Sexual Life of Savages* (1929), his second major monograph, Malinowski wrote *Coral Gardens and Their Magic* (1935), a two-volume account of the economic, legal, and ritual activities associated with Trobriand yam cultivation. The hiatus between the publication of *Coral Gardens* (1935) and *Argonauts* (1922) marks a radical shift in which Malinowski perceived the importance of his Trobriand research in relation to the controversial issues raised by Freud's theory of psychoanalysis. Malinowski's growing interest in and criticisms of Freudian psychoanalysis made him sought out by members of psychoanalytic circles. He was a friend of Havelock Ellis, author of *Psychology of Sex*, and it was Ellis who penned the enthusiastic preface to the first edition of *The Sexual Life of Savages*. In 1926 Malinowski was invited to the United States where he attended, among other things, a psychoanalytic conference on sexology.[12] While in America he visited Ruth Benedict at Columbia, prompting her to write Margaret Mead, who was then doing fieldwork in Samoa: "He has the quick imagination and the by-play of mind that makes him a seven-days' joy. About psychoanalysis he's as skeptical as Papa Franz—nearly." (Mead 1959, 305)

To a greater extent than did Franz Boas, however, Malinowski found much of importance for anthropology in psychoanalytic theory. The open treatment of sex in psychoanalysis, shocking to many at the time, Malinowski felt was of the greatest value to science. Like Boas and some of his students such as Alfred Kroeber (1920), Malinowski refuted Freud's ethnocentric and evolutionary claims about the origins of human institutions and the notion of a "primal horde." Malinowski's book *Sex and Repression in Savage Society*, published in 1927, was his most polemical attack, and argued that Freud's theory of the universality of the Oedipus complex had to be revised because it was based on the emotional dynamics within the patriarchal Western family. In the Trobriands, Malinowski saw a different familial configuration, because Trobrianders reckon descent matrilineally. All persons are believed to be related by blood ties to their mother, their mother's mother, and so on, tracing their descent through women back to the founding ancestors. Lineage property and the authority to control it are passed through generations not from fathers to sons, as in a patriarchy, but from a woman's brother to her sons. Malinowski claimed that this difference created variations in the constitution of familial relationships that necessitated a rethinking of some of the universal claims of psychoanalysis.

During the next decade, Malinowski's interests shifted away from psychoanalytic issues to a range of other concerns. In addition to the completion of his last major Trobriand monograph, *Coral Gardens*, he devoted much attention to developing a more formalistic approach to his functional methodology, although his largely unsuccessful book *A Scientific Theory of Culture* (1945) was not published until after his death. During the 1930s Malinowski also took up more general questions of race and culture change. He traveled through South and East Africa, where he visited his students in the field and did some brief field survey work as well, which resulted in a series of essays, published posthumously as *The Dynamics of Culture Change: An Inquiry into Race Relations in Africa* (1945).

In 1935, Malinowski's wife died after suffering for many years from multiple sclerosis, leaving him with three young daughters.[13] In 1937, because of his own health problems, Malinowski left England to spend his sabbatical in the United States. With the threat of war in Europe, Malinowski was advised by the director of the London School of Economics to remain in America (Wayne 1985, 538), and he moved to New Haven when he was offered a visiting professorship at Yale University. In 1940 he married Valetta Swann, an artist, whom he had known previously in England. By then he had begun to write on topics reflecting the political crisis in Europe, and these essays on warfare, ethnicity, and nationalism were edited and published posthumously by his wife as *Freedom and Civilization* (1947).

In the summer of 1940 Malinowski began a new fieldwork project in collaboration with a Mexican research assistant, Julio de la Fuente, who later became professor at the Mexican School of Anthropology and History. Together with Valetta Swann Malinowska and De la Fuente, Malinowski spent two summers studying the Zapotec Indians' regional peasant market in Oaxaca, Mexico (Malinowski and De la Fuente 1982),[14] returning to his earlier and extensive interest in economics. At the beginning of 1942, Malinowski was appointed professor of anthropology at Yale. Tragically, on 16 May of the same year, he suffered a fatal heart attack. When Frazer died the year before, Malinowski wrote an obituary which Raymond Firth, his student and closest colleague, said could equally apply to Malinowski himself: "he had an artist's power to create with great integrative capacity a world of his own . . . and he had the true scientist's intuitive discrimination between relevant and adventitious, fundamental and secondary issues" (1981, 137).

Malinowski's creative insights and scientific discriminations are uniquely evident in *The Sexual Life of Savages*. At one level, the book, like the earlier *Argonauts*, was a demonstration of Malinowski's functional method and a general refutation of nineteenth-century ethnocentric ideas about "savage" mentality. Unlike *Argonauts*, however, *The Sexual Life of Savages* was less complete and more polemical. Originally Malinowski envisioned that the body of material he had collected on Trobriand sexuality and the family would be published in a large monograph, while he would write a small book on the subject of psychoanalysis as applied to anthropological fieldwork and would, in yet another volume, take up more directly general problems of kinship analysis. Malinowski's unpublished notes reveal an outline of chapters for a book on Freudian psychoanalysis in which he planned to critique each aspect of Freud's theory.[15] This project was never undertaken and Malinowski's attempt to revise the ethnocentric universal premises in Freudian psychoanalysis, especially in relation to the Oedipus complex, was restricted to essays published in the 1920s and later republished as the first part of *Sex and Repression in Savage Society*. The often-promised book on kinship never appeared either, although Malinowski's other unpublished notes (MY; MLSE) contain numerous outlines for such a book. Many of the chapters in *The Sexual Life of Savages* were already published as individual essays in the mid-1920s and so the book itself never held any radically new views on Trobriand kinship and the family.

Yet the publication of *The Sexual Life of Savages* represents much more than kinship analyses or the details of Trobriand love-making, for it marks the culmination of six years of enormously productive work during which Malinowski marshaled the Trobriand data as ethnographic evidence to counter two major intellectual issues of the time, both of which involved sexuality and the family, namely, the evolutionary theories of human society and Freud's theory of psychoanalysis. Sexuality, marriage, and the family had long been of primary importance in the universal evolutionary schemes that formed the basis for much of nineteenth-century anthropological writing. These controversies about the origin of the family and marriage lasted into the 1920s and made sexuality a major anthropological concern. At the same time, the publication of Freud's *Totem and Taboo* (1913) and *Three Contributions to the Theory of Sex* (1905) stirred wide interest and debate. One aspect of Freud's thought —that the conflicts and emotions surrounding the relation between an infant and its mother, father, and siblings result in the formation of unconscious feelings that later in life affect the individual's relationships to others—held potential significance for anthropological analyses. Yet from an anthropological perspective, psychoanalysis was deeply plagued by ethnocentric biases taken from evolutionary and diffusionist reconstructions of the past. Malinowski, sensitive to the need to disprove these still popular ideas about origins, and eager to give the young discipline of modern anthropology validation as a scientific endeavor, was equally aware of his own historical role in the development of the field.[16] He found in his Trobriand data the evidence that would set right the major debates about the origins of the family and the ethnocentric biases and reductionism in psychoanalysis.

Under the earlier tutelage of Westermarck, Malinowski had been well grounded in the nineteenth-century controversies surrounding sexuality and the family. Many scholars, such as Bachofen, McLennon, and Morgan, who drew primarily on antiquarian-type information that pictured "savages" living in a primoridal state of "unbridled sexual license" or in "primeval sexual communism," believed that the evolution of human society originated with promiscuity and group marriage. Their speculative reconstructions claimed that from these earliest societies matriarchy had evolved, followed by polygamy and only most recently by patriarchy and monogamous marriage. Other scholars, most notably Westermarck, had countered these theories by trying to prove that the family and individual marriage must have been primary. By the 1920s, the lines were still drawn between those, like Westermarck, who believed in the primacy of the family and monogamous marriage, and those, like Rivers and Frazer, who held to the view that the primary stages of social life began with promiscuity and group marriage.

Even in Malinowski's early publication on the Australian Aborigine family he showed which side he favored. In 1922 Malinowski reviewed Westermarck's expanded and revised study *The History of Human Marriage,* and wrote that those who held to the promiscuity hypothesis used it "constantly as a skeleton-key to open all questions of sex" (Malinowski 1922c, 119). What Malinowski saw as significant about Westermarck's study was his contention that even in the most "primitive" kinds of social groupings, feelings such as modesty, jealousy, and sexual attraction must have been present, thereby regulating sexual desires. Further, "a union between man and wife, based on personal affection springing out of sexual attachment, based on economic conditions, on mutual services, but above all on a common relation to the children, such a union is the origin of the human family" (ibid., 120).

For Malinowski, this expression of the fundamental nature of marriage and sexuality served as the basis for illuminating how Trobriand kinship functioned, and as early as 1923 he expressed this position in an essay in *Psyche*.[17] At this time, Malinowski did not reject the concern with origins, but instead took a specific position within the evolutionists' debates against those who asserted the primacy of promiscuity. Malinowski saw his task as illuminating how sexuality is transformed and organized to create a stable relationship within the family. By extension, these familial bonds would grow beyond the family to include other relatives, clan and tribal members. Thus, for Malinowski, individuals within the nuclear family unit developed their primary emotional attachments to each other which in turn served as prototypes for other more distant relationships. In evolutionary terms, the family had to be primary in all human societies. Regardless of the level of promiscuity and sexual "license" in a society, sexuality was always controlled in certain ways that orchestrated the social and legal forms of kinship relations.

Malinowski also still held to the idea that those living in "primitive" societies believed that men made no contribution to biological reproduction. Initially basing his assumptions on the early data from Australian Aborigine studies and on evidence he found for the same beliefs among the Mailu, Malinowski also discovered that Trobrianders did not believe in physical paternity either. In fact, the first essay (1916) Malinowski wrote about the Trobriands during his break from fieldwork in Australia focused on these beliefs. With his own extensive data, Malinowski could now prove his side of the "origin" argument, namely, that marriage in these societies functioned to legitimate parenthood. Malinowski's analysis of Trobriand matrilineality further revealed that, as fathers, men were nurturing and loving toward their children and did not act in an authoritarian manner, as the role of father in Western patriarchal societies mandated. Rather, the mother's brother held the position of authority and thus Malinowski opposed matriliny or "mother-right" to "father-love."

By 1910, Freud had defined the libido theory in which sex was viewed as an essential part of the personality. This theory enabled Freud to make universal assumptions about the sex drive and establish a theoretical framework for his earlier work on neurosis. In *Totem and Taboo*, Freud developed more fully his universal theory of the Oedipus complex. Arguing also that the family and individual marriage were primary in the evolution of human societies, Freud claimed that within this family, the dominance of the patriarchal father in opposition to the loving and nurturing mother was the emotional nexus for precipitating the Oedipus complex in the child.

While Malinowski was in the Trobriands, Seligman sent him some books on psychoanalysis that stimulated him to "reflect on the manner in which the Oedipus complex and other manifestations of the 'unconscious' might appear in a community founded on mother-right." [18] Not until he had finished *Argonauts*, however, did Malinowski take up the issues in which Trobriand matrilineality would play such an important role for both psychoanalysis and anthropology, and would establish him as an important "Freudian revisionist" (Stocking 1986, 35). [19] Malinowski's refutation of the universality of the Oedipus complex based on his example of the Trobriand "matrilineal nuclear complex," however, was repudiated by Ernest Jones in two papers read at scientific meetings in 1924. [20] In these essays, Jones not only rejected Malinowski's example but used the historical reconstructions of Elliot Smith and William Perry, the leaders of the diffusionist school, whose work Malinowski and others opposed, as ethnographic proof of the scientific value of psychoanalytic interpretations. The last two sections of *Sex and Repression* were Malinowski's rebuttal to Jones, criticizing his naïve assumptions based on these speculative reconstructions. The debate stayed at this polemical level, however, with each participant talking past the other, and the Trobriand example never precipitated revisions by Freud or Jones about either the Oedipus theory or psychoanalysis generally.

The issues raised by the Trobriand case continue to generate debate.[21] Recently, Melford Spiro, espousing the view of Jones and Freud, has called into question Malinowski's original analysis, stating that Malinowski's data are "slim, confusing, and contradictory" (1982, 39). Spiro then reanalyzed the Trobriand data himself and claimed that not only do Trobriand boys develop an Oedipus complex, but the complex is so strongly repressed that it becomes pathological in adult life. Therefore, according to Spiro, the Oedipus complex is far more potent in the Trobriands than it is in Western society. As a result, Trobriand men never lose their Oedipal desires to possess their mothers sexually. In adult life these repressed longings induce in them "fear and hatred of the dreaded vagina" (ibid., 129), and this pathology gives rise to many deviant behaviors where women act as the victimizers, e.g., the sexual orgies Malinowski described in *The Sexual Life of Savages*. While Malinowski made Trobrianders appear rational and pragmatic, even given adolescent indulgence and freedom in sexual behavior, Spiro reversed matters, presenting adult Trobriand men as beset by "bad mother" representations, a "sadomasochistic sexual orientation," and a "strong castration anxiety" (ibid., 141).

Spiro's claims, however, are ethnographically exaggerated and ethnocentrically biased (see Weiner 1985),[22] thus illustrating, sixty years later, exactly what Malinowski saw as most distorting and limiting in Freudian psychoanalysis.

The original Jones-Malinowski debate over the Oedipus complex, however, did not bring forth the revisions in psychoanalysis that Malinowski hoped for, and as a result he argued more emphatically that the subject of sex could not be studied in isolation but required a synthesis of all aspects of family and kinship relations. Whereas Freud reduced everything to the sexual impulse, Malinowski would prove through his ethnographic analysis of sexuality among Trobrianders the significance of social and cultural factors (1932, xxxv). As early as 1922 he wrote: "The universally human conception of sex must be explained, I think, by its function within culture rather than by mere reference to primitive psychology and the early conditions of life" (1922c, 128). He held to this view and made it the focus of *The Sexual Life of Savages*: "the problem of sex, family, and kinship presents an organic unity which cannot be disrupted" (1932, xx–xxi), for to understand adolescent sexual freedom, it is necessary to study courtship, then marriage, then the family.

What followed in *The Sexual Life of Savages* was Malinowski's final plea to the followers of psychoanalysis to broaden their investigations of sexuality. Malinowski hoped that the book would be discussed and criticized on the basis of his functioned method, for it was his methodology in the study of sexuality that would expose the flaws in psychoanalysis. Yet this was the very aspect of the book that was ignored, prompting Malinowski to write a lengthy Special Foreword to the third edition that was published in 1932. Instead of being elated over the book's excellent reception, Malinowski was disappointed. He thought that the reviewers tended to pick out only the most sensational aspects of love-making and "the notorious ignorance of primitive paternity" and therefore, they had missed the major point of the book: "its achievement in field-work and in methods of exposition" (1932, xix).

Until this time, however, Malinowski had never defined his functional methodology in any explicit way. Writing in 1926, he said that functionalism

> aims at the explanation of anthropological facts at all levels of development by their function, by the part which they play within the integral system of culture, by the manner in which they are related to each other within the system, and by the manner in which this system is related to the physical surroundings. It aims at the understanding of the nature of culture, rather than at conjectural reconstructions of its evolution or of past historical events. (1926b, 132)

Only when he had finished writing *The Sexual Life of Savages* did Malinowski begin to formulate the specifics of his functional theory of needs, in which each basic human biological need triggers a cultural response. In this way, procreation demands kinship associations, just as bodily comforts require shelter and so forth.[23] In its crystallized form, Malinowski's functional scheme became a highly reductionist view in which an individual's psychological state derived from physiological needs, which left little room in the analysis of culture for anything other than the pragmatics of individuals' behaviors. Yet, earlier, it was exactly this kind of reductionism that Malinowski himself found so limiting in psychoanalytic theory. In *The Sexual Life of Savages*, however, his functional method was directed primarily to nothing more explicit than a general theory of how to do fieldwork. This theory was to "guide and orientate the observer" to study the society as "a self-contained reality" (1932, xxxi).

By using the concept of functionalism only as the empirical means to comprehend and analyze all aspects of Trobriand sexuality within the context of Trobriand kinship, Malinowski thought that he could illuminate the reductionism in psychoanalytic theory. A *cultural* account of sexuality was of absolute necessity for any psychological study of sexual life. Today, this idea seems obvious, yet in 1929 it was a radical position.[24] It was, however, a position that Malinowski reached after having confronted the issues surrounding evolutionary and diffusionist reconstructions. In *The Sexual Life of Savages*, Malinowski for the first time relinquished his earlier ideas on evolutionary theories. In the Special Foreword he recanted his past position on the origins of human society and noted that he had "grown more and more indifferent to the problems of origins—origins, that is, conceived in the naive way in which I treated them in my previous utterances" (1932, xxiii). Malinowski eliminated all references to evolutionary phases or historical reconstructions from the earlier essays that were incorporated into *The Sexual Life of Savages* and replaced this theoretical position with one that called for the establishment of "the laws of a process"—the regularities of growth, development, and their correlations.[25]

Thus *The Sexual Life of Savages* is a landmark identifying significant changes in Malinowski's theoretical approach to his ethnographic data. To read *The Sexual Life of Savages* from its *author's* point of view is to situate the ethnographic data in their historical context. Reading this book over a half century after it was first written can illuminate the way theoretical issues of that time stimulated not only certain controversies, but also Malinowski's perceptions of these issues and the revisionism in his own thinking. Malinowski's seminal idea—that the total range of fieldwork data must fit together and make sense—was, as Leach noted (1957, 120), one of his great contributions. But it was the issue of sexuality that presented Malinowski with the theoretical premises against which he could test not a total range of data, but a highly selective aspect of them. "The sex book," as Malinowski and his wife called it,[26] would differ dramatically from *Argonauts* and *Coral Gardens*, not only in subject matter, but in its theoretical grounding and purpose as well.

For all its original influence, one must still evaluate *The Sexual Life of Savages* in relation to subsequent developments in anthropology. Cultural and social anthropology has grown enormously over the past fifty years, and as it has revealed greater and greater complexity in human societies and cultures it has refuted Malinowski's narrow functional methodology. Since the 1950s, even our assumptions about Trobriand life have altered somewhat as other anthropologists have done extensive field research there, making contributions that counter and revise some of Malinowski's most cherished and well-known interpretations of Trobriand culture.[27]
Meyer Fortes, another of Malinowski's esteemed students, argued that Malinowski never wrote his promised book on Trobriand kinship because he could see kinship only as " 'the facts of sexuality, marriage, family and clanship' inter-related in 'one integral institution—the Procreative Institution of Mankind' " (1957, 162).[28] As opposed to Rivers, Radcliffe-Brown, and Fortes himself, Malinowski rejected what he repeatedly called "kinship algebra," kinship analyses achieved through the genealogical method whereby a structural ordering of relationships can be discerned. Malinowski was unwilling to change his views on kinship; he saw classificatory kinship terminologies as little more than metaphors and homonyms and he failed to appreciate jural implications that underwrite kin and affinal relationships. Fortes and others have judged such views to be the very limitation that prevented

INTRODUCTION

Malinowski from conceptualizing kinship as a theoretical issue in its own right.

Like the debates over the Oedipus complex, these issues are still controversial and reflect assumptions about kinship that themselves are historically grounded.[29] It is, however, the hiatus between the writing of *Argonauts* and *Coral Gardens* to which we must turn again. The differences between these two monographs and *The Sexual Life of Savages* take on particular meaning when we consider the most limiting problem in Malinowski's general ideas about his functional method. The essential flaw in *The Sexual Life of Savages* stems from Malinowski's separation of his interest in exchange from his interest in kinship. In writing *Argonauts*, Malinowski confronted the major issues that evolutionary theorists claimed represented the economics of "savages," who were described as self-serving and irresponsible in their rudimentary economic pursuits of gain. To combat these views, Malinowski examined labor-intensive projects such as Trobriand gardening and *kula* exchange and showed them to be rational, systematic, and highly organized. *Argonauts*, more than any other study at the time, dealt a death blow to the current ideas about a preeconomic stage of development and, subsequently, Malinowski's Trobriand data on exchange became the basis for other important theoretical positions within anthropology.[30]

Shortly after the publication of *Argonauts*, Marcel Mauss wrote his seminal essay on exchange (1923–24), stimulated in large part by Malinowski's analysis of *kula*. Mauss raised important issues about exchanges as "total social phenomena," calling attention to the fact that the thing given has embedded within it the "spirit" of the giver. Malinowski's *Crime and Custom* (1926a) was, in part, his response to Mauss, a response that rejected any symbolic configuration. For Malinowski, the pragmatics of obligatory give and take were dictated by custom. Thus custom became the legal force instigating and controlling reciprocal returns.[31] Even though Malinowski called attention to reciprocity as the maintenance of social relationships, he kept kinship and exchange theoretically isolated.

The result of this artificial separation is most succinctly represented in Malinowski's analysis of the Trobriand father, the basis of his frame of reference for Trobriand kinship. Malinowski's descriptive tag "father-love" obscured the deep economic importance of a man to his children throughout his children's lives.[32] This relationship was formed and bounded by exchange obligations that continued even after a man died. Malinowski's informants told him that throughout a man's life he is always called "stranger" (*tomakava*) by his children. They also told him that men play no biological role in the reproduction of children. Yet he also saw how nurturing men behaved toward their children and how important it was for a child to resemble its father. Further, a woman's brother played a significant role in her married life, since her sons would inherit lineage property from him rather than from their own father. The most unusual information about the whole system of familial relationships was that each year men gave their harvested yams to their married sisters rather than to their own wives. Clearly, here was a complex system that involved a social, economic, and legal ordering of relationships far different from that of Western society.

We can easily understand how Malinowski came to situate the father in a passive role in opposition to the authoritative role of his brother-in-law. It was not that the facts were only partially disclosed to him or that he had to invent his own "fiction." By taking the emotional and legal obligations between a woman, her brother, her husband, and child as the core situation, Malinowski could use

INTRODUCTION

his data to refute the intellectual issues of his time.
The same problem appears in the controversy over
Trobriand "virgin birth." [33] Procreation for Malinowski was a genetic fact and since Trobrianders
had such different assumptions about these biological processes, the question was how to relate the
ethnographic data to Trobrianders' perceptions
about sexuality and the family. Thus Malinowski
pointed out in the Special Foreword that Trobrianders have "a complicated attitude towards the
facts of maternity and paternity" (1932, xxi), in
that they lack some kinds of knowledge and have
other kinds. Because the issue of "original ignorance" of physical paternity had been so central in
Malinowski's earlier thinking, he focused almost
exclusively on making a case for the paramount
importance of the sociological role of the father.
When he gave up his concern with "origins," he
emphasized that paternity was difficult to reduce to
an either-or situation, pointing in the direction of
a more complex answer to the question of "virgin
birth."

As my own research demonstrates, Trobriand
beliefs about reproduction do revolve around dual
aspects of kinship in which matrilineal substance
is thought to be transmitted through a woman to
her child while her husband adds to this endowment with elements from his own matrilineage
(Weiner 1976; 1987). Thus, through the connection between a woman's blood and an ancestral
spirit, a child is conceived, but men are believed
to add to the birth process by continual sexual
intercourse, which contributes to the growth of the
fetus. In this way, a father's procreative role is
linked to the child's growth and development, and
this support, publicly marked by the fact that an
infant resembles its father, continues throughout
the life of the child. Only when a woman becomes
pregnant without being married does this resemblance go publicly unmarked. To do otherwise

would be dangerous because men play a role in the lives of their children that involves the ongoing circulation of precious resources that can be fully repaid only at death.

In *The Sexual Life of Savages* Malinowski wrote that if he were to describe the mortuary exchanges that took place following each death, it would necessitate an even longer book. Yet it is precisely in these exchanges that the long-term relationships between men and their children are given their due. The exchanges at death trace out the strengths and weaknesses of individual relationships and, from a societal perspective, demonstrate what is most meaningful about kinship and its relation to the political and cosmological domains. Here the role of Trobriand women is paramount. In *The Sexual Life of Savages*, Malinowski often noted the high status of Trobriand women, but he never mentioned that women manufacture and control their own wealth, which consists of banana-leaf bundles and skirts and is of the utmost importance at every death.[34] Malinowski observed the exchanges of women's wealth because he photographed them (MY; *The Sexual Life of Savages*) and even wrote in a field note (MMM) that these bundles were important at death. However, he never pursued the economic value associated with these flimsy-looking objects or noted the fact that the circulation of bundles directly affects the wealth of men. Not only is women's wealth involved in the yam harvests that men present to their sisters, but in its distribution at a death, in the form of bundles and skirts, it gives women political prominence, because through their exchanges they reproduce the most essential features of Trobriand kinship.

The answers Malinowski and I received from Trobriand informants were not so dissimilar, and it is not difficult to retrace how Malinowski analyzed what Trobrianders told him, given the issues of his time and what was then generally known about

matrilineal kinship. Had he not ignored the economics of women's wealth, he would have been far
more sensitive to the role of Trobriand men as
fathers and mothers' brothers. Yet Malinowski was
by no means the only anthropologist to think of
economics and politics as solely the priorities of
men. Only very recently have we recognized the
importance of accounting for what women control,
not only to elucidate the women's side of things but
also to learn more than we ever understood about
the men's side of things. This traditional lack of
interest in studying women, which persists in some
quarters even today, gives us a prime contemporary
example against which we can evaluate Malinowski's
fieldwork and ethnographic analyses. Despite his
imperfections, Malinowski's genius took us far beyond the boundaries of anthropology in the early
1920s. From today's perspective his fieldwork was
flawed, yet history makes us all victims of such flaws.
This is, however, the way a discipline grows. As in
all the sciences, the more we learn about a subject,
the more we refine and revise earlier assumptions.

Malinowski certainly recognized the importance of
ethnographic revision in deciding to present his
own rethinking in an appendix at the end of *Coral
Gardens* (1935, 479–81), the last part of his Trobriand magnum opus. Here Malinowski confessed
that his "most serious shortcoming" was his dismissal of how Trobrianders had been affected by European influences. For fifty years prior to Malinowski's
fieldwork, whalers, adventurers, and traders had
made the Trobriands a port of call. By the turn of
the century, missionaries and colonial government
officials were already instituting changes in Trobriand life. Yet resistance to fundamental changes,
especially regarding the practice of polygamy and
the sexual freedom of adolescents, remained strong.
In 1971, on my first field trip to the Trobriands, I
was amazed at how similar to Malinowski's descrip-

tions village life still was, and I was duly impressed when a missionary told me that he and his colleagues had given up all hope of trying to change Trobrianders' ideas about sexuality.

In 1975 the Trobriand Islands became part of the independent country of Papua New Guinea. Some young Trobrianders who have read Malinowski's books at the University of Papua New Guinea complain that Malinowski is responsible for the Trobriands being known as the "Islands of Free Love." Actually, travel agents and filmmakers have been the major contemporary promoters of this image, which still exerts a powerful attraction upon tourists, beachcombers, writers, television producers, and anthropologists. Some Trobrianders travel and work abroad and some have taken university degrees in Australia and the United States. Many young Trobrianders work and live in Port Moresby, the capital of Papua New Guinea, and even there they have transported some of their most important traditional harvest and mortuary exchanges directly to this urban setting.[35] In the Trobriands, during the months of July and August, unmarried teen-agers still adorn themselves for harvest festivities with all the care and magical preparation that Malinowski first described. Even though the missions have been able to eliminate a few of the sexual "orgies" that Malinowski described, during these months following the harvest tourists still flock to the Trobriands to witness the all-night dancing and sexual revelries that seem to come straight out of *The Sexual Life of Savages*.

If Malinowski made mistakes in his analysis of Trobriand kinship, he was brilliant in his focus on Trobriand sexuality. His major purpose was to illustrate that, despite the seemingly unbridled sexual liaisons among young people, certain rules limited their behavior and therefore, given these adolescent circumstances, marriage was not the licensing of sexual intercourse but the licensing of parenthood. Contemporary legal concerns about changes in reproductive strategies, such as surrogate motherhood, suddenly make Malinowski's ideas extremely relevant today. Furthermore, Malinowski emphasized in *The Sexual Life of Savages* that attracting lovers is not a frivolous, adolescent pastime. By focusing on the variables of exchange once again, we see that this sexual freedom is the first step toward entering the adult world, which includes not only marriage in Malinowski's sense, but also the task of learning the fine distinction between influencing others while not allowing others to gain control of one's self.

Sexual liaisons give adolescents the time and opportunity to experiment with all the possibilities and problems that adults face in creating relationships with those who are not kin. Any notion of idyllic "Islands of Free Love" misrepresents the drama and significance of adolescent life. Sexual freedom and autonomous behavior are limited by jealousy, taboos about one's public behavior, and enticement through gifts and magic spells. Individual wills clash and the achievement of resolution requires patience, hard work, and determination. The world of love-making has its own dangers and disillusionments. Young people must learn to be careful and fearless. Ultimately, one relationship leads to marriage and an adult world in which success demands productive work and networks of supporting kin. The beauty and vitality of youth, with its power of allurement, is transformed slowly into the power of seduction through wealth. After marriage the game is played not for sexual, but for political advantage. The underlying dynamics of those processes of social interaction and exchange that adolescents experiment with and gradually learn through their sexuality prepares them for an adult world where the same basic principles of desire, autonomy, and control still apply. It is no accident that adults return to draw on the power of adolescent sexuality at particular times by using the same seductive techniques of beauty and love magic to establish their power over others. As in other societies, Trobriand sexuality must be recognized as an inherent part of the political domain.

Although Malinowski's *The Sexual Life of Savages* may appear to situate us in the arguments of time past, yet, as we have seen, it is a past that has significant implications for the future. Malinowski's ethnography itself can still be appreciated on its own terms, for it makes us understand how far we have come in our own research. Yet the monograph has more than retrospective value. The search for ethnographic "truth," like the search for truth in all sciences, may be partial at any one moment, but it is the accumulation of ethnographic data and interpretations, situated in the historical context of their time, that makes ethnography a powerful tool that allows us to uncover continually and elucidate what is most significant about human beings and the cultures in which they live. In the 1920s, Malinowski wrote that anthropology was in crisis, a claim that some anthropologists make today about the current state of the discipline. Malinowski saw the future development of ethnographic investigation as "hand-maiden to a general theory of human society, a theory trying to achieve a deeper grasp of human nature and of human history" (1922a, 218–19). Even though we now know that our subject matter is highly complex, these themes bear repeating today. Malinowski's voice, speaking to us through his ethnography, revitalizes our commitment to this awesome, at times elusive, but undeniably essential undertaking.

NOTES

I thank T. O. Beidelman, William E. Mitchell, and Helena Wayne for their comments on the manuscript of this introduction.

 1. The publication of Malinowski's diaries (1967) precipitated

INTRODUCTION

outraged debates among anthropologists, prompting Clifford
Geertz to acknowledge that anthropology's "archetypal field-
worker" indeed had clay feet (1967, 12). See also Clifford 1986a;
Payne 1981; Stocking 1974; 1983.

2. In his published field diaries, Malinowski first mentioned
his plan to write an article about the "new humanism" (1967,
254–55) and even to form a scientific association (ibid., 267) devoted to the study of living peoples rather than obsolete facts.

3. Clifford argues that ethnographies are "fictions" (1986b, 6).
They are not only "something made or fashioned" but also things
that are invented and made up. See also the essays in Clifford
and Marcus 1986 and Marcus and Fisher 1986. This view would
have been repugnant to Malinowski and is questionable to me, as
this essay is intended to show.

4. See Bronislaw Średniawa 1981 for a more extensive discussion of Malinowski's years of study at the University of Kraków.

5. As a child he had almost died of peritonitis and he suffered
with eye problems that almost developed into blindness. As a
result, most of his early schooling took place at home under the
direction of his mother (Wayne 1985, 530).

6. Malinowski also had been introduced to ethnography
through his father's interests and through his travels to other
parts of Europe, the Mediterranean, North Africa and the Canary
Islands (Średniawa 1981; Wayne 1985).

7. See Seligman 1910.

8. One exception in New Guinea research was the Russian
anthropologist Nickolai N. Mikloucho-Maclay, who spent almost
three years on the north coast in the 1870s. His field diaries have
recently been translated into English (Mikloucho-Maclay 1975).
In its own way, Franz Boas's year-long study (1888) among the
Central Eskimo in 1883 had already established the tradition of
long-term fieldwork in American anthropology.

9. Young (1984) discusses Malinowski's fieldwork choices and
why he decided to stay in the Trobriands.

10. See Wayne (1985, 535), who describes at length the editorial
help Malinowski received from his wife, both before and throughout thir marriage. Beginning in 1922, Malinowski and his wife,
Elsie, also planned, talked over, and edited *The Sexual Life of
Savages*, although Raymond Firth did the major editing on this
monograph (Wayne, personal communication).

11. See especially *Crime and Custom in Savage Society* (1926a);
the collection of three essays in *Magic, Science and Religion*
(1945); *The Father in Primitive Psychology* (1927a) reprinted with
revisions as chapter 1, section 1, and chapter 7 in *The Sexual Life
of Savages*; and *Sex and Repression in Savage Society* (1927b).

12. The next year he attended a sex congress in Berlin. I am
grateful to Helena Wayne, Malinowski's youngest daughter, for
this and other information.

13. See Wayne 1985 for a discussion of these years.

14. The preliminary report of this study was originally published in Spanish translation in 1957.

15. In these notes Malinowski wrote that Freud's theories are an exaggerated version of the general trend of modern psychology: Freud "gets the vital point but elaborates and exaggerates, sees himself as prophet" (MYII-26, 218).

16. From passages in his Trobriand diary (Malinowski 1967), we can observe this awareness. See also Leach 1957.

17. This essay, entitled "The Psychology of Sex and the Foundations of Kinship in Primitive Societies," (Malinowski 1923), was reprinted as *The Father in Primitive Psychology* (1927a) and was incorporated with some changes into *The Sexual Life of Savages*; see note 11 above.

18. Malinowski (1927b, 6) never noted what literature Seligman sent, but from his unpublished notes, Stocking surmises that Seligman probably sent Malinowski the book by Rivers, *Dreams and Primitive Culture*, "and a book on 'insanity from the modern point of view,' encouraging him to collect dreams from his Trobriand informants" (1986, 31).

19. See Stocking 1986 for details on Malinowski's role as "Freudian revisionist." According to Stocking (pp. 32–33), Malinowski's response to psychoanalysis may have been more than intellectual. Rivers, the most eminent figure at the time in British anthropology, died suddenly in 1922, leaving a vacuum in leadership. Stocking suggests that because Rivers had a long interest in psychoanalysis, Malinowski, in taking up psychoanalytic debates, strengthened his bid against the diffusionists William Perry and Elliot Smith, to become Rivers's successor.

20. Jones (1974) read the paper "Psycho-Analysis and Anthropology" before the Royal Anthropological Institute on 19 February 1924, and on 19 November of the same year he read "Mother-Right and the Sexual Ignorance of Savages" before the British Psycho-Analytical Society.

21. See, e.g., Fortes 1977, Róheim 1950, Parsons 1964.

22. Geertz (1984, 270–71), remarking on an earlier paper by Spiro (1978), noted that Spiro's view of universal human nature still seems to have some ethnocentric bias clinging to it. Neither Spiro nor Jones took seriously Malinowski's discussion of the relationship between a Trobriand woman and her brother and why he gave it such importance despite limited and contradictory data (see Weiner 1985; also Parsons 1964).

23. Malinowski's earliest formulation of his theory of needs can be found in the essay "Culture" (1931), and the most complete synthesis in *The Scientific Study of Culture* (1944), edited after his death from lecture notes.

24. Mead's *Coming of Age in Samoa* (1928), although not framed so directly, also was aimed in part at the Freudian posi-

INTRODUCTION

tion, and tried similarly to show the importance of cultural variables to an understanding of adolescent sexuality.

25. This reflects the changes that Malinowski made when he incorporated *The Father in Primitive Psychology* into *The Sexual Life of Savages*. See notes 11 and 17 above. Leach (1957, 125) argues that even though Malinowski recanted, in 1930 he still used an evolutionary comparison between "savage" societies and "early" societies (Malinowski 1930, 113, 123). But in his ethnographic analysis, as he made clear in the Special Foreword in 1932, he recanted his earlier position.

26. Malinowski's publishers originally wanted him to call the book *Courtship and Marriage*, but Malinowski held out for the title *The Sexual Life of Savages*. In 1928 his publishers became apprehensive about publishing the book and wanted to censor it, making the abridged part available to the general public and publishing the descriptions of sexual intercourse and so on in a separate appendix that only specialists could buy. After a confrontation with two editors, Malinowski succeeded in having it published as he wished with only a few minor deletions from section 12, chapter 10 (Wayne, personal communication).

27. Field research has been done on Kiriwina Island by Hutchins (1980), J. W. Leach (e.g., 1978), Powell (e.g., 1960), and Weiner (e.g., 1976). Campbell (e.g., 1983) worked on Vakuta Island, Scoditti (1980) on Kitava Island, and Montague (e.g., 1974) and Senft (1986) on Kaileuna Island. See also Battaglia 1986 on urban harvest activities. See Uberoi 1962 for a reanalysis of *kula* based on Malinowski's data. The essays in Leach and Leach 1983 reevaluate *kula*, especially those by recent enthnographers working on other Massim Islands; see also Weiner 1983. See Watson 1956 for a correction by a Trobriander of Malinowski's ranking of chiefly lineages.

28. This view is quoted from Malinowski's essay on parenthood (1930).

29. Malinowski's analysis of Trobriand kinship sparked many long-standing controversies. See, e.g., Fortes 1957; Homans and Schneider 1955; E. R. Leach 1958; Lounsbury 1965; Needham 1962; Powell 1969a and 1969b; and Weiner 1978.

30. See Firth 1957 for a discussion of Malinowski's contributions and limitations in economic anthropology. See also Malinowski's influence on, e.g., Lévi-Strauss (1969), Polanyi (1958), and Sahlins (1972); cf. Weiner 1980.

31. In *Argonauts* (1922b), however, Malinowski was much more sensitive to the symbolic meanings that gave value to specific objects. This is most notable in his comparisons between the Crown Jewels and *kula* shells (p. 89).

32. See Weiner 1976 and 1987.

33. Within anthropology, debates continued over whether or not Trobrianders actually believed that sexual intercourse was

unnecessary for pregnancy to occur (Spiro 1968 and 1982) or whether these ideas were only abstract beliefs that no one actually accepted (E. R. Leach 1966 and 1967). See also Delaney 1986; Schneider 1968; Weiner 1974 and 1987.

34. See Weiner 1976 and 1987 for details.

35. After a high-ranking Trobriand chief died in 1982, urban Trobrianders held the traditional women's wealth distribution in Port Moresby. Battaglia (1986) reports that during 1985 Port Moresby Trobrianders grew large amounts of yams for a traditional harvest competition (see Malinowski 1935; Weiner 1987).

REFERENCES CITED

References to Malinowski's unpublished field notes are from three sources: Yale University Library (MY); the Museum of Mankind, London (MMM); and the London School of Economics (MLSE).

Battaglia, D. 1986. Urban gardens and their magic. Report submitted to the Institute for Social and Economic Study. Borkoko, Papua New Guinea.

Benedict, R. 1929. The family, with a difference. *The New York Herald Tribune Books*, Sunday, 28 July.

Boas, F. 1888. The central Eskimo. Sixth Annual Report of the Bureau of Ethnology, 399–669. Washington, D.C.: Smithsonian Institution.

Campbell, S. 1983. Kula in Vakuta: The mechanics of keda. In *The Kula: new perspectives on Massim exchange*, edited by J. W. Leach and E. Leach, 201–28. Cambridge: Cambridge University Press.

Clifford, J. 1986a. On ethnographic self-fashioning: Conrad and Malinowski. In *Reconstructing individualism*, edited by M. Sosna, D. Wellbury, and T. Heller. Stanford: Stanford University Press.

———. 1986b. Introduction: Partial truths. In *Writing culture: The poetics and politics of ethnography*, 1–26. Berkeley: University of California Press.

Clifford, J., and G. Marcus, eds. 1986. *Writing culture: The poetics and politics of ethnography*. Berkeley: University of California Press.

Delaney, C. 1986. The meaning of paternity and the virgin birth controversy. *Man*, n.s. 21:494–513.

Firth, R. 1957. The place of Malinowski in the history of economic anthropology. In *Man and culture: An evaluation of the work of Bronislaw Malinowski*, edited by R. Firth, 209–28. London: Routledge & Kegan Paul.

———, ed. 1957a. *Man and culture: An evaluation of the work of Bronislaw Malinowski*. London: Routledge & Kegan Paul.

INTRODUCTION

————. 1981. Bronislaw Malinowski. In *Totems and teachers: Perspectives of the history of anthropology*, edited by S. Silverman, 101–40. New York: Columbia University Press.

Fortes, M. 1957. Malinowski and the study of kinship. In *Man and culture: An evaluation of the work of Bronislaw Malinowski*, edited by R. Firth, 157–88. London: Routledge & Kegan Paul.

————. 1977. Custom and conscience in anthropological perspective. *International Review of Psychoanalysis* 4:127–54.

Freud, S. 1913 [1918]. *Totem and taboo.* London: A. A. Brill.

————. 1905 [1910]. *Three contributions to the study of sex.* New York: A. A. Brill.

Geertz, C. 1967. Under the mosquito net. *New York Review of Books* 9:12–13.

————. 1984. Distinguished lecture: Anti anti-relativism. *American Anthropologist* 86(2):263–78.

Homans, G., and D. Schneider. 1955. *Marriage, authority, and final causes: a study of unilineal cross-cousin marriage.* Glencoe: Free Press.

Hutchins, E. 1980. *Culture and inference: A Trobriand Island case study.* Cambridge, Mass.: Harvard University Press.

Jones, E. 1974. *Psycho-myth, psycho-history: Essays in applied psychoanalysis*, 114–73. 2 vols. New York: Hillstone Publishing.

Kroeber, A. 1920. Totem and taboo: An ethnologic psychoanalysis. *American Anthropologist* 22:48–55.

Leach, E. R. 1957. The epistemological background to Malinowski's empiricism. In *Man and culture: An evaluation of the work of Bronislaw Malinowski*, edited by R. Firth, 119–38. London: Routledge & Kegal Paul.

————. 1958. Concerning Trobriand clans and the kinship category *tabu*. In *The developmental cycle in domestic groups*, edited by Jack Goody, 120–45. Cambridge: Cambridge University Press.

————. 1966. Virgin birth. *Proceedings of the Royal Anthropological Institute*, 39–50.

————. 1967. Correspondence: Virgin birth. *Man*, n.s. 3:655–56.

Leach, J. W. 1978. The Kabisawali movement in the Trobriand Islands. Ph. D. dissertation, Cambridge University.

Leach, J. W., and E. R. Leach, eds. 1983. *The kula: New perspective on Massim exchange.* Cambridge: Cambridge University Press.

Lévi-Strauss, C. 1969. *The elementary structures of kinship.* Boston: Beacon Press.

Lounsbury, F. 1965. Another view of the Trobriand kinship categories. In *Formal Semantic Analysis*, edited by E. Hammel. American Anthropologist Special Publication 67(2):142–85.

Malinowski, B. K. 1913. *The family among Australian Aborigines.* London.

————. 1915. The natives of Mailu: Preliminary results of the Robert Mond Research Work in British New Guinea. Transactions and Proceedings of the Royal Society of South Australia 39:494–706.

————. 1916. *Baloma*: The spirits of the dead in the Trobriand Islands. *Journal of the Royal Anthropological Institute* 45. Reprinted in Malinowski 1945.

————. 1922a. Ethnology and the study of society. *Economica* 2:208–19.

————. 1922b. *Argonauts of the western Pacific: An account of native enterprise and adventure in the archipelagoes of Melanesian New Guinea*. New York: E. P. Dutton.

————. 1922c. Pioneers in the study of sex and marriage. In Malinowski 1962, 114–31.

————. 1923. The psychology of sex and the foundations of kinship in primitive societies. *Psyche* 4:98–128.

————. 1926a. *Crime and custom in savage society*. New York and London: International Library of Psychology, Philosophy, and Scientific Method. [Patterson Littlefield, Adams. 1962.]

————. 1926b. *Encyclopaedia Britannica*, 13th edition, s.v. "anthropology," 131–40.

————. 1927a. *The father in primitive psychology*. London: Psyche Miniatures.

————. 1927b. *Sex and repression in savage society*. London: International Library of Psychology, Philosophy, and Scientific Method.

————. 1929. *The sexual life of savages in north-western Melanesia: An ethnographic account of courtship, marriage and family life among the natives of the Trobriand Islands*. 1st edition. With a preface by Havelock Ellis. London: Routledge & Kegan Paul.

————. 1930. Parenthood the basis of social structure. In *The New Generation*, edited by V. F. Calverton and S. D. Schmalhausen, 113–68. London: Macaulay.

————. 1931. Culture. *Encyclopaedia of the Social Sciences*, 4:621–46. New York: Macmillan.

————. 1932. Special foreword. In *The sexual life of savages in north-western Melanesia*, xix–xliv. Third edition.

————. 1935. *Coral gardens and their magic: A study of the methods of tilling the soil and of agricultural rites in the Trobriand Islands*. 2 vols. New York: American Book Co. [Bloomington: Indiana University Press, 1965.]

————. 1944. *A scientific theory of culture and other essays*. Chapel Hill: University of North Carolina Press.

————. 1945. *The dynamics of culture change: An inquiry into race relations in Africa*. Edited by P. Kayberry. New Haven: Yale University Press.

INTRODUCTION

————. 1947. *Freedom and civilization*. Preface by Valetta Malinowska . New York: Roy Publishers.

————. 1962. *Sex, culture, and myth*. New York: Harcourt, Brace & World.

————. 1967. *A diary in the strict sense of the term*. Preface by V. Malinowska, introduction by R. Firth. New York: Harcourt, Brace & World.

Malinowski, B., and J. de la Fuente. 1982. *Malinowski in Mexico: The economics of a Mexican market system*. Edited and introduction by S. Drucker-Brown. London: Routledge & Kegan Paul.

Marcus, G., and M. Fisher. 1986. *Anthropology as cultural critique: An experimental moment in the human sciences*. Chicago: University of Chicago Press.

Mauss, M. 1923–24. Essai sur le don: Forme et raison de l'échange dans les sociétés archaïques. In *Année Sociologique*, nouvelle série 1. Translated as *The Gift*. Ian Cunnison, trans. Glencoe, Ill.: Free Press, 1954.

Mead, M. 1928. *Coming of age in Samoa: A psychological study of primitive youth for western civilization*. New York: Morrow.

————. 1959. *An anthropologist at work: Writings of Ruth Benedict*. Boston: Houghton Mifflin.

Mikloucho-Maclay, N. 1975. *New Guinea diaries 1871–1883*. Madang, Papua New Guinea: Kristen Press.

Montague, S. 1974. The Trobriand society. Ph.D. dissertation, University of Chicago.

Needham, R. 1962. *Structure and sentiment: A test case in social anthropology*. Chicago: University of Chicago Press.

New Statesman. 1929. Sex amongst savages [anonymous review]. *Literary supplement*, 4 May, x.

Parsons, A. 1964. Is the Oedipus complex universal? The Jones-Malinowski debate revisited and a south Italian "nuclear complex." In *The psychoanalytic study of society*, vol. 3, edited by W. Muensterberger and S. Axelrad, 278–328. New York: International Universities Press.

Payne, H. C. 1981. Malinowski's style. *Proceedings of the American Philosophical Society* 125(6):416–40.

Pitt-Rivers, G. 1929. Sex in savagery. *Nature* (7 December): 870–72

Polanyi, K. 1958. The market as instituted process. In *Trade and markets in early empires*, edited by K. Polanyi, C. Arensberg, and H. W. Pearson, 243–70. New York: The Free Press.

Powell, H. A. 1960. Competitive leadership in Trobriand political organization. *Journal of the Royal Anthropological Institute* 90:118–48.

————. 1969a. Genealogy, residence, and kinship in Kiriwina. *Man*, n.s. 4:117–202.

xlvii

———. 1969b. Territory, hierarchy, and kinship in Kiriwina. *Man*, n.s. 4:580–604.

Róheim, G. 1950. *Psychoanalysis and anthropology*. New York: International Universities Press.

Sahlins, M. 1972. *Stone age economics*. Chicago: Aldine.

Scoditti, G. 1980. *Fragmenta ethnographica*. New York and Rome: Serafini Editore.

Seligman, C. G. 1910. *The Melanesians of British New Guinea*. Cambridge: Cambridge University Press.

Senft, G. 1986. *Kilivila: The language of the Trobriand Islanders*. Berlin: Mouton de Gruyter.

Schneider, D. M. 1968. Correspondence: Virgin birth. *Man*, n.s. 3:126–29.

Slaughter, J. W. 1929. Savage mentality and sex. *The New Republic*, 18 September, 129–30.

Spencer, B., and F. J. Gillen. 1904. *The northern tribes of central Australia*. London.

Spiro, M. 1968. Virgin birth, parthenogenesis, and physiological paternity: An essay in cultural interpretation. *Man*, n.s. 3:242–61.

———. 1978. Culture and human nature. In *The making of psychological anthropology*, edited by G. Spindler, 330–60. Berkeley: University of California Press.

———. 1982. *Oedipus in the Trobriands*. Chicago: University of Chicago Press.

Średniawa, B. 1981. The anthropologist as a young physicist: Bronislaw Malinowski's apprenticeship. *Isis* 72:613–20.

Stocking, G. W., Jr. 1974. Empathy and antipathy in the heart of darkness. In *Readings in anthropology*, edited by R. Darnell, 281–87. New York: Harper & Row.

———. 1983. The ethnographer's magic: The development of fieldwork in British anthropology from Tylor to Malinowski. *History of Anthropology* 1:70–120.

———. 1986. Anthropology and the science of the irrational: Malinowski's encounter with Freudian psychoanalysis. *History of Anthropology* 4:13–49.

Uberoi, J. P. Singh. 1962. *Politics of the kula ring: an analysis of the findings of Bronislaw Malinowski*. Manchester: Manchester University Press.

Watson, L. 1956. Trobriand Island clans and chiefs. *Man*, n.s. 56:164.

Wayne, H. 1985. Bronislaw Malinowski: The influence of various women on his life and works. *American Ethnologist* 12(3): 529–40.

Weiner, A. B. 1976. *Women of value, men of renown: New perspectives in Trobriand exchange*. Austin: University of Texas Press.

———. 1978. Trobriand kinship from another view: The reproductive power of women and men. *Man*, n.s. 14:328–48.

———. 1980. Reproduction: A replacement for reciprocity. *American Ethnologist* 7(1):71–85.

———. 1983. "A world of made is not a world of born": Doing kula in Kiriwina. In *The kula: New perspectives on Massim exchange*, edited by J. W. Leach and E. Leach, 147–70. Cambridge: Cambridge University Press.

———. 1985. Oedipus and ancestors. *American Ethnologist* 12:758–62.

———. 1987. *The Trobrianders of Papua New Guinea*. New York: Holt Rinehart and Winston.

Young, M. W. 1984. The intensive study of a restricted area, or, why did Malinowski go to the Trobriand Islands? *Oceania* 55:1–26.

PREFACE

By Havelock Ellis

THE sexual life of savages has long awaited its
natural historian. Owing to sex taboos, that
weigh at least as much on the civilized as on the
savage mind, this subject has always been veiled
in mystery. The mystery has been fascinating or
sombre according to the general attitude to savagery
that happened to prevail. In the eighteenth century
it was fascinating. That century, especially in its
French mode, virtually discovered what is loosely and
incorrectly termed " Primitive Man ", and found
his finest embodiment in the new and Paradisiacal
world of America and Oceania. These French
voyagers and missionaries (though there were some
notable but more sober-minded English and other
sailors among them) were delighted and intoxicated
as these strange manners and customs, often so
gracious and fantastic, opened out before their
astonished vision. They were incapable of understanding them, and they had no time to penetrate
below the surface, but the enthusiastic impressions
they honestly set down seemed a revelation to the
Parisian world with its own widely unlike
artificialities and conventions. Then was developed
the conception of the " noble " savage of whom
Tacitus had caught a glimpse in primeval German
forests living in " a state of Nature ". The
nineteenth century grew contemptuous of what
seemed to it Rousseau's superficial and imaginative
vision of the natural man. But Rousseau had
really been a careful student of the narratives of
explorers in his time, as there is clear evidence to
show. The conclusions he drew were not more
extravagant than those at the opposite extreme drawn

by later generations and sometimes still persisting to-day. Diderot, likewise, when he wrote his famous *Supplément au Voyage de Bougainville*, to exhibit to his fellow-countrymen the superior reasonableness in matters of sexual ethics of the Tahitian, brought forward various correct facts—already set down in the attractive narrative of the great French navigator—but misleadingly, because he was ignorant of the social framework to which they belonged.

In the nineteenth century the more sombre view prevailed. The explorers were now mainly English, and they carried with them the Anglo-Saxon Puritanism for which all sexual customs that are unfamiliar are either shocking or disgusting. " Obscene " was the word commonly used, and it was left to the reader's imagination to picture what that might mean. The sexual behaviour of savages seemed mostly unspeakable. The urethral subincision practised by some Australian tribes was mysteriously named " the terrible rite ". A similar mutilation of the nose or ear, or anywhere a little higher up or a little lower down, would not have seemed " terrible " ; but at that particular spot it aroused a shuddering and shamefaced awe.

In the twentieth century we have moved towards a calmer attitude. We are learning to view our own sex taboos a little less solemnly. At the same time we are acquiring a more scientific spirit in the investigation of the few remaining peoples yet not too completely under the influence of our own civilization, no longer regarding them with either adulation or contempt, but as valuable witnesses to unfamiliar aspects of our common human nature. The Cambridge Expedition to Torres Straits with its scientifically trained observers, and all that that expedition led to in subsequent observations in other parts of the world by such distinguished workers as Rivers and Seligman, may be regarded as a landmark. But we still pined in vain for a picture

PREFACE

of the sexual life of any unspoilt people. One or
two investigators, like Roth in Queensland, noted a
few precise objective facts of the sex life, and
more recently Felix Bryk, in his *Neger-Eros*, has
produced a valuable study of the erotic life in
Equatorial Africa, but it has not been easy to find
any really comprehensive picture.

Such a task needed, indeed, a rare combination
of qualifications ; not only a scientific equipment
but a familiarity with various new fertilizing ideas,
not always considered scientific, which have of
late been thrown into the anthropological field ;
a long and intimate knowledge of the people to be
investigated and of their language, for it is not only
in civilization that the sexual life tends to be shy
and recessive ; not least, there was required in the
investigator a freedom alike from the traditions of
Anglo-Saxon Puritanism, however estimable in
their own place, and from the almost equally
unfortunate reactions to which the revolt against
those traditions may lead.

All these qualifications are in a rare degree
combined in Dr. Malinowski : the scientific outfit,
the sensitive intelligence, the patience in observation,
the sympathetic insight. He is known by numerous
monographs on various sociological aspects of savage
culture, mostly based on his research among the
Trobriand Islanders off the east coast of New Guinea,
among whom he lived in close touch for two years.
His *Argonauts of the Western Pacific*—the original
and elaborate analysis of the peculiar *Kula* exchange
system of the Trobriands—is recognized as a
brilliant achievement of ethnographic research. It
is, indeed, more than merely ethnographic, and as
Sir James Frazer, who introduced the book, pointed
out, it is characteristic of Dr. Malinowski's method
that he takes full account of the complexity of human
nature. An institution that, at the first glance,
might seem to be merely economic, is found in his
searching hands to be not merely commercial, but

bound up with magic and ministering to the emotional and æsthetic needs of the people who exercise it.

In the field of sex, as I have remarked, it is only to-day that investigation has become possible. And this not simply because our sex taboos have at last lost something of their stringency. It is only to-day that it has here become possible to ask those right questions which, as Bacon said, are the half of knowledge. A quarter of a century ago the study of sex was merely the study of extravagant aberrations, and, outside this, just sentimental rhapsody. It has now become—accordingly as we approach it—either a field of natural history, to be studied in the ordinary spirit of the field naturalist, or else a department of psychological dynamics where forces are at play which may often be traced beneath the surface and take on strange forms and influence even those modes of activity which seem most remote from sex. In this department, the genius of Freud—as some think, in ways that are exaggerated—has given an impetus to the study of the sexual impulse and to its possible manifestations even in the myths and customs of savages. To these developments Dr. Malinowski is fully alive. He was even prepared at one time to be much more nearly a Freudian than we can now describe him. To-day he is neither Freudian nor anti-Freudian ; he recognizes the fertilizing value of Freud's ideas, and he is prepared to utilize them whenever they seem helpful in elucidating the phenomena under investigation. These phenomena he views with a charactistically wide outlook ; while not neglecting the precise technique of the erotic art among the Trobriand Islanders, he duly investigates their whole sexual life in its æsthetic, emotional, family, and social implications. Now that he has shown the way, other students doubtless will be inspired to follow. But in this field not all who are called are chosen. The special combination of needed qualifications can rarely be found, and meanwhile the opportunities are every year diminishing. It may safely be said that *The Sexual Life of Savages in North-Western Melanesia* will become a classic of which the value must increase with the passage of time.

So far I have been speaking of this work in its relation to science. But I believe that it also has wider relations. It may interest not only those who are concerned with origins and with what they may perhaps consider exotic forms of social life, but also those who are concerned with the present or the future, and the forms of social life at home.

We often overlook the fact, which is yet well established, that the rate and level of evolution are not at every point equal. We do not place the negro at the summit of human development ; but at some points he is further evolved in physical form than the white man. Or, if we take a wider range, it has long been clear that the forefoot of the horse has reached a higher stage of evolution than that of other animals in general much higher in the scale. So, also, on the psychic side, we are accustomed to regard the civilization of classic antiquity in some respects higher than our own which yet has progressed much further along other lines.

In the life of sex we are concerned with an impulse of profound interest to mankind from the first. It occupies a field, one may note, which may be cultivated even by peoples whose level of culture is, in many important respects far from high. It may even be said that an absorption in other fields of culture is actually detrimental to culture in the sexual field, and, as we know, a marvellous expansion of the mechanical arts and exalted achievements in the intellectual sphere may co-exist with a sexual culture thrust back into conventions and routines which are scarcely even regarded as open to discussion. It is possible to be sensitive and alive to achievement in the more complex human arts and yet, at the same time, remain crude in the more fundamental arts. The reverse development is also possible.

So it may happen that, in presence of the picture Dr. Malinowski here presents to us, we become aware, not only of a unique contribution to anthropological research, but of suggestions bearing on civilized life and its efforts towards social reform. The Trobriand Islanders are a small community living in a confined space ; they only supply one of the patterns of savage life, though it may well be a fairly typical pattern. When we study it we find not merely that in this field the savage man is very like the civilized man, with the like vices and virtues under different forms, but we may even find that in some respects the savage has here reached a finer degree of civilization than the civilized man. The comparisons we can thus make furnish suggestions even for the critical study of our own social life.

H. E.

SPECIAL FOREWORD TO THE THIRD EDITION

I AM writing this somewhat lengthy Foreword to the new edition of *The Sexual Life of Savages* because the book has been a disappointment to me, and that in spite of a reception on the whole extremely benevolent and encouraging. The book has appeared in four languages, with separate English and American editions ; other translations are being prepared ; the reviewers have been invariably kind and pleasant—and yet I am not satisfied. No author, I expect, ever is satisfied that his book has been taken in the spirit in which it was given, or understood as it was meant to be understood, and this is, of course, always the author's own fault.

I am disappointed in the reception of this book because I wanted it to be regarded as an achievement in field-work and in methods of exposition, an achievement—or perhaps an experiment—to be questioned, discussed, criticized, rejected in parts, but not to be ignored. But this experimental and ambitious aim has not, so far as I can judge, received the attention which I wished it to receive.

So that I want to take the opportunity of explaining this aim, that is of stating the significance of the functional method in field-work and in the synthetic description of ethnographic material.

Sex as a Cultural Force.

My object in publishing this monograph was to demonstrate the main principle of the functional method : I wanted to show that only a synthesis of facts concerning sex can give a correct idea of what sexual life means to a people. The effect of the book, on the other hand, was that merely sensational details were picked out, and wondered or laughed at, while the synthesis, the integration of details, the correlation of aspects, the whole functional mechanism in short was missed.

I intended to give a concrete example showing that a subject like sex cannot be treated except in its institutional setting, and through its manifestations in other aspects of culture. Love, sexual approaches, eroticism, combined with love-magic and the mythology of love, are but a part of customary courtship in the Trobriands. Courtship, again, is a phase, a preparatory phase, of marriage, and marriage but one side of family life. The family itself ramifies into the clan, into the relations between matrilineal and patriarchal kindred ; and all these subjects, so intimately bound up with one another, constitute really one big system of kinship, a system which controls the social relations of the tribesmen with each other, dominates their economics, pervades their magic and mythology, and enters into their religion and even into their artistic productions.

So that, starting with the problem of sex, I was led to give a full account of the kinship system, and of its function within the Trobriand culture. I have left out, or, rather, I have only briefly indicated, the linguistic aspect of the question—the ill-omened kinship nomenclatures—a subject so wildly over-discussed, so often exaggerated in records of field-work, that one is sometimes led to suspect that it is nothing but an avenue to anthropological insanity. This aspect of kinship I have reserved for publication in a separate volume, hoping that by an overdose of terminological documentation and linguistic detail I can administer a cathartic cure to social anthropology.

My main aim in this book, however, was to show that from whichever side you approach it, the problem of sex, family, and kinship presents an organic unity which cannot be disrupted. I somehow feel that the synthetic or constructive part of my book did not " get across ". Havelock Ellis saw the significance of my main argument and commented on it in the Preface. Bertrand Russell fully appreciated the functional significance of the Trobriand facts as regards paternity and made use of them in his pioneering work on *Marriage and Morals*. A brilliant American writer, Floyd Dell, used my evidence with a clear grasp of the essentials in his *Love in the Machine Age*—a book which I should like everyone to read. But apparently most other readers have not been aware of the wider purpose of my book. What has aroused general interest has been sensational details—the notorious ignorance of primitive paternity, the technicalities of love-making, certain aspects of love-magic (a subject unquestionably attractive), and one or two eccentricities of the so-called matriarchal system.

The Ignorance of Paternity and the Social Dynamics of a Native Doctrine.

The " ignorance of paternity " seems to be the most popular subject in this book. And here I feel that most of those who have commented upon my material have missed two points. First of all, the Trobrianders do not suffer from a specific complaint, an *ignorantia paternitatis*. What we actually find among them is a complicated attitude towards the facts of maternity and paternity. Into this attitude there enter certain elements of positive knowledge, certain gaps in embryological information. These cognitive ingredients again are overlaid by beliefs of an animistic nature, and influenced by the moral and legal principles of the community and by the sentimental leanings of the individual.

The second point which I should like emphatically to make here is that in this book I am not pronouncing any opinion as to whether there was any " original ignorance of paternity " throughout primitive mankind and whether the Trobrianders still suffer from it ; or whether what they believe is the result of the direct influence of the matrilineal system of social organization upon their physiological knowledge. I have contributed towards the confusion perhaps by committing myself in a previous publication to the view that the Trobrianders represent the state of " original ignorance ". This was as early as 1916, when, in an article published in the *Journal of the Royal Anthropological Institute*, I. gave the preliminary statement about the Trobrianders' beliefs concerning reincarnation and procreative processes. I still believe that most of what I said there was plausible, but as a fieldworker I should have made my theoretical conjectures entirely distinct from my descriptions of fact, and there is no doubt that I committed myself then to certain evolutionary views, which at present I regard as irrelevant, even though unimpeachable.

An Evolutionist's Recantation.

This, I think, is a good opportunity of making a clean breast of it in the form of a recantation. In 1916 I defended the evolutionary thesis of Sidney Hartland about the universal ignorance of paternity in primitive mankind. I also tried to prove that the Trobrianders as well as a number of other peoples in New Guinea and Central Australia are still under the sway of this primitive ignorance of paternity.

In 1923 and again in 1927 I reiterated " my firm conviction that the ignorance of paternity is an original feature of primitive psychology, and that in all speculations about the origins of marriage and the evolution of sexual customs, we must bear in mind this fundamental ignorance ".[1] But the reader of Chapter VII of this book, which appeared in 1929, will find no such statements about " origins ",

[1] *The Father in Primitive Psychology*, p. 93. Cf. also " The Psychology of Sex in Primitive Societies ", *Psyche*, Oct., 1923.

" primeval states ", and other fundamentals of evolutionism, not even echoes of them. The fact is that I have ceased to be a fundamentalist of evolutionary method, and I would rather discountenance any speculations about the " origins " of marriage or anything else than contribute to them even indirectly. So that the complete elimination of all evolutionary or reconstructive attitudes from this book is not merely the outcome of a greater puritanism in method, the maintenance of the sacred rule in all exposition which makes the statement of fact kept clear from any conjectural opinions. The change in my presentation of material is also due to the fact that I have grown more and more indifferent to the problems of origins—origins, that is, conceived in the naïve way in which I treated them in my previous utterances. In 1916 I was still interested in the question : " Is this state of ignorance primitive, is it simply the absence of knowledge, due to insufficient observation and inference, or is it a secondary phenomenon, due to an obscuring of the primitive knowledge by superimposed animistic ideas ? " [1] Now this problem and problems of this type have become meaningless to me. The original state of any knowledge or any belief or any ignorance must have no doubt been a complete blank. Pithecanthropus as it became man had not even language to express its interests. Evolution in this case as in any other was a gradual growth and differentiation of ideas, customs, institutions.

Professions of a Disguised Antiquarian.

I still believe in evolution, but what appears to me really relevant is not how things started or how they followed one another, but rather the statement of the elements and factors which control the growth

[1] " Baloma," *Journal of the Royal Anthropological Institute*, 1916, p. 413.

of culture and of social organization. In the present case I would ask what were the social and moral forces which could have contributed to the development of embryological knowledge or its obscuring? Under what circumstances was man likely to become aware about physiological paternity and what are the constellations which would place this knowledge on a very distant plane of interest? Now such questions, however reconstructively we put them, can only be empirically answered by the study of the mechanisms which still can be observed in present-day stone-age communities.

If we find out that ideas about procreation are invariably correlated with the reckoning of kinship; if we can establish that in patriarchal societies there is generally greater emphasis on female chastity, hence a greater opportunity for empirical correlation between the sexual act and pregnancy; if, again, we find that in patriarchal communities the father's procreative share is emotionally more important— we learn a great deal about the mechanisms of the process by which sexual relations and knowledge, marriage, and kinship must have evolved. And such information is the real foundation on which all our speculations about the development of domestic institutions have to rest. Such speculations may, at times even must, go beyond the strictly empirical basis. As long as we are aware that we move in the realm of hypothesis, of probabilities, of things imagined or tentatively reconstructed, there is no harm in flights of speculative antiquarianism.

My indifference to the past and to its reconstruction is therefore not a matter of tense, so to speak; the past will always be most attractive to the antiquarian, and every anthropologist is an antiquarian, myself certainly so. My indifference to certain types of evolutionism is a matter of method. I wish the past to be reconstructed on the foundations of sound scientific method, and science teaches us above all that we can reconstruct only when we know the regularities of a process, when we know laws of growth, development, and correlation. As long as we are ignorant of these laws and regularities, we can have only flights of imagination and not a scientific reconstruction. After we have established the laws of a process, we can then, within limits, reconstruct the past.

The Sentimental Charm, The Philosophic Interest, and The Scientific Value of Anthropology.

If I had to balance sentiment, imagination, and reason I should definitely state that romantically, that is allowing sentiment to dominate my imagination, I am a full-blooded antiquarian. Philosophically, that is allowing my reason to be swayed by imagination, the facts of anthropology attract me mainly as the best means of knowing myself. But scientifically I have to claim that unless we use the comparative method from the functional point of view, and through this obtain the laws of correlation, of cultural process, and of the relationship between various aspects of human civilization, we shall inevitably be building all our vast edifices of reconstructive hypothesis or philosophical reflection on sand.

Cuvier was able to reconstruct his antediluvian monster from a tiny bone only because he knew the correlation of the bone to the rest of the skeleton. It is in the relation between a detail of structure to the whole that its meaning and its reconstructive virtue lies, and in the science of culture to tear out a custom which belongs to a certain context, which is part of it, the very existence of which would determine all the work which it does within that context—to tear it out, to dote upon it in a collectioneering or curio-hunting spirit, leads nowhere. And in the item of culture which we study, in the doctrine of bodily identity as derived from procreation, it is only the significance of this doctrine as a basis of matrilineal descent, as determining the father's relationship to the child, and as entering more or less directly into most aspects of kinship, that we find its significance.

The hunt for origins then should lead us to the study of laws of structure, of laws of process. In recanting my evolutionary adherence to the dogma of "primitive ignorance", I am not altogether renegade from evolutionism. I still believe in evolution, I am still interested in origins, in the process of development, only I see more and more clearly that answers to any evolutionary questions must lead directly to the empirical study of the facts and institutions, the past development of which we wish to reconstruct.

The Trobriand Belief in Reincarnation.

Returning to my present views as compared to my previous interests, I have to recant my affirmation that "if we are at all justified in speaking of certain 'primitive' conditions of mind, the ignorance in question is such a primitive condition ".[1] I recant this statement precisely because I do not think that we are justified in speaking about "primitive views of man" or of anything else, using *primitive* in the absolute sense of the word. But I fully abide by my view that " a state of ignorance similar to that found in the Trobriands obtains among a wide range of the Papuo-Melanesians of New Guinea ".[2] I also abide by my view that what with the laxity in sexual conduct and its early beginning in life, the natives of the Trobriands have extremely unpropitious conditions for any empirical observations on embryology.

I said in 1916 that had the Trobrianders had favourable opportunities, they probably would have obtained a much clearer insight into the facts of impregnation than they actually have. " Given such (favourable)

[1] *Baloma*, p. 418.   [2] Op. cit., p. 414.

conditions, the natives would probably have discovered the causal connection (between copulation and pregnancy), because the native mind works according to the same rules as ours ; his powers of observation are keen, whenever he is interested, and the concept of cause and effect is not unknown to him." [1] I am still convinced that there is nothing extraordinary in the Trobrianders' incomplete realization of embryological facts.

The Trobrianders' Ignorance of Relativity.

Let me here briefly justify this theoretical conviction. I think it is rather inconsistent to get excited about the faulty knowledge of the Trobrianders when it comes to processes of sexual fertilization, while we are perfectly satisfied that they possess no real knowledge as to processes of nutrition, or metabolism, the causes of disease and health, or any other subject of natural history— that they have no correct knowledge and cannot have it. These natives, in fact, do not know very much about Einstein's theory of relativity, nor about the Newtonian laws of motion, nor yet about the systems of Copernicus and Keppler. Their knowledge of astronomy and physics is limited, their beliefs concerning anatomy and physiology crude. On botany and geology we would not expect them to give us any scientifically valid observations. Why, then, do we demand full and precise ideas on embryology ? It would be much more incredible if the natives "knew the connection between sexual intercourse and pregnancy ", as we are so often told about one tribe or another. The verb "know" in this context cannot mean "to possess correct knowledge ", it must always cover a great confusion of the elements of knowledge and ignorance.

Every open-minded reader can see from the

[1] Op. cit., pp. 417, 148.

relevant chapters of this book that the natives have a knowledge, however incomplete, of the correlation between sexual intercourse and pregnancy. Their strong matrilineal principles of law make the recognition of paternity a remote question to them, and the supernatural version of the causes of childbirth has the strongest hold on their imagination and the greatest influence on their institutional life.

The Social Function of Procreative Ideas.

I have given in this book the native theory of bodily and spiritual identity derived from procreation. I have shown how the scanty gleanings of physical and physiological fact are overshadowed by mythological beliefs concerning the reincarnation of spirits—beliefs which are embedded in their whole animistic system. My account is an answer to the questions : What are the actual facts of the Trobrianders' knowledge, beliefs, ignorances, institutionalized attitudes about maternity, paternity, and the physiological and spiritual foundations of kinship ? Incidentally, my account is a methodological challenge for future field-work. It constitutes a demand that in future we should have neither affirmations nor denials, in an empty wholesale verbal fashion, of native " ignorance " or " knowledge ", but instead, full concrete descriptions of what they know, how they interpret it, and how it is all connected with their conduct and their institutions.

There is then nothing miraculous or even unexpected in the Trobriand configuration of belief, moral conduct, embryological knowledge, and social institution as regards paternity. We might feel incredulous if we were told we could find there *perfect knowledge* or *absolute ignorance*. This is exactly what we do not find in the Trobriands. The search for such clear-cut, absolute facts in black and white seems to me always futile. The functional method insists on the complexity of sociological facts ; on the concatenation of various often apparently contradictory elements in one belief or conviction ; on the dynamic working of such a conviction within the social system ; and on the expression of social attitudes and beliefs in traditionally standardized behaviour.

The functional method, therefore, not merely leads the theory-maker to a reframing of facts, above all it drives the field-worker to new types of observation. It is thus a theory which, begun in field-work, leads back to field-work again.

As we have seen, the functional method develops the interest in the relations between isolated customs, institutions, and aspects of culture. All the ligatures which connect social and moral forces, dogmatic beliefs, ritual acts, cannot be reconstructed from the armchair—they must be discovered in the study of a native community as it lives its beliefs and as it does or does not practise its moral and legal rules.

The Functional School.

I have been speaking of the *functional method* as if it were an old-established school of anthropology. Let me confess at once : the magnificent title of the Functional School of Anthropology has been bestowed by myself, in a way on myself, and to a large extent out of my own sense of irresponsibility. The claim that there is, or perhaps that there ought to be, a new school based on a new conception of culture and that this school should be called " functional ", was made first in the article s.v. " Anthropology " in the 13th edition of *The Encyclopædia Britannica* (1926). Among the various tendencies of modern anthropology, I there claimed a special place for " the Functional Analysis of Culture ". And I briefly defined this method as follows : " This type of theory aims at the explanation of anthropological facts at all levels of development by their function, by the part which they play within the integral system of culture, by the manner in which they are related to each other within the system, and by the manner in which this system is related to the physical surroundings. It aims at the understanding of the nature of culture, rather than at conjectural reconstructions of its evolution or of past historical events." [1]

I was fully aware then that I was speaking of a New Movement, which hardly existed, and that in a way I was making myself into the captain, the general staff, and the body of privates of an army which was not yet there. The only thing which I can claim in extenuation of this act of self-appointment was that it was not done without some sense of humour.

> " Oh, I am the cook and the captain bold,
> And the mate of the *Nancy* brig :
> And the bo'sun tight
> And the midship mite
> And the crew of the captain's gig . . . ."

(. . . and, as many of my colleagues would suggest, for the same reason . . .).

But the " Functional School " has come to stay. It is now generally admitted that such a school is needed. As to myself, from the very outset of my anthropological work, I felt it was high time to precipitate into existence, to consolidate and define a tendency which, old as the hills in all studies of human culture and society, has only gradually been coming to the fore, a tendency, however, which imperatively demanded explicit recognition and reorganization. The reason for this need of a rapid crystallizing of principles is the fact that at present specialized and scientifically competent field-work among primitive peoples has to be done against time : it must be accomplished within the next few decades or never. Now the modern specialist in the field becomes aware at once that in order to do his work effectively and within the short space of time which he has at his disposal, he has to develop

---

[1] This article has been reprinted in the 14th edition of *The Encyclopædia Britannica*, s.v. "Social Anthropology."

methods, principles, and theories of a different type to those which were sufficient for the long-stay amateur or the old travelling curio-hunter. The rapid collecting of really relevant documents, the possibility during a sojourn of necessity all too short, of obtaining correct and reliable information directly from native sources, requires a special theoretical grounding.

The Functional Method as the Theory of Field-work.

Modern field-work therefore needs a theory of a purely empirical nature, a theory which does not go beyond inductive evidence, but which provides for a clear understanding of how human culture in its primitive forms works. The field-worker is bound to make mistakes, and to frame his material within a wrong perspective if he is under the obsession of any reconstructive diffusionist or evolutionary doctrines.

The scientific field-worker should study the culture of his tribe in its own right so to speak, and as a self-contained reality. The comparative work as well as reconstructive speculations on his material can be done later on from the armchair. The observations on what exists, on how it works, and what it means to the natives—the full reality of culture as it works in full swing—this has to be seized and related by the man in the field. No one will be able to accomplish it after he has left his tribe, not even the man himself.

And here a very important point has to be made: while without a theory in the right empirical sense, that is, a theory which serves to guide and orientate the observer, no effective field-work can be done, conjectural and reconstructive theories have a directly bad influence on field-work. The reconstructive theorist, whether evolutionary or diffusionist, is bound to regard every element of culture as extraneous to the context in which it is found. For the evolutionist is mainly interested in a fact as a survival of a past stage, while the diffusionist sees in it above all a mechanically conveyed importation from another geographical region. The one places it in a past time, the other in a distant space. But both remove the fact far from the actual surroundings where it now lives. Thus every element of culture, the idea, the custom, the form of organization, the word, has to be torn out of its context and fitted into some imaginary schéme.

How the Discovery of " Group Marriage " followed its Invention.

It is this isolating of loose items or " traits ", this dissecting of culture which makes the reconstructive attitude dangerous in the field. Thus, take an apparently innocent, theoretical pastime : speculations about the " origins of marriage ". One school, and a very powerful school, believes in group marriage, that is, in a state when individual marriage was unknown and instead of that human beings were sexually united into group marriage— something very immoral, terribly prurient, in fact, so unthinkable that it has never been clearly defined ! Can you imagine Morgan, the respectable Puritan of New England, entering into details of his own famous hypothesis, " group marriage," explaining how it really took place ? The fact is that Morgan never did analyse or define his fundamental categories of primitive organization : " promiscuity," " group marriage," " consanguine family," and so on. This was, perhaps, excusable, certainly comprehensible, in a man of his moral outlook and with a lack of sociological training. He was a pioneer, in many ways a great pioneer, but he was not a schooled student of human society. What is really shocking to the modern sociologist is that not one of his numerous followers ever exercised his creative imagination sufficiently to give us a clear vision and definition of those imaginary modes of human mating.

But postulated and affirmed they were, and they became an obsession to the amateur field-worker as well as to the theoretical student.

"Numerous instances" of "group marriage" were found all over the world and brought triumphantly to Morgan and laid at his puritanic doorstep. Thus we have the famous *pirrauru* institution of Central Australia made into a "form of group marriage". This was done by tearing the *pirrauru* out of its context, failing completely to inquire into its non-sexual aspects, and over-emphasizing its sexual side. By identifying in the special puritanic euphemism *sexual relations* with *marital relations*, *pirrauru* was made into "an actually existing form of group marriage". In reality this is neither marriage nor a group relationship, but a form of seriatim cicisbeism (cf. my *Family among the Australian Aborigines*, ch. v, 1913). And all this happened because the writers who were describing it were looking for "traces of group marriage", and were not interested in a full all-round description of the working institutions as they really existed and functioned within a concrete and complex sociological context. In Central Australia individual marriage, which is real marriage, does exist. The question which our first-hand observers should have answered is: "What is the relation between the *pirrauru* institution and marriage; what actual services do the *pirrauru* partners render to one another besides occasional mutual sexual enjoyment?" Such an analysis would have shown that while marriage in Central Australia is a domestic, ceremonial, legal, religious, and procreative institution, the *pirrauru* is mainly a legalized sexual relationship.

The Passing of Rites de Passage.

Another typical dangerous label is that of *rites de passage*. Valuable as M. Van Gennep's contribution has been, it was mainly a formal scheme not based on the real functional analysis of the various rites lumped together because of their formal similarity. The essence of an initiation ceremony lies in its sociological, educational, and religious significance. The analysis of secret societies and initiation ceremonies given by Schurtz, Cunow, and Hutton Webster were made in a much more functional spirit and are therefore more useful than the formal classifications under the several sub-headings of *rites de passage*. Yet innumerable field-workers have been gripped by the clever label, and very good material such as that of Rattray's, or of Junod, is vitiated by the formalism of its setting.

" Classificatory systems of kinship," mother-right, and father-right, the dual organization, the clan system, solar or lunar mythology—all these are labels manufactured often by armchair theorists who never saw the enlivening actuality of native tribal life, and had a tendency towards the abstract and detached formulation of cultural realities. Many an amateur field-worker, again, fascinated by the learned-sounding title, hypnotized into the belief that in order to be scientific you have to go far away from what is under your nose, used these labels in at times a ridiculously inadequate and naïve fashion.

Sex is not Everything.

I have been speaking of sex because this is the subject matter of the present book. Any other topic would have led us to the same conclusions and I could exemplify the synthetic principle of the Functional School on the problems of nutrition, of economic pursuits, of religious and magical beliefs, or on any other anthropological theme. To take nutrition as an example, food becomes in all primitive—and, of course, in all civilized—societies, a centre of social grouping, a basis of systems of value, and the nucleus of ritual acts and religious beliefs. We need only remember that the central rite of our own religion is a nutritive act.

Everything which refers to food should be studied in a synthetic manner, by analysing the integration of social grouping, of systems of value, and of ritualism round this main biological need and mental interest of man. No culture can be understood unless all its nutritive institutions are worked out in direct reference to the preparing and eating of food, to the quest for food, to its distribution and storage. It is one of the remarkable paradoxes of social science that while a whole school of economic metaphysics has erected the importance of material interests—which in the last instance are always food interests—into the dogma of materialistic determination of all historical process, neither anthropology nor any other special branch of social science has devoted any serious attention to food. The anthropological foundations of Marxism or of anti-Marxism are still to be laid down.

Again, while sex has been discussed and is being discussed *ad nauseam*, while the psycho-analytic school are reducing everything to the sexual impulse, no one as far as I know has thought of devoting the same amount of attention and emphasis to the twin interest, that in food—to nutrition, the other need of the human organism, as fundamental as procreation. Nutrition is, of course, being studied by biologists, by hygienists, and by medical men, but, on the one hand, to study the physiology of nutrition without its cultural setting constitutes a great loss to both aspects of the subject, and, on the other hand, the whole of the science of culture is sterile as long as the second great foundation of human society, the quest for food, is not brought fully to the attention of anthropologists.

The functional school, which ultimately aims at tracing all cultural phenomena to the essential wants of the human organism, is bound to remedy this evil. As a matter of fact, Dr. A. I. Richards, in her work, *Food in Savage Society*, dealing with the sociology of nutrition and which is shortly to be published, has made an important contribution to this subject. It is to be hoped that her pioneering lead will be soon followed by others of this school.

The Study of Primitive Economics.

But functionalism does not hinge only on sex or food or on both of these. The functional method recognizes perhaps above all that the satisfaction of biological needs implies and develops a system of derivative requirements. Man living under conditions of culture obtains his bread indirectly through co-operation and exchange. He has to procure it in complicated economic pursuits. Culture therefore creates new requirements, requirements for implements, weapons, and means of transport, for social co-operation, for institutions which ensure an ordinary and lawful working of human groups and which allow of organized co-operation.

The function therefore of many features of human culture is not the direct satisfaction of nutritive or sexual needs, but rather the satisfaction of what might be called *instrumental needs*, that is, needs for instruments, for means to an end, the end being the biological well-being of the individual, the procreation of the species, and also the spiritual development of the personality and the establishment of a give-and-take in social co-operation. Instrumental needs, again, that is the body of artifacts and social organization, imply other requirements. The whole production is based on knowledge, while social organization is based on morality, religion, and magic. We have, therefore, cultural wants of a yet higher degree of derivation, and I like to call them *integrative needs:*

Some preparatory work in the direction of coping with the instrumental aspect of culture has been done by economists and anthropologists, in the discussion of the economic organization of primitive peoples. The extraordinary preconceptions as to the simplicity of primitive economic organization has led to the later theories of the four or five stages of economic development. The only problem known to early anthropology and comparative economics was the problem of sequence in occupational stages. Did hunting precede a pastoral life, or did agriculture come first ? Was the tilling of the soil invented by women, by men, or by priests ? These and such like were the questions discussed by Liszt, by Schmoller, by Wagner, and even in the recent works of Hahn and Max Schmidt.

A certain over-simplification of the problem still dominates the pioneering attempts of Karl Bücher, from which really modern discussions on primitive economics begin. Dr. R. W. Firth's book on *The Primitive Economics of the Maori* is perhaps the first full monograph treating primitive economics from the functional point of view. And an analysis of that book—which welds together magic and economic activities, æsthetic interests and incentives to labour, economic values and religious ideas— an analysis of Dr. Firth's arguments would show us quite as well as an analysis of the present book what functionalism really means. In writing my *Argonauts of the Western Pacific*, I was made to realize also how the study of one economic institution inevitably forces us to place it within the general context of tribal economics, and to trace out its relations to other social aspects of the community. The real definition of such an institution as the inter-tribal trading round Eastern New Guinea is really made not by this or that activity but by establishing the relation between magic, mythology, social organization, purely commercial interests, and a half ceremonial, half æsthetic system of values, built round objects whose primary function was adornment, but which soon became simply repositories of a traditional and competitive principle of value.

I wish only briefly to indicate here that the functional theory is not merely the statement that what functions must have a function, but that it leads us to an analysis of the nature of culture and of cultural processes. Since I have given a preliminary outline of such a functional theory of culture (article s.v. " Culture " in the *American Encyclopædia of the Social Sciences*, edited by Edwin Seligman and Alvin Johnson), it will be enough for me to refer to it, indicating here merely the width and scope of modern anthropological work on functional lines.

Returning, however, to the present book, let me once more illustrate by another example the point which I was making at the outset, viz. that the little curiosities or self-contained facts and stories which were picked out and discussed are in themselves of little consequence, and that the real significance becomes only apparent if we place them within their institutionalized context.

The Antiquarian Aspect of Culture.

I shall take the one aspect of primitive culture which is usually regarded as leading an independent existence, detached from present-day concerns, idle and useless—except perhaps as a form of stimulating pastime or entertainment. I mean folk-lore, the body of stories, legends and myths related by a tribe. The current view is that myths are a mere intellectual hobby, a sort of cross-word puzzle of primitive man. Folk-lore, we are told, contains " the earliest attempts to exercise reason, imagination, and memory . . . Myths are stories which, however marvellous and improbable to us, are, nevertheless, related in all good faith because they are intended, or believed by the teller, to *explain* by means of something concrete and intelligible, an *abstract* idea or such *vague* and *difficult* conceptions as Creation, Death, distinctions of race or animal species, the different occupations of men and women ; the origins of rites and customs, or striking natural objects or prehistoric monuments ;

the meaning of the names of persons or places. Such stories are sometimes described as *aetiological*, because their *purpose is to explain why something exists or happens.*" (The italics are mine.) I have quoted here from the last edition but one of *Notes and Queries*,[1] a statement written, in collaboration with the late Miss C. S. Burne, by one of our greatest authorities, Professor J. L. Myres, than whom no one is more competent to summarize the views of the classical anthropology of to-day.

And yet this statement cannot be accepted by those holding functional points of view—and it is the functionalist who is entitled to judge it because this statement concerns the function of myth. We read about " explanations ", " abstract ideas ", the relation of myth to " vague and difficult conceptions ". Mythology then would be a primitive form of science. It would be, in fact, an incomplete or warped science, because, while our own science is an integral part of modern culture, the foundation of our technology, the source of our philosophic, even of our religious inspiration, mythology or primitive science would of necessity remain idle and unconnected with primitive economics or pragmatic *Weltanschauung* for the very simple reason that it is not knowledge but fancy. The function of folk-lore, then, according to modern anthropologists, would be to provide primitive man with a fanciful, useless, and completely self-contained system of warped scientific explanations.

Is such a functional definition of myth acceptable? Certainly not. The functionalist field-worker finds that myths are by no means told when questions of "why" or "for what reason" arise. They are not used as exercises of intelligence, imagination, or memory. In the first place they are not mere stories idly told. Myths to the native are enacted in ritual, in public ceremony, in dramatic performances. His sacred tradition lives to him in his sacramental

[1] *Notes and Queries on Anthropology*, 4th ed., 1912, p. 210.

acts, in his magical performances, in his social order and his moral outlook. It is not of the nature of fiction, such as we cultivate in our novels or moving pictures, or even in our drama. It is not a scientific doctrine such as we apply in present-day theory and carry out in practice. It is to the native a living reality believed to have once happened in primeval times and to have established a social, moral, and physical order.

This perhaps may seem a mere modified restatement of the previous quotation. But there is a fundamental difference between explaining, such as a scientific instructor does, and laying down a sacred rule as is done by the modern religious teacher who " explains " the doctrine of original sin by reference to the Biblical myth of Adam and Eve. To confuse mythological causality, which is essentially dogmatic, religious, and mystical, with scientific causality, is an epistemological and logical mistake, which has, however, dominated most of the work done on mythology.

The Functional Character of Myth.

Glance at the myths of Central Australia. Are they mere stories to the natives ? They are danced, enacted, performed ritually at initiation and during the Intichiuma ceremonies. This re-enactment of mythology influences rain and wind and the growth of plants. The myths constitute the charter of the totemic order, of the local rights, of the rules of descent, inheritance, and sexual relationship. They are the foundation of magical technique and the guarantee of magical effectiveness. Indirectly they also influence the economics of this tribe. But in all this, myth does not function as a real science, but as a charter of moral and social order, as the precedent on which modern life must be built if it is to be good and effective.

Exactly the same applies to the legends of the Polynesians with the long pedigrees forming the

foundation of the aristocratic order of their society ;
to the mythology of West Africa or of North
America ; or for that matter to our own myth
about Adam and Eve and the Garden of Eden. The
myths of the Old Testament are the foundation of
our doctrines of moral responsibility and original
sin, of our patriarchal order of kinship, and of many
of our ideas about social duty and personal conduct ;
they are the basis of our Christian views of human
nature and of the relation between man and God.
The stories of the New Testament, again, are
to the Roman Catholics the very backbone of their
main religious rite, the Holy Mass. Whenever
a new religion is founded by a Joseph Smith or a
Mrs. Eddy, by a Stalin or a Mussolini, some special
myth has to be created, revived, or reinterpreted,
in order to give a supernatural validity to the new
religion. Would we regard such modern myth as
in any way equivalent to science ? Certainly not.
But if our myths are not science, why should we
assume that primitive myths are so? Since the
function of both is the same, their nature is identical,
and they must be studied by anthropologists from
the same point of view.

The Myth of Incest in the Trobriands.

But let us turn once more to the present book.
We have a moving and dramatic myth of primitive
incest which lies at the foundation of Trobriand
folk-lore and which is deeply associated with their
social organization, above all, with the powerful
taboo on brother and sister relationship. Does this
myth *explain* anything ? Perhaps incest ? But
incest is strictly forbidden; it is to the natives an
almost unthinkable event, the occurrence of which
they do not even want to admit. They cannot tell
stories in explanation of things to them unthinkable.

A moral lesson the myth does contain : the death
of the two incestuous lovers is a precedent and a
pattern, but a moral lesson is not an explanation.

The myth also contains no exercises in imagination ; such an exercise would be really repugnant to the natives when it comes to incest ; nor in memory, since whenever incest occurs they try hard to forget it. The reader of the present volume will see that the function of the myth of Kumilabwaga is to provide the charter for love-magic, to show how through the power of spell and rite even the strong repulsion of incest can be broken. The myth also contains a potential excuse for such transgressions of incestuous and exogamous rules as sometimes occur, and it sanctions the forces which give an exclusiveness in the practice of magic to certain communities.

But what is the net and practical result of our functional reformulation of mythology ? Here, again, it is not a mere verbal resetting. Whereas the older conception of myth encouraged the field-worker to do nothing but note down stories and find out what they " explain ", the functionalist has a much harder task. He has to study the myth in its concrete embodiment. Are certain stories enacted ritually ; are others constantly referred to in discussions of moral and social rules ; are, again, others told invariably on certain occasions ? All such problems can only be worked out in that most difficult type of field-work which consists in living native life side by side with the natives, in following them into their concerns and activities, and not merely taking down statements on paper. The relation between myth and magic, for instance, can be learned best in seeing magical rites enacted. The function of the present myth, the myth of love and of love-magic, I was able to grasp mainly by listening to echoes of dramatic occurrences, by following up village gossip and being aware of what actually was happening in the villages. The myth of Iwa and Kumilabwaga lives in the love-making and the courtship of the Trobrianders ; in the relations between brother and sister, and between those who are allowed to mate ; also in the rivalries between the community of Iwa and that of Kumilabwaga.

We have thus shown that the most antiquarian side of primitive culture appears alive, active, dynamic, once we study it in relation to the full context of tribal life, and not merely as a set of stories written down by the ethnographer in his note-book.

The Function of Material Culture.

We may rest confident that the other aspects of culture are also imbued with function, that means, with the capacity to go on working, to satisfy the needs, to be correlated with human wants. The field-worker in his observations sees every implement constantly used. In his study of material culture, therefore, he is quickly weaned from the vision of Museum specimens ranged in comparative or diffusionist series. He becomes impressed with the fact that it is in the manual use of a material object that we find its prima facie significance to the natives. He also finds that the manual use of a weapon, a tool, a magical gewgaw, or a religious image, shades imperceptibly into what might be called mental or spiritual use ; that is, that material objects are deeply embedded in the beliefs, customary attitudes, and types of social organization of a tribe.

Take again material objects of more directly sociological character, such as dwellings, means of locomotion, places of magical or religious worship, arrangements for public gatherings, schemes of human settlement—the field-worker who wishes to squeeze the full meaning out of the physical matter, out of the shaped environment of his tribe, is more and more driven to the study of function. And by function here I mean the manner in which a house, or a canoe, or a ceremonial site is correlated with the bodily and spiritual needs of the tribesmen. Thus even in material culture, the simple interest in technology or in typological arrangements on the pattern of a museum case, must give way in field-work to the economics of human possessions, to the sociological concatenations of the monuments of a tribe, to the magical, religious, mythological, and spiritual significance of every object which man produces, owns, and uses.

Functional field-work consists always in the study of concatenations or the correlation of aspects in actual usage. And by usage I mean not merely manipulation, not merely the direct or instrumental satisfaction of needs, but the bodily attitudes in the widest behaviouristic sense in which body embraces mind ; that is the ideas, beliefs, and values which centre round an object.

Obviously the explanation of customs must go on the same lines. A custom, that is a traditionally standardized habit, or as a modern physiologist would call it, conditioned reflex, is always an integral part of a bigger compound. Detailed analysis of social organization and culture would show us that most customs, in fact all customs, integrate into a number of institutions.

But I cannot enter any further into such detailed analysis. I have given enough references to my other writings, especially to my two concise but comprehensive statements in the American *Encyclopædia of the Social Sciences* (s.v. " Culture ") and in the *Encyclopædia Britannica* (s.v. "Anthropology", 13th edition, reprinted as " Social Anthropology " in the 14th edition). I have not been able here to give a full definition of what I understand by Functional Method. I have tried rather to stimulate the reader or perhaps to intrigue him. If I have succeeded in that, the purpose of this rambling foreword has been fulfilled.

B. MALINOWSKI.

TAMARIS,
October, 1931.

FOREWORD TO THE FIRST EDITION

I HAVE chosen for this book the plainest, that is the most truthful title, partly to contribute towards the rehabilitation of the indispensable and often misused term *sexual*, partly to announce directly what the reader has to expect in the most outspoken paragraphs. Sex is not a mere physiological transaction to the primitive South Sea Islander any more than it is to us ; it implies love and love-making ; it becomes the nucleus of such venerable institutions as marriage and the family ; it pervades art and it produces its spells and its magic. It dominates in fact almost every aspect of culture. *Sex*, in its widest meaning—and it is thus that I have used it in the title of this book— is rather a sociological and cultural force than a mere bodily relation of two individuals. But the scientific treatment of this subject obviously involves also a keen interest in the biological nucleus. The anthropologist must therefore give a description of the direct approaches between two lovers, as we find them in Oceania, shaped by their traditions, obeying their laws, following the customs of their tribe.

In Anthropology the essential facts of life must be stated simply and fully, though in scientific language, and such a plain statement cannot really offend the most delicately-minded nor the most prejudiced reader ; nor can it be of any use to the seeker after pornography ; least of all can it entice the unripe interest of the young. For pruriency consists in oblique day-dreaming and not in simple and direct statement. The reader will find that the natives treat sex in the long run not only as a source of pleasure, but, indeed, as a thing serious and even

sacred. Nor do their customs and ideas eliminate
from sex its power to transform crude material
fact into wonderful spiritual experience, to throw
the romantic glamour of love over the technicalities
of love-making. The institutions of the Trobriand
community allow mere brutal passion to ripen into
life-long love, to be shot through with personal
affinities, to be strengthened by the manifold bonds
and attachments created through the advent of
children, by the mutual anxieties and hopes, by the
common aims and interests of family life.

It is perhaps in the blending of the directly
sensual with the romantic and in the wide and
weighty sociological consequences of what to start
with is the most personal event—it is in this richness
and multiplicity of love that lies its philosophic
mystery, its charm for the poet and its interest for
the anthropologist. This many-sidedness of love
exists among the Trobrianders as well as with us,
and it brings nearer to us even that which to most
might at first appear crude and uncontrolled.

To ignore this latter aspect, however, to shirk
treating the material foundations of love would in
a scientific work mean completely to stultify all
results. It would be to commit the unpardonable
sin of evading the real issue. Anyone who does not
wish to be concerned with sex need not acquire
or read this book ; and those who approach the
subject in a non-scientific spirit may be warned
from the outset that they will find nothing suggestive
or alluring in the following chapters.

I want to make it quite clear that the comparisons
between native and European conditions scattered
here and there, especially in the later chapters, are
not meant to serve as a sociological parallel—for
that they are far too slight. Still less are the native-
European parallels of the present book meant to
provide a homily on our own failings or a pæan
on our virtues. They are given simply because, in

FOREWORD

order to explain strange facts, it is necessary to hark
back to familiar ones. The Anthropologist in his
observations has to understand the native through
his own psychology, and he must form the picture
of a foreign culture from the elements of his own and
of others practically and theoretically known to
him. The whole difficulty and art of field work
consists of starting from those elements which are
familiar in the foreign culture and gradually working
the strange and diverse into a comprehensible
scheme. In this the learning of a foreign culture
is like the learning of a foreign tongue : at first mere
assimilation and crude translation, at the end a
complete detachment from the original medium and
a mastery of the new one. And since an adequate
ethnographic description must reproduce in
miniature the gradual, lengthy, and painful processes
of field-work, the references to the familiar, the
parallels between Europe and the Trobriands have
to serve as starting points.

After all, to reach the reader I have to rely upon
his personal experiences which are built up in our
own society. Exactly as I have to write in English,
and translate native terms or texts into English, so
also I have, in order to make them real and comprehensible, to translate Melanesian conditions into
our own. Whatever error there is in either procedure
is inevitable. An Anthropologist may be well aware
of *traduttore traditore*, but he cannot help it—he
cannot banish his few patient readers for a couple
of years to a South Sea coral atoll, and make them
live the life for themselves ; he has, alas, to write
books about his savages and lecture on them !

One more point about the method of presentation.
Every conscientious scientific observer should state
not only what he knows and how he has come to
know it, but also indicate those gaps in his knowledge
of which he is aware, the failures and omissions in
his field work. I have given already (*Argonauts of*

the Western Pacific, ch. i) a full account of my credentials : length of time spent on the islands, linguistic qualifications, methods of collecting documents and statements. I shall not repeat this all here, and the few necessary additional remarks on the difficult study of native intimate life, the reader will find in the text (ch. ix, 9 ; ch. x, intro. ; chs. xii and xiii, intros.).

The competent and experienced ethnographer and anthropologist—and only such a one is interested in the margin of accuracy, in the methodology of evidence and in the gaps in information—will easily see from the data presented throughout this book, where the documentation is thin and where it is full. When I make a simple statement without illustrating it from personal observation or adducing facts, this means that I am mainly relying on what I was told by my native informants. This is, of course, the least reliable part of my material.

I am especially aware that my knowledge of obstetrical facts and of the women's attitude at pregnancy and childbirth is rather meagre. Again the father's behaviour at the time of childbirth and male psychology with regard to it, were not studied as fully as they should have been. Many minor points throughout the book are treated in a manner which will make clear to the specialist, not only where the information is incomplete, but also what further inquiry would be needed to fill out the gaps. On most points of fundamental importance, I am convinced that I have come down to bedrock.

One gap, regrettable but hardly to be remedied, is the small number of illustrations bearing directly on erotic life. Since this, however, takes place in deep shadow, literally as well as figuratively, photographs could only be faked, or at best, posed—and faked or posed passion (or sentiment) is worthless.

The many obligations incurred in the course of my fieldwork have been acknowledged elsewhere

(*Argonauts of the Western Pacific*) ; but I should like here to mention a very special indebtedness to my friend, Billy Hancock, trader and pearl-buyer in the Trobriands, whose mysterious death occurred while I was writing this book. He was ill, and awaiting the South-bound boat at Samarai, the European settlement in the east of New Guinea. One evening he disappeared, never to be seen or heard of again. He was not only an excellent informant and helpmate, but a real friend, whose company and assistance added a great deal of material comfort and moral support in a somewhat exacting and tedious existence.

In writing this book I was greatly stimulated by the interest taken in it by Mr. Havelock Ellis, whose work and whose example as a pioneer in honest thought and outspoken research I have always admired and revered. His preface materially enhances the value of this book.

The group of my friends, pupils, and colleagues who have been associated with Anthropological Research Work and Teaching at the London School of Economics for the last few years, have helped me greatly to clarify my ideas and to present my material, more especially on the subject of family life, kinship organization, and marriage law. The names of Mrs. Robert Aitken (Miss Barbara Freire-Marecco), of Dr. R. W. Firth (now in the Solomons), of Mr. E. E. Evans-Pritchard (now among the Azande), of Miss Camilla Wedgwood (now in Australia), of Dr. Gordon Brown (now in Tanganyika), of Dr. Hortense Powdermaker (now on the way to Papua), of Mr. I. Schapera (late of South Africa), of Mr. T. J. A. Yates (late of Egypt), of Miss Audrey Richards, will in my mind be always gratefully remembered in association with the drafting of the more difficult sociological chapters of this book.

My greatest debt in this book, as in most I have

FOREWORD

written, is to my wife. Her counsel and practical
co-operation have made the writing of the *Argonauts
of the Western Pacific* and of this an agreeable task
instead of a drudgery. If there is any value and
interest in these books for me personally, it comes
from her share in the common work.

B. M.

LONDON,
    January, 1929.

CHAPTER I

THE RELATIONS BETWEEN THE SEXES IN TRIBAL LIFE

MAN and woman in the Trobriand Islands—their relations in love, in marriage, and in tribal life—this will be the subject of the present study.

The most dramatic and intense stage in the intercourse between man and woman, that in which they love, mate, and produce children, must occupy the dominant place in any consideration of the sexual problem. To the average normal person, in whatever type of society we find him, attraction by the other sex and the passionate and sentimental episodes which follow are the most significant events in his existence, those most deeply associated with his intimate happiness and with the zest and meaning of life. To the sociologist, therefore, who studies a particular type of society, those of its customs, ideas, and institutions which centre round the erotic life of the individual should be of primary importance. For if he wants to be in tune with his subject and to place it in a natural, correct perspective, the sociologist must, in his research, follow the trend of personal values and interests. That which means supreme happiness to the individual must be made a fundamental factor in the scientific treatment of human society.

But the erotic phase, although the most important, is only one among many in which the sexes meet and enter into relations with each other. It cannot be studied outside its proper context, without, that is, being linked up with the legal status of man and woman ; with their domestic relations ; and with the distribution of their economic functions.

Courtship, love, and mating in a given society are influenced in every detail by the way in which the sexes face one another in public and in private, by their position in tribal law and custom, by the manner in which they participate in games and amusements, by the share each takes in ordinary daily toil.

The story of a people's love-making necessarily has to begin with an account of youthful and infantile associations, and it leads inevitably forward to the later stage of permanent union and marriage. Nor can the narrative break off at this point, since science cannot claim the privilege of fiction. The way in which men and women arrange their common life and that of their children reacts upon their love-making, and the one stage cannot be properly understood without a knowledge of the other.

This book deals with sexual relations among the natives of the Trobriand Islands, a coral archipelago lying to the north-east of New Guinea. These natives belong to the Papuo-Melanesian race, and in their physical appearance, mental equipment, and social organization combine a majority of Oceanic characteristics with certain features of the more backward Papuan population from the mainland of New Guinea.[1]

I

THE PRINCIPLES OF MOTHER-RIGHT

We find in the Trobriands a matrilineal society, in which descent, kinship, and every social relationship are legally reckoned through the mother only, and in which women have a considerable share in tribal life, even to the taking of a leading part in

[1] For a full general account of the Northern Massim, of whom the Trobrianders form a section, cf. the classical treatise of Professor C. G. Seligman, *Melanesians of British New Guinea*, Cambridge, 1910, which also shows the relation of the Trobrianders to the other races and cultures on and around New Guinea. A short account of Trobriand culture will also be found in my *Argonauts of the Western Pacific* (George Routledge and Sons, 1922).

economic, ceremonial, and magical activities—a fact which very deeply influences all the customs of erotic life as well as the institution of marriage. It will be well, therefore, first to consider the sexual relation in its widest aspect, beginning with some account of those features of custom and tribal law which underlie the institution of mother-right, and the various views and conceptions which throw light upon it ; after this, a short sketch of each of the chief domains of tribal life—domestic, economic, legal, ceremonial, and magical—will combine to show the respective spheres of male and female activity among these natives.

The idea that it is solely and exclusively the mother who builds up the child's body, the man in no way contributing to its formation, is the most important factor in the legal system of the Trobrianders. Their views on the process of procreation, coupled with certain mythological and animistic beliefs, affirm, without doubt or reserve, that the child is of the same substance as its mother, and that between the father and the child there is no bond of physical union whatsoever (see ch. vii).

That the mother contributes everything to the new being to be born of her is taken for granted by the natives, and forcibly expressed by them. " The mother feeds the infant in her body. Then, when it comes out, she feeds it with her milk." " The mother makes the child out of her blood." " Brothers and sisters are of the same flesh, because they come of the same mother." These and similar expressions describe their attitude towards this, their fundamental principle of kinship.

This attitude is also to be found embodied, in an even more telling manner, in the rules governing descent, inheritance, succession in rank, chieftain-ship, hereditary offices, and magic—in every regulation, in fact, concerning transmission by kinship. Social position is handed on in the mother-line from a man to his sister's children, and this

3

exclusively matrilineal conception of kinship is of paramount importance in the restrictions and regulations of marriage, and in the taboos on sexual intercourse. The working of these ideas of kinship can be observed, breaking out with a dramatic intensity, at death. For the social rules underlying burial, lamentation, and mourning, together with certain very elaborate ceremonies of food distribution, are based on the principle that people joined by the tie of maternal kinship form a closely knit group, bound by an identity of feelings, of interests, and of flesh. And from this group, even those united to it by marriage and by the father-to-child relation are sharply excluded, as having no natural share in the bereavement (see ch. vi, secs. 2–4).

These natives have a well-established institution of marriage, and yet are quite ignorant of the man's share in the begetting of children. At the same time, the term " father " has, for the Trobriander, a clear, though exclusively social, definition : it signifies the man married to the mother, who lives in the same house with her, and forms part of the household. The father, in all discussions about relationship, was pointedly described to me as *tomakava*, a " stranger ", or, even more correctly, an " outsider ". This expression would also frequently be used by natives in conversation, when they were arguing some point of inheritance or trying to justify some line of behaviour, or again when the position of the father was to be belittled in some quarrel.

It will be clear to the reader, therefore, that the term " father ", as I use it here, must be taken, not as having the various legal, moral, and biological implications that it holds for us, but in a sense entirely specific to the society with which we are dealing. It might have seemed better, in order to avoid any chance of such misconception, not to have used our word " father " at all, but rather the native

one *tama*, and to have spoken of the " *tama* relationship " instead of " fatherhood " ;· but, in practice,
this would have proved too unwieldy. The reader,
therefore, when he meets the word " father " in
these pages, should never forget that it must be
defined, not as in the English dictionary, but in
accordance with the facts of native life. I may add
that this rule applies to all terms which carry special
sociological implication, that is to all terms of
relationship, and such words as " marriage ",
" divorce ", " betrothal", " love ", " courtship", and
the like.

What does the word *tama* (father) express to the
native ?   " Husband of my mother " would be the
answer first given by an intelligent informant. He
would go on to say that his *tama* is the man in whose
loving and protecting company he has grown up.
For, since marriage is patrilocal in the Trobriands,
since the woman, that is to say, moves to her
husband's village community and lives in his house,
the father is a close companion to his children ;
he takes an active part in the cares which are
lavished upon them, invariably feels and shows a
deep affection for them, and later has a share in their
education. The word *tama* (father) condenses,
therefore, in its emotional meaning, a host of
experiences of early childhood, and expresses the
typical sentiment existing between a boy or girl
and a mature affectionate man of the same household ; while socially it denotes the male person who
stands in an intimate relation to the mother, and
who is master of the household.

So far *tama* does not differ essentially from
" father " in our sense. But as soon as the child
begins to grow up and take an interest in things
outside the affairs of the household and its own
immediate needs, certain complications arise, and
change the meaning of *tama* for him. He learns
that he is not of the same clan as his *tama*, that his
totemic appellation is different, and that it is identical

5

with that of his mother. At the same time he learns that all sorts of duties, restrictions, and concerns for personal pride unite him to his mother and separate him from his father. Another man appears on the horizon, and is called by the child *kadagu* ("my mother's brother"). This man may live in the same locality, but he is just as likely to reside in another village. The child also learns that the place where his *kada* (mother's brother) resides is also his, the child's, "own village"; that there he has his property and his other rights of citizenship; that there his future career awaits him; that there his natural allies and associates are to be found. He may even be taunted in the village of his birth with being an "outsider" (*tomakava*), while in the village he has to call "his own", in which his mother's brother lives, his father is a stranger and he a natural citizen. He also sees, as he grows up, that the mother's brother assumes a gradually increasing authority over him, requiring his services, helping him in some things, granting or withholding his permission to carry out certain actions; while the father's authority and counsel become less and less important.

Thus the life of a Trobriander runs under a two-fold influence—a duality which must not be imagined as a mere surface play of custom. It enters deeply into the existence of every individual, it produces strange complications of usage, it creates frequent tensions and difficulties, and not seldom gives rise to violent breaks in the continuity of tribal life. For this dual influence of paternal love and the matrilineal principle, which penetrates so far into the framework of institutions and into the social ideas and sentiments of the native, is not, as a matter of fact, quite well adjusted in its working.[1]

It has been necessary to emphasize the relationship between a Trobriander and his father, his mother, and his mother's brother, for this is the

[1] Cf. my *Crime and Custom in Savage Society*, Kegan Paul, 1926.

nucleus of the complex system of mother-right or matriliny, and this system governs the whole social life of these natives. The question is, moreover, specially related to the main theme of this book : love-making, marriage, and kinship are three aspects of the same subject ; they are the three facets which it presents in turn to sociological analysis.

2

A TROBRIAND VILLAGE

We have so far given the sociological definition of fatherhood, of the mother's brother's relation, and of the nature of the bond between mother and child ; a bond founded on the biological facts of gestation and the extremely close psychological attachment which results from these. The best way to make this abstract statement clear will be to display the inter-working of the three relationships in an actual community in the Trobriands. Thus we can make our explanations concrete and get into touch with actual life instead of moving among abstractions ; and, incidentally, too, we can introduce some personalities who will appear in the later parts of our narrative.

The village of Omarakana is, in a sense, the capital of Kiriwina, the main district of these islands. It is the residence of the principal chief, whose name, prestige, and renown are carried far and wide over the Archipelagoes, though his power does not reach beyond the province of Kiriwina.[1] The village lies on a fertile, level plain in the northern parts of the large, flat coral island of Boyowa (see fig. 2). As we walk towards it, from the lagoon anchorages on the western shore, the level road leads across monotonous stretches covered with low scrub,

[1] For further references to this eminent personage and for an account of chieftainship, see C. G. Seligman, *op. cit.*, chapters xlix and li ; also my *Argonauts of the Western Pacific, passim*, and " Baloma, Spirits of the Dead," *Journ. R. Anthrop. Inst.*, 1916.

here and there broken by a tabooed grove, or by a large garden, holding vines trained on long poles and looking, in its developed form, like an exuberant hop-yard. We pass several villages on our way ; the soil becomes more fertile and the settlement denser as we approach the long ridge of raised coral outcrop which runs along the eastern shore and shuts off the open sea from the inland plains of the island.

A large clump of trees appears at a distance— these are the fruit-trees, the palms and the piece of uncut virgin jungle which together surround the village of Omarakana. We pass the grove and find ourselves between two rows of houses, built in concentric rings round a large open space (see fig. 1 and plate 1). Between the outer ring and the inner one a circular street runs round the whole of the village, and in it, as we pass, we see groups of people sitting in front of their huts (see pl. 4). The outer ring consists of dwelling-houses, the inner of store-huts in which the *taytu*, a variety of yam, which forms the staple food of the natives, is kept from one harvest to the next. We are struck at once by the better finish, the greater constructive elaboration, and the superior embellishment and decoration which distinguish the yam-houses from the dwellings (see pl. 31). As we stand on the wide central space we can admire the circular row of storehouses in front of us, for both these and the dwellings always face the centre. In Omarakana a big yam-house belonging to the chief stands in the middle of this space. Somewhat nearer the ring, but still well in the centre stands another large building, the chief's living hut (see pls. 1 and 2).

This singularly symmetrical arrangement of the village is of importance, for it represents a definite sociological scheme. The inner place is the scene of the public and festive life. A part of it is the old-time burial ground of the villagers, and at one end is the dancing ground, the scene of all ceremonial

8

and festive celebrations. The houses which surround it, the inner ring of store-huts that is, share its quasi-sacred character, a number of taboos being placed upon them. The street between the two rows is the theatre of domestic life and everyday occurrence (see pls. 4 and 39). Without over-labouring the point, the central place might be called the male portion of the village and the street that of the women.

Let us now make preliminary acquaintance with some of the more important inhabitants of Omarakana, beginning with the present chief, To'uluwa (see pls. 2 and 41). He and his family are not only the most prominent members of the community, but they occupy more than half of the village. As we shall see (ch. v, sec. 4), the chiefs in the Trobriands have the privilege of polygamy. To'uluwa, who lives in the large house in the middle of the village, has a number of wives who occupy a whole row of huts (A—B on the plan, fig. 1). Also his maternal kinsmen, who belong to his family and sub-clan called Tabalu, have a separate space in the village for themselves (A—C). The third section (B—C) is inhabited by commoners who are not related to the chief either as kinsmen or as children.

The community is thus divided into three parts. The first consists of the chief and his maternal kinsmen, the Tabalu, all of whom claim the village as their own, and consider themselves masters of its soil with all attendant privileges. The second consists of the commoners, who are themselves divided into two groups : those claiming the rights of citizenship on mythological grounds (these rights are distinctly inferior to those of the chief's sub-clan, and the claimants only remain in the village as the chief's vassals or servants) ; and strangers in the hereditary service of the chief, who live in the village by that right and title. The third part consists of the chief's wives and their offspring.

These wives, by reason of patrilocal marriage,

9

have to settle in their husband's village, and with them, of course, remain their younger children. But the grown-up sons are only allowed to stay in the village through the personal influence of their father. This influence overrules the tribal law that every man ought to live in his own—that is his mother's—village. The chief is always much more attached to his children than to his maternal kinsmen. He prefers their company ; like every typical Trobriand father, he takes, sentimentally at least, their side in any dispute ; and he invariably tries to grant them as many privileges and benefits as possible. This state of affairs is naturally not altogether appreciated by the chief's legal successors, his maternal kinsmen, the children of his sister ; and frequently considerable tension and sharp friction arise between the two sections in consequence.

Such a state of tension revealed itself recently in an acute upheaval, which shook the quiet tribal life of Omarakana and for years undermined its internal harmony.[1] There was a feud of long standing between Namwana Guya'u, the chief's favourite son, and Mitakata, his nephew and third in succession to the rule (see pl. 3). Namwana Guya'u was the most influential man in the village, after the chief, his father : To'uluwa allowed him to wield a great deal of power, and gave him more than his share of wealth and privilege.

One day, about six months after my arrival in Omarakana, the quarrel came acutely to a head. Namwana Guya'u, the chief's son, accused his enemy, Mitakata, the nephew and one of the heirs, of committing adultery with his wife, brought him before the White Resident Magistrate, and thereby caused him to be imprisoned for a month or so. The news of this imprisonment reached the village from

[1] The following account has been already published (in *Crime and Custom*, pp. 101 sq.). Since it is an almost exact reproduction of the original entry in my field-notes, I prefer to give it here once more in the same form, with a few verbal alterations only.

the Government compound, a few miles distant, at sunset, and created a panic. The chief shut himself up in his personal hut, full of evil forebodings for his favourite, who had thus rashly outraged tribal law and feeling. The kinsmen of the imprisoned heir to chieftainship were boiling with suppressed anger and indignation. As night fell, the subdued villagers settled down to a silent supper, each family over its solitary meal. There was nobody on the central place. Namwana Guya'u was not to be seen, the chief To'uluwa remained secluded in his hut, most of his wives and their children staying indoors also. Suddenly a loud voice rang out across the silent village. Bagido'u, the heir apparent and eldest brother of the imprisoned man, standing before his hut, cried out, addressing the offender of his family :

" Namwana Guya'u, you are a cause of trouble. We, the Tabalu of Omarakana, allowed you to stay here, to live among us. You had plenty of food in Omarakana. You ate of our food. You partook of the pigs brought to us as a tribute, and of the flesh. You sailed in our canoe. You built a hut on our soil. Now you have done us harm. You have told lies. Mitakata is in prison. We do not want you to stay here. This is our village ! You are a stranger here. Go away ! We drive you away ! We drive you out of Omarakana."

These words were uttered in a loud, piercing voice, which trembled with strong emotion : each short sentence was spoken after a pause ; each, like an individual missile, was hurled across the empty space to the hut where Namwana Guya'u sat brooding. Next, the younger sister of Mitakata rose and spoke, and then a young man, one of their maternal nephews. Their words were in each case almost the same as Bagido'u's, the burden being the formula of dismissal or driving away, the *yoba*. These speeches were received in deep silence. Nothing stirred in the village. But, before the night

was over, Namwana Guya'u had left Omarakana
for ever. He had gone over and settled a few miles
away, in Osapola, his " own " village, whence his
mother came. For weeks she and his sister wailed
for him with loud lamentations as for the dead.
The chief remained for three days in his hut, and
when he came out he looked aged and broken by
grief. All his personal interest and affection were
on the side of his favourite son, yet he could do
nothing to help him. His kinsmen had acted strictly
within their rights, and, according to tribal law,
he could not possibly dissociate himself from them.
No power could change the decree of exile. Once
the words " Go away "—*bukula*, " we drive thee
away "—*kayabaim*, had been pronounced, the man
had to go. These words, very rarely uttered in
earnest, have a binding force and an almost ritual
power when pronounced by citizens against a resident
outsider. A man who would try to brave the dreadful
insult involved in them and remain in spite of them,
would be dishonoured for ever. In fact, anything but
immediate compliance with a ritual request is
unthinkable for a Trobriand Islander.

The chief's resentment against his kinsmen was
deep and lasting. At first he would not even speak
to them. For a year or so, not one of them dared to
ask to be taken on overseas expeditions by him,
although they were fully entitled to this privilege.
Two years later, in 1917, when I returned to the
Trobriands, Namwana Guya'u was still resident in
the other village and keeping aloof from his father's
kinsmen, though he frequently visited Omarakana
in order to be in attendance on his father, especially
when To'uluwa went abroad. His mother had died
within a year after his expulsion. As the natives
described it : " She wailed and wailed, refused to
eat, and died." The relations between the two
main enemies were completely broken, and Mitakata,
the young chieftain who had been imprisoned, had
repudiated his wife, who belonged to the same sub-

clan as Namwana Guya'u. There was a deep rift
in the whole social life of Kiriwina.

This incident was one of the most dramatic which
I have ever witnessed in the Trobriands. I have
described it at length, as it contains a striking
illustration of the nature of mother-right, of the
power of tribal law, and of the passions which
work against and in spite of these. It shows
also the deep, personal attachment which a
father feels for his children, the tendency which
he has to use all his personal influence to
give them a strong position in the village, the
opposition which this always evokes among his
maternal kinsmen, and the tension and rifts thus
brought about. Under normal conditions, in a
smaller community where the contending powers
are humbler and less important, such tension would
merely mean that, after the father's death, the
children would have to return to his maternal
kinsmen practically all the material benefits they
had received from him during his lifetime. In any
case, a good deal of discontent and friction and many
roundabout methods of settlement are involved in
this dual play of paternal affection and matrilineal
authority: the chief's son and his maternal nephew
can be described as predestined enemies.

This theme will recur in the progress of the
following narrative. In discussing consent to
marriage, we shall see the importance of paternal
authority and the functions of the matrilineal
kinsmen. The custom of cross-cousin marriage is
a traditional reconciliation of the two opposing
principles. The sexual taboos and prohibitions of
incest also cannot be understood without a clear
grasp of the principles discussed in this section.

So far we have met To'uluwa, his favourite wife
Kadamwasila, whose death followed on the village
tragedy, their son Namwana Guya'u, and his enemy
Mitakata, son of the chief's sister, and these we
shall meet again, for they were among my best

informants. We shall also become acquainted with
the other sons of the chief, and of his favourite wife,
and with some of his maternal kinsmen and kinswomen. We shall follow several of them in their love
affairs, and in their marriage arrangements ; we shall
have to pry into their domestic scandals, and to take
an indiscreet interest in their intimate life. For all
of them were, during a long period, under ethnographic observation, and I obtained much of my
material through their confidences, and especially
from their mutual scandal-mongering.

Many examples will also be given from other
communities, and we shall make frequent visits
to the lagoon villages of the western shore, to places
on the south of the island, and to some of the
neighbouring smaller islands of the Archipelago.
In all these other communities more uniform and
democratic conditions prevail, and this makes some
difference in the character of their sexual life.

3

FAMILY LIFE

In entering the village we had to pass across
the street between the two concentric rows of
houses.[1] This is the normal setting of the everyday
life of the community, and thither we must return
in order to make a closer survey of the groups
of people sitting in front of their dwellings
(see pl. 4). As a rule we find that each group
consists of one family only—man, wife, and
children—taking their leisure, or engaged in some
domestic activity which varies with the time of
day. On a fine morning we would see them hastily
eating a scanty breakfast, and then the man and
woman preparing the implements for the day's

[1] A good glimpse of the " street " can be obtained on pl. 12, where
two dwelling huts, right and left, can be seen behind the two yam
houses in the middle.

work, with the help of the bigger children, while the
baby is laid out of the way on a mat. Afterwards,
during the cool hours of the forenoon, each family
would probably set off to their work, leaving the
village almost deserted. The man, in company
with others, may be fishing or hunting or building
a canoe or looking for timber. The woman may have
gone collecting shell-fish or wild fruits. Or else
both may be working in the gardens, or paying a
visit. The man often does harder work than the
woman, but when they return in the hot hours of
the afternoon he will rest, while the woman busies
herself with household affairs. Towards evening,
when the descending sun casts longer, cooler
shadows, the social life of the village begins. At this
time we would see our family group in front of their
hut, the wife preparing food, the children playing,
the husband, perhaps, seated amusing the smallest
baby. This is the time when neighbours call on
one another, and conversation may be exchanged
from group to group.

The frank and friendly tone of intercourse, the
obvious feeling of equality, the father's domestic
helpfulness, especially with the children, would at
once strike any observant visitor. The wife joins
freely in the jokes and conversation ; she does her
work independently, not with the air of a slave or
a servant, but as one who manages her own department. She will order the husband about if she needs
his help. Close observation, day after day, confirms
this first impression. The typical Trobriand
household is founded on the principles of equality
and independence of function : the man is considered to be the master, for he is in his own village
and the house belongs to him, but the woman has,
in other respects, a considerable influence ; she and
her family have a great deal to do with the food
supply of the household ; she is the owner of separate
possessions in the house ; and she is—next to her
brother—the legal head of her family.

The division of functions within the household is, in certain matters, quite definite. The woman has to cook the food, which is simple, and does not require much preparation. The main meal is taken at sunset, and consists of yams, taro, or other tubers, roasted in the open fire—or, less frequently, boiled in a small pot, or baked in the ground—with the occasional addition of fish or meat. Next morning the remains are eaten cold, and sometimes, though not regularly, fruit, shell-fish, or some other light snack may be taken at mid-day.

In some circumstances, men can and do prepare and cook the food : on journeys, oversea voyages, fishing or hunting expeditions, when they are without their women folk. Also, on certain occasions, when taro or sago dumplings are cooked in the large clay pots, men are required by tradition to assist their wives (pl. 5). But within the village and in normal daily life the man never cooks. It would be considered shameful for him to do so. " You are a he-cook " (*tokakabwasi yoku*) would be said tauntingly. The fear of deserving such an epithet, of being laughed at or shamed (*kakayuwa*), is extreme. It arises from the characteristic dread and shame, found among savages, of not doing the proper thing, or, worse still, of doing something which is intrinsically the attribute of another sex or social class (see ch. xiii, secs. 1–4).

There are a number of occupations strictly assigned by tribal custom to one sex only. The manner of carrying loads is a very noteworthy example. Women have to carry the special feminine receptacle, the bell-shaped basket, or any other kind of load upon their heads ; men must carry only on the shoulder (pls. 6, 7, and 28). It would be with a real shudder, and a profound feeling of shame, that an individual would regard carrying anything in the manner proper to the opposite sex and nothing would induce a man to put any load on his head, even in fun.

An exclusively feminine department is the water supply. The woman has the water bottles of the household in her charge. These are made out of the woody shell of a mature coconut, with a stopper of twisted palm-leaf. In the morning or near sunset she goes, sometimes a full half-mile, to fill them at the water-hole : here the women fore-gather, resting and chatting, while one after the other fills her water-vessels, cleans them, arranges them in baskets or on large wooden platters, and, just before leaving, gives the cluster a final sprinkling of water to cover it with a suggestive gloss of fresh-ness. The water-hole is the woman's club and centre of gossip, and as such is important, for there is a distinct woman's public opinion and point of view in a Trobriand village, and they have their secrets from the male, just as the male has from the female.

We have already seen that the husband fully shares in the care of the children. He will fondle and carry a baby, clean and wash it, and give it the mashed vegetable food which it receives in addition to the mother's milk almost from birth. In fact, nursing the baby in the arms or holding it on the knees, which is described by the native word *kopo'i*, is the special rôle and duty of the father (*tama*). It is said of the children of unmarried women who, according to the native expression, are " with-out a *tama* " (that is, it must be remembered, without a husband to their mother), that they are "·unfortunate " or " bad " because " there is no one to nurse and hug them (*gala taytala bikopo'i*) ". Again, if anyone inquires why children should have duties towards their father, who is a " stranger " to them, the answer is invariably : " because of the nursing (*pela kopo'i*)," " because his hands have been soiled with the child's excrement and urine " (cf. ch. vii).

The father performs his duties with genuine natural fondness : he will carry an infant about for hours, looking at it with eyes full of such love and pride as are seldom seen in those of a European father. Any praise of the baby goes directly to his heart, and he will never tire of talking about and exhibiting the virtues and achievements of his wife's offspring. Indeed, watching a native family at home or meeting them on the road, one receives a strong impression of close union and intimacy between its members (see pls. 7, 26). Nor, as we have seen, does this mutual affection abate in later years. Thus, in the intimacy of domestic life, we discover another aspect of the interesting and complicated struggle between social and emotional paternity, on the one hand, and the explicitly acknowledged legal mother-right on the other.

It will be noticed that we have not yet penetrated into the interior of a house, for in fine weather the scene of family life is always laid in front of the dwelling. Only when it is cold and raining, at night, or for intimate uses, do the natives retire into the interior. On a wet or windy evening in the cooler season we would find the village streets deserted, dim lights flickering through small interstices in the hut walls, and voices sounding from within in animated conversation. Inside, in a small space heavy with dense smoke and human exhalation, the people sit on the floor round the fire or recline on bedsteads covered with mats.

The houses are built directly on the ground and their floors are of beaten earth. On the adjoining diagrammatic plan we see the main items of their very simple furniture : the fireplace, which is simply a ring of small stones with three large ones to support a pot ; wooden sleeping bunks, placed one over the other against the back and side walls opposite the fireplace (cf. pl. 8) and one or two shelves for nets, cooking pots, women's grass petticoats, and other household objects. The chief's personal dwelling is built like an ordinary house, but is larger. The yam houses are of somewhat

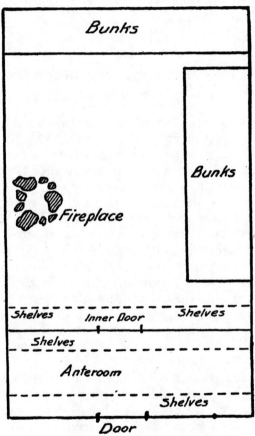

PLAN OF A DWELLING HOUSE

[*Ch. I*, 3]

different and more complicated construction, and
are slightly raised above the ground.

A normal day in a typical household forces the
family to live in close intimacy—they sleep in the
same hut, they eat in common and spend the best
part both of their working and of their leisure
hours together.

4

THE DIVISION OF PROPERTY AND DUTIES ACCORDING
TO SEX

Members of the household are also bound together
by community of economic interest. On this point,
however, a more detailed statement is necessary,
as the subject is important and complicated. To
begin with the right of ownership, it must be
realized that personal possession is a matter of
great importance to the native. The title *toli-*
("owner" or "master", used as a prefix to the
object possessed) has a considerable value in itself
as conferring a sort of distinction, even when it
does not give a claim to rights of exclusive use.
This term and the conception of ownership, are, in
every particular case, very well defined, but the
relationship varies with different objects, and it is
impossible to summarize it in one formula covering
all cases.[1]

It is remarkable that in spite of the close union
within the household, domestic utensils and the
many objects littering the hut are not owned in
common. Husband and wife have each his or her
own possessions. The wife owns her grass petticoats,
of which there are usually some twelve to
twenty in her wardrobe, for use on various occasions.
Also she relies on her own skill and industry to
procure them. So that in the question of toilet,
a Kirwinian lady depends solely upon herself. The

---

[1] Cf. *Argonauts of the Western Pacific*, ch. vi, and *passim*.

water vessels, the implements for dressmaking, a number of articles of personal adornment, are also her own property. The man owns his tools, the axe and adze, the nets, the spears, the dancing ornaments, and the drum, and also those objects of high value, called by the natives *vaygu'a*, which consist of necklaces, belts, armshells, and large polished axe-blades.

Nor is private ownership in this case a mere word without practical significance. The husband and the wife can and do dispose of any article of their own property, and after the death of one of them the objects are not inherited by the partner, but distributed among a special class of heirs. When there is a domestic quarrel a man may destroy some of his wife's property—he may wreak his vengeance on the water bottles or on the grass petticoats—and she may smash his drum or break his dancing shield. A man also has to repair and keep his own things in order, so that the woman is not the housekeeper in the general European sense.

Immovable goods, such as garden-land, trees, houses, as well as sailing-vessels, are owned almost exclusively by men, as is also the live stock, which consists mainly of pigs. We will have to touch on this subject again, when we speak of the social position of women, for ownership of such things goes with power.

Passing now from economic rights to duties, let us consider the partition of work according to sex. In the heavier type of labour, such as gardening, fishing, and carrying of considerable loads, there is a definite division between man and woman. Fishing and hunting, the latter of very slight importance in the Trobriands, are done by men, while only women engage in the search for marine shell-fish. In gardening, the heaviest work, such as cutting the scrub, making fences, fetching the heavy yam supports, and planting the tubers, is done

exclusively by men. Weeding is the woman's special
duty, while some of the intermediate stages, in which
the plants have to be looked after, are performed
by mixed male and female labour. Men do such
tending as there is to be done of the coco- and
areca-nut palms and of the fruit-trees, while it is
chiefly the women who look after the pigs.

All oversea expeditions are made by men, and the
building of canoes is entirely their business. Men
have to do most of the trading, especially the
important exchange of vegetable food for fish
which takes place between the inland and coastal
villagers. In the building of houses, the framework
is made by men, and the women help with the
thatching. Both sexes share in the carrying of
burdens; the men shoulder the heavier ones,
while the women make up by carrying more
frequently. And, as we have seen, there is a
characteristic sexual distinction in the mode of
placing the burden.

As regards the minor work of manufacturing small
objects, the women have to make the mats and
plait the armlets and belts. Of course, they alone
fashion their personal dress, just as men have to
tailor their own not very extensive but very carefully
finished garment, the pubic leaf. Men do the wood
carving, even in the case of objects used exclusively
by women; they manufacture lime gourds for betel
chewing and, in the old days, they used to polish and
sharpen all stone implements.

This specialization of work according to sex gives,
at certain seasons, a characteristic and picturesque
touch to village life. When harvest approaches
new skirts of the coloured variety have to be made,
ready to wear when the crops are brought in and
at the subsequent festivities. Quantities of banana
and pandanus leaf are brought to the villages, and
are there bleached and toughened at the fire. At night
the whole village is bright with the shining of these
fires, at each of which a couple of women sit opposite

each other and pass the leaf to and fro in front of
the flame (see pl. 9).   Loud chatter and song enlivens
the work, gay with the anticipation of the coming
entertainments.   When the material is ready, it has
still to be cut, trimmed, and dyed.   Two kinds of
roots are brought from the bush for the dyeing, one
giving a deep purple, and the other a bright crimson.
The dye is mixed in large bowls made of giant clam
shells ; in these the leaf strips are steeped, and then
they are hung up in thick bunches to dry in the
central place, enlivening the whole village with
their gay colour (see pl. 10). After a very complex
process of piecing together, a resplendent
" creation " results ; the golden yellow of the
pandanus, the soft hay-green or dun of the banana-
leaf, the crimson and purple of the dyed layers form
a really beautiful harmony of colour against the
smooth, brown skin of the woman.

Some manufactures are carried out by men and
women together. Both sexes, for example, take part
in the elaborate process which is necessary in
preparing certain shell ornaments,[1] while nets and
water-vessels may be made by either sex.

It will have been seen, then, that women do not
bear the brunt of all the drudgery and hard work.
Indeed, the heaviest tasks in the gardens and the
most monotonous ones are performed by men. On
the other hand, women have their own province
in economic activity ; it is a conspicuous one, and
through it they assert their status and importance.

[1] Cf. ch. xv of *Argonauts of the Western Pacific.*

CHAPTER II

THE STATUS OF WOMAN IN NATIVE SOCIETY

THE ideas of the native concerning kinship and descent, with their assertion of the mother's exclusive part in propagation ; the position of woman within the household, and her considerable share in economic life : these imply that woman plays an influential rôle in the community, and that her status cannot be low or unimportant. In this section it will be necessary to consider her legal status and her position in the tribe ; that is, her rank, her power, and her social independence of man.

In the first section of the previous chapter we have discussed the kinship ideas of the natives, founded on the matrilineal principle that everything descends through the mother. We have also seen that the real guardianship of her family remains not with herself, but with her brother. This can be generalized into the formula that, in each generation, woman continues the line and man represents it ; or, in other words, that the power and functions which belong to a family are vested in the men of each generation, though they have to be transmitted by the women.

I

THE PRIVILEGES AND BURDENS OF RANK

Let us examine some of the consequences of this principle. For the continuation and very existence of the family, woman as well as man is indispensable ; therefore both sexes are regarded by the natives as being of equal value and importance. When you discuss genealogies with a native, the question of continuity of line is constantly considered in relation to the number of women alive. This was noticeable whenever a man of a sub-clan of high rank, such as the Tabalu of Omarakana, discussed the ethnographic census of its members with me : the fact that there were a great number of women would be emphasized with pleasure, and said to be good and important. That there were only two women of that sub-clan of high rank in Omarakana, while there were several male members, was obviously a sore point, and every Tabalu informant volunteered the statement that there were, however, more women in the younger line of Olivilevi, a village in the south of the island also ruled by the Tabalu. A man of any clan would often, in speaking of his family relations, expatiate on the number of his sisters and of their female children as being a matter of real importance to his lineage. Thus girls are quite as welcome at birth as boys, and no difference is made between them by the parents in interest, enthusiasm, or affection. It is needless to add that the idea of female infanticide would be as absurd as abhorrent to the natives.

The general rule that women hand on the privileges of the family and men exercise them, must be examined as it works. When we do so we shall be able to understand the principle better and even to qualify it somewhat. The idea of rank—that is, of an intrinsic, social superiority of certain people as their birthright—is very highly developed among the Trobriand Islanders ; and a consideration of the way in which rank affects the individual will best explain the working of the general principle.

Rank is associated with definite hereditary groups of a totemic nature, which have already been designated here as *sub-clans* (see also ch. xiii, sec. 5). Each sub-clan has a definite rank ; it claims to be higher than some, and admits its inferiority to others. Five or six main categories of rank can, broadly speaking, be distinguished, and within these the minor grades are of but small importance. For the sake of brevity and clarity, I shall chiefly concern myself with a comparison of the sub-clan of Tabalu, the highest of all in rank, with its inferiors.

Every village community " belongs to " or is " owned by " one such sub-clan, and the eldest male is the headman of the village. When the sub-clan is of highest rank, its oldest male is not only headman of his own village, but exercises over-rule in a whole district, and is what we have called a chief. Chieftainship and rank are, therefore, closely associated, and rank carries with it, not only social distinction, but also the right to rule. Now, one of these two attributes, but one only, social distinction, is shared by men and women alike. Every woman of the highest rank, that of Tabalu, enjoys all the personal privileges of nobility. The male members of the clan will perhaps say that man is more aristocratic, more *guya'u* than woman, but probably this merely expresses the general assumption of male superiority. In all concrete manifestations of rank, whether traditional or social, the two sexes are equal. In the extensive mythology referring to the origin of the various sub-clans, a woman ancestress always figures beside the man (her brother), and there are even myths in which a woman alone inaugurates a line.[1]

Another important manifestation of rank is the complex system of taboos, and this is equally binding on man and woman. The taboos of rank include numerous prohibitions in the matter of food, certain animals especially being forbidden, and there are some other notable restrictions, such as that prohibiting the use of any water except from water-holes in the coral ridge. These taboos are enforced by supernatural sanction, and illness follows their breach, even if it be accidental. But the real force by which they are maintained is a strong conviction on the part of the taboo keeper that the forbidden food is intrinsically inferior, that it is

---

[1] Cf. my *Myth in Primitive Psychology*, ch. ii.

disgusting and defiling in itself. When it is suggested to a Tabalu that he should eat of stingaree or bush pig he shows unmistakable signs of repulsion ; and cases are quoted in which a man of rank has vomited, with every sign of nausea, some forbidden substance which he had taken unwittingly. A citizen of Omarakana will speak of the stingaree eaters of the lagoon villages with the same disgusted contempt as the right-minded Briton uses towards the frog- and snail-eaters of France, or the European towards the puppy- and rotten-egg-eaters of China.

Now a woman of rank fully shares in this disgust, and in the danger from breaking a taboo. If, as does occasionally happen, she marries a man of lower rank, she must have all food, all cooking utensils, dishes, and drinking vessels separate from her husband, or else he must forego all such diet as is taboo to her ; the latter is the course more usually adopted.

Rank entitles its possessors to certain ornaments, which serve both as its insignia and as festive decorations. For instance, a certain kind of shell ornament, the red spondylus shell-discs, may only be worn on the forehead and on the occiput by people of the highest rank. As belts and armlets they are also permitted to those next in rank. Again, an armlet on the forearm is a mark of the first aristocracy. Varieties and distinctions in personal adornment are very numerous, but it will be enough to say here that they are observed in exactly the same manner by male and female, though the ornaments are more frequently made use of by the latter.

Certain house decorations, on the other hand, such as carved boards and ornaments of shell (pls. 2, 20, and 23), which are in pattern and material exclusive to the several higher ranks, are primarily made use of by the male representatives. But a woman of rank who marries a commoner would be fully entitled to have them on her house.

The very important and elaborate ceremonial of respect observed towards people of rank is based on the idea that a man of noble lineage must always remain on a physically higher level than his inferiors. In the presence of a noble, all people of lower rank have to bow the head or bend the body or squat on the ground, according to the degree of their inferiority. On no account must any head reach higher than that of the chief. Tall platforms are always built on to the chief's house, and on one of these he will sit so that the people may freely move below him during tribal gatherings (see pl. 2, where we see the chief leaning against such a platform). When a commoner passes a group of nobles seated on the ground, even at a distance, he has to call out *tokay* (" arise "), and the chiefs immediately scramble to their feet and remain standing while he crouches past them.[1] One would think that so uncomfortable a ceremonial of homage would have been circumvented in some way ; but this is not the case. Many times when I was sitting in the village in conversation with the chief, a commoner would pass through the village grove, and call out *tokay*, and though this would happen every quarter of an hour or so, my friend had to rise while the other, bending low, walked slowly by.[2]

Women of rank enjoy exactly the same privilege in this matter. When a noble woman is married to a commoner, her husband has to bend before her in public, and others have to be still more careful to do so. A high platform is erected for

---

[1] *Tokay*, as noun, also means " commoner ". The noun is perhaps derived etymologically from the verb.

[2] When To'uluwa, the paramount chief of the Trobriands, was put in jail by the resident magistrate, the latter, mostly, I am afraid, because he wanted to humiliate his native rival, forbade the commoners incarcerated with the chief to crouch before him. In spite of this, I have been told on good authority by several eye-witnesses that all the commoners in jail did constantly move bending, except when the white satrap appeared upon the scene. This is an example of the short-sighted policy of the typical white official, who thinks that his authority can only be maintained at the expense of the native chiefs, and thus undermines native tribal law and introduces a spirit of anarchy.

her and she sits upon it alone at tribal assemblies, while her husband moves or squats below with the rest of the crowd.

The sanctity of the chief's person is particularly localized in his head, which is surrounded by a halo of strict taboos. More especially sacred are the forehead and the occiput with the neck. Only equals in rank, the wives and a few particularly privileged persons, are allowed to touch these parts, for purposes of cleaning, shaving, ornamentation, and delousing. This sanctity of the head extends to the female members of the noble sub-clans, and if a noble woman marries a commoner, her brow, her occiput, her neck and shoulders, should not— in theory at least—be touched by the husband even during the most intimate phases of conjugal life.

Thus in myth, in the observance of taboo, and in the ceremonial of bending, the woman enjoys exactly the same privileges of rank as the man; but she never exercises the actual power associated with it. No woman is ever the head of any sub-clan, and thus she cannot be a chieftainess. What would happen should there be no male members in a given generation I cannot say, for there are no actual cases of this on record; but the interim regency of a woman seems by no means incompatible with the ideas of the Trobrianders. But, as we shall see later on (ch. v, sec. 4), the privilege of polygamy is the foundation of a chief's or headman's power, and women, of course, have no such similar privilege of polyandry.

Many other social functions of rank are directly exercised by men alone, the women participating only in the social prestige. Thus ownership of canoes, for instance, is vested in the headman— though all the villagers enjoy definite rights in them —but his kinswomen only have the benefit of the renown (butura), that is, the privilege of talking in proprietary terms of the canoes and of boasting about them.[1] Only in exceptional cases do they accompany their men-folk on oversea expeditions. Again, all sorts of rights, privileges, and activities connected with the *kula*, a special system of exchange in valuables, are the prerogatives of men. The woman, whether the man's wife or sister, is only occasionally drawn personally into the matter. For the most part she but basks in reflected glory and satisfaction. In war, men have the field of action entirely to themselves, though the women witness all the preparations and preliminary ceremonies, and even take an occasional peep at the battle-field itself.[2]

It is important to note that in this section, when comparing the parts played by the sexes, we have had quite as often to set the brother and sister side by side as the husband and wife. Within the matrilineal order, the brother and the sister are the naturally linked representatives of the male and female principle respectively in all legal and customary matters. In the myths concerning the origin of families, the brother and sister emerge together from underground, through the original hole in the earth. In family matters, the brother is the natural guardian and head of his sister's household, and of her children. In tribal usage, their respective duties and obligations are strictly regulated, and these form, as we shall see, one of the main strands in the social fabric. But in their personal relations the strictest taboo divides brother from sister—and prevents any sort of intimacy between them.[3]

As woman is debarred from the exercise of power, land ownership, and many other public privileges, it

---

[1] These questions have been discussed in detail in *Argonauts of the Western Pacific*, ch. iv, secs. iv and v, and ch. xi, sec. ii. Cf. also ch. vi of that book, and *Crime and Custom*.

[2] For a full description of the *kula*, see *Argonauts* ; fighting has been described in the article on " War and Weapons among the Natives of the Trobriand Islands ", *Man*, 1920.

[3] Cf. ch. xiii, sec. 6, and ch. xiv.

follows that she has no place at tribal gatherings
and no voice in such public deliberations as are held
in connection with gardening, fishing, hunting,
oversea expeditions, war, ceremonial trade, festivities
and dances.

2

MORTUARY RITES AND FESTIVITIES

On the other hand, there are certain ceremonial
and festive activities in connection with which
women have a great deal both to say and to do.   The
most important of these in solemnity and sanctity,
as well as the most imposing in display and extent,
are the mortuary ceremonies.   In the tending of
the corpse, the parade of grief, the burial with
its manifold rites and long series of ceremonial
food distributions; in all these activities, which
begin immediately after the death of any important
tribesman and continue at intervals for months
or even years afterwards, women play a large part
and have their own definite duties to fulfil.   Certain
women, standing in a special relationship to the
deceased, have to hold the corpse on their knees,
and fondle it; and while the corpse is tended in
the hut, another category of female relatives performs
a remarkable rite of mourning outside : a number
of them, some in couples facing each other and some
singly, move in a slow dance, forwards and backwards across the central place, to the rhythm of
the wailing dirge (see pl. 11). As a rule, each
of them carries in her hand some object worn or
possessed by the deceased.   Such relics play a
great part in mourning and are worn by the women
for a long time after their bereavement.   The
wrapping up of the corpse and the subsequent
vigil over the grave is the duty of yet another
category of the dead man's womenkind.

Some functions of burial, notably the gruesome
custom of cutting up the corpse, are performed by

men. In the long period of mourning which follows, the burden of the dramatic expression of grief falls mostly on· the women ; a widow always mourns longer than a widower, a mother longer than a father, a female relative longer than a male of the same degree. In the mortuary distributions of food and wealth, based on the idea that the members of the deceased's sub-clan give payment to the other relatives for their share in the mourning, women play a conspicuous rôle, and conduct some parts of the ceremonial distributions themselves (see pl. 12).

I have barely touched on the mortuary ceremonies, as we shall have to return to them presently (ch. vi, secs. 3 and 4), but I have said enough to show how large a share women take in this class of religious or ceremonial display. Some tribal ceremonies in which women alone are active will be described in detail later, and it is only necessary here to state briefly that in the long and complicated ceremonial of first pregnancy (ch. viii, secs. 1 and 2) and in the rites of beauty magic at festivities (ch. xi, secs. 2–4) women are the main actors. On certain occasions, such as first pregnancy ritual and the first appearance after childbirth, as well as at big tribal dances and *kayasa* (competitive displays), women appear in full dress and decoration (pl. 13), which correspond to the men's full festive attire (as seen on pls. 14 and 79).

An interesting incident occurs during the *milamala*, the annual season of dancing and feasting held after the harvest. This period is inaugurated by a ceremony, the principal aim of which is to break the taboo on drums. In this initial feast there is a distribution of food, and the men, adorned in full dancing attire, range themselves for the performance, the drummers and the singers in the centre of a ring formed by the decorated dancers. As in a normal dance, standing in the central place, the singers intone a chant, the dancers begin to

move slowly and the drummers to beat time. But
they are not allowed to proceed : almost at the first
throb of the drums, there breaks forth from inside
the huts the wailing of those women who are still
in mourning ; from behind the inner row of houses,
a crowd of shrieking, agitated female figures rush
out and attack the dancers, beat them with sticks,
and throw coconuts, stones, and pieces of wood at
them. The men are not bound by custom to display
too considerable courage and in a trice the drummers,
who had so solemnly initiated the performance,
have entirely disappeared ; and the village lies
empty, for the women pursue the fugitives.
But the taboo is broken and, on the afternoon of
the same day, the first undisturbed dance of the
festivities is held.

In full dress dancing (see pls. 14, 58, 65, 73, 82),
it is mainly the men who display their beauty and
skill. In some dances, such as those performed in
a quick tempo with carved dancing boards or with
bunches of streamers or in conventionalized imitation
of animals, men alone may participate (pls. 65, 73,
82). Only in one traditional type of dance, for
which men put on the fibre petticoats of the female
(see pls. 3, 58), are women not debarred by custom
from participation. But though I witnessed scores
of performances of this type, I only once saw a
woman actually dance, and she was of the very
highest rank. As passive witnesses and admirers,
however, women form a very important adjunct to
this form of display.

There are many other long, continuous periods
of amusement in the Trobriands besides the dancing
season, and in these women take a more active share.
The nature of the amusement is fixed in advance,
and has to remain the same during the whole period.
There are different kinds of *kayasa*, as these entertainments are called (see ch. ix, secs. 2–4). There
is a *kayasa* in which, evening after evening, groups
of women, festively adorned, sit on mats and sing ;

in another, men and women, wearing wreaths and garlands of flowers, exchange such ornaments with each other ; or a *kayasa* is announced, the main theme of which is a general daily display of a certain type of ornament. Sometimes the members of a community prepare small toy sailing canoes and hold a miniature regatta daily on shallow water. There can be also a *kayasa* of erotic pastimes. Some of these entertainments are exclusively feminine (singing and certain ornaments) ; in others both sexes participate (flowers, erotics, and hair decoration) ; in others only men (the toy canoes).

In all the public festivals and entertainments, whether women take an active part or no, they are never excluded from looking on or freely mixing with the men ; and this they do on terms of perfect equality, exchanging banter and jokes with them and engaging in easy conversation.

3

WOMAN'S SHARE IN MAGIC

One aspect of public life is very important to the Trobriander and stands apart as something peculiar and specific. The native sets on one side a certain category of facts, one type of human behaviour, and designates these by the word *megwa*, which may be quite adequately translated as " magic ". Magic is very intimately associated with economic life and indeed with every vital concern ; it is also an instrument of power and an index of the importance of those who practise it. The position of women in magic deserves therefore very special consideration.

Magic constitutes a particular aspect of reality. In all important activities and enterprises in which man has not the issue firmly and safely in hand,

34

magic is deemed indispensable. Thus appeal is made to it in gardening and fishing, in building a large canoe, and in diving for valuable shell, in the regulation of wind and weather, in war, in matters of love and personal attraction, in securing safety at sea and the success of any great enterprise ; and, last but not least, in health and for the infliction of ailments upon an enemy. Success and safety in all these matters is largely and sometimes entirely dependent upon magic, and can be controlled by its proper application. Fortune or failure, dearth or plenty, health or disease are felt and believed to be mainly due to the right magic rightly applied in the right circumstances.

Magic consists of spells and rites performed by a man who is entitled by the fulfilment of several conditions to perform them. Magical power resides primarily in the words of the formula, and the function of the rite, which is as a rule very simple, is mainly to convey the magician's breath, charged with the power of the words, to the object or person to be affected. All magical spells are believed to have descended unchanged from time immemorial, from the beginning of things.

This last point has its sociological corollary ; several systems of magic are hereditary, each in a special sub-clan, and such a system has been possessed by that sub-clan since the time it came out from underground. It can only be performed by a member, and is, of course, one of the valued attributes and possessions of the sub-clan itself. It is handed on in the female line, though usually, as with other forms of power and possession, it is exercised by men alone. But in a few cases such hereditary magic can also be practised by women.

The power given by magic to its performer is not due merely to the effects of its specific influence. In the most important types of magic the rites are intimately interwoven with the activities which they accompany and are not merely superimposed upon them. Thus, in garden magic, the officiator plays an economically and socially important rôle and is the organizer and director of the work. It is the same in the building of a canoe and its magic, and in the rites associated with the conduct of an oversea expedition : the man who technically directs and is the leader of the enterprise has also the duty or privilege of performing the magic.[1] Both functions, the directive and the magical, are indivisibly united in the same person. In other types of magic, which are placed by the natives in the category of *bulubwalata* (black magic)— and this comprises all sorcery and, among others, the charms for drought or rain—the practitioner has an immense and direct influence over other tribesmen. Magic is indeed by far the most efficient and frequently used instrument of power.

As magic is so intimately bound up with the activity which it accompanies, it is clear that, in certain types of occupation, the division of functions between the sexes will involve a corresponding division in magical performance. Those types of work which customarily only men perform will demand a man as officiating magician ; where women are occupied with their own business, the magician must be female. Thus, looking at the table given below, we see that in fishing and hunting, as well as in wood carving, activities in which no woman ever participates, magic is exclusively practised by men. War magic, too, which is now in abeyance, was an hereditary system of spells and rites always practised by a man of a certain sub-clan. The long and complex series of spells which accompany the building of a sea-going canoe can never be made by a woman, and, as no woman ever goes on a ceremonial overseas expedition, the magic of safety and of *kula* which then has to be performed can only be done by a man.

[1] Cf. *Argonauts of the Western Pacific*, esp. chs. iv, v, vii, and xvii.

DIVISION OF MAGIC BETWEEN THE SEXES

Male.	Female.	Mixed.
Public garden magic (*Towosi*)	Rites of first pregnancy	Beauty magic
Fishing	Skirt making	Love magic
Hunting	Prevention of dangers at birth	Private garden magic
Canoe building	Toothache	
Magic of *kula* (*Mwasila*)	Elephantiasis, swellings	
Weather (sun and rain)'	Affections of the genitals with discharge (Gonorrhœa ?)	
Wind	Abortion	
War magic (*Boma*)	Female witchcraft (*Yoyova* or *Mulukwausi*)	
Safety at sea (*Kayga'u*)		
Wood carving (*Kabitam*)		
Sorcery (*Bwaga'u*)		

Again there are some important types of magic which are obviously adapted to female hands and lips, for they are attached to activities or functions which by their nature or by social convention exclude the presence of men. Such is the magic associated with the ceremony of first pregnancy (see ch. viii, secs. 1 and 2); the magic of the expert which gives skill in the manufacture of fibre petticoats ; and the magic of abortion.

There are, however, mixed spheres of activity and influence, such as gardening or love-making, the control of the weather or human health, where at first glance there appears to be no association with one sex rather than the other. Yet garden magic is invariably a man's concern and women never perform the important public rites, most scrupulously observed and highly valued by the natives, which are carried out by the village magician over the gardens of the whole community.[1] Even those phases of gardening, such as weeding, which are undertaken exclusively by women, have to be inaugurated by the male garden magician in an

[1] In the Amphlett Islands, on the other hand, garden magic is made mainly if not exclusively by women. Among the natives of Dobu Island and on the north-eastern shores of Dawson Straits in the d'Entrecasteaux Archipelago, women also play a preponderating rôle in garden magic.

official ceremony. Wind, sunshine, and rain are also controlled entirely by male hands and mouths.

In certain mixed activities a man or a woman can equally well perform the required magic, and some minor rites of private garden magic, used by each individual for his or her own benefit, can be carried out indiscriminately by men or women. There is the magic of love and beauty, of which the spells are recited by anyone who suffers from unrequited love or needs to enhance his or her personal charm. Again, on certain occasions, such, for instance, as the big tribal festivals, the spells of beauty are publicly recited by women over men (ch. xi, sec. 3), and, at other times, men apply a form of beauty magic to their own persons and ornaments.[1]

The most definite allocation of magical powers to one or other of the sexes is to be found in the dark and dreaded forces of sorcery : those forces which most profoundly affect human hope and happiness. The magic of illness and health, which can poison life or restore its natural sweetness, and which holds death as it were for its last card, can be made by men and women alike ; but its character changes entirely with the sex of the practitioner. Man and woman have each their own sorcery, carried on by means of different rites and formulæ, acting in a different manner on the victim's body and surrounded by an altogether different atmosphere of belief. Male sorcery is much more concrete, and its methods can be stated clearly, almost as a rational system. The sorcerer's supernatural equipment is restricted to his power of vanishing at will, of emitting a shining glow from his person, and of having accomplices among the nocturnal birds. Extremely poor means of super-natural action if we compare them with the achievements of a witch !

[1] Cf. *Argonauts of the Western Pacific*, ch. xiii, sec.

A witch—and be it remembered that she is always a real woman and not a spiritual or non-human being—goes out on her nightly errand in the form of an invisible double ; she can fly through the air and appears as a falling star ; she assumes at will the shape of a fire-fly, of a night bird or of a flying-fox ; she can hear and smell at enormous distances ; she is endowed with sarcophagous propensities, and feeds on corpses.

The disease which witches cause is almost incurable and extremely rapid in its action, killing, as a rule, immediately.   It is inflicted by the removal of the victim's inside, which the woman presently consumes.   The wizard, on the other hand, never partakes of his victim's flesh, his power is much less effective, he must proceed slowly, and the best he can hope for is to inflict a lingering disease, which may, with good luck, kill after months or years of steady labour.   Even then another sorcerer can be hired to counteract his work and restore the patient. But there is little chance of combating a witch, even if the help of another witch be sought immediately.

A witch, when she is not old, is no less desirable sexually than other women.   Indeed, she is surrounded by a halo of glory due to her personal power, and usually she has also that strong individuality which seems to accompany the reputation for witchcraft.   The attraction which a marriageable young witch has for the other sex need not be altogether disinterested, for witchcraft is occasionally a source of income and of personal influence in which it is pleasant to have a share.   But the profession of witch, unlike that of sorcerer, is not exercised openly ; a witch may receive payment for healing, but she never undertakes to kill for a fee.   In this again she differs from the sorcerer who derives the greater part of his income from black rather than from curative practice.   Indeed, even when a woman is generally known to be a witch, she is never supposed to admit it explicitly, even to her husband.

Witchcraft is inherited from mother to daughter, and an early initiation has to take place. In later life, the art of female necromancy is sometimes further enhanced by less reputable means. Some women are said to have sexual relations with non-human, highly malignant beings called *tauva'u* who bring epidemics and various evils upon the people (see ch. xii, sec. 4). By them they are further instructed in the art of harming, and such women are greatly feared. Several of my personal acquaintance were definitely pointed out as having a leman from the sphere of *tauva'u*, notably the wife of the headman of Obweria, a very intelligent and enterprising character, who is seen, as the main performer, on plates 77 and 78.

From the point of view of the investigating sociologist, the most important difference between male and female sorcery lies in the fact that the wizard actually carries on his trade, while the witch's activity exists only in folk-lore and in the imagination of the native. That is to say, a sorcerer actually knows the magic of his trade; when called upon he will utter it over the proper substances; will go out at night to waylay his victim or visit him in his hut; and in certain cases, I suspect, may even administer poison. The witch, on the other hand, however much she may be believed to play the part of a *yoyova*, does not—needless to say—really fly or abstract the insides of people, and she knows no spells or rites, since this type of female magic lives merely in legend and fiction.

There are a number of minor ailments, among them toothache, certain tumours, swelling of the testicles and genital discharge (gonorrhœa ?), which woman can inflict on man by means of magic. Toothache is exclusively a female speciality, and one woman will be called in to cure it when some other has caused it. A witch can produce it through her magical power over a small beetle called *kim*, which is very similar to the one which makes holes in taro. The resemblance between dental caries and the cavities bored by the beetle in taro is a sufficient proof that similar effects have been produced by similar causes. But some of my informants had actually seen the small black scarab fall out of a man's mouth while a woman was performing the curative formula.

There are, as we have seen, forms of hereditary magic which can be carried on only by male members of a sub-clan, or, exceptionally, by the son of such a member. (And in the latter case he has to relinquish it at his father's death.) Now, if the males of a certain generation were to die out, a woman could learn such magic, though she would not be allowed to practise it, and when she bore a male heir to her sub-clan, would teach him the formula for his future use. Thus woman can tide over the gap of one generation, carrying in her memory a system of garden magic, or weather and wind charms, or spells for fishing, hunting, canoe building, and oversea trade. She can even preserve a system of war magic, but she must never learn the formula of masculine sorcery, which is strictly taboo to the female sex. Nor is there any necessity for her to do so, since this magic is never strictly hereditary within a sub-clan.

Thus we see that the strong tribal position of women is also buttressed by their right to exercise magic—that toughest and least destructible substance of belief.

And now, in order to summarize briefly the results of this chapter and the previous one, let us imagine that we are taking a bird's eye view of a native village, and are trying to form a compound moving picture of the life of the community. Casting our glance over the central place, the street, and the surrounding grove and garden land, we see them peopled by men and women mixing freely and on terms of equality. Sometimes they go together to work in the garden, or to collect food-stuffs in the jungle or on the sea-shore. Or else they separate, each sex forming a group of workers engaged‾ in some special activity, and performing it efficiently and with interest. Men predominate on the central place, discussing, perhaps, in a communal gathering the prospects of the garden, or preparing for an oversea expedition or for some ceremony. The street is peopled by women, busying themselves with household work, and there the men will presently join them, helping them to amuse the children or in some domestic task. We can hear the women scold their husbands, usually in a very good-natured manner.

Let us suppose our attention to be drawn to some singular event, to a death, a tribal squabble, a division of inherited wealth, or to some ceremony. We watch it with understanding eyes, and see, side by side, the workings of tribal law and custom, and the play of personal passion and interest. We see the influence of matrilineal principles, the working of paternal rule, usages of tribal authority, and the results of totemic division in the clans and sub-clans. In all this there is a balance between the influence of male and female, the man wields the power while the woman determines its distribution.

Or perhaps the central place is thronged by a mixed gathering, gay with festive dress and decorations. Women move with a soft swaying motion in their holiday attire, coquettishly aware of the lines of their bodies and the elegant swish-swish of their full, crimson, purple, and golden skirts. The men are more soberly dressed, and affect a stiff, immovable dignity. They move very little, unless they are among the performers in the dance or other festive function. These last are covered gorgeously with ornaments, and are instinct with life and motion. The performance starts ; it is carried on sometimes by men only, and sometimes by women. As it progresses, later in the afternoon or in the evening, the young men and women begin to show some interest in each other : here and there snatches of conversation, bursts of laughter and giggling can be heard. Nothing in the slightest degree obscene, indecent, or sexually improper can be observed in their behaviour, though their vocabulary is by no means prim. But, since we understand this community, we know that assignations are being made and intrigues inaugurated. Thus we are led up to the closer study of the erotic phase of native life ; and we now proceed to a systematic description of this subject.

CHAPTER III

THE Trobrianders are very free and easy in their sexual relations. To a superficial observer it might indeed appear that they are entirely untrammeled in these. This, however, is not the case ; for their liberty has certain very well-defined limits. The best way of showing this will be to give a consecutive account of the various stages through which a man and a woman pass from childhood to maturity—a sort of sexual life-history of a representative couple.

We shall have first to consider their earliest years, for these natives begin their acquaintance with sex at a very tender age. The unregulated and, as it were, capricious intercourse of these early years becomes systematized in adolescence into more or less stable intrigues, which later on develop into permanent liaisons. Connected with these latter stages of sexual life, there exists in the Trobriand Islands an extremely interesting institution, the bachelors' and unmarried girls' house, called by the natives *bukumatula* ; it is of considerable importance, as it is one of those arrangements sanctioned by custom which might appear on the surface to be a form of " group-marriage ".

I

THE SEXUAL LIFE OF CHILDREN

Children in the Trobriand Islands enjoy considerable freedom and independence. They soon become emancipated from a parental tutelage which has never been very strict. Some of them obey their parents willingly, but this is entirely a matter

44

of the personal character of both parties : there is no idea of a regular discipline, no system of domestic coercion. Often as I sat among them, observing some family incident or listening to a quarrel between parent and child, I would hear a youngster told to do this or that, and generally the thing, whatever it was, would be asked as a favour, though sometimes the request might be backed up by a threat of violence. The parents would either coax or scold or ask as from one equal to another. A simple command, implying the expectation of natural obedience, is never heard from parent to child in the Trobriands.

People will sometimes grow angry with their children and beat them in an outburst of rage ; but I have quite as often seen a child rush furiously at his parent and strike him. This attack might be received with a good-natured smile, or the blow might be angrily returned ; but the idea of definite retribution, or of coercive punishment, is not only foreign, but distinctly repugnant to the native. Several times, when I suggested, after some flagrant infantile misdeed, that it would mend matters for the future if the child were beaten or otherwise punished in cold blood, the idea appeared unnatural and immoral to my friends, and was rejected with some resentment.

Such freedom gives scope for the formation of the children's own little community, an independent group, into which they drop naturally from the age of four or five and continue till puberty. As the mood prompts them, they remain with their parents during the day, or else join their playmates for a time in their small republic (see pls. 15, 16, and 17). And this community within a community acts very much as its own members determine, standing often in a sort of collective opposition to its elders. If the children make up their minds to do a certain thing, to go for a day's expedition, for instance, the grown-ups and even the chief himself, as I often observed, will not be able to stop them. In my ethnographic work I was able and was indeed forced to collect my information about children and their concerns directly from them. Their spiritual ownership in games and childish activities was acknowledged, and they were also quite capable of instructing me and explaining the intricacies of their play or enterprise (see pl. 15).

Small children begin also to understand and to defer to tribal tradition and custom ; to those restrictions which have the character of a taboo or of a definite command of tribal law, or usage or propriety.[1]

The child's freedom and independence extend also to sexual matters. To begin with, children hear of and witness much in the sexual life of their elders. Within the house, where the parents have no possibility of finding privacy, a child has opportunities of acquiring practical information concerning the sexual act. I was told that no special precautions are taken to prevent children from witnessing their parents' sexual enjoyment. The child would merely be scolded and told to cover its head with a mat. I sometimes heard a little boy or girl praised in these terms : " Good child, he never tells what happens between his parents." Young children are allowed to listen to baldly sexual talk, and they understand perfectly well what is being discussed. They are also themselves tolerably expert in swearing and the use of obscene language. Because of their early mental development some quite tiny children are able to make smutty jokes, and these their elders will greet with laughter.

Small girls follow their fathers on fishing expeditions, during which the men remove their pubic

---

[1] The processes by which respect for tribal taboo and tradition is instilled in the child are described throughout this book, especially in ch. xiii. Custom must not be personified nor is its authority absolute or autonomous, but it is derived from specific social and psychological mechanisms. Cf. my *Crime and Custom*, 1926.

leaf. Nakedness under these conditions is regarded as natural, since it is necessary. There is no lubricity or ribaldry associated with it. Once, when I was engaged in the discussion of an obscene subject, a little girl, the daughter of one of my informants, joined our group. I asked the father to tell her to go away. " Oh no," he answered, " she is a good girl, she never repeats to her mother anything that is said among men. When we take her fishing with us we need not be ashamed. Another girl would describe the details of our nakedness to her companions or her mothers.[1] Then these will chaff us and repeat what they have heard about us. This little girl never says a word." The other men present enthusiastically assented, and developed the theme of the girl's discretion. But a boy is much less in contact with his mother in such matters, for here, between maternal relations, that is, for the natives, between real kindred, the taboo of incest begins to act at an early age, and the boy is removed from any intimate contact of this sort with his mother and above all with his sisters.

There are plenty of opportunities for both boys and girls to receive instruction in erotic matters from their companions. The children initiate each other into the mysteries of sexual life in a directly practical manner at a very early age. A premature amorous existence begins among them long before they are able really to carry out the act of sex. They indulge in plays and pastimes in which they satisfy their curiosity concerning the appearance and function of the organs of generation, and incidentally receive, it would seem, a certain amount of positive pleasure. Genital manipulation and such minor perversions as oral stimulation of the organs are typical forms of this amusement. Small boys and girls are said to be frequently initiated by their somewhat older companions,

---

[1] That is, "classificatory mothers" mother, maternal aunts, etc. Cf. ch. xiii, secs. 5 and 6.

who allow them to witness their own amorous dalliance. As they are untrammelled by the authority of their elders and unrestrained by any moral code, except that of specific tribal taboo, there is nothing but their degree of curiosity, of ripeness, and of " temperament " or sensuality, to determine how much or how little they shall indulge in sexual pastimes.

The attitude of the grown-ups and even of the parents towards such infantile indulgence is either that of complete indifference or of complacency—they find it natural, and do not see why they should scold or interfere. Usually they show a kind of tolerant and amused interest, and discuss the love affairs of their children with easy jocularity. I often heard some such benevolent gossip as this : " So-and-so (a little girl) has already had intercourse with So-and-so (a little boy)." And if such were the case, it would be added that it was her first experience. An exchange of lovers, or some small love drama in the little world would be half-seriously, half-jokingly discussed. The infantile sexual act, or its substitute, is regarded as an innocent amusement. " It is their play to *kayta* (to have intercourse). They give each other a coconut, a small piece of betel-nut, a few beads or some fruits from the bush, and then they go and hide, and *kayta*." But it is not considered proper for the children to carry on their affairs in the house. It has always to be done in the bush.

The age at which a girl begins to amuse herself in this manner is said to coincide with her putting on the small fibre skirt, between, that is, the ages of four and five. But this obviously can refer only to incomplete practices and not to the real act. Some of my informants insisted that such small female children actually have intercourse with penetration. Remembering, however, the Trobriander's very strong tendency to exaggerate in the direction of the grotesque, a tendency not altogether devoid

48

of a certain malicious Rabelaisian humour, I am inclined to discount those statements of my authorities. If we place the beginning of real sexual life at the age of six to eight in the case of girls, and ten to twelve in the case of boys, we shall probably not be erring very greatly in either direction. And from these times sexuality will gradually assume a greater and greater importance as life goes on, until it abates in the course of nature.

Sexual, or at least sensuous pleasure constitutes if not the basis of, at least an element in, many of the children's pastimes. Some of them do not, of course, provide any sexual excitement at all, as for instance those in imitation of the grown-up economic and ceremonial activities (see pl. 17), or games of skill or childish athletics; but all sorts of round games, which are played by the children of both sexes on the central place of the village, have a more or less strongly marked flavour of sex, though the outlets they furnish are indirect and only accessible to the elder youths and maidens, who also join in them. Indeed, we shall have to return later (chs. ix and xi) to a consideration of sex in certain games, songs, and stories, for as the sexual association becomes more subtle and indirect it appeals more and more to older people alone and has, therefore, to be examined in the contexts of later life.

There are, however, some specific games in which the older children never participate, and into which sex directly enters. The little ones sometimes play, for instance, at house-building, and at family life. A small hut of sticks and boughs is constructed in a secluded part of the jungle, and a couple or more repair thither and play at husband and wife, prepare food and carry out or imitate as best they can the act of sex. Or else a band of them, in imitation of the amorous expeditions of their elders, carry food to some favourite spot on the sea-shore or in the coral ridge, cook and eat vegetables there, and " when they are full of food, the boys sometimes fight with each other, or sometimes *kayta* (copulate) with the girls". When the fruit ripens on certain wild trees in the jungle they go in parties to pick it, to exchange presents, make *kula* (ceremonial exchange) of the fruit, and engage in erotic pastimes.[1]

Thus it will be seen that they have a tendency to palliate the crudity of their sexual interest and indulgence by associating it with something more poetic. Indeed, the Trobriand children show a great sense of the singular and romantic in their games. For instance, if a part of the jungle or village has been flooded by rain, they go and sail their small canoes on this new water ; or if a very strong sea has thrown up some interesting flotsam, they proceed to the beach and inaugurate some imaginative game around it. The little boys, too, search for unusual animals, insects, or flowers, and give them to the little girls, thus lending a redeeming æsthetic touch to their premature eroticisms.

In spite of the importance of the sexual motive in the life of the youngest generation, it must be kept in mind that the separation of the sexes, in many matters, obtains also among children, Small girls can very often be seen playing or wandering in independent parties by themselves. Little boys in certain moods—and these seem their more usual ones—scorn the society of the female and amuse themselves alone (pl. 17). Thus the small republic falls into two distinct groups which are perhaps to be seen more often apart than together ; and, though they frequently unite in play, this need by no means be necessarily sensuous.

It is important to note that there is no interference by older persons in the sexual life of children. On rare occasions some old man or woman is suspected of taking a strong sexual interest in

[1] For a description of the real *kula*, cf. *Argonauts of the Western Pacific.*

the children, and even of having intercourse with some of them. But I never found such suspicions supported even by a general consensus of opinion, and it was always considered both improper and silly for an older man or woman to have sexual dealings with a child. There is certainly no trace of any custom of ceremonial defloration by old men, or even by men belonging to an older age class.

2

Age Divisions

I have just used the expression " age class ", but I did so in a broad sense only : for there are no sharply distinguished age grades or classes among the Trobriand natives. The following table of age designations only roughly indicates the stages of their life ; for these stages in practice merge into one another.

Designations of Age

1. *Waywaya* (fœtus ; infant till the age of crawling, both male and female).
2. *Pwapwawa* (infant, till the stage of walking, male or female).
3. *Gwadi* (child, till puberty, male or female).
4. *Monagwadi* (male child)　　4. *Inagwadi* (female child)

I. Stage : *Gwadi*—Word used as a generic designation for all these stages 1–4, meaning *child*, male or female, at any time between birth and maturity

5. *To'ulatile* (youth from puberty till marriage)
6. *Tobubowa'u* (mature man)
6a. *Tovavaygile* (married man)

5. *Nakapugula* or *Nakubukwabuya* (girl from puberty till marriage)
6. *Nabubowa'u* (ripe woman)
6a. *Navavaygile* (married woman)

II. Stage : Generic designations—*Ta'u* (man), *Vivila* (woman).

7. *Tomwaya* (old man)
7a. *Toboma* (old honoured man)

7. *Numwaya* (old woman)

III. Stage : Old age.

The terms used in this table will be found to overlap in some instances. Thus a very small infant may be referred to as *waywaya* or *pwapwawa* indiscriminately, but only the former term as a rule would be used in speaking of a fœtus or referring to the pre-incarnated children from Tuma.[1] Again, you might call a few months' old child either *gwadi* or *pwapwawa*, but the latter term would be but seldom used except for a very small baby. The term *gwadi* moreover can be used generically, as "child" in English, to denote anything from a fœtus to a young boy or girl. Thus, it will be seen that two terms may encroach on each other's field of meaning, but only if they be consecutive. The terms with sex prefixes (4) are normally used only of elder children who may be distinguished by their dress.

There are, besides these more specific subdivisions, the three main distinctions of age, between the ripe man and woman in the full vigour of life and the two stages—those of childhood and of old age—which limit manhood and womanhood on either side. The second main stage is divided into two parts, mainly by the fact of marriage. Thus, the words under (5) primarily designate unmarried people and to that extent are opposed to (6a), but they also imply youthfulness or unripeness, and in that respect are opposed to (6).

The male term for old age, *tomwaya* (7) can also denote rank or importance. I myself was often so addressed, but I was not flattered, and much preferred to be called *toboma* (literally "the tabooed man"), a name given to old men of rank, but stressing the latter attribute rather than the former. Curiously enough, the compliment or distinction implied in the word *tomwaya* becomes much weaker, and almost disappears in its feminine equivalent. *Numwaya* conveys that tinge of scorn or ridicule inseparable from "old woman" in so many languages.

[1] Cf. ch. vii, sec. 2.

3

THE AMOROUS LIFE OF ADOLESCENCE

When a boy reaches the age of from twelve to fourteen years, and attains that physical vigour which comes with sexual maturity, and when, above all, his increased strength and mental ripeness allow him to take part, though still in a somewhat limited and fitful manner, in some of the economic activities of his elders, he ceases to be regarded as a child (*gwadi*), and assumes the position of adolescent (*ulatile* or *to'ulatile*). At the same time he receives a different status, involving some duties and many privileges, a stricter observance of taboos, and a greater participation in tribal affairs. He has already donned the pubic leaf for some time; now he becomes more careful in his wearing of it, and more interested in its appearance. The girl emerges from childhood into adolescence through the obvious bodily changes : " her breasts are round and full ; her bodily hair begins to grow ; her menses flow and ebb with every moon," as the natives put it. She also has no new change in her attire to make, for she has much earlier assumed her fibre skirt, but now her interest in it from the two points of view of elegance and decorum is greatly increased.

At this stage a partial break-up of the family takes place. Brothers and sisters must be segregated in obedience to that stringent taboo which plays such an important part in tribal life.[1] The elder children, especially the males, have to leave the house, so as not to hamper by their embarrassing presence the sexual life of their parents. This partial disintegration of the family group is effected by the boy moving to a house tenanted by bachelors or by elderly widowed male relatives or friends. Such a house is called *bukumatula*, and in the next section we shall become acquainted with the details of its arrangement. The girl sometimes goes to

[1] Cf. ch. xiii, 6, and ch. xiv.

the house of an elderly widowed maternal aunt or other relative.

As the boy or girl enters upon adolescence the nature of his or her sexual activity becomes more serious. It ceases to be mere child's play and assumes a prominent place among life's interests. What was before an unstable relation culminating in an exchange of erotic manipulation or an immature sexual act becomes now an absorbing passion, and a matter for serious endeavour. An adolescent gets definitely attached to a given person, wishes to possess her, works purposefully towards this goal, plans to reach the fulfilment of his desires by magical and other means, and finally rejoices in achievement. I have seen young people of this age grow positively miserable through ill-success in love. This stage, in fact, differs from the one before in that personal preference has now come into play and with it a tendency towards a greater permanence in intrigue. The boy develops a desire to retain the fidelity and exclusive affection of the loved one, at least for a time. But this tendency is not associated so far with any idea of settling down to one exclusive relationship, nor do adolescents yet begin to think of marriage. A boy or girl wishes to pass through many more experiences ; he or she still enjoys the prospect of complete freedom and has no desire to accept obligations. Though pleased to imagine that his partner is faithful, the youthful lover does not feel obliged to reciprocate this fidelity.

We have seen in the previous section that a group of children forming a sort of small republic within the community is conspicuous in every village. Adolescence furnishes the community with another small group, of youths and girls. At this stage, however, though the boys and girls are much more bound up in each other as regards amorous interests, they but rarely mix in public or in the daytime. The group is really broken up into two, according

to sex (pls. 18 and 19; see also pls. 59 and 61).
To this division there correspond two words,
to'ulatile and *nakubukwabuya*, there being no one
expression—such as there is to describe the younger
age group, *gugwadi*, children—to define the
adolescent youth of both sexes.

The natives take an evident pride in this, " the
flower of the village ", as it might be called.   They
frequently mention that " all the *to'ulatile* and
nakubukwabuya (youths and girls) of the village
were there ".   In speaking of some competitive
game, or dance or sport, they compare the looks or
performance of their own youths with those of some
other village, and always to the advantage of their
own.   This group lead a happy, free, arcadian
existence, devoted to amusement and the pursuit
of pleasure.

Its members are so far not claimed by any serious
duties, yet their greater physical strength and ripeness give them more independence and a wider
scope of action than they had as children.   The
adolescent boys participate, but mainly as free-
lances, in garden work (see pl. 19), in the fishing
and hunting and in oversea expeditions ; they get
all the excitement and pleasure, as well as some of
the prestige, yet remain free from a great deal of
the drudgery and many of the restrictions which
trammel and weigh on their elders.   Many of the
taboos are not yet quite binding on them, the burden
of magic has not yet fallen on their shoulders.   If
they grow tired of work, they simply stop and rest.
The self-discipline of ambition and subservience
to traditional ideals, which moves all the elder
individuals and leaves them relatively little personal
freedom, has not yet quite drawn these boys into
the wheels of the social machine.   Girls, too, obtain
a certain amount of the enjoyment and excitement
denied to children by joining in some of the activities
of their elders, while still escaping the worst of the
drudgery.

Young people of this age, besides conducting their love affairs more seriously and intensely, widen and give a greater variety to the setting of their amours. Both sexes arrange picnics and excursions and thus their indulgence in intercourse becomes associated with an enjoyment of novel experiences and fine scenery. They also form sexual connections outside the village community to which they belong. Whenever there occurs in some other locality one of the ceremonial occasions on which custom permits of licence, thither they repair, usually in bands either of boys or of girls, since on such occasions opportunity of indulgence offers for one sex alone (see ch. ix, esp. secs. 6 and 7).

It is necessary to add that the places used for love-making differ at this stage from those of the previous one. The small children carry on their sexual practices surreptitiously in bush or grove as a part of their games, using all sorts of makeshift arrangements to attain privacy, but the *ulatile* (adolescent) has either a couch of his own in a bachelors' house, or the use of a hut belonging to one of his unmarried relatives. In a certain type of yam-house, too, there is an empty closed-in space in which boys sometimes arrange little " cosy-corners ", affording room for two. In these, they make a bed of dry leaves and mats, and thus obtain a comfortable *garçonnière*, where they can meet and spend a happy hour or two with their loves. Such arrangements are, of course, necessary now that amorous intercourse has become a passion instead of a game.

But a couple will not yet regularly cohabit in a bachelors' house (*bukumatula*), living together and sharing the same bed night after night. Both girl and boy prefer to adopt more furtive and less conventionally binding methods, to avoid lapsing into a permanent relationship which might put unnecessary restraint upon their liberty by becoming generally known. That is why they usually prefer a small nest in the *sokwaypa* (covered yam-house), or the temporary hospitality of a bachelors' house.

We have seen that the youthful attachments between boys and girls at this stage have ripened out of childish games and intimacies. All these young people have grown up in close propinquity and with full knowledge of each other. Such early acquaintances take fire, as it were, under the influence of certain entertainments, where the intoxicating influence of music and moonlight, and the changed mood and attire of all the participants, transfigure the boy and girl in each other's eyes. Intimate observation of the natives and their personal confidences have convinced me that extraneous stimuli of this kind play a great part in the love affairs of the Trobrianders. Such opportunities of mutual transformation and escape from the monotony of everyday life are afforded not only by the many fixed seasons of festivity and permitted licence, but also by that monthly increase in the people's pleasure-seeking mood which leads to many special pastimes at the full of the moon.[1]

Thus adolescence marks the transition between infantile and playful sexualities and those serious permanent relations which precede marriage. During this intermediate period love becomes passionate and yet remains free.

As time goes on, and the boys and girls grow older, their intrigues last longer, and their mutual ties tend to become stronger and more permanent. A personal preference as a rule develops and begins definitely to overshadow all other love affairs. It may be based on true sexual passion or else on an affinity of characters. Practical considerations become involved in it, and, sooner or later, the man thinks of stabilizing one of his liaisons by marriage. In the ordinary course of events, every marriage is preceded by a more or less protracted period of

[1] Cf. ch. ix.

sexual life in common. This is generally known and spoken of, and is regarded as a public intimation of the matrimonial projects of the pair. It serves also as a test of the strength of their attachment and extent of their mutual compatibility. This trial period also gives time for the prospective bridegroom and for the woman's family to prepare economically for the event.

Two people living together as permanent lovers are described respectively as " his woman " (*la vivila*) and " her man " (*la ta'u*). Or else a term, also used to describe the friendship between two men, is applied to this relationship (*lubay-*, with pronominal suffixes). In order to distinguish between a passing liaison and one which is considered preliminary to marriage, they would say of the female concerned in the latter : " *la vivila mokita ; imisiya yambwata yambwata* "—" his woman truly ; he sleeps with her always always." In this locution the sexual relationship between the two is denoted by the verb " to sleep with " (*imisiya*), the durative and iterative form of *masisi*, to sleep. The use of this verb also emphasizes the lawfulness of the relation, for it is used in talking of sexual intercourse between husband and wife, or of such relations as the speaker wishes to discuss seriously and respectfully. An approximate equivalent in English would be the verb " cohabit ". The natives have two other words in distinction to this. The verb *kaylasi*, which implies an illicit element in the act, is used when speaking of adultery or other forms of non-lawful intercourse. Here the English word " fornicate " would come nearest to rendering the native meaning. When the natives wish to indicate the crude, physiological fact, they use the word *kayta*, translatable, though pedantically, by the verb " copulate with ".

The pre-matrimonial, lasting intrigue is based upon and maintained by personal elements only. There is no legal obligation on either party. They may enter into and dissolve it as they like. In fact, this relationship differs from other liaisons only in its duration and stability. Towards the end, when marriage actually approaches, the element of personal responsibility and obligation becomes stronger. The two now regularly cohabit in the same house, and a considerable degree of exclusiveness in sexual matters is observed by them. But they have not yet given up their personal freedom ; on the several occasions of wider licence affianced couples are invariably separated and each partner is " unfaithful " with his or her temporary choice. Even within the village, in the normal course, the girl who is definitely going to marry a particular boy will bestow favours on other men, though a certain measure of decorum must be observed in this ; if she sleeps out too often, there will be possibly a dissolution of the tie and certainly friction and disagreement. Neither boy nor girl may go openly and flagrantly with other partners on an amorous expedition. Quite apart from nocturnal cohabitation, the two are supposed to be seen in each other's company and to make a display of their relationship in public. Any deviation from the exclusive liaison must be decent, that is to say, clandestine. The relation of free engagement is the natural outcome of a series of trial liaisons, and the appropriate preliminary test of marriage.

4

THE BACHELORS' HOUSE

The most important feature of this mode of steering towards marriage, through gradually lengthening and strengthening intimacies, is an institution which might be called " the limited bachelors' house ", and which, indeed, suggests at first sight the presence of a " group concubinage ". It is clear that in order to enable pairs of lovers permanently to cohabit, some building is needed which will afford them seclusion. We have seen the makeshift arrangements of children and the more comfortable, but not yet permanent love-nests of adolescent boys and girls, and it is obvious that the lasting liaisons of youth and adult girls require some special institution, more definitely established, more physically comfortable, and at the same time having the approval of custom.

To meet this need, tribal custom and etiquette offer accommodation and privacy in the form of the *bukumatula*, the bachelors' and unmarried girls' house of which mention has already been made (see pls. 20 and 21). In this a limited number of couples, some two, three, or four, live for longer or shorter periods together in a temporary community. It also and incidentally offers shelter for younger couples if they want amorous privacy for an hour or two.

We must now give some more detailed attention to this institution, for it is extremely important and highly significant from many points of view. We must consider the position of the houses in the village, their internal arrangements and the manner in which life within the *bukumatula* shapes itself.

In the description of the typical village in the Trobriands (ch. i, sec. 2), attention was drawn to its schematic division into several parts. This division expresses certain sociological rules and regularities. As we have seen, there is a vague association between the central place and the male life of the community ; between the street and feminine activities. Again, all the houses of the inner row, which consists principally of storehouses (pls. 10 and 82), are subject to certain taboos, especially to the taboo of cooking, which is believed to be inimical to the stored yam. The outer ring, on the other hand, consists of household dwellings, and there cooking is allowed (pls. 4 and 5). With this distinction is associated the fact that all the establishments of married people have to stand in the outer ring, whereas a bachelor's house may be allowed among the storehouses in the middle. The inner row thus consists of yam-houses (*bwayma*), personal huts of a chief and his kinsmen (*lisiga*) (pl. 1), and bachelor's houses (*bukumatula*). The outer ring is made up of matrimonial homes (*bulaviyaka*), closed yam-houses (*sokwaypa*), and widows' or widowers' houses (*bwala nakaka'u*). The main distinction between the two rings is the taboo on cooking. A young chief's *lisiga* (personal hut) is as a rule used also to accommodate other youths and thus becomes a *bukumatula* with all that this implies (pl. 20).

At present there are five bachelors' establishments in Omarakana, and four in the adjoining village of Kasana'i. Their number has greatly diminished owing to missionary influence. Indeed, for fear of being singled out, admonished and preached at, the owners of some *bukumatula* now erect them in the outer ring, where they are less conspicuous. Some ten years ago my informants could count as many as fifteen bachelors' homes in both villages, and my oldest acquaintances remember the time when there were some thirty. This dwindling in number is due, of course, partly to the enormous decrease of population, and only partly to the fact that nowadays some bachelors live with their parents, some in widowers' houses, and some in the missionary compounds. But whatever the reason, it is needless to say that this state of affairs does not enhance true sex morality.

The internal arrangements of a *bukumatula* are simple. The furniture consists almost exclusively of bunks with mat coverings. Since the inmates lead their life in association with other households in the day-time, and keep all their working implements in other houses, the inside of a typical *bukumatula* is strikingly bare. It lacks the feminine touch, the impression of being really inhabited.

In such an interior the older boys and their temporary mistresses live together. Each male owns his own bunk and regularly uses it. When a couple dissolve their liaison, it is the girl who moves, as a rule, to find another sleeping-place with another sweetheart. The *bukumatula* is, usually, owned by the group of boys who inhabit it, one of them, the eldest, being its titular owner. I was told that sometimes a man would build a house as a *bukumatula* for his daughter, and that in olden days there used to be unmarried people's houses owned and tenanted by girls. I never met, however, any actual instance of such an arrangement.

At first sight, as I have said, the institution of the *bukumatula* might appear as a sort of " Group Marriage " or at least " Group Concubinage ", but analysis shows it to be nothing of the kind. Such wholesale terms are always misleading, if we allow them to carry an extraneous implication. To call this institution " Group Concubinage " would lead to misunderstanding ; for it must be remembered that we have to deal with a number of couples who sleep in a common house, each in an exclusive liaison, and not with a group of people all living promiscuously together ; there is never an exchange of partners, nor any poaching nor " complaisance ". In fact, a special code of honour is observed within the *bukumatula*, which makes an inmate much more careful to respect sexual rights within the house than outside it. The word *kaylasi*, indicating sexual trespass, would be used of one who offended against this code ; and I was told that " a man should not do it, because it is very bad, like adultery with a friend's wife."

Within the *bukumatula* a strict decorum obtains. The inmates never indulge in orgiastic pastimes, and it is considered bad form to watch another couple during their love-making. I was told by my young friends that the rule is either to wait till all the others are asleep, or else for all the pairs of a house to undertake to pay no attention to the rest. I could find no trace of any " voyeur " interest taken by the average boy, nor any tendency to exhibitionism. Indeed, when I was discussing the positions and technique of the sexual act, the statement was volunteered that there are specially unobtrusive ways of doing it " so as not to wake up the other people in the *bukumatula*."

Of course, two lovers living together in a *bukumatula* are not bound to each other by any ties valid in tribal law or imposed by custom. They foregather under the spell of personal attraction, are kept together by sexual passion or personal attachment, and part at will. The fact that in due course a permanent liaison often develops out of a temporary one and ends in marriage is due to a complexity of causes, which we shall consider later ; but even such a gradually strengthening liaison is not binding until marriage is contracted. *Bukumatula* relationships, as such, impose no legal tie.

Another important point is that the pair's community of interest is limited to the sexual relation only. The couple share a bed and nothing else. In the case of a permanent liaison about to lead to marriage, they share it regularly ; but they never have meals together ; there are no services to be mutually rendered, they have no obligation to help each other in any way, there is, in short, nothing which would constitute a common ménage. Only seldom can a girl be seen in front of a bachelors' house as in plate 21, and this as a rule means that she is very much at home there, that there has been a liaison of long standing and that the two are going to be married soon. This must be clearly realized, since such words as " liaison " and " concubinage ", in the European use, usually imply a community of household goods and interests. In the French language, the expression *vivre en ménage*, describing typical concubinage, implies a shared domestic economy, and other phases of life in common, besides sex. In Kiriwina this phrase could not be correctly applied to a couple living together in the *bukumatula*.

In the Trobriands two people about to be married must never have a meal in common. Such an act would greatly shock the moral susceptibility of a native, as well as his sense of propriety. To take a girl out to dinner without having previously married her—a thing permitted in Europe—would be to disgrace her in the eyes of a Trobriander. We object to an unmarried girl sharing a man's bed—the Trobriander would object just as strongly to her sharing his meal. The boys never eat within, or in front of, the *bukumatula*, but always join their parents or other relatives at every meal.

The institution of the *bukumatula* is, therefore, characterized by : (1) individual appropriation, the partners of each couple belonging exclusively to one another ; (2) strict decorum and absence of any orgiastic or lascivious display ; (3) the lack of any legally binding element ; (4) the exclusion of any. other community of interest between a pair, save that of sexual cohabitation.

Having described the liaisons which lead directly to marriage, we end our survey of the various stages of sexual life previous to wedlock. But we have not exhausted the subject—we have simply traced the normal course of sexuality and that in its main outlines only. We have yet to consider those licensed orgies to which reference has already been made, to go more deeply into the technique and psychology of love-making, to examine certain sexual taboos, and to glance at erotic myth and folk-lore. But before we deal with these subjects, it will be best to carry our descriptive narrative to its logical conclusion—marriage.

CHAPTER IV

THE AVENUES TO MARRIAGE

THE institution of marriage in the Trobriands, which is the theme of this and the following chapter, does not present on its surface any of those sensational features which would endear it to the " survival " monger, the " origin " hunter, and the dealer in " culture contacts ". The natives of our Archipelago order their marriages as simply and sensibly as if they were modern European agnostics, without fuss, or ceremony, or waste of time and substance. The matrimonial knot, once tied, is firm and exclusive, at least in the ideal of tribal law, morality, and custom. As usual, however, ordinary human frailties play some havoc with the ideal. The Trobriand marriage customs again are sadly lacking in any such interesting relaxations as *jus primæ noctis*, wife-lending, wife-exchange, or obligatory prostitution. The personal relations between the two partners, while most illuminating as an example of the matrilineal type of marriage, do not present any of those " savage " features, so lurid, and at the same time so attractive to the antiquarian.

If, however, we dig beneath the surface and lay bare the deeper aspects of this institution, we shall find ourselves face to face with certain facts of considerable importance and of a somewhat unusual type. We shall see that marriage imposes a permanent economic obligation on the members of the wife's family : for they have to contribute substantially towards the maintenance of the new household. Instead of having to buy his wife, the man receives a dowry, often relatively as tempting as that of a modern European or American heiress.

This fact makes marriage among the Trobrianders a pivot in the constitution of tribal power, and in the whole economic system ; a pivot, indeed, in almost every institution. Moreover, as far as our ethnological records go, it sets aside their marriage customs as unique among those of savage communities.

Another feature of Trobriand marriage which is of supreme importance to the sociologist is the custom of infant betrothal. This is associated with cross-cousin marriage, and will be seen to have interesting implications and consequences.

I

MOTIVES FOR MARRYING

The gradual strengthening of the bonds between two partners in a liaison, and the tendency to marry displayed at a certain stage of their mutual life in the *bukumatula*, have already been described in the foregoing chapter. We have seen how a couple who have lived together for a time and found that they want to marry, as it were advertise this fact by sleeping together regularly, by showing themselves together in public, and by remaining with each other for long periods at a time.

Now this gradual ripening of the desire for marriage requires a more minute consideration than we have yet given it, especially as it is one of those general, seemingly obvious questions which do not challenge attention. Yet, if in a closer sociological study we try to place it in its proper perspective, and to bring it into harmony with other features of native life, a real problem at once becomes evident. To us marriage appears as the final expression of love and the desire for union ; but in this case we have to ask ourselves why, in a society where marriage adds nothing to sexual freedom, and, indeed, takes

66

a great deal away from it, where two lovers can possess each other as long as they like without legal obligation, they still wish to be bound in marriage. And this is a question to which the answer is by no means obvious.

That there is a clear and spontaneous desire for marriage, and that there is a customary pressure towards it, are two separate facts about which there can be not the slightest doubt. For the first there are the unambiguous statements of individuals—that they married because they liked the idea of a life-long bond to that particular person—and for the second, the expression of public opinion, that certain people are well suited to each other and should therefore marry.

I came across a number of cases in which I could observe this desire for marriage developing over a prolonged period. When I came to Omarakana, I found several couples engaged to be married. The second youngest brother of Namwana Guya'u, Kalogusa (pl. 22), had been previously engaged to Dabugera, a girl of the highest rank, his father's sister's daughter's granddaughter (i.e. the matrilineal grand-niece of To'uluwa, the present chief and father of Kalogusa, see below, sec. 5). During a particular absence of her betrothed, which lasted for a year, the girl married another man. On his return, Kalogusa consoled himself by upsetting the engagement of his elder brother, Yobukwa'u, and taking the latter's betrothed, Isepuna, for himself. These two, Kalogusa and Isepuna were very fond of each other ; they were always together, and the boy was very jealous. The elder brother did not take his loss very seriously ; he started a liaison with another girl, rather plain, lazy, trained in a Mission, and altogether unsatisfactory. Both brothers married their fiancées a few months after I became acquainted with them (see pl. 4, where Kalogusa is seen standing near the hut and Yobukwa'u in the centre, each behind his wife).

Another man, Ulo Kadala, one of the less privileged sons of the chief, was deeply enamoured of a girl whose people, however, did not approve of the match. When I returned again after two years, these two were still not married, and I had an opportunity of witnessing the man's culminating failure to bring about the wedding. I often received confidences from boys longing to marry and faced by some obstacle. Some of them hoped to obtain material help from me, others to be backed by the white man's authority. It was clear that, in all such cases, the pair were already living sexually with each other, but that the thing which they specially desired was marriage. A great friend of mine, Monakewo, had a long and lasting intrigue with Dabugera, the niece of To'uluwa just mentioned, and who by that time had divorced her first husband. He knew that he would never be able to marry her, for her rank was too high for him, and he was genuinely unhappy on this account.

Such instances show clearly that young people want to marry, even when they already possess each other sexually, and that the state of marriage has real charm for them. But before I could entirely understand all the reasons and motives for this desire, I had to grasp the complexities and deeper aspects of the institution, and its relation to other elements in the social system.

The first thing to be realized is that the Trobriander has no full status in social life until he is married. As we saw in the table of age designations, the current term for a man in the prime of life is *tovavaygile* (married man). A bachelor has no household of his own, and is debarred from many privileges. There are, in fact, no unmarried men of mature age, except idiots, incurable invalids, old widowers and albinos. Several men were widowed during my stay in the Islands, and others were deserted by their wives. The former re-married almost as soon as their mourning was over, the latter as soon as their attempts at reconciliation had proved fruitless.

The same applies to women. Provided she is at all sexually tolerable, a widow or divorcée will not have long to wait. Once released from mourning, a widow again becomes marriageable. She may sometimes delay a little, in order to enjoy the sexual freedom of her unmarried state, but such conduct will ultimately draw on her the censure of public opinion, and a growing reputation for " immorality ", that is disregard of tribal usage, will force her to choose a new mate.

Another very important reason for marriage, from the man's point of view, is economic advantage. Marriage brings with it a considerable yearly tribute in staple food, given to the husband by the wife's family. This obligation is perhaps the most important factor in the whole social mechanism of Trobriand society. On it, through the institution of rank and through his privilege of polygamy, rests the authority of the chief, and his power to finance all ceremonial enterprises and festivities. Thus a man, especially if he be of rank and importance, is compelled to marry, for, apart from the fact that his economic position is strengthened by the income received from his wife's family, he only obtains his full social status by entering the group of *tovavaygile*.

There is, further, the natural inclination of a man past his first youth to have a house and a household of his own. The services rendered by a woman to her husband are naturally attractive to a man of such an age ; his craving for domesticity has developed, while his desire for change and amorous adventure has died down. Moreover, a household means children, and the Trobriander has a natural longing for these. Although not considered of his own body nor as continuing his line, they yet give him that tender companionship for which, when he reaches twenty-five or thirty, he begins to crave. He has become used, it should be remembered, to playing with his sister's children and with those of other relatives or neighbours.

These are the reasons—social, economic, practical and sentimental—which urge a man towards marriage. And last, though not least, personal devotion to a woman and the promise of prolonged companionship with one to whom he is attached, and with whom he has sexually lived, prompt him to make certain of her by means of a permanent tie, which shall be binding under tribal law.

The woman, who has no economic inducement to marry, and who gains less in comfort and social status than the man, is mainly influenced by personal affection and the desire to have children in wedlock.

This personal motive comes out very strongly in the course of love affairs which do not run smoothly, and brings us from the reasons for marriage in general to the motives which govern the individual's particular choice.

In this matter it must first be realized that the choice is limited from the outset. A number of girls are excluded completely from a man's matrimonial horizon, namely those who belong to the same totemic class (see ch. xiii, sec. 5). Further-more, there are certain endogamous restrictions, though these are by no means so precisely defined as those imposed by exogamy. Endogamy enjoins marriage within the same political area, that is within some ten to twelve villages of the same district. The rigidity of this rule depends very much on the particular district. For instance, one area in the north-west corner of the island is absolutely endogamous, for its inhabitants are so despised by the other Islanders that the latter would not dream either of marrying or of having sexual relations within it. Again, the members of the most aristocratic province of Kiriwina seldom marry outside their own district, except into the neigh-bouring island of Kitava, or into certain eminent families from one or two outside villages (see also ch. xiii, sec. 5).

Even within this limited geographical area, there are further restrictions on the choice of a mate, and these are due to rank. Thus, members of the highest sub-clan, the Tabalu, and more especially their women, would not marry into a sub-clan of very low caste, and a certain correspondence in nobility is considered desirable even in marriage between less important people.

It follows that choice must be made from among persons who are not of the same clan, who are not widely different in rank, who reside within the convenient geographical area, and who are of a suitable age. In this limited field, however, there is still sufficient freedom of selection to allow of *mariages d'amour, de raison, et de convenance*; and, as with Kalogusa and Isepuna of whom I have spoken, individual preference and love are often the determining factors of choice. And many other married couples, whom I knew well personally, had been governed in their choice by the same motive. This could be gathered from their history, and from the happy, harmonious tone of their common life.

There are also *mariages de convenance*, where wealth, that is the quantity of yams which a girl's family can provide, or pedigree, or status have determined the choice. Such considerations have, of course, a special importance in marriage by infant betrothal, of which we shall speak presently.

2

THE CONSENT OF THE WIFE'S FAMILY

Permanent liaisons which are on the point of ripening into marriage become known and are talked about in the village, and now the girl's family, who, so far, have taken no interest in her love affairs, who have, indeed, kept ostentatiously aloof, must face the fact about to be accomplished, and make up their minds whether or no they will approve it. The man's family, on the other hand, need show little interest in a matter in which they have practically no say. A man is almost entirely independent with regard to matrimony, and his marriage, which will be a matter of constant and considerable effort and worry to his wife's family, will continue to lie completely outside the sphere of his own people's concerns.

It is remarkable that, of all the girls' family, the person who has most to say about her marriage, although legally he is not reckoned as her kinsman (*veyola*), is her father. I was astonished when this information was given to me early in the course of my field work, but it was fully confirmed later on by observation. This paradoxical state of affairs becomes less incomprehensible, however, if we bring it into relation with certain rules of morals and etiquette, and with the economic aspect of marriage. One would naturally expect a girl's brothers and maternal kinsmen to take the most important part in deliberations concerning her marriage, but the strict taboo which rules that the brother must have nothing at all to do with the love affairs of his sister, and her other maternal kinsmen but little, debars them from any control over her matrimonial plans.

Thus, although her mother's brother is her legal guardian, and her own brothers will in the future occupy the same position with regard to her own household, they must all remain passive until the marriage is an accomplished fact. The father, say the natives, acts in this matter as the spokesman of the mother, who is the proper person to deliberate upon her daughter's love intrigues and marriage. It will also be seen that the father is closely concerned in the work of his sons from the economic standpoint, and that, after the marriage of their sister, these will have to divide the fruits of their labour between her and their mother, instead of, as previously, giving them all to the parental household. When two lovers have decided on marriage, the young man becomes assiduous in his attentions to his sweetheart's family, and perhaps her father will, on his own initiative, say : " You sleep with my child : very well, marry her." As a matter of fact, if the family are well disposed to the youth, they will always take this initiative either by such a direct declaration or else by asking him for small gifts, an equally unambiguous indication that he is accepted.

When the family are, definitely opposed to the match and give no sign of goodwill, the boy may take the initiative and plead on his own behalf. If he is refused it may be either because he is of too low a rank, or because he is notoriously lazy, and would be too great a drag on his future relatives-in-law, or else because the girl is intended for someone else. After such a refusal, the pair may relinquish their plans, or, if they are strong enough to fight the matter out, they may try to bring about their marriage in the teeth of opposition. If they decide to do this, the bride stays in her lover's house (that is, in his parents' house), as if she were really married, and the news is spread abroad that the man is attempting to wed her in spite of her people. Sometimes the two actually elope and go to another village in the hope of impressing and mortifying their hard-hearted opponents. In any case, they stay indoors all day, and do not eat any food to see if this will soften the hearts of her family. This abstention from the common meal, which, as we know, constitutes a definite declaration of marriage, shows that they are still waiting for her family's consent.

In the meantime, the boy's father or maternal uncle may go as an ambassador to the girl's family and offer them a gift of high value to melt their resistance. Under this combined pressure the latter may give in, and send the customary present to the young couple. If, on the other hand, they do not relent, they repair in great numbers to the spot where the girl stays with the youth and " pull her back ", a customary and technical expression, but one which also indicates what actually occurs. The boy's relatives and friends may possibly oppose the " pulling back ", and then a scuffle will ensue. But the girl's people always have the whip hand, for, as long as they withhold their consent, nobody can force them to supply the pair with food, and without this the household is soon dissolved in the natural course.

A few examples of such abortive marriage occurred in my own experience. Mekala'i, a boy whom I often used as a temporary servant, became enamoured of Bodulela, a really attractive young girl, and the step-daughter of the headman of Kabululo, who, as was well known in the village, lived incestuously with her (see ch. xiii, sec. 6). Mekala'i made an heroic attempt to abduct and retain her in his parents' house in Kasana'i, but he had no wealthy relatives or powerful friends to back him up. On the first afternoon of their joint life, the headman of Kabululo simply walked over to Kasana'i, took his abashed and truant step-daughter by the hand, and led her back to his own house ; that was the end.

Another and a more complicated case was that of Ulo Kadala, who was mentioned in the last section. He wooed a girl during my first stay in Omarakana and was refused by her parents. The couple attempted to settle down to married life, but the family pulled the girl back by force. Ulo Kadala still continued his faithful courtship. On my second visit to Omarakana two years later, the girl came to the village once more and took up her abode in the house of Isupwana, the adoptive mother of Ulo Kadala, a stone's throw from my tent. This second attempt at marriage lasted, I think, for a

day or two, while To'uluwa was making some not
very energetic efforts towards reconciliation. One
afternoon the parents arrived from the neighbouring
village, and laid hold of the girl and unceremoniously
carried her away. The procession passed in front
of my tent, the wailing girl led by her father and
followed by vociferous partisans, who hurled abuse
at each other. The girl's people said quite explicitly
what they thought of Ulo Kadala, of his laziness,
his incapacity for doing anything properly, and his
well-known greed. " We do not want you, we shall
not give her any food." This argument clinched
the refusal, and that was the last attempt which the
two young people made.

When the parents are well disposed and signify
their pleasure in the match by asking the intended
for a small present, the engaged couple must still wait
for a little in order to give necessary time for
the preparations. But one day the girl instead of
returning in the morning to her parents' house, will
remain with her husband, take her meals in the
house of his parents and accompany him throughout
the day. The word goes round : " Isepuna is
already married to Kalogusa." Such proceedings
constitute the act of marriage. There is no
other rite, no other ceremony to mark the
beginnings of wedlock. From the morning on which
she has remained with the bridegroom, the girl
is married to him, provided, of course, the consent
of the parents has been given. Without this, as we
have seen, the act constitutes only an attempt at
marriage. Though utterly simple, this act of
remaining with the man, of openly sharing a meal
with him, and of staying under his roof, has a legally
binding force. It is the conventional public
declaration of marriage. It has serious consequences,
for it changes the life of the two concerned, and it
imposes considerable obligations on the girl's
family, obligations associated in turn with counter-
obligations on the part of the bridegroom.

3
MARRIAGE GIFTS

This simple declaration of marriage is followed by that exchange of gifts which is so typical of any social transaction in the Trobriands. Each gift is definite in nature and quantity, each has to take its proper place in a series and each is reciprocated by some corresponding contribution. The subjoined table will help to make clear the description which follows it :—

MARRIAGE GIFTS

I **G—B**	1. *Katuvila*—cooked yams, brought in baskets by the girl's parents to the boy's family. 2. *Pepe'i*—several baskets of uncooked yams, one given by each of the girl's relatives to the boy's parents. 3. *Kaykaboma*—cooked vegetables, each member of the girl's family bringing one platter to the boy's house.
II **B—G**	4. *Mapula Kaykaboma*—repayment of gift (3), given in exactly the same form and material by the boy's relatives to the girl's family. 5. *Takwalela Pepe'i*—valuables given by the boy's father in repayment of gift (2) to the girl's father.
III **G—B**	6. *Vilakuria*—a large quantity of yam-food offered at the first harvest after the marriage to the boy by the girl's family.
IV **B—G**	7. *Saykwala*— gift of fish brought by the boy to his wife's father in repayment of (6). 8. *Takwalela Vilakuria*—a gift of valuables handed by the boy's father to the girl's father in payment of (6).

G—B (girl to boy), gifts from the girl's family ; B—G, return gifts from the boy's relatives to the girl's.

The girl's family have to make the first offering to signify their consent to the marriage. Since their agreement is absolutely essential, this gift, in conjunction with the public declaration of the union of the partners, constitutes marriage. It is a small gift, a little cooked food brought in baskets and offered by the girl's father to the boy's parents. It is set down in front of their house with the words *kam katuvila*, " thy *katuvila* gift." It must be given on the day on which the two remain together, or on the morning of the next day. As we have seen, when the consent of the girl's family is doubtful the two partners often abstain from food till this gift is brought.

Soon afterwards, usually on the same day, the girl's relatives bring a bigger present. Her father, her maternal uncle, and her brothers who now for the first time emerge from the inaction imposed on them by the specific brother-sister taboo, each bring a basket of uncooked yam food, and offer it to the boy's parents. This gift is called *pepe'i*. But even this is not enough. A third offering of food is brought to the boy's parents, cooked this time and carried on large platters, such as can be seen on plates 4 and 5. This gift is called *kaykaboma*.[1]

The boy's family must not delay long before they reciprocate. The last gift, cooked food on trays, is returned almost immediately and in exactly the same form as it was received. A more important gift follows. The boy's father has already prepared certain valuables of the *vaygu'a* type, that is to say, large, polished axe-blades of green stone, necklaces of polished spondylus shell discs, and armlets made of the *conus* shell ; also, when the second gift of uncooked food was brought to him by the girl's family, he made a small distribution of it among his own relatives, and they in turn now bring him other valuables to add to his own. All these he presents to the girl's family ; he has kept the baskets in which the food was brought to him ; he puts the valuables into these, and they are carried by himself and his family to the girl's house. This gift is called *takwalela pepe'i* or " repayment in valuables of the *pepe'i* gift ".

The reader is perhaps weary of all these petty details, but this meticulous absorption in small gifts and counter-gifts is highly characteristic of the Trobrianders. They are inclined to boast of

---

[1] The reader who has grasped the complex psychology of ceremonial gifts in the *kula* and in associated activities will understand the great importance of the exchanges which accompany so many social transactions in the Trobriands. Cf. *Argonauts of the Western Pacific*, especially chs. iii and vi.

their own gifts, with which they are entirely satisfied, while disputing the value and even quarrelling over what they themselves receive, but they regard these details as most important and observe them scrupulously. In the exchange of marriage gifts, as a rule, they are less cantankerous than on other occasions, and a more generous and friendly spirit prevails. After the *takwalela pepe'i* there is a long pause in the exchange of gifts, which lasts until the next harvest. During this time and while the couple's own dwelling is being built, the wife usually remains with her husband in his father's house. At harvest time they will receive the first substantial gift due from the girl's family, and of this they will themselves make a distribution by way of payment to those who have helped in the building of their new home.

To resume, then, the girl's family give a present of considerable value at the next harvest, and from then on at every harvest they will have to help the new household with a substantial contribution of fresh yams. The first present of this sort, however, has a special name (*vilakuria*), and is surrounded by a ceremonial of its own. Prism-shaped receptacles (*pwata'i*) are constructed of poles, in front of the young couple's yam-house (see pls. 23 and 24), and the girl's family, after selecting a large quantity, a hundred, two hundred, or even three hundred basketfuls of the best yams, arrange them in these receptacles with a great amount of ceremony and display.

This gift also must be repaid without any too great delay. Fish is considered a proper counter-offering. In a coastal village, the husband will embark with his friends on a fishing expedition. If he lives inland, he has to purchase the fish in one of the coastal villages, paying for them in yams.

The fish is laid in front of the girl's parents' house, with the words " *Kam saykwala* " (thy *saykwala* gift). Sometimes, if the young husband is very rich, or else if he and his family were not able previously to repay the *pepe'i* present, a gift of *vaygu'a* (valuables) will be given at this point in answer to the first harvest offering. This is called *takwalela vilakuria* (repayment by valuables of the *vilakuria* present), and closes the series of initial marriage gifts.

This series of gifts appears at first sight unnecessarily complicated. But, if we examine it more closely, we find that it represents a continuous story, and is no mere disconnected jumble of incident. In the first place it expresses the leading principle in the economic relation which will subsequently obtain for the whole duration of the marriage : that the girl's family provide the newly-established household with food, being occasionally repaid with valuables. The small initial gifts (1, 2, and 3), express the consent of the girl's family, and are a sort of earnest of their future and more considerable contributions. The return offering of food (4), made immediately by the boy's family, is a characteristically Trobriand answer to a compliment. And the only really substantial gifts from the bridegroom's family to the bride's (5, or 8, or both) exert a definitely binding force on the husband, for if the marriage be dissolved, he does not recover them save in exceptional cases. They are about equivalent in value to all the other first year's gifts put together. But this present from the husband must emphatically not be considered as purchase money for the bride. This idea is utterly opposed both to the native point of view and to the facts of the case. Marriage is meant to confer substantial material benefits on the man. These he repays at rare intervals with a gift of valuables, and it is such a gift that he has to offer at the moment of marriage. It is an anticipation of the benefits to follow, and by no means a price paid for the bride.

It may be mentioned that not all of this series of gifts are equally indispensable. Of the first three,

only one (either 1 or 2) must be given at all costs.
Of the rest, 6 and 7 are never omitted, while
either 5 or 8 are absolutely obligatory.

It is necessary, as I have already said, to enter
into such minute details as these if we would
approximate to the savage point of view. Closely
observing the care and anxiety with which the gifts
are gathered and given, it is possible to determine
the psychology of the acts themselves. Thus
Paluwa, the father of Isepuna, worried good-
humouredly as to how he might collect sufficient
food to offer to a chief's son, his daughter's future
husband ; and he discussed his troubles with me
at length. He was faced by the difficulty of having
three daughters and several female relatives, and
only three sons. Everybody's working power had
already been taxed to provide food for the other
married daughters. And now Isepuna was going to
wed Kalogusa, a man of high rank in his own right,
and also a son of To'uluwa, the paramount chief.
All his people exerted themselves to the utmost to
produce as big a crop as possible that season, in
order to be able to give a fine *vilakuria* present.
And To'uluwa, the bridegroom's father, on his
side, revealed to me his own anxiety. Could he
provide a worthy counter gift ? Times were hard,
and yet something fine had to be given. I inspected
several of the chief's valuables, and discussed their
respective suitability with him. There was an
under-current of suggestion, in the conversation of
both parties, that some tobacco from the white
man would be a much appreciated addition to
either gift.

4
INFANT BETROTHAL AND CROSS-COUSIN MARRIAGE

There is another way of arranging marriages in
the Trobriands beside the ordinary method of
courtship, and in many respects the two are in sharp
contrast to each other. Normal marriage is brought

about by free choice, by trial, and by the gradual strengthening of bonds which assume a legal obligation only after marriage. In marriage by infant betrothal, a binding agreement is made by the parents in the children's infancy ; the boy and girl grow up into the relationship, and find themselves bound to each other before they have had an opportunity to choose for themselves.

The great importance of this second type of marriage lies in the fact that infant betrothal is always associated with cross-cousin marriage. The two people who, according to native ideas, are most suited for marriage with each other—a man's son and the daughter of his sister—are betrothed in infancy. When the father's sister's daughter is too old to be betrothed to her male infant cousin, her daughter may replace her. By the native legal system the two are equivalent, for the purposes of this marriage.

The significance of this institution can only be understood if we return to a consideration of the compromise between father-love and matriliny.[1] Cross-cousin marriage is an arrangement whereby both tribal law, which enjoins matrilineal succession, and the promptings of paternal love, which incline the father to bestow all possible privileges on his son, find equitable adjustment and adequate satisfaction.

Let us take a concrete instance. A chief, a village headman—or, indeed, any man of rank, wealth, and power, will give to a favourite son all that he can safely alienate from his heirs ; some plots in the village lands, privileges in fishing and hunting, some of the hereditary magic, a position in the *kula* exchange, a privileged place in the canoe and precedence in dancing. Often the son becomes in some sort his father's lieutenant, performing magic instead of him, leading the men in tribal council, and displaying his personal charm and influence on

[1] Cf. also *Crime and Custom.*

all those occasions when a man may win the much-coveted *butura* (renown). As examples of this tendency, which I have found in every community where there was a chief of outstanding influence, we may take the arrogant Namwana Guya'u, before his banishment the leading figure in the village life of Omarakana (see ch. i, sec. 2). Again, in the sister village of Kasana'i, the chief's son Kayla'i, a modest and good-natured fellow, wielded the power of thunder and sunshine in virtue of the supreme system of weather-magic which his father had imparted to him. And the coastal villages of Kavataria, Sinaketa, Tukwa'ukwa, each had its leader in a son of the chief. But such privileged positions are invidious and insecure, even while they last; as the rightful heirs and owners in matriliny resent being pushed aside during the lifetime of the chief; and, in any case, all such benefits cease with the father's death. There is only one way by which the chief can establish his son permanently in the village with rights of full citizenship for himself and his progeny, and secure possession of all the gifts until death; and that is by contracting the son in paternal cross-cousin marriage, marriage with his sister's daughter or with this daughter's daughter. The following diagram will help to make the genealogy of the relation clear.

DIAGRAMMATIC GENEALOGY OF CROSS-COUSIN MARRIAGE

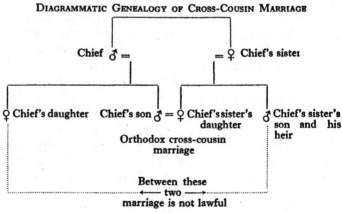

82

Our diagrammatical chief has a sister; and she has a son, the chief's heir and successor, and a daughter, the chief's niece by his sister, a girl who will continue the aristocratic line. The husband of this girl will enjoy a very privileged position, into which he will step on the day of his marriage. By native law and custom he will have a definite claim on his wife's brother or brothers and other male relatives, who will be obliged to give him annual tribute of food, and will be considered his *ex-officio* allies, friends, and helpers. He also acquires the right to live in the village if he choose, and to participate in tribal affairs and in magic. It is clear, therefore, that he will occupy practically the same position as that enjoyed by the chief's son during his father's lifetime, and from which he is ousted by the rightful heir at his father's death. This type of marriage differs from the ordinary one also in that the husband comes to live in his wife's community. Cross-cousin marriage is thus matrilocal in contradistinction to the ordinary patrilocal usage.[1]

The obvious and natural solution, therefore, of the chief's difficulty is to marry his son to his niece or grand-niece. Usually all parties benefit by the transaction. The chief and his son get what they want; the chief's niece marries the most influential man in the village, and in so doing confirms this influence; and an alliance is established between the son of the chief and his lawful heirs which frustrates the potential rivalry between them. The girl's brother cannot oppose the marriage, because of the taboo (see ch. xiii, sec. 6); nor, as it is contracted in the chief's son's infancy, would he normally be in a position to do so.

---

[1] I think that any man could settle in his wife's community if he wished. But by doing so, he would both degrade himself and suffer disabilities. A chief's son, however, is an exception owing to his position in the village and his vested interests.

5

MATRIMONIAL ALLIANCES IN A CHIEF'S FAMILY

Whenever there is a possibility of it, a cross-cousin marriage will always be arranged, a fact which is well illustrated in the family of To'uluwa (see the adjacent pedigree).

When Namwana Guya'u, the eldest son of To'uluwa's favourite and most aristocratic wife, was born, there was no marriageable girl available for him in his father's family, that is to say, among To'uluwa's maternal kinswomen. Ibo'una and Nakaykwase were, by that time, almost marriageable and could not be affianced to a little child, and their daughters were yet unborn. And the pedigree shows no other female in the sub-clan of the Tabalu, To'uluwa's matrilineal lineage. But by the time a younger son, Kalogusa, was born to To'uluwa, his grand-niece, Ibo'una, had a small daughter, Dabugera; therefore the two were betrothed. In this case the cross-cousin-marriage failed, for, as we have seen (see above, sec. 1), the girl married another man during her fiancé's absence abroad.

In the same pedigree we can take another example from the previous generation. Purayasi, the penultimate chief of Omarakana, had a son called Yowana, who belonged to the same sub-clan as Namwana Guya'u. Yowana was a man of great talent and strong personality; he was renowned for his mastery of several systems of important magic which he performed for his father, and for his skill as a gardener, sailor, and dancer. He married Kadubulami, Purayasi's grand-niece, and lived all his life in Omarakana in the enjoyment of his personal privileges. He instructed his son, Bagido'u, the present heir apparent, in all his magical and other accomplishments.

In his turn Bagido'u had a son by his first wife, but he died in infancy. This child, soon after birth, had been betrothed to an infant daughter of

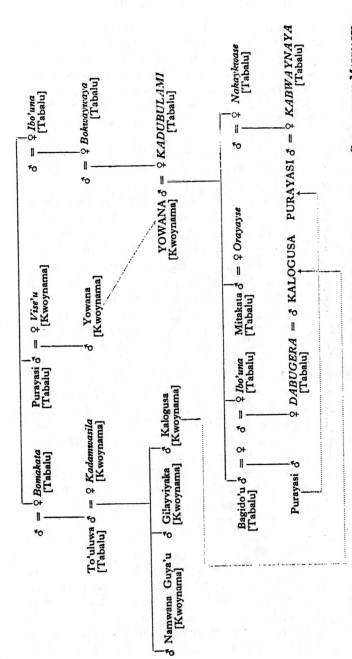

PEDIGREE SHOWING THE ALLIANCES BETWEEN THE SUBCLANS TABALU AND KWOYNAMA, AND THEIR CROSS-COUSIN MARRIAGES,
WHICH ARE INDICATED BY CAPITAL LETTERS.

[page 85

Bagido'u's youngest sister Nakaykwase. Thus, in one small pedigree, we see three cases of cross-cousin marriage arranged by infant betrothal. It must be remembered, however, that this pedigree includes the noblest family of the chieftains of Omarakana and the sub-clan Kwoynama of Osapola, both regarded as especially suitable for entering into matrimonial alliance.

Cross-cousin marriage is, undoubtedly, a compromise between the two ill-adjusted principles of mother-right and father-love ; and this is its main *raison d'être*. The natives are not, of course, capable of a consistent theoretical statement ; but in their arguments and formulated motives this explanation of the why and wherefore of the institution is implicit, in an unmistakable though piecemeal form. Several points of view are expressed and reasons given by them which throw some further light on their ideas, but all, if pushed to a conclusion, point to the same ultimate reason for cross-cousin marriage. Sometimes, for instance, it will be stated as a rider to the principle of exogamy that " the marriage between brother and sister is wrong " (" brother and sister " in the extended sense, all people of opposite sex and of the same generation related through the mother). " To marry a *tabula* (cross-cousin) is right ; the true *tabula* (the first cross-cousin) is the proper wife for us."

Let us make clear one more point : among all the marriages possible between cousins, only one is lawful and desirable for the Trobriander. Two young people of opposite sex, whose mothers are sisters, are, of course, subject to the strict sexual taboo which obtains between brother and sister. A boy and a girl who are the children of two brothers stand in no special relation to each other. They may marry if they like, but there is no reason why they should ; no special custom or institution is connected with such a relationship, since in a matrilineal society it is irrelevant. Only a boy and a girl, descendants of a brother and sister respectively, can conclude a marriage which is lawful and which, at the same time, stands out from mere haphazard alliances; for here, as we have seen, a man gives his own kinswoman to his son for a wife. But an important point must here be noted: the man's son has to marry the woman's daughter, and not the man's daughter the woman's son. Only in the former combination do the two people call each other *tabugu*, a term which implies lawfulness of sexual intercourse. The other couple joined by a dotted line on the diagram (sec. 4) stand in a different relation according to native ideas of kinship (see the discussion of these kinship terms in ch. xiii, sec. 6). A girl calls the son of her father's sister *tamagu* " my father ". Marriage with the real father or with the father's brother is incestuous and strictly tabooed. Marriage with the *tama* (" father " = father's sister's son) is not incestuous, but it is viewed with disfavour and happens only rarely. Such a marriage offers few inducements. A chief might like his daughter to be married to another chief or to a man of rank in his own family, but she would not thus acquire any specially high or privileged position. On the other hand, as his daughter will have to be supported by the same men who now work for her mother, the chief's wife, he may prefer for his own sake to marry her to a humbler and less exacting person than his heir. It all depends on his relations with his heir, which are, as we have seen, by no means so uniformly friendly and intimate as those with his own son.

The advantages of cross-cousin marriage were put to me from another point of view by Bagido'u, when I asked him why he had wanted his little son Purayasi to marry Kabwaynaya. " I wanted a daughter-in-law who would be my real kinswoman," he said. " I wanted, when I got old, to have someone of my family to look after me; to cook my food; to bring me my lime-pot and lime-stick, to pull out my grey hairs. It is bad to have a stranger to do that. When it is someone of my own people, I am not afraid." His fear was, of course, of sorcery. It should be realized that since marriage is patrilocal, and since the son, in the case of important people, often remains near the father, this latter has good reasons to be interested in his daughter-in-law. Since she is his kinswoman there is yet another justification for his son's residence in the father's community. Thus we are brought back to cross-cousin marriage as the reconciling compromise between the claims of father-love and matriliny. The man may have to rely, in his old age, on the attentions of his son and his son's wife, but neither of them are his real kindred unless the daughter-in-law is also his sister's child. In spite of his personal affection for his son, he prefers to have someone of his own *veyola* (maternal kindred) about him, and this can only be achieved if the son marries the right cross-cousin, that is the father's sister's daughter or her daughter.

6

CEREMONIES OF INFANT BETROTHAL

Now that we have grasped the principles of cross-cousin marriage, a brief account must be given of the steps and ceremonies by which it is brought about. The initiative is always taken by the brother, who, on behalf of his son, asks his sister for the hand of her daughter in marriage. A man has a definite right to make such a request ; as the natives say: " Is he not the *kadala* (maternal uncle) of the girl ? Are his sister and her child not his real *veyola* (maternal kindred) ? Has he not raised the *urigubu* (annual harvest contribution) for the household ? "

The request may be made when the son is born, if his sister has a daughter, or perhaps a grand-daughter (daughter's daughter), who will not be too old to become the wife of the new-born infant later on. The disparity of age should never exceed two or three years.

Or the boy's father may wait, and if within ten years or so a girl is born to his sister, he may requisition her as a future daughter-in-law. His sister is not allowed to refuse his application. Soon after the preliminary agreement has been concluded, the man has to take a *vaygu'a* (valuable), a polished axe-blade or shell ornament, and give it to his sister's husband, the father (*tama*) of the infant bride. " This is the *katupwoyna kapo'ula* for your child," he says, and adds that it is given " so that she may not sleep with men, nor make *katuyausi* (licentious escapades), nor sleep in the *bukumatula* (bachelor's house). She must sleep in her mother's house only." Shortly after this, three gifts of food are offered by the girl's family to the boy's father. They are similar in nature to the three initial gifts in ordinary marriage, and are designated by the same names : *katuvila*, *pepe'i*, and *kaykaboma*.

The natives regard *vaypokala* (infant betrothal) as equivalent to actual marriage. The betrothed are spoken of as husband and wife, and thus address each other. As in adult wedding, the three gifts are considered to conclude the marriage and the infant bridegroom's family have to repay the last present by a return gift of food—*mapula kaykaboma*. At the next harvest, the girl's father brings a *vilakuria* (substantial contribution of yam food) to the boy's parents. This latter fact is interesting, since it is a reversal, on account of the anticipated marriage, of what happens in the previous generation. The boy's father, who is the brother of the girl's mother, has to give a harvest gift year by year to the girl's parents ; and this at the time of his sister's marriage he had inaugurated by a gift of *vilakuria*. Now he receives on behalf of his infant son a *vilakuria* gift from his sister's husband, who acts as the representative of his own son or sons, that is the brother or brothers of the future bride, who later on will annually bring substantial harvest offerings to the household, when it becomes such. As yet, however, the yearly *urigubu* (harvest gifts) do not follow the first offering of crops (the *vilakuria*), and this interval in the exchange of gifts lasts until betrothal culminates in actual marriage.

This concludes the preliminary exchange of gifts at infant betrothal. Although it is called by the natives a marriage, the *de facto* difference between betrothal and marriage is recognized in the explicit statements of the natives and in custom, for when the two grow up they have to marry again. The bride, that is, has to go officially to the bridegroom's house, share his bed there, take her meals with him and be publicly announced to have married him. The initial gifts of ordinary marriage, however (Nos. 1–4 of the table in sec. 3) are omitted on this occasion. Only the large harvest gift (*vilakuria*), and its repayment (*takwalela vilakuria*) are exchanged.

But before this stage is reached and the two are safely married, a somewhat difficult course has to be steered. Although nobody seriously expects the young people to be chaste and faithful to each other, appearances have to be kept up. A flagrant transgression of the obligation to the betrothed would be resented by the offended party, and with some exaggeration called " adultery ". It is considered a great shame to the girl if her fiancé openly has a liaison with someone else, and she on her side must not make a *bukumatula* her permanent abode either in the company of her betrothed or of anyone else ; nor may she go to other villages on those avowedly sexual expeditions called *katuyausi* (see ch. ix, sec. 7). Both parties to the betrothal must carry on their amours discreetly and *sub rosa*. This, of course, is neither easy nor pleasant for them, and they tread the straight path of superficial decorum only under heavy pressure. The boy knows what he has to lose, so he is as careful as he can bring himself to be. Also, the father controls his son to some extent, and at the same time exercises some authority over his future daughter-in-law, through his status of maternal uncle. A man who had betrothed his son and niece to each other put the matter thus to me : " She is afraid that she might die (that is, by sorcery), or that I might hit her." And, of course, her mother is very careful and does what she can to conceal and make light of her daughter's delinquencies.

In spite of this, friction is common and ruptures not unknown. One of my earliest informants was Gomaya of Sinaketa, an enterprising, but very lazy and dishonest man, and a great *coureur de femmes*. I got his story partly from himself, partly from gossip, and partly by personal observation. He was betrothed to his cross-cousin, but in spite of this, entered into a flagrant intrigue with a good-looking girl, one Ilamweria of Wakayse, a village near Omarakana (see ch. vii, sec. 4). Once, when he brought this girl to Sinaketa, the kinsmen of his fiancée wanted to kill her and she had to run away. When Gomaya grew tired of his amour and went back to his native village, he wished to sleep with his betrothed, but she refused. " You always sleep with Ilamweria," she said, " so go to her." He at once applied to a man acquainted with love magic and asked for a spell, saying : " I want to sleep with my wife (that is, my fiancée) ; she refuses me. I must make some magic over her." And it was only after the required rites had been performed that she yielded. The marriage, however, was never completed, for in the end her parents dismissed him as a lazy good-for-nothing. The presents were not returned, for this is not customary when a cross-cousin betrothal is dissolved. We have also seen that the betrothal between Kalogusa and Dabugera never resulted in marriage. But in my opinion both these failures, which are of recent date, were largely due to the subversive influence of the white man on native custom.

In the foregoing sections we have given an account of the various inducements to marriage and of the two modes of contracting it. In the next chapter we shall pass to a description of the phases of wedded life itself, and of the sociological features of marriage as an institution.

CHAPTER V

Marriage

HUSBAND and wife in the Trobriands lead their common life in close companionship, working side by side, sharing certain of the household duties, and spending a good deal of their leisure with each other, for the most part in excellent harmony and with mutual appreciation. We have already visited a native household, while taking a general survey of the relations between the sexes, and have gained this impression from our preliminary inspection. With our present greater knowledge of Trobriand sociology, and better understanding of sexual matters, we must now reconsider the subject of the personal relations between husband and wife.

I

Husband and Wife as Companions

We left the young couple starting their common life in the hut of the bridegroom's parents ; here they remain until the protracted series of marriage gifts and counter-gifts, and the redistribution of every one of these among more distant relatives, has been completed. Only about the time of the next harvest do they build their own home ; until then they have to spend a protracted " honeymoon " under the parental roof. This must seem a most unsatisfactory state of affairs to the European reader. But he must avoid drawing too close a parallel to our own conditions. The young people have left the passionate stages of their life together behind them in the *bukumatula*, and the initial months of matrimony, on which they now enter, are not of predominantly sexual interest to them.

Now it is the change in their social status, and the alteration which their relations undergo, both towards their own families and towards the other people in the village, which mainly preoccupy them.

Although there is no definite sexual taboo at this time, the newly-wedded couple probably think less of love-making during the stage which corresponds to our honeymoon than they have done for a long time previously. I have heard this statement volunteered : " We feel ashamed in the house of our mother and father. In the *bukumatula* a man has intercourse with his sweetheart before they marry. Afterwards they sleep on the same bunk in the parental house, but they do not take off their garments." The young couple suffer from the embarrassment of new conditions. The earlier nights of marriage are a natural period of abstinence.

When the pair move on to their own hut, they may or may not share the same bunk ; there seems to be no rule in this matter. Some of my native authorities specifically informed me that married couples always sleep in the same bed at first, but later on they separate and come together only for intercourse. I suspect, however, that this is rather a piece of cynical philosophy than a statement of accepted usage.

It must be remembered that it is impossible to get direct information from any man concerning his own conjugal life ; for in this matter a very strict etiquette has to be observed. In speaking to a husband the slightest allusion to this must be avoided. Nor is any reference allowed to their common sexual past, nor to the woman's previous love adventures with other men. It would be an unpardonable breach of etiquette were you to mention, even unwittingly and in passing, the good looks of a wife to her husband : the man would walk away and not come near you for a long time. The Trobriander's grossest and most unpardonable form of swearing or insult is *Kwoy um kwava* (copulate with thy wife). It leads to murder, sorcery, or suicide (see ch. xiii, sec. 4).

There is an interesting and, indeed, startling contrast between the free and easy manner which normally obtains between husband and wife, and their rigid propriety in matters of sex, their restraint of any gesture which might suggest the tender relation between them. When they walk, they never take hands or put their arms about each other in the way, called *kaypapa*, which is permitted to lovers and to friends of the same sex. Walking with a married couple one day, I suggested to the man that he might support his wife, who had a sore foot and was limping badly. Both smiled and looked on the ground in great embarrassment, evidently abashed by my improper suggestion. Ordinarily a married couple walk one behind the other in single file. On public and festival occasions they usually separate, the wife joining a group of other women, the husband going with the men. You will never surprise an exchange of tender looks, loving smiles, or amorous banter between a husband and wife in the Trobriands.

To quote a terse statement of the case made by one of my informants : " A man who puts his arm round his wife on the *baku* (central place of the village, i.e. in public) ; a man who lies down beside his wife on his yam-house platform—he is a fool. If we take hold of our wife by the hand—we act as fools. If a husband and wife catch each other's lice on the *baku*—that is correct " (see pl. 25). With the possible exception of the last point, it will be conceded that married couples in the Trobriands push their etiquette to a point which would seem unnaturally exaggerated and burdensome to us.

This punctilio, as we know, does not preclude good-humoured familiarity in other respects. Husband and wife may talk and exchange banter in public as long as any allusion to sex is rigidly excluded. Generally speaking, husband and wife remain on excellent terms, and show a marked liking for each other's company. In Omarakana, Oburaku, Sinaketa, and in the many other places where I became intimately acquainted with the domestic life of the people, I found the majority of couples united by unwavering sexual attachment or by real congeniality of temperament. Kalogusa and his wife, to take an instance from among friends already mentioned, I found as good comrades after two years of marriage as in the days of courtship. And Kuwo'igu, the wife of my best informant and chief favourite, Tokulubakiki, made him a good mate, for the two were well-matched in looks, in dignity, in decency of character and in sweetness of temper (see pl. 26). Mitakata and his wife Orayayse, before their divorce, Towese'i and Ta'uya; Namwana Guya'u and Ibomala were all, in spite of occasional differences, excellent friends and companions. Between older couples also a real affection is sometimes found. The chief, To'uluwa, for instance, was genuinely attached to his wife, Kadamwasila. But affection, in some cases, is not sufficient to stand against the stress of circumstance. Thus Mitakata and Orayayse, an exemplary couple when I first knew them in 1915, were forced apart by the quarrel between the husband and the wife's kinsman, Namwana Guya'u (ch. i, sec. 2). Two of the finest looking people whom I knew in the Trobriands, Tomeda of Kasana'i, and his wife, Sayabiya, whom I had supposed most tenderly attached during my first visit, were already divorced on my return. But the existence of attachments lasting into old age shows that conjugal affection in the Trobriands can be real, even though perhaps it is not always deep.

I seldom witnessed quarrels or heard bad language among married people. If a woman is a shrew (*uriweri*) and the husband not sufficiently dominated to bear the fact meekly, or *vice versa*, marriage is so easily dissolved that there is hardly ever an unsuccessful match which survives the first outbreak long. I can remember only two or three households, where relations between husband and wife were outwardly and chronically strained. Two married people in Oburaku frequently indulged in lengthy quarrels, to such a degree that the matter became a serious nuisance to me and disturbed my field-work. As their hut was next door to my tent, I could hear all their domestic differences—it almost made me forget that I was among savages and imagine myself back among civilized people. Morovato, a reliable informant and friend of mine, was ordered about by his wife and badly henpecked, and I could cite perhaps one more really unfortunate marriage in Sinaketa. That there are fewer matches in which the man, and not the woman, is the aggressor in the quarrel is probably due to the fact that it is a rather more serious loss to a man to break up a good home than it is to a woman (see next chapter). A couple living in Liluta used to have difficulties owing to the man's aggressive and jealous temper. Once, when he scolded and ill-treated his wife very brutally for making *kula* (ceremonial exchange) of aromatic wreaths of the *butia* flower with another man, she went away to her own village. I saw an embassy of several men come from the husband to the wife, bringing her reconciliation presents (*lula*). This was the only case of wife-beating which actually occurred during my stay in Kiriwina, and it was done in a fit of jealousy.

2

ADULTERY AND SEXUAL JEALOUSY

Jealousy, with or without adequate reason, and adultery are the two factors in tribal life which put most strain on the marriage tie. In law, custom and public opinion, sexual appropriation is exclusive. There is no lending of wives, no exchange, no waiving of marital rights in favour

of another man. Any such breach of marital
fidelity is as severely condemned in the Trobriands
as it is in Christian principle and European law ;
indeed the most puritanical public opinion among
ourselves is not more strict. Needless to say,
however, the rules are as often and as easily broken,
circumvented, and condoned as in our own society.

In the Trobriands the norms are strict, and
though deviations from them are frequent, they are
neither open nor, if discovered, unatoned ; they
are certainly never taken as a matter of course.

For example, in October 1915, during one of
the chief's long absences overseas, the village of
Omarakana was put under the usual taboo. After
sunset, no people were supposed to leave their
houses, no young men from the neighbourhood
were allowed to pass through, the village was
deserted save for one or two old men who had
been appointed to keep watch. Night after night,
when I was out in search of information, I found
the streets empty, the houses shut, and no lights to
be seen. The village might have been dead.
Nor could I get anyone from Omarakana or the
neighbourhood to come to my tent. One morning
before I was up, a great commotion arose at the
other end of the village, and I could hear loud
quarrelling and screaming. Startled, I hurried to
make inquiries and was able to find one or two of
my special friends in the angry, vociferating crowd,
who told me what had occurred. Tokwaylabiga,
one of the less noble sons of To'uluwa, the chief,
who had not accompanied his father, had left
Omarakana on a visit. Returning before he was
expected, he was told that his wife, Digiyagaya,
had slept in his absence with another son of
To'uluwa, Mwaydayle, and that they had that very
morning gone together to the gardens, the woman
taking her water-bottles as a pretext. He ran
after them and, according to gossip, found them
under compromising conditions, though the real

facts will never be known. Tokwaylabiga, not a very bloodthirsty man, vented his passion and revenged himself on his wife by smashing all her water-bottles. Obviously a philosopher like M. Bergeret, he did not want to cause any serious trouble, and yet was not willing to suppress his injured feelings altogether. The commotion which had attracted my attention was the reception given to husband and wife on their return to the village ; for the taboo had been broken, and all the citizens were out taking sides with one party or the other. The same evening I saw the outraged husband sitting beside his wife in perfect harmony.[1]

Another case of adultery has been previously mentioned in the account of Namwana Guya'u's expulsion. Rightly or wrongly, he suspected his father's nephew and heir, Mitakata, of having committed adultery with his wife, Ibomala. But he also did not push his conjugal vindictiveness beyond bringing the case before the white magistrate, and after he left the capital, he and his wife were to be seen together in his own village apparently on excellent terms.

There are more serious cases of conjugal infidelity on record, however. In a small village near Omarakana, there lived a man called Dudubile Kautala, who died in 1916, apparently of old age, and whose funeral I attended. I remember his wife, Kayawa, as a terrible old hag, shrivelled like a mummy and smeared all over with grease and soot as a sign of mourning ; and I can still feel the dreadful atmosphere pervading her little widow's cage, where I paid her a visit soon after her bereavement. History tells us, however, that once she was fair and tempting, so that men were driven to suicide for her. Molatagula, chief of a neighbouring village, was among those who succumbed to her

---

[1] Another case of breach of the sexual taboo imposed on the village during the chief's absence has been described in *Argonauts of the Western Pacific*, p. 484. See also pp. 205–6 of that book.

beauty. One day, when the husband had gone to procure fish from a lagoon village, the love-sick chieftain entered Kayawa's house knowing her to be indoors—a gross breach of usage and manners. The story runs that Kayawa lay asleep naked upon her bed, offering a most alluring sight to the intruder, as the natives somewhat crudely put it. He approached her and took advantage of her sleep and helplessness, without, says my version, still gallantly partial to the lady, any connivance on her part. But when the husband returned, panting under a load of fish, he found them together. Both were undressed and there was more besides to compromise them. The adulterer tried to carry it off with effrontery, and said he had only come to fetch some fire. But the evidence was against him, and when the husband seized an axe, the offender tore a big hole in the thatch and escaped. Public opinion was unfavourable and the villagers insulted and ridiculed Molatagula. So he took some of the fish poison which is, as a matter of fact, the resource of those who wish to leave a loop-hole in the suicide forced upon them. He was, in fact, saved by emetics, and lived in all honour and good health for some time afterwards.

A more tragic story is that told in Omarakana about a man called Taytapola, belonging to a generation now passed away. He caught his wife Bulukwau'ukwa in the very act of adultery with Molukwayawa, a man of the same village. The adulterer succeeded in making his escape. The husband pursued him spear in hand, but failing to overtake him, came back to his hut and blew the conch shell. His maternal kinsmen (*veyola*) rallied round him ; and they all repaired to the adversary's end of the village, where they accused the culprit and insulted him in front of his sub-clan. A village fight ensued, the two principals facing each other, each supported by his kinsmen. The offender was speared and died. In such a case, the attack was probably concentrated on him personally, and the defence of the wrongdoer lacked the impetus of conviction.

Kouta'uya, a chief of the compound village of Sinaketa, went on a *kula* expedition to Gumasila.[1] One of his wives, Bogonela, had a lover, by name Kaukweda Guya'u. Both men are still alive and well known to me. The eldest wife of the absent chief, Pitaviyaka, was suspicious of her fairer companion and watched her. Hearing a noise one night, she went to Bogonela's hut and found the two lovers together. A great scandal broke out in the village. The guilty wife was publicly harangued and insulted by the female relatives of her husband : " You like carnal pleasures too much ; you are too fond of male charms." Bogonela did as the custom and ideal of personal honour dictated. In her best attire and adorned with all her valuable ornaments, she climbed a tall coconut palm on the central place of the village. Her little daughter, Kaniyaviyaka, stood under the tree and cried. Many people were assembled. She commended her child to the care of the eldest wife and jumped from the tree. She was killed on the spot.

There are many such stories which prove the existence of strong passions and complex sentiments among the natives. Thus a man of Sinaketa named Gumaluya was married to Kutawouya, but fell in love with Ilapakuna, and entered into a regular liaison with her. His wife refused to cook for him or to bring him water, so he had to receive these from a married sister. One evening, at the time when a village is socially astir with families sitting over their supper or gossiping round the fire, Kutawouya made a scene in public, and her scolding rang right through the village : " You are too fond of dissipation ; you are in a constant

---

[1] He and his sailings are familiar to readers of *Argonauts of the Western Pacific*.

state of sexual excitement; you never tire of copulation "; these were fragments of her speech, retailed to me in a vividly coloured narrative. She goaded herself into a fury, and insulted the man in such shocking words that he also became blinded by passion, and seized a stick and beat her into senselessness. Next day she committed suicide by taking the gall-bladder of the *soka* fish (a species of globe-fish), a poison which acts with lightning rapidity.

Isakapu, a fine-looking young woman, virtuous and hard-working, was, if we are to believe the testimony of historical gossip, quite faithful to her husband, yet wrongfully suspected by him. One day, returning home after a prolonged absence, he fell into a fury of jealousy; he accused and insulted her in a loud voice, and beat her mercilessly. She wept and lamented, crying : " I am sore all over, my head aches, my back aches, my buttocks ache. I shall climb a tree and jump down." A day or two after the quarrel, she adorned herself, climbed a tree and cried aloud to her husband : " Kabway- naka, come here. Look at me as I see you. I never committed adultery. You beat and insulted me without reason. Now I shall kill myself." The husband tried to reach her in time to stop her, but when he was half-way up the tree, she threw herself down and thus ended her life.

For some reason Bolobesa, one of the wives of Numakala, the predecessor of the present chief of Omarakana, left her husband for a time and returned to her own village, Yalumugwa. Her maternal uncle, Gumabudi, chief of that village, sent her back to her husband. She refused to go and turned back again half-way, although, I was told, she quite intended to return to her husband ultimately. Her uncle insisted, and insulted her so grossly that she committed suicide.

In each of these cases it was open to the woman simply to leave her husband ; or, in the last quoted incident, to return to him. In each, she was evidently prevented from adopting this easy solution by some strong attachment, or by *amour propre* and a sense of personal honour. Death was preferable to life in the village where she had been dishonoured, preferable too to life in any other village. It was unbearable to live with the man, and impossible to live without him, a state of mind which, though it might seem incredible among savages whose sexual life is so easy and carnal, yet can exercise real influence on their married life.

3

THE ECONOMIC TRIBUTE FROM THE WIFE'S FAMILY

We now come to the most remarkable and, one might say, sociologically sensational feature of Trobriand marriage. It is so important that I have already had to anticipate my statement of it several times. Marriage puts the wife's family under a permanent tributary obligation to the husband, to whom they have to pay yearly contributions for as long as the household exists. From the moment when they signify by the first gift that they accept the marriage, they have to produce, year after year by their own labour, a quantity of yams for their kinswoman's family. The size of the offering varies with the status of both partners, but covers about half the annual consumption in an average household.

When, after their " honeymoon " in the boy's parental house, the couple set up for themselves, they have to erect a yam-store as well as a dwelling-hut, and the former, as we know, will stand in the inner ring facing the latter. The yam-house has a ceremonial compartment, contained between the beams of a square well, and into this the annual contribution of the wife's family is regularly stowed at harvest. At the same time the master of the new household is himself delivering a large quantity of yams to his own sister or female relatives. He keeps for himself only the inferior tubers, stowed under the thatch in the top compartment and in the inferior yam-houses, *sokwaypa*. He also produces his own seed yams and all other vegetables : peas, pumpkins, *taro* and *viya*.

Thus everyone keeps back a fraction of his garden-yield for himself. The rest goes to his female relatives and their husbands. When a boy is young, his duty is to provide for his nearest female relative, his mother. Later on, he has to maintain his sister when she marries ; or perhaps a maternal aunt, or a maternal aunt's daughter, if these have no nearer male kinsmen to provide for them.

There are several types of garden, each of a different nature and with a different name. There are the early gardens, *kaymugwa*, planted with mixed crops, which begin to yield new food after the last year's harvest has been exhausted. This keeps the household going until the new, main harvest has begun. And there is the *taro* garden, *tapopu*. Both of these every family makes for its own use. Then there is the main garden, *kaymata*, the yield of which is chiefly devoted to the supply of the female relatives. All that the man produces for his own use is called by the generic term *taytumwala* ; what he grows for his women-folk and their husbands is called *urigubu*.

The harvest of the main gardens inaugurates a long and elaborate series of activities, associated with the offering of annual gifts. The members of each household—for digging is always done *en famille*—repair to their own garden-plot within the large, communal enclosure. The yams of the small variety, called *taytu*, which are by far the most important of all native vegetables, are then dug up by means of pointed sticks and carried to a shady arbour (*kalimomyo*) made of poles and yam vine, where the family group sit down and carefully clean the dug-up tubers, shaking the earth from

them and shaving off the hairs with sharpened
shells. Then a selection is made. The best yams
are placed in a large conical heap in the middle,
and this is the *urigubu* yield (see pl. 27). The rest
are stowed away in the corners in less regular and
much smaller heaps. The main heap is constructed
with almost geometrical precision, with the best
yams carefully distributed all over its surface, for
it will remain in the little shed for some time, to be
admired by people from the village and neighbouring
communities. All this part of the work, which,
as can easily be seen, has no utilitarian value, is
done eagerly, with interest and *con amore*, under
the stimulus of vanity and ambition. The chief
pride of a Trobriander is to gain renown as a
" master-gardener " (*tokway-bagula*). And to
achieve this, he will make great efforts and till many
plots in order to produce a considerable number
of heaps with a large quantity of yams in each. It
must also be remembered that the marriage gift
is the chief and most ostentatious product of the
garden work.

In about a week or a fortnight, the *taytu* (small
yams) are brought in from the gardens to the
village. The owner then engages a number of
helpers—men, women, and children—to carry the
gift to his sister's husband, perhaps right at the
other end of the district (pl. 28). These put
on semi-festive dress (see pl. 61), paint their
faces, adorn themselves with flowers and set out
in a merry crowd ; this is a time for gaiety and
rejoicing. The carrier parties walk about all over
the gardens, inspect and admire or criticize the
crops. Perhaps a man, through special luck or
excess of zeal in labour, has an outstandingly good
yield, and the renown (*butura*) of this has spread.
Or there may be a famous master-gardener in
the village, and his crops have to be viewed and
compared with his previous achievements. Sometimes a village community, or several of them,

agree to have a *kayasa* (competitive) harvest, and all strive to the utmost to do themselves and their community credit. The rivalry is so strong that in old days there was seldom a *kayasa* harvest without a war, or at least fights, to follow.

The gardens have a picturesque and festive appearance at this time. The uprooted heaps of *taytu* vine litter the soil with large, decorative leaves, shaped like those of the fig or of the grape. Among them groups of people are seated cleaning the yams and arranging them, while gay parties of sightseers come and go through the welter of leaves. The copper-colour of their bodies, the red and gold of the girls' gala petticoats, the crimson of the hibiscus, the pale yellow pandanus, and the green of the garlands of trailing foliage, catching at limb or breast, make up a half Bacchic, half-idyllic South Sea pastoral.

After they have rested and admired the gardens, the crowd of carriers engaged for the occasion repair to the owner's plot. There the yams are dealt out and measured with a standard basket. For each basketful, a small petal is torn off a cycas leaf. Each tenth petal is left standing, to mark the tithe. For a big plot, several cycas leaves may have to be used. The carriers then proceed to the recipient's village, men and women mixing together, with jokes and laughter. The owner supplies them with dainties on the road : coco-drinks to quench their thirst, betel-nut as a stimulant, succulent bananas to refresh them. The village is entered at high speed ; the men run ahead, pandanus petals streaming from their armlets, and the women follow closely. As they come among the houses, a collective litany is shouted, the fore-runner repeating a series of meaningless traditional words very quickly at the top of his voice : " *Bomgoy, yakakoy, siyaloy* . . ." while the whole crowd thunder back in unison a loud and strident " Yah ". Then in front of the recipient's yam-house, they build the yams into a circular heap, quite as fine as the one made before in the garden (pl. 29). It is only after a few days that the next ceremonial event takes place, when the vegetables are removed to the inside of the yam-house.

Returning now to the sociological and economic importance of the annual marriage endowment, it not only has very considerable effect on the marriage institution itself, but on the whole economy and constitution of the tribe. Looked at from the point of view of the recipient, it is clear that every man has to guide his marital choice according to his needs, and to his prospective wife's endowment. For he will be dependent, not only on his own industry and capacity, but also on that of his relatives-in-law. A fortune-hunter will lay siege to a girl who is the only sister of several brothers—the very existence of whom would at once cool the ardour of a European with a similar end in view. Only a man who could face destitution with equanimity would court a girl who had several sisters and but a single brother. As a man's wife bears sons and they grow up, he acquires as it were home-made relatives-in-law—for in a matrilineal society children are naturally classed with relatives-in-law—and their first duty is to provide for the parental household. Ordinarily the husband receives the main part of his wife's endowment from one relative-in-law only ; but in the case of a chief or a man of importance, though one man will nominally be responsible, many others will co-operate with him to provide a suitable gift. Even a commoner, however, receives, besides the *urigubu* from his chief donor, a number of smaller gifts named *kovisi* or *taytupeta* from his wife's other relatives. They are all presented at harvest time and consist of several baskets of yams and other vegetables.

A man also receives from his relatives-in-law

various services, given as occasion demands. They have to assist him when he builds a house or canoe, arranges for a fishing expedition, or takes part in one of the public festivals. In illness, they must keep watch over him against sorcerers, or carry him to some other place where he hopes to get better. In feuds or in other emergencies he may, given certain circumstances, command their services. Finally, after his death, the bulk of mortuary duties will fall upon them. Only from time to time has the man to repay the annual services of his relatives in-law by a gift of valuables—such occasional gifts being called *youlo*.

The most interesting question about this institution of annual harvest gifts, and the most difficult to understand, is this : what are the legal, social, or psychological forces which impel a man to give freely and liberally year after year, and to strain his working power to the utmost in so doing ? The answer is : tribal custom and personal pride. There are no definite punishments to enforce this duty ; those who neglect it merely sink in the public esteem and have to bear public contempt.

A Trobriander is extremely ambitious and there are two points at which his ambition is specially sensitive. One of them is his family pride. A man's sister is his nearest relation, and her honour, her position and her dignity he identifies with his own. The other point of honour is concerned with food supply. Scarcity of food, hunger, lack of superabundance are considered very shameful indeed.[1] Thus, when it is necessary to uphold the honour of his family by providing his sister with food, a Trobriander, unless he is entirely devoid of decency and morality, works with a will. When his sister's husband is a man of higher rank than himself, then all the weight of the latter's prestige is added to the stimulus of ambition ;

[1] For this psychology of food honour, compare *Argonauts of the Western Pacific*, esp. ch. vi, and *Crime and Custom*.

and if the husband is of a rank lower than himself, then the sister's status must be the more enhanced. In short, the sense of what is right, the pressure of public opinion, and inequalities of rank in either direction, produce strong psychological incentives which only in very rare and exceptional cases fail in their effect.

From the point of view of tribal economy, this system of annual marriage endowment introduces extraordinary elements of complication : there is all the additional work associated with display and ceremonial offering ; there is the sorting, cleaning, and arrangement of the heaps ; there is the building of an arbour. In addition there is the work of transport, which is sometimes very considerable ; for a man has to make his garden in the place where he lives and to transport the produce to his brother-in-law's village, perhaps six or eight miles away at the other end of the district. Sometimes, where the distance is exceptionally great, a few hundred basketfuls of yams have to be carried in relays to a coastal village, transported thence by canoe, and afterwards carried again. It is easy to see the enormous amount of waste involved in all this. But if a benevolent white reformer, and there are, alas, many such at work even in the Trobriands, tried to break down the native system, the good would be very doubtful and the harm most certain. In general, the destruction of any tribal custom is subversive of order and morals. And more than this : if we examine the roundabout methods of native economy more closely, we see that they provide a powerful incentive to industrial efficiency. If he worked just to satisfy his own immediate wants, and had only the spur of directly economic considerations, the native, who has no means of capitalizing his surplus, would have no incentive to produce it. The deep-rooted motives of ambition, honour, and moral duty, have raised him to a relatively high level of efficiency and organization which, at seasons of drought and scarcity, allows him to produce just enough to tide over the calamity.

In this extraneous economic endowment of households, we see again the dual workings of father-right and matriliny. The husband is only partially the head of the household ; he is also only partially its provider. His wife's brother, who according to tribal law remains the guardian of the wife and her children, has heavy economic duties towards the household. Thus there is an economic counterpart to the wife's brother's interference with household affairs. Or in other words, the husband, through his marriage, acquires an economic lien on his male relatives-in-law, while they, in exchange for their services, retain a legal authority over the wife and her children. This, of course, is a formulation in abstract terms of the state of affairs as the sociologist sees it, and contains no hypothesis as to the relative priority in time or importance of father-right and mother-right. Nor does it represent the point of view of the natives, who would be incapable of producing such an abstract formula.

4

POLYGAMY OF CHIEFS

Monogamy is so much the rule among the Trobrianders, that our treatment of their marriage customs has, so far, assumed the existence of one wife only. In a way this is not misleading, since if a man has several wives, all that has been said refers to each union separately. But a few supplementary notes must be added on plurality of wives. Polygamy (*vilayawa*) is allowed by custom to people of higher rank or to those of great importance, such as, for instance, the sorcerers of renown. In certain cases, indeed, a man is obliged to have a great number of wives by virtue of his position.

This is so with every chief, that is to say, every headman of high rank who exercises an over-rule in a more or less extended district. In order to wield his power and to fulfil the obligations of his position, he must possess wealth, and this in Trobriand social conditions is possible only through plurality of wives.

It is a very remarkable fact in the constitution of the tribe of which we are speaking, that the source of power is principally economic, and that the chief is able to carry out many of his executive functions and to claim certain of his privileges only because he is the wealthiest man in the community. A chief is entitled to receive tokens of high respect, to command observance and require services; he can ensure the participation of his subjects in war, in any expedition and in any festival; but he needs to pay heavily for all these things. He has to give great feasts and finance all enterprises by feeding the participants and rewarding the chief actors. Power in the Trobriands is essentially plutocratic. And a no less remarkable and unexpected feature of this system of government is that, although the chief needs a large revenue, there is nothing of the sort directly attached to his office : no substantial tributes are paid him by the inhabitants as from subject to chief. The small annual offerings or tribute in special dainties—the first fish caught, vegetable primitiæ, special nuts and fruits—are by no means a source of revenue ; in fact the chief has to repay them at full value. For his real income he has to rely entirely on his annual marriage contribution. This, however, in his case, is very large, for he has many wives, and each of them is far more richly dowered than if she had married a commoner.

A statement of the specific conditions will make matters clearer. Each chief has a tributary district comprising several villages—a few dozen in the

case of Kiriwina ; a dozen or so in Luba or Tilataula ;
one or two in the cases of some minor chiefs—
and this district is tributary through marriage.
Each subject community renders a considerable
contribution to the chief, but only and exclusively
in the form of a dowry, paid annually in yams.
Each village—and in the case of a compound
village each constituent part of it—is " owned "
by a sub-clan (see ch. i, sec. 2) and ruled by the
head man of that sub-clan. From every one of
these sub-clans the chief takes a wife and she is,
as it were, perpetual, since on her death another
wife, her substitute (*kaymapula*), is immediately
wed to him from the same sub-clan. To the
dowry of this one woman, the chosen representative
of the sub-clan, all its male members contribute
their share, though the whole is presented
collectively by the headman. Thus every man
in a district works for his chief, but he works for
him as for his relative-in-law, however distant.

The headman of Omarakana, and chief of
Kiriwina, is supreme in rank, power, extent of
influence and renown. His tributary grasp, now
considerably restricted by white men and crippled
by the disappearance of some villages, used to
reach all over the northern half of the island and
comprise about five dozen communities, villages,
or sub-divisions of villages, which yielded him up
to sixty wives (of whom a remnant may be seen
on pl. 30). Each of these brought him in a
substantial yearly income in yams. Her family had
to fill one or two storehouses each year (pl. 31)
containing roughly five to six tons of yams. The
chief would receive from 300 to 350 tons of yams
per annum.[1] The quantity which he disposes
of is certainly sufficient to provide enormous feasts,
to pay craftsmen for making precious ornaments,
to finance wars and oversea expeditions, to hire

---

[1] This rough computation was made for me by a trader who was
engaged among other things in exporting yams for the mainland plantations. As I was unable to check it, it must be received with caution.

dangerous sorcerers and assassins—to do all, in short, which is expected of a person in power.

Thus wealth emphatically forms the basis of power, though in the case of the supreme chief of Omarakana, it is reinforced by personal prestige, by the respect due to his tabooed or holy character, and by his possession of the dreaded weather magic through which he can make or mar the prosperity of the whole country. The smaller chiefs have usually only a few villages to draw upon ; the smallest merely the other component parts of their own settlement. In every case their power and status depend entirely on their privilege of polygamy and on the exceptionally rich dowry due to a woman who marries a chief.

This account though short and necessarily incomplete will yet be sufficient to indicate the enormous and manifold influence of marriage and polygamy on the constitution of power and on the whole of social organization in the Trobriands.[1]

5

THE DOMESTIC ASPECT OF POLYGAMY

Turning now to the domestic aspect of polygamy, let us consider the steps by which a chief acquires his several wives. It will be best to take a specific instance ; that of To'uluwa, for example. He began his sexual life in the ordinary way, passing through the stages of complete freedom, then of a liaison in the *bukumatula*, and finally of a permanent attachment. His first choice fell on Kadamwasila, of the clan of Lukwasisiga, the sub-clan Kwaynama of Osapola village (see pl. 4 and diag. in ch. iv, sec. 5). It was quite a suitable match, for this sub-clan is the very one from which a Tabalu chief ought to

[1] I cannot enter here more deeply into the political nature of chieftain-ship ; I have treated the subject somewhat more fully elsewhere (*Argonauts*, ch. ii, sec. v, pp. 62–70). Nor can I deal *in extenso* with the economic aspect of power ; this has been examined in " The Primitive Economics of the Trobriand Islanders," *Economic Journal*, March, 1921.

choose his principal wife. The girl must have been very good-looking, and she certainly was a " real lady ", possessing charm, dignity, and simple honesty. The two were deeply attached to each other and remained so ; and the union was blessed by five boys and a girl, the youngest child. I have called Kadamwasila " the chief's favourite wife ", meaning by that that their's was a union of love, a real companionship, and undoubtedly in its early years, a passionate relation. The chief, however, even before his accession, took to himself other wives, each from one of the communities which have to supply him with an annual contribution. It often happens that when a chief's wife dies, the community from which she came supplies the heir apparent, instead of the actual chief himself, with a girl who counts as substitute for the deceased. To'uluwa had become possessed of three or four wives of this kind, when his elder brother and predecessor died. Then he inherited the late chief's widows, who automatically and immediately became his wives, while their children became part of his household. The majority of the widows were fairly old, some having passed through the hands of three husbands. It seems that the chief would not have any obligation to live sexually with such inherited wives, but of course he could do so if he wished. Subsequently To'uluwa married four other wives, from such communities as were not represented among his complement at the time. The marriage of a chief does not differ from that of a commoner, except that his wife is brought to him by her parents openly, and that the gifts exchanged are more substantial.

At present a stop is being gradually put to the whole system of the chief's polygamy. The first administrators, benevolently conceited and megalomaniacally sensitive as all those with arbitrary power over an " inferior " race are apt to be, were not guided by any sympathetic understanding of native custom and institutions. They did not grope, but proceeded at once to hit about them in the dark. They tried to destroy such native power as they found, instead of using it and working through it. Polygamy, a practice uncongenial to a European mind and indeed regarded by it as a sort of gross indulgence, seemed a weed proper for extirpation. So the chiefs, and especially he of Omarakana, though allowed to retain such wives as they had, were forbidden to fill the place left by each death, as would have been done in olden days. This prohibition was, by the way, an arbitrary act on the part of the white Resident, since it was justified by no law or regulation of the colony.[1] Now To'uluwa's wealth and influence are declining, and would already have ceased to exist if it had not been for the faithful obedience of his subjects to native custom. They were openly encouraged to forego payment of the annual gifts, and the wives were invited to leave their husband; but so far loyalty and tradition have prevailed. At the death of the present chief, however, a complete disorganization is sure to take place among the natives of the Trobriands, and is certain to be followed by a gradual disintegration of culture and extinction of the race.[2]

Returning to the chief's household, it is clear that his relations with his different wives cannot be the same. Three classes of these latter may be roughly distinguished.

The first of these consists of wives acquired from his predecessor, a man much older than himself. These should be regarded as dowager tribute-bringers, who cannot be repudiated, and are

---

[1] I am unable to say whether the Magistrate's taboo on polygamy was ever embodied in a definite statement or order, or only verbally given to the natives. But I know that chiefs and headmen have not acquired recently any new wives and that they not only allege, as a reason for this, a taboo from the white authorities, but that they are genuinely afraid of defying this taboo, and also deeply resent it.

[2] Cf. the excellent analysis of such conditions in other parts of Melanesia in G. Pitt-Rivers's *Clash of Culture*, pp. 134 sq. and *passim*.

living in dignity and retirement, but hardly exercise sexual allurement. Some of them, indeed, play an important rôle and enjoy a high degree of prestige. The eldest wife of To'uluwa, Bokuyoba (fourth from right on pl. 30), whom he inherited from his elder brother, has, though childless, a right of precedence in many matters, and is considered the head of the *giyovila* (chief's wives) whenever, for ceremonial or festival purposes or during private receptions, they act as a body. Next come Bomiyototo, Bomidabobu, and others, and there is also Namtawa, mother of two strapping fellows, sons of the last chief, who take next place after To'uluwa's own sons. The chief has probably never actually lived sexually with these venerable relicts of the former régime.

The second class of wives are those whom the chief married in his youth, women acquired and not inherited. There is usually one favourite among these : Kadamwasila filled this position in youth, and in her old age she was highly respected and had considerable influence. This influence was exercised directly and also indirectly through her sons, one of whom is the banished Namwana Guya'u.

The third class consists of younger women, adopted in exchange for such older ones as have died. Some of them are really pretty, for the most attractive women are always chosen for the chief. The method of choice is simple ; the chief simply indicates which of the girls pleases him best, and, irrespective of her previous attachments, she is given to him. With these younger women their husband unquestionably has sexual intercourse, but the same degree of intimacy and companionship as with the wives of his youth does not, as a rule, obtain.

The latest acquisition of To'uluwa, Ilaka'ise (second from right on pl. 30, and on pl. 31) is one of the best-looking girls in the Trobriands. But the chief is seldom seen in her company. Isupwana (pl. 18), the eldest of the third class of acquisitions, really stands on the border-line between the second and the last category. She is the present favourite of the chief, and is often to be seen with him in the garden, or on visits,.or in front of his personal hut. But he always used to prefer to take his meals at the house of Kadamwasila during her life-time, and—apart from his own personal hut—made it his home.

The outward relations of the chief's wives towards each other are noticeably good. Nor could I discover from indiscreet village gossip the existence of any violent rivalries and hatreds among them. Bokuyoba, the oldest wife, who, as has been said, enjoyed a privileged position among them, is undoubtedly popular and liked by them all. She is also supposed to keep an eye on their morals, a somewhat invidious task which always falls to the oldest wife. It will be remembered that Pitaviyaka, the first wife of Kouta'uya, one of the chiefs of Sinaketa, actually discovered an act of adultery among her colleagues, a discovery which, as we have seen, ended so tragically in the suicide of the guilty one. In Omarakana, however, the first wife is less of a Mrs. Grundy.

Scandal reports many breaches of marital fidelity among To'uluwa's wives, especially and naturally on the part of the youngest ones. The point on which village gossip centres its most eager and malicious interest is the fact that several of the most prominent sons of the chief himself are among the adulterers. Of course, this relation.has not the same incestuous flavour as it would possess for us, since the bodily tie between father and son is not recognized ; but it is bad enough to scandalize the natives, or rather to arouse their interest by its piquancy. Ilaka'ise, the youngest wife, a girl of not more than twenty-five and, with her tall figure, soft and well-developed contour, and shapely face, a model of Melanesian beauty, has a permanent intrigue with Yobukwa'u. He is the third son of To'uluwa and Kadamwasila, and one of the finest-looking, best-mannered, and really most satisfactory fellows of my acquaintance. As the reader may remember, he has recently married a girl who is not his equal either in character or personal charm (see ch. iv, sec. 1). His friends smiled at the suggestion that his marriage might mean a rupture with Ilaka'ise.

Isupwana, the chief's favourite of his younger wives and a woman who has the air of a stately yet comely matron, is enamoured, among others, of Yabugibogi, a young son of the chief. This youth, though good-looking enough and endowed, according to the scandal-mongers, with great attractions for a jaded feminine taste, is perhaps the most obnoxious waster in the whole community.

Namwana Guya'u, the eldest son of Kadamwasila and his father's favourite, does not consider this fact a sufficient reason for being more abstemious than his brothers. He has chosen Bomawise for his mistress, the least attractive of the few younger wives of his father. Both before his marriage and after it, he lived in a faithful though incestuous relation with her, which only ended with his banishment.

The greatest scandal of all was caused by Gilayviyaka, the second son of Kadamwasila, a fine and intelligent native, who died soon after my first departure from the Trobriands. Unfortunately for himself, he married a very attractive girl, Bulubwaloga, who seems to have been passionately fond and very jealous of him. Before his marriage, he had an intrigue with Nabwoyuma, one of his father's wives, and did not break it off after the wedding. His wife suspected and spied upon him. One night, the guilty couple were caught *in flagrante delicto* in Nabwoyuma's own hut by the adulterer's wife.

The alarm was given, and a dreadful public scandal ensued. The outraged wife left the village immediately. A great social upheaval took place in Omarakana, and a permanent estrangement ensued between the father and son. For, though the chief probably knows a good deal of what goes on and condones it, once a scandal becomes public, custom demands the punishment of the offenders. In olden days they would have been speared, or destroyed by sorcery or poison. Now that the chief's power is paralysed, nothing so drastic can happen ; but Gilayviyaka had to leave the village for some time, and after his return was always under a cloud. His wife never returned to him. The chief's wife remained with a stain on her character, and in great disfavour with her husband.

I heard many other items of scandalous gossip which space forbids me to retail. It is sufficient to say that the behaviour of the eldest sons of Kadamwasila is typical. The chief's other male children seem to have no such permanent intrigues with special wives, but they are not held in greater public esteem because of that, since they are known to take any opportunity of a temporary affair with any one of their father's wives. Nowadays, when the law and the moral pretence of the white rule have done much to rot away the real morality and sense of what is right among the natives, all these inter-family adulteries are committed much more openly and shamelessly. But, even in the old days, as some of my more ancient informants told me with a reminiscent smile, the young wives of an old chief would never suffer a sad lot in resignation, and would always seek comfort, with discretion, but not without success. Polygamy in the Trobriands was never a cruel and inhuman institution.

In this chapter we have discussed marriage in its domestic aspect, and in the aspect of the economic and legal obligations which it imposes on the wife's family with regard to the household. Finally we have discussed the effect on public and political life which it exerts through the fact of the chief's polygamy. In the next chapter we shall see what light is thrown on marriage in the Trobriands by the modes of its dissolution through divorce and death.

CHAPTER VI

DIVORCE AND THE DISSOLUTION OF MARRIAGE BY DEATH

THE nature of matrimonial bonds reveals itself in their breaking in life by divorce, as it does also in their dissolution by death. In the first instance we can observe the strain to which they are submitted; we can see where they are strong enough to resist and where they most easily yield. In the second we can estimate the strength of the social ties and the depth of personal sorrow by their expression in the ceremonial of mourning and burial.

I

DIVORCE

Divorce, called by the natives *vaypaka* (*vay* = marriage; *paka*, from *payki*, to refuse), is not infrequent. Whenever husband and wife disagree too acutely, or whenever bitter quarrels or fierce jealousy make them chafe too violently at the bond between them, this can be dissolved—provided the emotional situation does not lead instead to a more tragic issue (see sec. 2 of the previous chapter). We have seen why this solution, or rather dissolution, of the difficulty is a weapon used by the woman rather than the man. A husband very seldom repudiates his wife, though in principle he is entitled to do so. For adultery, he has the right to kill her; but the usual punishment is a thrashing, or perhaps merely remonstrance or a fit of the sulks. If he has any other serious grievance against her, such as bad temper or laziness, the husband, who is little hampered by marriage ties, easily finds consolation outside his household, while he still benefits by the marriage tribute from his wife's relatives.

There are, on the other hand, several instances on record of a woman leaving her husband because of ill-treatment or infidelity on his part, or else because she had become enamoured of someone else. Thus, to take a case already described, when Bulubwaloga caught her husband, Gilayviyaka, *in flagrante delicto* with his father's wife, she left him and returned to her family (see ch. v, sec. 5). Again, a woman married to Gomaya, the ne'er-do-well successor to one of the petty chiefs of Sinaketa, left him because, in his own words, she found him an adulterer and also " very lazy ".   Bolobesa, the wife of the previous chief of Omarakana, left him because she was dissatisfied or jealous, or just tired of him (ch. v, sec. 2). Dabugera, the great-grand-niece of the present chief, left her first husband because she discovered his infidelities and found him, moreover, not to her taste. Her mother, Ibo'una, the chief's grand-niece, took as a second husband one Iluwaka'i, a man of Kavataria and at that time interpreter to the resident magistrate.   When he lost his position she abandoned him, not only, we may presume, because he was less good-looking without his uniform, but also because power attracts the fair sex in the Trobriands as elsewhere. These two ladies of rank display an exacting taste in husbands, and indeed the fickleness of those privileged by birth has become proverbial in the Trobriands : " She likes the phallus as a woman of *guya'u* (chief) rank does."

But among people of lower rank, also, there are many instances of a woman leaving her husband simply because she does not like him. During my first visit to the Trobriands, Sayabiya, a fine-looking girl, bubbling over with health, vitality, and temperament, was quite happily married to Tomeda, who was a handsome, good-natured and honest, but stupid man   When I returned, she had gone back to live in her village as an unmarried girl, simply because she was tired of her husband. A very good-looking girl of Oburaku, Bo'usari, had left two husbands, one after the other, and, judging from her intrigues, was looking for a third. Neither from her, nor from the intimate gossip of the village, could I get any good reason for her two desertions, and it was obvious that she simply wanted to be free again.

Sometimes extraneous conditions, more especially quarrels between the husband and the wife's family, lead to divorce. Thus as one result of the quarrel between Namwana Guya'u and Mitakata, Orayayse, Mitakata's wife, had to leave her husband because she belonged to his enemy's family. In a dispute between two communities, marriages are often dissolved for the same reason.

An interesting case of matrimonial misfortune which led to divorce is that of Bagido'u, the heir apparent of Omarakana (pl. 64). His first wife and her son died, and he then married Dakiya, an extremely attractive woman who bore traces of her good looks even at the somewhat mature age at which I first saw her. Dakiya's younger sister Kamwalila was married to Manimuwa, a renowned sorcerer of Wakayse. Kamwalila sickened, and her sister Dakiya went to nurse her. Then between her and her sister's husband evil things began. He made love magic over her. Her mind was influenced, and they committed adultery then and there. When, after her sister's death, Dakiya returned to her husband Bagido'u, matters were not as before. He found his food tough, his water brackish, the coconut drinks bitter, and the betel nut without a bite in it. He would also discover small stones and bits of wood in his lime pot, twigs lying about in the road where he used to pass, pieces of foreign matter in his food. He sickened and grew worse and worse, for all these substances were, of course, vehicles of evil magic, performed by his enemy, the

sorcerer Manimuwa, assisted in this by the faithless
wife. In the meantime, his wife trysted with her
leman.

Bagido'u scolded and threatened her until one
day she ran away and went to live with Manimuwa,
an altogether irregular procedure. The power
of the chiefs being now only a shadow, Bagido'u
could not use special force to bring her back ;
so he took another wife—a broad-faced, sluggish,
and somewhat cantankerous person by the name of
Dagiribu'a. Dakiya remained with her wizard
lover, and married him. The unfortunate Bagido'u
who obviously suffers from consumption, a disease
with which all his family are more or less tainted,
attributes his ills to his successful rival's sorcery,
even now, as he believes, active against him. This
is very galling, for he has the injury of black magic
added to the insult of his wife's seduction. When
I came back to Omarakana in 1918, I found my
friend Bagido'u much worse. By now (1928), this
man of extraordinary intelligence, good manners, and
astounding memory, the last worthy depository
of the family tradition of the Tabalu, is no doubt
dead.

The formalities of divorce are as simple as those
by which marriage is contracted. The woman
leaves her husband's house with all her personal
belongings, and moves to her mother's hut, or to
that of her nearest maternal kinswoman. There
she remains, awaiting the course of events, and in
the meantime enjoying full sexual freedom. Her
husband, as likely as not, will try to get her back.
He will send certain friends with " peace offerings "
(*koluwvi*, or *lula*) for the wife and for those with
whom she is staying. Sometimes the gifts are
rejected at first, and then the ambassadors are sent
again and again. If the woman accepts them,
she has to return to her husband, divorce is ended
and marriage resumed. If she means business, and
is determined not to go back to her wedded life,

PLATE I

THE CENTRAL PLACE OF OMARAKANA

The Chief's large yam house is in the centre, behind it resting shelters for visitors; to the left the Chief's personal hut, and in the background one or two houses of the wide ring. [Ch. I, 2; ch. III, 4]

PLATE 2

THE CHIEF AND HIS SONS

*To'uluwa leaning against the platform, Namwana Guya'u on his
right, and beyond other less important sons. Mwaydayli in the
background. The large conch shell and the decorated gable are
symbols of chieftainship.* [*Ch. I, 2; also ch. II, 1*]

PLATE 3

TWO HEREDITARY ENEMIES

The Chief's son and the heir apparent in dancing dress before their quarrel. [Ch. I, 2 ; also ch. II, 2 ; ch. X, intro.]

PLATE 4

THE CHIEF'S FAVOURITE WIFE AND HER FAMILY

Kadamwasila is seated in front of her living hut between her two daughters-in-law; behind stand their husbands, Kalogusa on the left and Yobukwa'u on the right. Their young sister Kenoria is taking a shower bath. Boiled yams and bananas are ready for a family meal. [Ch. I, 2 and 3; ch. III, 4; ch. IV, 1 and 3]

PLATE 5

CEREMONIAL COOKING OF TARO

The dumplings on platters (left) are first prepared by women and then thrown into large clay pots and stirred with long spatula. Note the miniature yam house (left centre) belonging to the small boy in front of it. We are looking from between dwellings across the store houses towards the central place. [Cb. I, 3 ; cb.IV, 3, and cb. XI, 2]

PLATE 6

WOMEN WITH CARRYING PADS

Resting at the wayside with loads off, the pads remaining in position. The central figure wears a mourning relic over her shoulder. [Ch. I, 3; cb. VIII, 4, footnote]

PLATE 7

A FAMILY ON THE ROAD

The woman is carrying large yams in a basket, and the child in a characteristic position on her hip ; the man has an adze on his shoulder. The child evidently feels safest clinging to both father and mother. [Ch. I, 3]

PLATE 8

NATIVE INTERIOR

Two bunks run across the back wall. Besides a Chinese trade trunk and a piece of calico there are water bottles, folded mats and a basket on the lower bunk. On the top bunk, note the lime pot stuck into the round basket and a few coils of pandanus leaf. [Ch. I, 3]

PLATE 9

A Stage in Skirt Making

Pandanus leaves are being made tough and supple by beating before a fire. One woman is shaved in sign of mourning. [Cb. I, 4]

PLATE 10

DRYING SKIRT FIBRE

The bunches of frayed banana leaves are hung in the sun after having been stained with crimson and purple.
In the inner ring of this lagoon village (Teyava) only yam houses can be seen. [Ch. I, 4; also ch. III, 4]

PLATE 11

THE MORTUARY DANCE

Held at Oburuku after the death of Ineykoya. *Compare plate 33.*
[*Ch. II, 2 ; also ch. VI, 3*]

PLATE 12

DISTRIBUTION OF SKIRTS IN MORTUARY RITUAL
[*Ch. II, 2*]

PLATE 13

DECORATED WOMEN
[*Ch. II, 2*]

PLATE 14

Men in Full Festive Attire
[*Ch. II*, 2]

PLATE 15

CHILDREN SHOWING A GAME TO THE ETHNOGRAPHER
[*Ch. III, 1*]

PLATE 16

THE CHILDREN'S REPUBLIC

Sometimes in the course of an ethnographic demonstration, a general discussion breaks out, which is easier to " snap " than to take down in notes. [Ch. III, 1]

PLATE 17

SMALL BOYS PLAYING AT *SAGALI*

The ceremonial distributions (sagali) are of great importance in native life ; they arouse the ambition and passion of the adult and appeal to the imagination of children. [Ch. III, 1].

PLATE 18

A GROUP OF GIRLS

Three adolescent girls of Omarakana visiting Isupwana, one of the Chief's wives. On the right Itana, second from the left Geumwala. The three girls on the left are wearing the underskirt only. [Ch. III, 3 ; also ch. X, sec. 4]

PLATE 19

BOYS IN THE YAM GARDEN
[*Ch. III*, 3]

PLATE 20

A DECORATED BACHELORS' HOUSE

This is a personal hut (lisiga) of an unmarried chief in Vakuta—hence its decorated boards—used also as a regular bukumatula. [Ch. III, 4; also ch. II, 1]

PLATE 21

GIRL IN FRONT OF *BUKUMATULA*
Scraping and fraying banana leaves for a grass skirt. [*Ch. III, 4*]

KALOGUSA, THE CHIEF'S SON

[*Cb. IV*, 1]

PLATE 23

MARRIAGE GIFT IN PREPARATION

A young husband of rank stands to the left of his newly-built and decorated store-house; the pwata'i is still in construction; the wife's brother is putting the final touches to it. Some food has already been brought in and is seen in baskets round the prism-shaped erection. [Cb. IV, 5; also cb. II, 1]

PLATE 24

THE MARRIAGE GIFT DISPLAYED

An exceptionally large pwata'i *erected on the outskirts of the village, filled with* taytu *(staple small yams) capped with* kuvi *(large yams) and taro.* [Ch. IV, 3]

PLATE 25

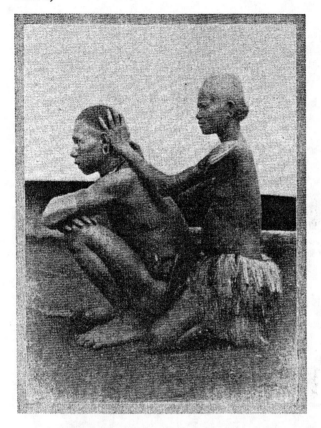

MITAKATA AND ORAYAYSE

She is lousing him, one of the few intimate attentions allowed in public between husband and wife. [*Ch. V*, 1 ; *also ch. X*, 3]

PLATE 26

A HAPPY FAMILY

*Tokulubakiki and his wife Kuwo'igu in front of their yam house ; their
little daughter is in the usual position on the mother's hip.* [Ch. V, 1]

PLATE 27

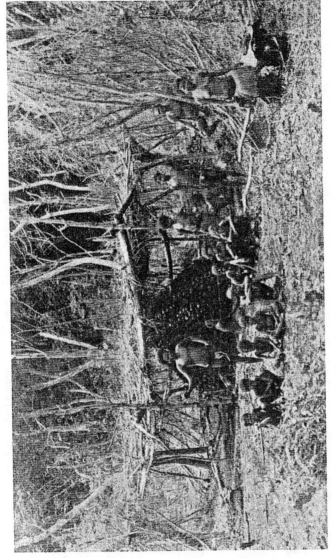

THE MARRIAGE TRIBUTE IN THE GARDEN

During a competitive harvest for the chief, people are admiring the yams arranged in the centre. Behind are one or two smaller heaps of inferior tubers, some of which have already been removed. [Ch. V, 3]

PLATE 28

CARRYING THE HARVEST GIFT

A small party, the men carrying the weight on their shoulders, the women on the head.
At a competitive harvest long files of people crowd the road. [*Ch. V, 3 ; also ch. I, 3*]

PLATE 29

THE URIGUBU IN THE VILLAGE

*The carriers arrange the yams again into a conical heap in front of the
store house, to which they will be transferred after a time.* [Cb. V, 3]

PLATE 30

A POLYGAMOUS FAMILY

The chief To'uluwa during a canoe launching festivity on the beach of Omarakana seated on a platform specially erected for the occasion. He is surrounded by some of his wives and his children, with his son, Gilaywiyaka, on his right. [Ch. V, 4]

PLATE 31

A Chief's Wife and Her Annual Dowry

Ilakai'ise in front of the store-houses which yearly have to be filled at harvest by her brothers and maternal kinsmen. [Ch. V, 4; also ch. I, 2]

PLATE 32

DECORATED CORPSE

Body of a young and beautiful woman carried off by sudden death and sincerely mourned by the widower, who is seen supporting the corpse for the photograph. Her face is painted; shell necklaces, belt and armlets adorn her; she wears coloured elaborate skirts. Her legs have been tied, but not her arms, nor have her nostrils, etc., yet been stuffed with fibre. [Ch. VI, 3]

the presents are never accepted ; then the husband
has to adjust himself as best he may, which means
that he begins to look for another girl. The dissolution of marriage entails in no case the restitution
of any of the inaugural marriage gifts exchanged,
unless, as we shall see, the divorced woman should
re-marry.

The girl, if she is still young enough, now resumes
her pre-nuptial life and leads the free, untrammelled
existence of a *nakubukwabuya* (unmarried girl),
entering upon liaison after liaison, and living in
bachelors' houses. One of the liaisons may
lengthen out and develop into a new marriage.
Then the new husband must present a valuable
object (*vaygu'a*) to his predecessor, in recompense for the one given to the wife's family at
the beginning of the first marriage. The new
husband must also give another *vaygu'a* to his
wife's relatives, and he then receives from them the
first annual harvest gift—*vilakuria*—and the subsequent yearly tribute in yams. It seemed to me
that a divorcée was much more independent of
family interference in choosing her new husband
than an ordinary unmarried girl. The initial gifts
of food (*pepe'i*, etc.) are not given in the case of
such a remarriage. There is, apparently, no social
stigma on a girl or a man who has been married
and divorced, although as a matter of *amour propre*
no one wishes to own that he or she has been
abandoned by the other.

It goes without saying that the children, in case
of divorce, always follow their mother ; and this
is no doubt another reason why divorce is less
popular with men than with women. During the
interim, when their mother is living as a spinster,
they remain in the household of her nearest married
maternal relative.

2

Death and the Bereaved

When a man dies, his wife is not set free by the event. It may be said without paradox that, in a way, the strictest and heaviest shackles of marriage are laid on her after the real tie has been dissolved by death. Custom compels her to play the burdensome rôle of chief mourner ; to make an ostentatious, dramatic, and extremely onerous display of grief for her husband from the moment of his demise until months, at times years, afterwards. She has to fulfil her part under the vigilant eyes of the public, jealous of exact compliance with traditional morals, and under the more suspicious surveillance of the dead man's kindred, who regard it as a special and grievous offence to their family's honour if she flags for a single moment in her duty. The same applies in a smaller degree to a widower, but in his case the mourning is less elaborate and burdensome, and the vigilance not so relentless.

The ritual in the early stages of widowhood reveals in a direct and intimate manner a most interesting complex of ideas—some very crude and quaint—concerning kinship, the nature of marriage, and the purely social ties between father and children. The whole mortuary ritual is, in fact, perhaps the most difficult and bewildering aspect of Trobriand culture for the investigating sociologist. In the overgrowth of ceremonial, in the inextricable maze of obligations and counter-obligations, stretching out into a long series of ritual acts, there is to be found a whole world of conceptions— social, moral, and mythological—the majority of which struck me as quite unexpected and difficult to reconcile with the generally accepted views of the human attitude towards death and mourning.

Throughout this ritual, the unfortunate remains of the man are constantly worried. His body is twice exhumed ; it is cut up ; some of its bones are peeled out of the carcase, are handled, are given to one party and then to another, until at last they come to a final rest. And what makes the whole performance most disconcerting is the absence of the real protagonist—Hamlet without the Prince of Denmark. For the spirit of the dead man knows nothing about all that happens to his body and bones, and cares less, since he is already leading a happy existence in Tuma, the nether-world, having breathed of the magic of oblivion and formed new ties (see ch. xii, sec. 5). The ritual performances at his twice-opened grave and over his buried remains, and all that is done with his relics, is merely a social game, where the various groupings into which the community has re-crystallized at his death play against each other. This, I must add with great emphasis, represents the actual contemporary view of the natives, and contains no hypothetical reference to the origins or past history of this institution. Whether the dead man always had his spiritual back turned on the Trobriand mortuary ritual, or whether his spirit has gradually evaporated from it—it is not for the field-worker to decide. In this context we shall have to confine ourselves to the study of mortuary practices in their barest outline only. A complete account of them would easily fill a volume of the present size. We shall, therefore, select such features as throw light on the ties of marriage, and on the ideas of kinship and relationship ; and even this will have to be done in a somewhat schematic and simplified form.[1]

Let us take the death of a man of consequence in the fulness of age, leaving behind a widow, several children and brothers. From the moment of his death, the distinction between his real, that

---

[1] Compare the brief account of these ceremonies among the Northern Massim, by Professor C. G. Seligman, *The Melanesians of British New Guinea.*

is matrilineal, kinsmen (*veyola*) on the one hand, and his children, relatives-in-law and friends on the other, takes on a sharp and even an outwardly visible form. The kinsmen of the deceased fall under a taboo ; they must keep aloof from the corpse. They are not allowed either to wash or adorn or fondle or bury it ; for if they were to touch or to come near it, pernicious influences from the body would attack them and cause their disease and death. These pernicious influences are conceived in the form of a material exhalation, issuing from the corpse and polluting the air. It is called *bwaulo*, a word which also designates the cloud of smoke which surrounds a village especially on steamy, calm days. The necrogenic *bwaulo*, invisible to common eyes, appears to a witch or sorcerer as a black cloud shrouding the village. It is innocuous to strangers, but dangerous to kinsmen (ch. xiii, sec. 1).

The kindred must also not display any outward signs of mourning in costume and ornamentation, though they need not conceal their grief and may show it by weeping. Here the underlying idea is that the maternal kinsmen (*veyola*) are hit in their own persons ; that each one suffers because the whole sub-clan to which they belong has been maimed by the loss of one of its members. " As if a limb were cut off, or a branch lopped from a tree." Thus, though they need not hide their grief, they must not parade it. This abstention from outward mourning extends, not only to all the members of the sub-clan beyond the real kinsmen, but to all the members of the clan to which the dead man belonged. On the other hand, the taboo against touching the corpse applies primarily to the members of the sub-clan and especially to the actual kinsmen, to whom, of course, the temptation to touch the corpse, as an expression of love, would be strongest.

Quite different, in the native idea, is the relation

of the widow, and of the children and relatives-in-law, to the dead and to his corpse. They ought, according to the moral code, to suffer and to feel bereaved. But in feeling thus they are not suffering directly; they are not grieving for a loss which affects their own sub-clan (*dala*) and therefore their own persons. Their grief is not spontaneous like that of the *veyola* (maternal kinsmen), but a duty almost artificial, springing as it does from acquired obligations. Therefore they must ostentatiously express their grief, display it, and bear witness to it by outward signs. If they did not, they would offend the surviving members of the dead man's sub-clan. Thus an interesting situation develops, giving rise to a most strange spectacle : a few hours after the death of a notable, the village is thronged by people, with their heads shaven, the whole body thickly smeared with soot, and howling like demons in despair. And these are the non-kinsmen of the dead man, the people not actually bereaved. In contrast to these a number of others are to be seen in their usual attire, outwardly calm and behaving as if nothing had happened. These represent the sub-clan and clan of the deceased, and are the actually bereaved. Thus by a devious reasoning, tradition and custom produce the reverse of what would seem natural and obvious to us or any observer from almost any other culture.

Among those who display their grief, it is easy to distinguish several groups and grades. There is the rank and file of mourners, comprising all the people belonging to the remaining three clans; for, when a notable dies, everyone in the village community puts on mourning, except the members of his own clan. A small group is busy about the body and the grave; this consists of the male children and brothers-in-law of the deceased. Nearest to the corpse and plunged most deeply in the mimicry of grief are seated a few women, among whom one, the widow, is conspicuous, supported by her daughters and sisters. In this group, and it may be in that of the sons also, an observer well acquainted with these natives would be able to distinguish an interesting interplay of feigned and merely histrionic grief with real and heartfelt sorrow.

3
FUNERAL CEREMONIES AND THE OBLIGATIONS OF MOURNING

With this sociological scheme before us, we can now follow the sequence of event and ritual which begins automatically with a man's death. When death is seen to be approaching, the wife and children, kinsmen and relatives-in-law crowd round the bed, filling the small hut to overflowing. The consummation of death is marked by a frantic outburst of wailing. The widow, who generally stands at the head of the dying man, utters the first piercing shriek, to which immediately other women respond, till the village is filled with the strange harmonies of the melodious dirge. From this moment all the varied activities of the days, and even weeks, which follow will be carried on to the choral accompaniment of a long-drawn wail which never stops for one instant. At times it swells up in violent and discordant gusts; then ebbs again into soft, melodious strains, musically well expressing sorrow. To me, this powerful uneven stream of sound, flowing over the village and enveloping as it were all these human beings in a feeble, imbecile protest against death, became symbolic of all that was deeply human and real in the otherwise stiff, conventional, incomprehensible ritual of mourning.

First the corpse is washed, anointed, and covered with ornaments (pls. 32 and 33), then the bodily apertures are filled with coconut husk fibre, the legs tied together, and the arms bound to the sides. Thus prepared, it is placed on the knees of a row of women who sit on the floor of the hut, with the widow or widower at one end holding the head.[1] They fondle the corpse, stroke the skin with caressing hands, press valuable objects against chest and abdomen, move the limbs slightly and agitate the head. The body is thus made to move and twist with slow and ghastly gestures to the rhythm of the incessant wailing. The hut is full of mourners, all intoning the melodious lamentation. Tears flow from their eyes and mucus from their noses, and all the liquids of grief are carefully displayed and smeared over their bodies or otherwise conspicuously disposed. Outside, certain women, usually relatives-in-law of the dead man, perform a slow rhythmic dance (the *vaysali*) with relics in their hands (pl. 11).

The sons in the meantime dig the grave, which in olden days was always on the central place of the village, but which now, by the white man's decree, must be on the outskirts. A few hours after death the body is laid in it, wrapped in mats, and is covered with logs, which leave a shallow space above. On this layer of logs the widow lies down to keep vigil over the corpse. Her daughter may be beside her; round the brink of the grave are her sisters, kinswomen and friends, and the other relatives-in-law of the dead man. As night draws on, the central place fills with people; for even nowadays the white man's regulations against burial in the *baku* are circumvented by making a temporary grave there, or placing the corpse on the ground. Here the mourners, the kinsmen, all the villagers and many guests from far afield congregate to hold a most remarkable wake (*yawali*).

The chief mourners and kinsmen in appropriate groups keep the central position round the grave.

---

[1] Cf. pl. lxv in *Argonauts of the Western Pacific*, where this act is reconstructed outside the hut for purposes of photography and the widow is replaced by the son.

Outside this inner ring, the villagers and guests are seated, each community in a separate body, their mood and behaviour becoming less tragic as they are farther removed from the corpse, until on the outskirts of the crowd, we find people in animated conversation, eating and chewing betel nut. The central group of mourners intones the deep wail of sorrow, the others sing songs, and, as the night goes on, people will stand up and recite fragments of magic in honour of the departed, chanting them over the heads of the crowd.

The body is not allowed to remain long in peace—if the weird, noisy, and discordant din of singing, wailing, and haranguing can be so described. On the following evening, the body is exhumed, and inspected for signs of sorcery (see pl. 33). Such an inspection yields most important clues, as to who caused the death by witchcraft and for what motive this was done. I have assisted at this ceremony several times ; the photograph for plate 33 was taken during the first exhumation of Ineykoya, wife of Toyodala, my best informant in Oburaku.[1]

Before daybreak after the first exhumation, the body is taken out of the grave, and some of the bones are removed from it. This anatomical operation is done by the man's sons, who keep some of the bones as relics and distribute the others to certain of their relatives. This practice has been strictly forbidden by the Government—another instance of the sacrifice of most sacred religious custom to the prejudice and moral susceptibilities of the " civilized " white. Yet the Trobrianders are so deeply attached to this custom that it is still clandestinely performed, and I have seen the jaw-bone of a man with whom I had spoken a few days before dangling from the neck of his widow (see pls. 34, 35, and 36).

---

[1] For further information about the signs of sorcery, see *Crime and Custom*, pp. 87-91.

The excision of the bones and their subsequent use as relics is an act of piety; the process of detaching them from the putrifying corpse, a heavy, repugnant, and disgusting duty. The sons of the deceased are expected by custom to curb and conceal their disgust, and to suck some of the decaying matter when they are cleaning the bones. Speaking with virtuous pride they will say : " I have sucked the radius bone of my father ; I had to go away and vomit ; I came back and went on." After they have cleansed the bones, which is always done on the seashore, they return to the village, and the dead man's kinswomen ceremonially " wash their mouths " by giving them food and purify their hands with coconut oil. The bones are converted to various purposes, serviceable and ornamental : the skull is made into a lime pot to be used by the widow ; the jaw-bone is turned into a neck ornament to hang on her breast ; the radius, ulna, tibia, and some other bones are carved into lime spatulæ to be used with betel and areca nut.

A curious mixed sentiment underlies this complex of customs. On the one hand, it should be the wish of the widow and children to keep a part of the beloved dead. " The relic (*kayvaluba*) brings the departed back to our mind and makes our inside tender." On the other hand, the use of these relics is regarded as a harsh and unpleasant duty, as a sort of pious repayment for all the benefits received from the father. As it was explained to me : " Our mind is grieved for the man who has fed us, who has given us dainties to eat ; we suck his bones as lime spatulæ." Or again : " It is right that a child should suck the father's ulna. For the father has held out his hand to its excrement and allowed it to make water on to his knee " (compare similar locutions quoted in section 3 of chapter i). Thus the use of relics is at the same time a relief to the bereaved widow and children, and an act of filial piety which must be rigorously observed.

To the dead man's maternal kinsmen (*veyola*) the use of his bones is strictly tabooed. If they break this taboo they would fall ill, their bellies would swell and they might die. The contact is most dangerous when the bone is still wet with the dead man's bodily juices. When, after a few years, the bones are handed over to the kinsmen, they are presented carefully wrapped in dry leaves, and are then only gingerly handled by them. They are finally deposited on rocky shelves overlooking the sea. Thus the bones pass several times from hand to hand before they come to their final rest.

More distant relatives-in-law and friends of the dead man have his nails, teeth and hair, which they make into all sorts of mourning ornaments and wear as relics. The dead man's personal possessions are used in the same way, and nowadays, when the bodily relics have frequently to be concealed, this practice is very much in favour (see plate 92).

After the second exhumation the body is buried, the wake is over, and the people disperse; but the widow, who, during all this time, has not stirred from her husband's side, nor eaten nor drunk nor stopped in her wailing, is not yet released. Instead she moves into a small cage, built within her house, where she will remain for months together, observing the strictest taboos. She must not leave the place; she may only speak in whispers; she must not touch food or drink with her own hands, but wait till they are put into her mouth; she remains closed up in the dark, without fresh air or light; her body is thickly smeared over with soot and grease, which will not be washed off for a long time. She satisfies all the necessities of life indoors, and the excreta have to be carried out by her relatives. Thus she lives for months shut up in a low-roofed, stuffy, pitch-dark space, so small that with outstretched hands she can almost touch the walls on either side; it is often filled with

people who assist or comfort her, and pervaded by
an indescribable atmosphere of human exhalations,
accumulated bodily filth, stale food, and smoke.
Also she is under the more or less active control
and surveillance of her husband's matrilineal
relatives, who regard her mourning and its inherent
privations as their due. When the term of her
widowhood has almost run its course—its length
depends upon the status of her husband and varies
from about six months to two years—she is gradually
released by the dead man's kinsmen. Food is
put into her mouth according to a ritual which
gives her permission to eat with her own hands.
Then, ceremonially, she is allowed to speak ;
finally she is released from the taboo of confinement
and, still with appropriate ritual, requested to walk
forth. At the ceremony of her complete release
by the female *veyola* of the dead man, the widow
is washed and anointed, and dressed in a new gaudy
grass skirt in three colours. This makes her
marriageable again.

4

THE IDEOLOGY OF MOURNING

Throughout the rigorous ritual of mourning,
in which the widow, the orphans, and to a much
lesser degree the other relatives-in-law of the
deceased are caught and held as in a vice, we can
observe the working of certain ideas belonging to
the tribal tradition of the Trobrianders. One
especially, the taboo on maternal kinsmen, which
forces them to keep aloof since it is both dangerous
to approach the corpse and superfluous to show
grief, is strikingly visible throughout the whole
course of burial, exhumation, and grave-tending.
The corresponding idea, that it is the imperative
duty of the widow and her relatives to show grief
and perform all the mortuary services, emphasizes
the strength and the permanence of marriage

bonds as viewed by tradition. . It is also a post-
humous continuation of the remarkable system
of services which have to be given to a married man
by his wife's family, including the woman herself
and her children.

In the mortuary phase of these services, however,
the dead man's sub-clan have to render payment
more strictly and more frequently than he had to do
in his life-time. Immediately after the bones
have been cut out and the remains buried, the
dead man's sub-clan organize the first big distribution of food and valuables, in which the widow,
children, and other relatives-in-law, as well as the
unrelated mourners, are richly paid for the various
services rendered in tending the corpse and digging
the grave. Other distributions follow at stated
intervals. There is one expressly for women
mourners; one for the tenders of the grave; one for
the rank and file of mourners; one, by far the largest,
in which presents of valuables and enormous
quantities of food are given to the widow and
children, in so far as they, in grief and piety, have
used the bones of the dead man for their lime-
chewing or as ornaments. This intricate series
of distributions stretches out into years, and it
entails a veritable tangle of obligations and duties;
for the members of the deceased's sub-clan must
provide food and give it to the chief organizer,
the headman of the sub-clan, who collects it and
then distributes it to the proper beneficiaries.
These, in their turn, partially at least, re-distribute
it. And each gift in this enormous complex
trails its own wake of counter-gifts and obligations
to be fulfilled at a future date.

The ostentation with which the widow and
children have to display their grief, the thickness—
literally and metaphorically speaking—with which
they put on their mourning are indeed striking;
and the underlying complex psychology of these
things must have become apparent in the above

account. In the first place, it is a duty towards the dead and towards his sub-clan, a duty strongly enjoined by the code of morals and guarded by public opinion, as well as by the kinsmen. " Our tears—they are for the kinsmen of our father to see," as one of the mourners simply and directly told me. In the second place, it demonstrates to the world at large that the wife and children were really good to the dead and that they took great care of him in his illness. Lastly, and this is very important, it allays any suspicion of their complicity in his murder by black magic. To understand the last queer motive, one has to realize the extreme fear, the ever-vigilant suspicion of sorcery, and the unusual lack of trust in anyone at all with reference to it. The Trobrianders, in common with all races at their culture level, regard every death without exception as an act of sorcery, unless it is caused by suicide or by a visible accident, such as poisoning or a spear thrust. It is characteristic of their idea of the bonds of marriage and fatherhood—which they regard as artificial and untrustworthy under any strain—that the principal suspicion of sorcery attaches always to the wife and children. The real interest in a man's welfare, the real affection, the natural innocence of any attempt against him are, by the traditional system of ideas, attributed to his maternal kinsmen. His wife and children are mere strangers, and custom persists in ignoring any real identity of interest between them.[1]

How utterly this traditional view is generally at variance with the economic and psychological reality, has been shown, and illustrated by many facts in chapter i, sections 1 and 2. For, apart from the personal attachment which always exists between husband and wife, father and children, it is clear

---

[1] Even this is a simplified account, one in which the ideal of native law and tradition is emphasized, as is always done by the natives themselves. The full account of native ideas about sorcery in relation to kinship and relationship by marriage will have to be postponed to a later publication.

that a man's children lose more at his death than do his kinsmen, who, as his heirs, always gain materially, especially in the case of a man of wealth, rank, and importance. And, in reality, the actual feelings of the survivors run their natural course independently of the mimic and official display of grief. The existence of an individual reality of thought, sentiment, and impulse, unfolding itself side by side with the conventional sentiment and idea contained in and imposed by a traditional pattern, is one of the most important subjects of social psychology—a subject on which we need more material from ethnological investigation, carried on with a good deal of detail and based upon personal knowledge of the savages observed.

In the Trobriands, the genuine sorrow of the widow and children is blurred, overlaid, and made almost unrecognizable by the histrionic display of grief. But their real feelings can be gauged by observing their behaviour at other times, especially under critical conditions. I have seen more than one case of a husband sitting night after night at his sick wife's bedside. I have seen his hopes surge and ebb, and unmistakable, even deep, despair set in as the apparent chances of survival waned. Differences are clearly distinguishable in the sorrow of widows and widowers, some merely conforming to custom, others genuinely grieving. To'uluwa, the chief, though a rather selfish and shallow character, could not speak about the death of Kadamwasila, his favourite wife, without visible and real emotion. Toyodala, the nicest man I knew in Oburaku (see pl. 33) was for weeks anxiously watching his wife's illness and hoping for her recovery. When she died, he behaved at first like a madman, and then, during his mourning confinement, in which I often visited him, he wept so bitterly that his eyesight suffered. There is no doubt at all that the kinsmen feel the personal loss much less. On the other hand, their conventional sentiment of bereavement and realization of the maiming of their group do not leave them unaffected. But here we enter upon a problem, that of feelings and ideas relating to the solidarity of the clan, which, if followed up, would take us too far away from our subject.

The study of marriage has led us away from the study of sex in the narrower sense of the word. We have had to consider questions of social organization, and the legal, economic, and religious setting of the relation between husband and wife, parents and children. This last subject, parenthood, will still occupy us in the next two chapters, before we pass to the detailed analysis of the sexual impulse in its cultural manifestations among our natives.

CHAPTER VII

PROCREATION AND PREGNANCY IN NATIVE BELIEF AND CUSTOM

THE dependence of social organization in a given society upon the ideas, beliefs, and sentiments current there is of primary importance to the anthropologist. Among savage races we often find unexpected and fantastic views about natural processes, and correspondingly extreme and one-sided developments of social organization as regards kinship, communal authority, and tribal constitution. In this chapter I shall give an account of the Trobrianders' idea of the human organism as it affects their beliefs about procreation and gestation, beliefs which are embodied in oral tradition, customs, and ceremonies, and which exercise a deep influence on the social facts of kinship and on the matrilineal constitution of the tribe.

I

THE MALE AND FEMALE ORGANISM AND THE SEXUAL IMPULSE IN NATIVE BELIEF

The natives have a practical acquaintance with the main features of the human anatomy, and an extensive vocabulary for the various parts of the human body and for the internal organs. They often cut up pigs and other animals, while the custom of *post mortem* dissection of corpses, and visits among their overseas cannibal neighbours supply them with an exact knowledge of the homologies of the human and animal organism. Their physiological theories, on the other hand, are remarkably defective ; there are many notable gaps in their knowledge about the functions of the most important organs, side by side with some fantastic and strange ideas.

Their understanding of sexual anatomy is, on the whole, limited in comparison with what they know about other parts of the human body. Considering the great interest which they take in this matter, the distinctions which they make are superficial and rough, and their terminology meagre. They distinguish and name the following parts: vagina (*wila*), clitoris (*kasesa*), penis (*kwila*), testes (*puwala*). They have no words to describe the *mons veneris* as a whole, nor the *labia majora* and *minora*. The *glans penis* they describe as the " point " of the penis (*matala kwila*) and the prepuce as the skin of the penis (*kanivinela kwila*). The internal female organs are called generically *bam*, and this comprises the uterus and the placenta. There is no special word for the ovaries.

Their physiological views are crude. The organs of sex serve for excretion and for pleasure. The excretive urinary processes are not associated with the kidneys. A narrow duct (*wotuna*) leads from the stomach directly to the bladder, from which it passes through the male and female genitals. Through this canal the water which we drink passes slowly till it is expelled, and on its way it becomes discoloured and sullied in the stomach by contact with excrement. For food begins to be changed into excrement in the stomach.

Their ideas about the sexual functions of the genitals are more complex and systematic, and present a sort of psycho-physiological theory. The eyes are the seat of desire and lust (*magila kayta*, literally " desire of copulation "). They are the basis or cause (*u'ula*) of sexual passion. From the eyes, desire is carried to the brain by means of the *wotuna* (literally, tendril or creeper; in the anatomical context, vein, nerve, duct, or sinew), and thence spreads all over the body to the belly, the arms, the legs, until it finally concentrates in the kidneys. The kidneys are considered the main or middle part or trunk (*tapwana*) of the system. From them, other ducts (*wotuna*) lead to the male organ. This is the tip or point (*matala*, literally eye) of the whole system. Thus, when the eyes see an object of desire they " wake up ", communicate the impulse to the kidneys, which transmit it to the penis and cause an erection. Hence the eyes are the primary motive of all sexual excitement : they are " the things of copulation " ; they are " that which makes us desire to copulate ". In proof of this the natives say : " A man with his eyes closed will have no erection " ; though they qualify this statement by admitting that the olfactory sense can sometimes replace the eyes, for " when a woman discards her grass petticoat in the dark, desire may be aroused ".

The process of sexual excitement in the female is analogous. Thus the eyes, the kidneys and the sexual organs are united by the same system of *wotuna* (communicating ducts). The eyes give the alarm, which passes through the body, takes possession of the kidneys, and produces sexual excitation of the clitoris. Both the male and female discharge are called by the same name (*momona* or *momola*), and they ascribe to both the same origin in the kidneys, and the same function, which has nothing to do with generation, but is concerned with lubricating the membrane and increasing pleasure.

I first obtained this account of the subject from Namwana Guya'u and Piribomatu, the former an amateur and the latter a professional sorcerer; both were intelligent men and both, in virtue of their profession, were interested in human anatomy and physiology. Thus it represents the highest development of Trobriand knowledge and theory. I obtained similar statements in other parts of the island, and in their main outline—such as the sexual functions of the kidneys, the great importance of the eyes and the olfactory sense, and the strict parallel between male and female sexuality—all were in agreement.

And on the whole, it is a fairly consistent, and not altogether nonsensical view of the psycho-physiology of sexual libido. The drawing of a parallel between the two sexes is consistent. The indication of the three cardinal points of the sexual system is sound, and characteristic of native canons of classification. In many subjects they distinguish these three elements : the *u'ula*, the *tapwana*, and the *matala*. The image is derived from a tree or a pillar or a spear : *u'ula*—in its literal sense the foot of the tree, the base, the foundation—has come, by extension, to mean cause, origin, source of strength ; *tapwana*, the middle part of the trunk, also means the trunk itself, the main body of any elongated object, the length of a road ; *matala*—originally eye, or point (as in a spear) and sometimes replaced by the word *dogina* or *dabwana*, the tip of a tree or the top of any high object—stands for the highest part, or, in more abstract metaphor, the final word, the highest expression.

The comparison as generally applied to the sexual mechanism is not, as we have said, altogether devoid of meaning, and only becomes nonsensical in ascribing a special function to the kidneys. These are regarded as a highly important and vital part of the human organism, and mainly because they are the source of the seminal fluid. Another view attributes male and female discharge, not to the kidneys, but to the bowels. In either case, the natives consider that something in the bowels is the actual agent of ejaculation : *ipipisi momona*—" it squirts out the discharge."

Very remarkable is their entire ignorance of the physiological function of the testes. They are not aware that anything is produced in this organ, and leading questions as to whether the male fluid (*momona*) has not its source there are answered emphatically in the negative. " See, women have

no testes and yet they produce *momona*." This
part of the male body is said to be only an ornamental
appendage (*katububula*). " Indeed, how ugly would
a penis look without the testes," a native æsthete
will exclaim. The testes serve " to make it look
proper " (*bwoyna*).

Love or affection (*yobwayli*) has its seat in the
intestines, in the skin of the belly, and of the arms,
and only to a lesser extent in those springs of desire,
the eyes. Hence, we like to look at those of whom
we are fond, such as our children, our friends,
or our parents, but when this love is strong we want
to hug them.

Menstruation the Trobrianders regard as a
phenomenon connected with pregnancy in a vague
manner : " the flow comes, it trickles, it trickles,
it ebbs—it is over." They denote it simply by
the word blood, *buyavi*, but with a characteristic
grammatical peculiarity. While ordinary bodily
blood is always mentioned with the pronoun of
nearest possession, which is affixed to all the parts
of a human body, menstruous blood is spoken of
with the same possessive pronouns as are used for
ornamentation and articles of apparel (second
nearest possession). Thus *buyavigu*, " blood-mine "
(" part of me—blood "), means bodily blood coming
from a cut or hæmorrhage ; *agu buyavi*, " my
blood " (" belonging to me—blood "), means
menstruous blood.

There is no pronounced masculine dislike or
dread of menstruous blood. A man will not cohabit
with his wife or sweetheart during her monthly
period, but he will remain in the same hut and
participate in the same food, and only refrains from
sleeping in the same bed. Women, during
menstruation, wash themselves daily, for purposes
of cleanliness, in the same large water hole from
which the whole village draws its drinking water,
and in which, also, males occasionally take a bath.
There are no special ablutions ceremonially carried

out at the end of the period, nor is any rite performed when a girl menstruates for the first time. The women have no special way of dressing during menstruation, except that at times they wear a longer skirt, and there is no particular modesty on the subject between the sexes.

2

REINCARNATION AND THE WAY TO LIFE THROUGH THE SPIRIT WORLD

The relation between menstruous blood and the formation of the fœtus has been observed and recognized by the natives, but their ideas about it are extremely vague. Such as they are, they are so mixed up with beliefs about the incarnation of spiritual beings, that physiological process and spiritual agencies will have to be considered together in this account. Thus we shall preserve the natural sequence and perspective of native doctrine. Since the new life, in Trobriand tradition, begins with death, we shall now have to move to the bedside of a dying man, and follow the progress of his spirit till we trace him back to earthly existence again.[1]

The spirit after death moves to Tuma, the Island of the Dead, where he leads a pleasant existence analogous to the terrestrial life—only much happier. Into the nature of this bliss we shall have to inquire in somewhat more detail, for sex plays an important part in it.[2] Here we are concerned with one of its features only : perpetual youth, preserved by the power of rejuvenation. Whenever the spirit (*baloma*)

[1] In my article " Baloma, the Spirits of the Dead " already quoted, I have given a short preliminary account of native beliefs concerning procreation. I also expressed certain opinions about primitive ignorance of paternity in general, some of which were challenged by Professor Westermarck (*History of Human Marriage*, 5th edition, vol, i, pp. 290 sq.) and by Professor Carveth Read (article, " No Paternity " in the *Journal of the Anthropological Institute*, 1917). The fuller evidence adduced in this chapter answers certain questions of fact raised by my critics.

[2] Cf. below, ch. xii, last section.

sees that bodily hair is covering his skin, that the skin itself is getting loose and wrinkled, and that his head is turning grey, he simply sloughs his covering and appears fresh and young, with black locks and smooth hairless skin.

But when a spirit becomes tired of constant rejuvenation, when he has led a long existence " underneath " as the natives call it, he may want to return to earth again ; and then he leaps back in age and becomes a small pre-born infant. Some of my informants pointed out that in Tuma, as on earth, there are plenty of sorcerers. Black magic is frequently practised, and can reach a spirit and make him weak, sick and tired of life ; then, and then only, will he go back to the beginnings of his existence and change into a spirit-child. To kill a spirit by black magic or accident is quite impossible ; his end will always mean merely a new beginning.

These rejuvenated spirits, these little pre-incarnated babies or spirit-children, are the only source from which humanity draws its new supplies of life. A pre-born infant finds its way back to the Trobriands and into the womb of some woman, but always of a woman who belongs to the same clan and sub-clan as the spirit child itself. Exactly how it travels from Tuma to Boyowa, how it enters the body of its mother, and how there the physiological processes of gestation combine with the spirit activity, are questions on which native belief is not altogether consistent. But that all spirits have ultimately to end their life in Tuma and turn into unborn infants ; that every child born in this world has first come into existence (*ibubuli*) in Tuma through the metamorphosis of a spirit ; that the only reason and real cause of every birth is spirit activity, are facts known to everybody and firmly believed by all.

Owing to its importance, I collected details and variants of this system of beliefs with special care.

The rejuvenation process is associated in a general
way with sea-water.   In the myth which describes
how humanity lost the privilege of regaining youth
at will, the scene of the last rejuvenation is laid on
the seashore in one of the lagoon inlets.[1]   In the
first account of rejuvenation which I obtained in
Omarakana, I was told that the spirit " goes to the beach
and bathes in the salt water ".   Tomwaya Lakwabulo
the Seer (pl. 37), who in his trances often goes
to Tuma and has frequent intercourse with the
spirits, told me : " The *baloma* go to a spring called
sopiwina (literally ' washing water ') ; it lies on
the beach.   There they wash their skin with brackish
water.   They become *to'ulatile* (young men)."
Likewise in the final rejuvenation, which makes them
return to the infant state, the spirits have to bathe
in salt water, and, when they become babies again,
they go into the sea and drift.   They are always
spoken of as floating on drift-logs, or on the leaves,
boughs, dead seaweed, sea-scum, and the other light
substances which litter the surface of the sea.
Tomwaya Lakwabulo says that they float all the
time around the shores of Tuma, wailing *wa, wa, wa*.
" At night I hear their wailing. I ask, ' What is it ? '
' Oh, children ; the tide brings them, they come.' "
The spirits in Tuma can see these pre-incarnated
infants, and so can Tomwaya Lakwabulo when he
descends into the spirit world.   But to ordinary
people they are invisible.   At times, however,
fishermen from the northern villages of Kaybola
and Lu'ebila, when they go far out into the sea after
shark, will hear the wailing—*wa, wa, wa*—in the
sighing of the wind and the waves.
    Tomwaya Lakwabulo and other informants main-
tain that such spirit children never float far away
from Tuma. They are transported to the Trobriands
by the help of another spirit. Tomwaya Lakwabulo

[1] This story is given in *Myth in Primitive Psychology*, pp. 80-106.
The village of Bwadela, where the loss of immortality occurred, is on
the west shore of the southern half of the main island.

gives the following account. " A child floats on a drift log. A spirit sees it is good-looking. She takes it. She is the spirit of the mother or of the father of the pregnant woman (*nasusuma*). Then she puts it on the head, in the hair, of the pregnant woman, who suffers headache, vomits, and has an ache in the belly. Then the child comes down into the belly, and she is really pregnant. She says : ' Already it (the child) has found me ; already they (the spirits) have brought me the child.' " In this account we find two leading ideas : the active intervention of another spirit—the one who somehow conveys the child back to the Trobriands and gives it to the mother—and the insertion of it through the head, with which (not in the statement quoted, but usually) is associated the idea of an effusion of blood, first to the head and then into the abdomen.

As to how the transportation is actually accomplished opinions vary : there are natives who imagine that the older spirit either carries the baby in some sort of receptacle—a plaited coco-nut basket or a wooden dish—or else simply in her arms. Others say candidly that they do not know. But the active control of another spirit is essentially important. When natives say that the children are " given by a *baloma* ", that " a *baloma* is the real cause of childbirth ", they refer always to this controlling spirit (as we might call it), and not to the spirit baby itself. This controlling spirit usually appears in a dream to the woman about to be pregnant (see ch. viii, sec. 1). As Motago'i, one of my best informants, volunteered : " She dreams her mother comes to her, she sees the face of her mother in a dream. She wakes up, and says : ' O, there is a child for me.' "

Frequently a woman will tell her husband who it was that brought the baby to her. And the tradition of this spiritual godfather or godmother is preserved. Thus the present chief of Omarakana knows that it was Bugwabwaga, one of his predecessors in office, who gave him to his mother. My best friend, Tokulubakiki, was a gift to his mother from her *kadala*, mother's brother. Tokulubakiki's wife received her eldest daughter from her mother's spirit. Usually it is some maternal relative of the prospective mother who bestows the gift; but it may be her father, as in Tomwaya Lakwabulo's statement.

The physiological theory associated with this belief has already been touched on. The spirit-child is laid by the bringer on the woman's head. Blood from her body rushes there, and on this tide of blood the baby gradually descends until it settles in the womb. The blood helps to build the body of the child—it nourishes it. That is the reason why, when a woman becomes pregnant, her menstruous flow stops. A woman will see that her menstruation has stopped. She will wait one, two, three moons, and then she will know for certain that she is pregnant. A much less authoritative belief maintains that the baby is inserted *per vaginam*.

Another version of the story of reincarnation ascribes more initiative to the pre-incarnated infant. It is supposed to be able to float of its own will towards the Trobriands. There it remains, probably in company with others, drifting about the shores of the island, awaiting its chance to enter the body of a woman while she bathes. Certain observances kept by girls in coastal villages are evidence that the belief has vitality. The spirit children are imagined, as around Tuma, to be attached to drift logs, scum, leaves, and branches, or else to the small stones on the bottom of the sea. Whenever, through wind and tide, much débris accumulates near the shore, the girls will not enter the water for fear they might conceive. Again, in the villages on the northern coast, there is a custom of filling a wooden baler with water from the sea which is then left overnight in the hut of a woman who wishes to conceive, on the chance that a spirit-child might have been caught in the baler and transfer itself during the night into the woman. But even in this case, the woman is said to be visited in her dream by the spirit of some deceased maternal relative, so that a controlling spirit is still essential to conception. It is important to note that the water must always be fetched by her brother or by her mother's brother ; that is, by a maternal kinsman. To give an example : a man from the village of Kapwani, on the northern shore, was asked by his sister's daughter to procure her a child. He went several times to the beach. One evening he heard a sound like the wailing of children. He drew water from the sea into the baler and left it in his *kadala's* (niece's) hut over night. She conceived a child, a girl. This child, unfortunately, turned out to be an albino, but this mischance was not due to the method of conception.

The chief points in which this belief differs from the one first described are that the pre-incarnated spirit child is endowed with more spontaneity— it can float across the sea and enter the bathing woman without help—and that its entry is effected *per vaginam*, or else through the skin of the abdomen if conception takes place in the hut. I found this belief prevalent in the northern part of the island, and especially in its coastal villages.

The nature of the spirit-child, or pre-incarnated baby, is not very clearly defined in traditional folk-lore. In answer to a direct question, the majority of informants said that they did not know what it was or what it looked like. One or two, however, who, through their superior intelligence, had worked out their beliefs in greater detail and with more consistency, said that it was like the fœtus in the womb which, they added, " looks like a mouse." Tomwaya Lakwabulo volunteered the statement that pre-incarnated infants look like very minute and fully-developed children, and that they are sometimes very beautiful. He had to say something, of course, since, on his own showing, he had

seen them frequently in Tuma. Even the nomenclature is not quite definite. Usually it is called
waywaya, small child or fœtus, but sometimes the
word *pwapwawa* is used, which, though almost
synonymous with *waywaya*, refers perhaps rather
to a child already born than to the fœtus or a
pre-incarnated baby. Quite as often, however, it is
spoken of simply as " child ", *gwadi* (plural,
gugwadi).

I was told, though I was not able to verify this
completely, that there is a magic performed over a
species of betel leaf (*kwega*) called *kaykatuvilena
kwega*, to induce pregnancy. A woman in
Yourawotu, a small village near Omarakana, knows
this magic, but unfortunately I was unable to get
into touch with her.[1]

Thus, as is always the case, this belief dissolves
into various and only partially consistent elements
when examined under the magnifying glass of detailed
research made over an extended area. The
divergencies are not wholly due to geographical
differences ; nor can they be assigned to special
social layers, for some of the inconsistencies occurred
in the account of one and the same man. Tomwaya
Lakwabulo, for instance, insisted that the children
cannot travel alone, but must be carried by a
controlling spirit and placed in the woman ; yet he
informed me that their wailing could be heard on the
north shore near Kaybola. Or, again, the man of
Kiriwina, who told me how the spirit child might
enter from a baler, also spoke of an older spirit
"giving" that child. Such inconsistencies are probably
the result of several mythological cycles of ideas,
meeting, so to speak, and intersecting on the locus
of this belief. One of these cycles contains the idea
of rejuvenation ; another that of fresh life floating

---

[1] A statement which I guardedly gave on the authority of a trader in
my article for the *Journal of the Anthropological Institute*, 1916, p. 404,
to the effect that there are " some stones in Sinaketa, to which a woman
who wants to become enceinte may have recourse ", I found quite baseless
after careful inquiries on the spot.

on the sea towards the island; another that a new member of the family comes as a gift from some ancestral spirit.

It is important, however, that, in all principal points, the various versions and descriptions agree, overlap and fortify one another; and we are left with a composite picture which, though blurred in some of its details, presents a strong outline when viewed from a distance. Thus all spirits rejuvenate; all children are incarnated spirits; the identity of sub-clan is preserved throughout the cycle; the real cause of childbirth is the spirit initiative from Tuma.

It must be remembered, however, that the belief in reincarnation is not one which exercises a great influence over custom and social organization in the Trobriands; rather it is one of those doctrines which lead a quiet and passive existence in folk-lore, and affect social behaviour only to a small extent. Thus, for instance, although the Trobrianders firmly believe that each spirit becomes a pre-born infant, and that this again becomes reincarnated into a human being, yet no consciousness of personal identity is preserved through the process. That is, no one knows whose incarnation the infant is—who he was in his previous existence. There is no remembrance of past life in Tuma or on earth. Any questioning of the natives makes it obvious that the whole problem appears to them irrelevant and indeed uninteresting. The only recognized rule which guides these metamorphoses is that the continuity of clan and sub-clan is preserved throughout. There are no moral ideas of recompense or punishment embodied in their reincarnation theory, no customs or ceremonies associated with it or bearing witness to it.

3

IGNORANCE OF PHYSIOLOGICAL PATERNITY

The correlation of the mystical with the physiological aspects in pregnancy belief—of the origin of the child in Tuma and its journey to the Trobriands with the subsequent processes in the maternal body, the welling up of the blood from the abdomen to the head and down again from the head to the womb—provides a co-ordinated and self-contained, though not always consistent, theory of the origin of human life. It also gives a good theoretical foundation for matriliny ; for the whole process of introducing new life into a community lies between the spirit world and the female organism. There is no room for any sort of physical paternity.

But there is another condition considered by the natives indispensable for conception and child-birth, which complicates their theory and blurs the clear outline of their belief. This condition is related to sexual intercourse, and brings us face to face with the difficult and delicate question : are the natives really entirely ignorant of physiological fatherhood ? Is it not rather a fact of which they are more or less aware, though it may be overlaid and distorted by mythological and animistic beliefs ? Is it not an instance of empirical knowledge possessed by a backward community, but never formulated because it is too obvious to need explicit statement, whereas the traditional legend which is the basis of their social structure is carefully expressed as a part of the body of authoritative dogma ? The facts which I am about to adduce contain an unambiguous and decisive answer to these questions. I shall not anticipate the conclusion, which, indeed, as we shall see, will be drawn by the natives themselves.

A virgin cannot conceive.

Tradition, diffuse folk-lore, certain aspects of

custom and customary behaviour, teach the natives this simple physiological truth. They have no doubt about it, and it will be seen from what follows that they can formulate it tersely and clearly.

This statement was volunteered by Niyova, a sound informant in Oburaku : " A virgin does not conceive, because there is no way for the children to go, for that woman to conceive. When the orifice is wide open, the spirits are aware, they give the child." This is quite clear ; but during the same sitting, the same informant had previously given me a detailed description of how the spirit lays the child on the woman's head. The words of Niyova, here quoted verbatim, imply an insertion *per vaginam*. Ibena, a clever old man of Kasana'i, gave me a similar explanation—in fact, it was he who first made it clear to me that virginity mechanically impedes spirit impregnation. His method of explanation was graphic. Holding out his closed fist, he asked : " Can anything enter ? " then, opening it, he continued : " Now, of course, it is easy. Thus it is that a *bulabola* (large orifice) conceives easily, and a *nakapatu* (small or closed entrance, a virgin) cannot do it."

I have quoted these two statements *in extenso*, as they are telling and characteristic ; but they are not isolated. I received a great number of similar declarations, all expressing the view that the way must be open for the child, but this need not necessarily be brought about by sexual intercourse. The point is quite clear. The vagina must be opened to remove the physiological obstacle, called simply *kalapatu* (her tightness). Once this has been done, in the normal way by sexual intercourse, there is no need for male and female to come together in order to produce a child.

Considering that there are no virgins in the villages—for every female child begins her sexual life very early—we may wonder how the natives arrived at this *conditio sine qua non*. Again, since

they have got so far, it may appear difficult to see
why they have not advanced just a little further and
grasped the fertilizing virtue of seminal fluid,
Nevertheless, there are many facts to prove that
they have not made this advance : as certainly as
they know the necessity of a mechanical opening of
the vagina, so they do not know the generative power
of the male discharge. It was in discussing the
mythological tales of mankind's beginnings on earth
(see below, ch. xiii, sec. 5) and fantastic legends
of distant lands, to the account of which I shall now
proceed, that I was made aware of this subtle yet
all-important distinction between mechanical
dilation and physiological fertilization ; and was
thus enabled to place native belief regarding
procreation in its proper perspective.

According to native tradition, mankind originated
from underground, whence a couple, a brother and
a sister, emerged at different specified places.
According to certain legends, only women
appeared at first. Some of my commentators
insisted upon this version : " You see, we are so
many on the earth because many women came first.
Had there been many men, we would be few." Now,
whether accompanied by her brother or not, the
primeval woman is always imagined to bear children
without the intervention of a husband or of any
other male partner ; but not without the vagina
being opened by some means. In some of the
traditions this is mentioned explicitly. Thus on the
island of Vakuta there is a myth which describes how
an ancestress of one of the sub-clans exposed her
body to falling rain, and thus mechanically lost her
virginity. In the most important Trobriand myth,
a woman, called Mitigis or Bolutukwa, mother of
the legendary hero Tudava, lives quite alone in a
grotto on the seashore. One day she falls asleep
in her rocky dwelling, reclining under a dripping
stalactyte. The drops of water pierce her vagina,
and thus deprive her of virginity. Hence her second

name, Bolutukwa : *bo*, female, prefix, *litukwa*,
dripping water. In other myths of origin the means
of piercing the hymen are not mentioned, but it is
often explicitly stated that the ancestress was
without a man, and could, therefore, have no
sexual intercourse. When asked in so many words
how it was that they bore children without a man,
the natives would mention, more or less coarsely
or jestingly, some means of perforation which they
could easily have used, and it was clear that no more
was necessary.

Moving into another mythological dimension—
into present-day legends of countries far to the
north—we find the marvellous land of Kaytalugi,
peopled exclusively by sexually rabid women.[1]
They are so brutally profligate that their excesses
kill every man thrown by chance upon their shores,
and even their own male children never attain
maturity before they are sexually done to death.
Yet these women are very prolific, producing many
children, male and female. If a native is asked how
this can be, how these females become pregnant
if there are no men, he simply cannot understand
such an absurd question. These women, he will
say, destroy their virginity in all sorts of ways if
they cannot get hold of a man to torture to death.
And they have got their own *baloma*, of course,
to give them children.

I have adduced these mythical instances first, for
they clearly demonstrate the native point of view ;
the need for perforation, and the absence of any
idea concerning the fertilizing value of the semen.
But there are some convincing present-day instances
which show that the natives believe that a girl can
be with child without previous sexual intercourse.
Thus, there are some women so ugly and repulsive
that no one believes that they can ever have had
intercourse (save, of course, for those few who
know better, but who are very careful to keep silent

[1] Cf. ch. xii, sec. 4.

from shame ; see. ch. x, sec. 2). There is Tilapo'i, now an old woman, who was famous for her hideousness in youth. She has become blind, was always almost an idiot, and had a repulsive face and deformed body. Her unattractiveness was so notorious that she became the subject of a saying : *Kwoy Tilapo'i* (" have connection with Tilapo'i "), a form of abuse used in mild chaff (ch. xiii, sec. 4). Altogether she is an infinite source and pivot of all kinds of matrimonial and obscene jokes, all based on the presumed impossibility of being Tilapo'i's lover or prospective husband. I was assured, over and over again, that no one ever could have had connection with her. Yet this woman has had a child, as the natives would triumphantly point out, when I tried to persuade them that only by intercourse can children be produced.

Again, there is the case of Kurayana, a woman of Sinaketa, whom I never saw, but who, I was told, was " so ugly that any man would be ashamed " to have intercourse with her. This saying implies that social shame would be an even stronger deterrent than sexual repulsion, an assumption which shows that my informant was not a bad practical psychologist. Kurayana, as thoroughly chaste as anyone could be—by necessity, if not by virtue— had no less than six children, five of whom died and one of whom still survives.[1]

Albinos, male and female, are considered unfit for sexual intercourse. There is not the slightest doubt that all the natives feel real horror of and disgust for these unfortunate beings, a horror perfectly comprehensible after one has seen specimens of such unpigmented natives (see pl. 38). Yet there are on record several instances of albino women who have brought forth a numerous progeny. " Why did they become pregnant ? Is it because

---

[1] In the already quoted article in the *Journal of the Anthropological Institute*, 1916, I did an injustice to Kurayana in stating on p. 412 that she was the mother of five children only. Six is the correct number, all produced without the assistance of a man.

they copulate at night time ? Or because a *baloma* has given them children ? " Such was the clinching argument of one of my informants, for the first alternative appeared obviously absurd. Indeed, the whole of this line of argument was volunteered to me in one of my early discussions of the subject, although I obtained confirmatory data by subsequent research. For as a means of testing the firmness of their belief, I sometimes made myself definitely and aggressively an advocate of the truer physiological doctrine of procreation. In such arguments the natives would quote, not only positive instances, such as those just mentioned, of women who have children without having enjoyed any intercourse ; but would also refer to the equally convincing negative aspect, that is, to the many cases in which an unmarried woman has plenty of intercourse and no children. This argument would be repeated over and over again, with specially telling concrete examples of childless persons renowned for profligacy, or of women who lived with one white trader after another without having any baby.

4

WORDS AND DEEDS IN TESTIMONY

Although I was never afraid of using a leading question, or of eliciting the natives' point of view by contradicting it, I was somewhat astonished at the fierce opposition evoked by my advocacy of physiological paternity. Only late in my Trobriand career did I find out that I was not the first to attack this part of native belief, having been preceded by the missionary teachers. I speak mainly of the coloured ones ; for I do not know what attitude was taken by the one or two white men who were in charge of the mission before my time, and those who came to the islands while I was there only held office for a short period and did not go into such details. But all my native informants corroborated the fact, once I had discovered it, that the doctrine and ideal of Paternity, and all that tends to strengthen it, is advocated by the coloured Christian teachers.

We must realise that the cardinal dogma of God the Father and God the Son, the sacrifice of the only Son and the filial love of man to his Maker would completely miss fire in a matrilineal society, where the relation between father and son is decreed by tribal law to be that of two strangers, where all personal unity between them is denied, and where all family obligations are associated with mother-line. We cannot then wonder that Paternity must be among the principal truths to be inculcated by proselytizing Christians. Otherwise the dogma of the Trinity would have to be translated into matrilineal terms, and we would have to speak of a God-*kadala* (mother's brother), a God-sister's-son, and a divine *baloma* (spirit).

But apart from any doctrinal difficulty, the missionaries are earnestly engaged in propagating sexual morality as we conceive it, in which endeavour the idea of the sexual act as having serious consequences to family life is indispensable. The whole Christian morality, moreover, is strongly associated with the institution of a patrilineal and patriarchal family, with the father as progenitor and master of the household. In short, a religion whose dogmatic essence is based on the sacredness of the father to son relationship, and whose morals stand or fall by a strong patriarchal family, must obviously proceed by confirming the paternal relation, by showing that it has a natural foundation. Only during my third expedition to New Guinea did I discover that the natives had been somewhat exasperated by having an " absurdity " preached at them, and by finding me, so " unmissionary " as a rule, engaged in the same futile argument.

When I found this out, I used to call the correct

physiological view " the talk of the missionaries ", and goad the natives into comment or contradiction. In this manner I obtained some of my strongest and clearest statements, from which I shall select a few.

Motago'i, one of my most intelligent informants, in answer to a somewhat arrogantly framed affirmation that the missionaries were right, exclaimed :—

" *Gala wala* ! *Isasopasi* : *yambwata yambwata*
  Not at all ! They lie : always   always

nakubukwabuya   momona   ikasewo
unmarried girls   seminal fluid it is brimful

litusi   gala."
children theirs not.

Which may be freely rendered : " Not at all, the missionaries are mistaken ; unmarried girls continually have intercourse, in fact they overflow with seminal fluid, and yet have no children."

Here, in terse and picturesque language, Motago'i expresses the view that, after all, if sexual intercourse were causally connected with child production, it is the unmarried girls who should have children, since they lead a much more intensive sexual life than the married ones—a puzzling difficulty which really exists, as we shall see later on, but which our informant exaggerates slightly, since unmarried girls do conceive, though not nearly as frequently as anyone holding the " missionary views " would be led to expect. Asked in the course of the same discussion : " What, then, is the cause of pregnancy ? " he answered : " Blood on the head makes child. The seminal fluid does not make the child. Spirits bring at night time the infant, put on women's heads—it makes blood. Then, after two or three months, when the blood [that is, menstruous blood] does not come out, they know : ' Oh, I am pregnant ! ' "

An informant in Teyava, in a similar discussion,

made several statements of which I adduce the
two most spontaneous and conclusive ones.
" Copulation alone cannot produce a child. Night
after night, for years, girls copulate. No child
comes." In this we see again the same argument from
empirical evidence ; the majority of girls, in spite of
their assiduous cultivation of intercourse, do not
bring forth.   In another statement the same
informant says : " They talk that seminal fluid
makes child.   Lie !   The spirits indeed bring
[children] at night time."

My   favourite   informant   in   Omarakana,
Tokulubakiki, on whose honesty, goodwill, and
dispassionate reflection I could always rely, when I
wanted a final test of my information, gave a clear,
though somewhat Rabelaisian, statement of the
native point of view :—

" *Takayta,*   *itokay*   *vivila*   *italagila*
  We copulate   she gets up   woman   it runs out

momona—   *iwokwo.*"
seminal fluid—   it is finished.

In other words, after the traces of sexual intercourse have been removed, there are no further
consequences.

These sayings are trenchant enough, as were those
previously quoted ; but, after all, an opinion is a mere
academic expression of belief, the depth and
tenacity of which can best be gauged by the test of
behaviour. To a South Sea native, as to a European
peasant, his domestic animals—that is, his pigs—
are the most valued and cherished members of the
household.   And if his earnest and genuine conviction can be seen anywhere, it will be in his care
for the welfare and quality of his animals. The South
Sea natives are extremely keen to have good, strong,
and healthy pigs, and pigs of a good breed.

The main distinction which they make in the
matter of quality is that between the wild or bush-
pigs, and the tame village pigs. The village pig is

considered a great delicacy, while the flesh of the bush-pig is one of the strongest taboos to people of rank in Kiriwina, the transgression of which they hold in genuine horror and disgust. Yet they allow the female domestic pigs to wander on the outskirts of the village and in the bush, where they can pair freely with male bush-pigs. On the other hand, they castrate all the male pigs in the village in order to improve their condition. Thus, naturally, all the progeny are in reality descended from wild bush sires. Yet the natives have not the slightest inkling of this fact. When I said to one of the chiefs : " You eat the child of a bush-pig," he simply took it as a bad joke ; for making fun of bush-pig eating is not considered altogether good taste by a Trobriander of birth and standing. But he did not understand at all what I really meant.

On one occasion when I asked directly how pigs breed, the answer was : " The female pig breeds by itself," which simply meant that, probably, there is no *baloma* involved in the multiplication of domestic animals. When I drew parallels and suggested that small pigs are brought by their own *balomas*, they were not convinced ; and it was evident that neither their own interest, nor the data supplied by tradition, went far enough to inspire any concern as to the procreation of pigs.

Very important was a statement volunteered to me by Motago'i : " From all male pigs we cut off the testes. They copulate not. Yet the females bring forth." Thus he ignored the possible misconduct of the bush-pigs, and adduced the castration of domestic hogs as final proof that intercourse has nothing to do with breeding. On another occasion, I instanced the only two goats in the Archipelago, one male and one female, which a trader had recently imported. When I asked whether the female would bear any young if the male were killed, there was no uncertainty about the answer : " Year after year she will breed." Thus they have the firm

conviction that if a female animal were entirely
cut off from any male of the species, this would by
no means interfere with her fecundity.

Another crucial test is provided by the recent importation of European pigs. In honour of the first
man who brought them, the late Mick George,
a Greek trader and a truly Homeric character,
they are called by the natives *bulukwa Miki* (Mick's
pigs), and they will give five to ten of the native
pigs in exchange for one of them. Yet when
they have acquired it, they will not take the slightest
precautions to make it breed with a male of the
same superior race, though they could easily do
so. In one instance when, having several small
pigs of European race they castrated all the males,
they were reproved by a white trader, and told
that by so doing they lowered the whole breed.
But they simply could not be made to understand,
and all over the district they continue to allow
their valued European pigs to mis-breed.

In the article already quoted (*Journal of the
Anthropological Institute*, 1916) I gave verbatim
a remark of one of my informants about pigs,
obtained early in the course of my field-work.
" They copulate, copulate, presently the female
will give birth." My comment was : " Thus
here copulation appears to be the *u'ula* (cause)
of pregnancy." This opinion, even in its qualified
form, is incorrect. As a matter of fact, during
my first visit to the Trobriands, after which this
article was written, I never entered deeply into
the matter of animal procreation. The concise
native utterance quoted above, cannot, in the light
of subsequent fuller information, be interpreted
as implying any knowledge of how pigs really
breed. As it stands, it simply means that vaginal
dilation is as necessary in animals as in human
beings. It also implies that, according to native
tradition, animals are not subject in this, as in many
other respects, to the same causal relations as man.

In man, spirits are the cause of pregnancy : in animals—it just happens. Again, while the Trobrianders ascribe all human ailments to sorcery, with animals disease is just disease. Men die because of very strong evil magic ; animals—just die. But it would be quite incorrect to interpret this as evidence that the natives know, in the case of animals, the natural causes of impregnation, disease, and death ; while in man they obliterate this knowledge by an animistic superstructure. The true summary of the native outlook is that they are so deeply interested in human affairs that they construct a special tradition about all that is vital for man ; while in what concerns animals, things are taken as they come, without any attempt at explanation, and also without any insight into the real course of nature.

Their attitude to their own children also bears witness to their ignorance of any causal relation between congress and the ensuing pregnancy. A man whose wife has conceived during his absence will cheerfully accept the fact and the child, and he will see no reason at all for suspecting her of adultery. One of my informants told me that after over a year's absence he returned to find a newly-born child at home. He volunteered this statement as an illustration and final proof of the truth that sexual intercourse has nothing to do with conception. And it must be remembered that no native would ever discuss any subject in which the slightest suspicion of his wife's fidelity could be involved. In general, no allusion is ever made to her sexual life, past or present. Her pregnancy and childbirth are, on the other hand, freely discussed.

There is another instance of a native of the small island of Kitava, who, after two years' absence, was quite pleased to find a few months' old baby at home, and could not in the slightest degree understand the indiscreet taunts and allusions of some white men with reference to his wife's virtue.

My friend Layseta, a great sailor and magician of Sinaketa, spent a long time in his later youth in the Amphlett Islands. On his return he found two children, borne by his wife during his absence. He is very fond of them and of his wife ; and when I discussed the matter with others, suggesting that one at least of these children could not be his, my interlocutors did not understand what I meant.

Thus we see, from these instances, that children born in wedlock during a prolonged absence of the husband, will yet be recognized by him as his own children, that is as standing to him in the social relation of child to father. An instructive parallel to this is supplied by cases of children born out of wedlock, but during a liaison as exclusive as a marriage. In such a case, the physiological father would be obvious to us ; yet a Trobriander would not recognize the children as his, and further, since for a girl it is dishonourable to bear children before she is married, he might refuse to marry her. Of this I had a good example : Gomaya, one of my early informants, whom we know already (ch. iv, sec. 6), had a liaison with a girl called Ilamweria (pl. 39). They lived together and were going to be married, but she became pregnant and gave birth to a girl, whereupon Gomaya abandoned her. He was quite convinced that she had never had any relations with another boy, so, if any question of physiological fatherhood had come into his mind, he would have accepted the child as his own, and married the mother. But, in accordance with the native point of view, he simply did not inquire into the question of fatherhood ; it was enough that there was pre-nuptial motherhood.

Thus of children born by a married woman, her husband is the father *ex officio*, but for an unmarried mother, there is " no father to the child ". The father is defined socially, and in order that there may be fatherhood there must be marriage. And traditional sentiment regards illegitimate children, as we have said, as improper on the part of the mother. Of course there is no implication of sexual guilt in this censure, but, to the native, to do wrong is simply to act contrary to custom And it is not the custom for an unmarried girl to have babies, although it is the custom for her to have as much sexual intercourse as she likes. When asked why it is considered bad, they will answer :—

" *Pela gala tamala, gala taytala bikopo'i* "
" Because no father his, no man he [who] might take [it] in his arms."

" Because there is no father to the child, there is no man to take it in his arms." In this locution, the correct definition of the term *tamala* is clearly expressed : it is the mother's husband, the man whose rôle and duty it is to take the child in his arms and to help her in nursing and bringing it up.

5

FATHERLESS CHILDREN IN A MATRILINEAL SOCIETY

This seems a convenient place to speak about the very interesting problem of illegitimate children, or, as the natives word it, " children born by unmarried girls," " fatherless children." Several questions must, no doubt, have already obtruded themselves on the reader. Since there is so much sexual freedom, must there not be a great number of children born out of wedlock ? If this is not so, what means of prevention do the natives possess ? If it is so, how do they deal with the problem, what is the position of illegitimate children ?

As to the first question, it is very remarkable to note that illegitimate children are rare. The girls seem to remain sterile throughout their period of licence, which begins when they are small

children and continues until they marry; when
they are married they conceive and breed, sometimes quite prolifically. I express myself cautiously
about the number of illegitimate children, for in
most cases there are special difficulties even in
ascertaining the fact. To have prenuptial children
is, as I have said, by an arbitrary ruling of doctrine
and custom, considered reprehensible. Thus, out
of delicacy towards people present, out of family
interest or local pride, the existence of such children
is invariably concealed. Such children are often
adopted by some relative, and the elasticity of
kinship terms makes it very difficult to distinguish
between actual and adopted children. If a married
man says : " This is my child," it may quite
easily be his wife's sister's illegitimate baby. So
that only an approximate estimate can be made
even in a community with which one is very well
acquainted. I was able to find roughly a dozen
illegitimate children recorded genealogically in the
Trobriands, or about one per cent. In this the
illegitimate children of the ugly, deformed, or
albino women mentioned above are not included,
as none of them happens to figure in the genealogical
records made by me.

Thus we are faced with the question : Why
are there so few illegitimate children ? On this
subject I can only speak tentatively, and I feel
that my information is perhaps not quite as full
as it might have been, had I concentrated more
attention upon it. One thing I can say with
complete confidence : no preventive means of any
description are known, nor the slightest idea of them
entertained. This, of course, is quite natural.
Since the procreative power of seminal fluid is
not known, since it is considered not only innocuous
but beneficient, there is no reason why the natives
should interfere with its free arrival into the parts
which it is meant to lubricate. Indeed, any suggestion of neo-Malthusian appliances makes them

shudder or laugh according to their mood or temperament. They never practise *coitus interruptus*, and still less have any notion about chemical or mechanical preventives.

But though I am quite certain on this point, I cannot speak with the same conviction about abortion, though probably it is not practised to any large extent. I may say at once that the natives, when discussing these matters, feel neither fear nor constraint, so there can be no question of any difficulties in finding out the state of affairs because of reticence or concealment. My informants told me that a magic exists to bring about premature birth, but I was not able either to obtain instances in which it was performed, nor to find out the spells or rites made use of. Some of the herbs employed in this magic were mentioned to me, but I am certain that none of them possess any physiological properties. Abortion by mechanical means seems, in fine, the only effective method practised to check the increase of population, and there is no doubt that even this is not used on a large scale.

So the problem remains. Can there be any physiological law which makes conception less likely when women begin their sexual life young, lead it indefatigably, and mix their lovers freely ? This, of course, cannot be answered here, as it is a purely biological question ; but some such solution of the difficulty seems to me the only one, unless I have missed some very important ethnological clue. I am, as I have said, by no means confident of my researches being final in this matter.

It is amusing to find that the average white resident or visitor to the Trobriands is deeply interested in this subject, and in this subject only, of all the ethnological problems opened to him for consideration. There is a belief prevalent among the white citizens of eastern New Guinea that the

Trobrianders are in possession of some mysterious and powerful means of prevention or abortion. This belief is, no doubt, explicable by the remarkable and puzzling facts which we have just been discussing. It is enhanced by insufficient knowledge, and the tendency towards exaggeration and sensationalism so characteristic of the crude European mind. Of insufficient knowledge, I had several examples ; for every white man with whom I spoke on the subject would start with the dogmatic assertion that unmarried girls among the Trobrianders never have children, saving those who live with white traders ; whereas, as we have seen, illegitimate children are on record. Equally incorrect and fantastic is the belief in mysterious contraceptives, for which not even the oldest residents, who are firmly convinced of their existence, can supply any basis in fact. This seems to be an example of the well-known truth, that a higher race in contact with a lower one has a tendency to credit the members of the latter with mysterious demoniacal powers.

Returning now to the question of " fatherless children ", we find among the Trobrianders a trend of public opinion with regard to illegitimacy which almost amounts to a moral rule. We, in our own society, share this opinion very emphatically ; but with us it is connected with our strong moral condemnation of unchastity. In theory at least, if not in practice, we condemn the fruits of sexual immorality, because of the cause and not because of the consequence. Our syllogism runs thus : " All intercourse out of wedlock is bad ; pregnancy is caused by intercourse ; hence all unmarried pregnant girls are bad." Thus, when we find in another society the last term of the syllogism endorsed, we jump to the conclusion that the other terms also obtain, especially the middle one. That is, we assume that the natives are aware of physiological paternity. We know, however, that the first proposition is not accepted in the Trobriands, for intercourse out of wedlock is quite free from censure unless it offends the special taboos of adultery, exogamy, and incest. Therefore the middle term cannot serve as a connecting link, and the fact that the natives endorse the conclusion proves nothing about their knowledge of fatherhood. I have developed this point in some detail, because it is a characteristic example of how difficult is emancipation from our own narrow modes of thinking and feeling, and our own rigid structures of social and moral prejudice. Although I myself should have been on my guard against such traps, and though at that time I was already acquainted with the Trobrianders and their ways of thinking, yet, on realizing their disapproval of children out of wedlock, I went through all this false reasoning before a fuller acquaintance with the facts forced me to correct it.

Fecundity in unmarried girls is discreditable ; sterility in married women is unfortunate. The same term *nakarige* (*na*, female prefix, *karige*, to die) is used of a childless woman as of a barren sow. But this condition brings no shame on the person concerned, and does not detract from the social status of such a woman. The oldest wife of To'uluwa, Bokuyoba, has no children, yet she ranks first among the wives as is the due of her age. Nor is the word *nakarige* considered to be indelicate ; a sterile woman will use it when speaking of herself, and others will apply it to her in her presence. But fertility in married women is considered a good thing. Primarily it affects her maternal kinsmen, and is a matter of great importance to them (see ch. i, sec. 1). "The kinsmen rejoice, for their bodies become stronger when one of their sisters or nieces has plenty of children." The wording of this statement expresses the interesting conception of collective clan unity, of the members being not only of the same flesh, but almost forming one body (see ch. vi and ch. xiii, sec. 5).

Returning again to the main trend of our argument, it must be noted that the scorn and disapproval levelled at illegitimacy is highly significant sociologically. Let us realize once more this interesting and strange constellation of facts : physical fatherhood is unknown ; yet fatherhood in a social sense is considered necessary and the "fatherless child" is regarded as something anomalous, contrary to the normal course of events, and hence reprehensible. What does this mean ? Public opinion, based on tradition and custom, declares that a woman must not become a mother before she marries, though she may enjoy as much sexual liberty as she likes within lawful bounds. This means that a mother needs a defender and provider of economic necessities. She has one natural master and protector in her brother, but he is not in a position to look after her in all matters where she needs a guardian. According to native ideas, a woman who is pregnant must, at a certain stage, abstain from all intercourse and "turn her mind away from men". She then needs a man who will take over all sexual rights in regard to her, abstain from exercising even his own privileges from a certain moment, guard her from any interference, and control her own behaviour. All this the brother cannot do, for, owing to the strict brother-sister taboo, he must scrupulously avoid even the thought of anything which is concerned with his sister's sex. Again, there is the need for a man to keep guard over her during childbirth, and "to receive the child into his arms", as the natives put it. Later it is the duty of this man to share in all the tender cares bestowed on the child (see ch. i, secs. 1 and 3 ; and ch. xiii, sec. 6). Only when the child grows up does he relinquish the greater part of his authority and hand it over to his wife's brother, retaining some of it in the case of female children, when it comes to marriage (see above, ch. iv).

Thus the part played by the husband is strictly defined by custom and is considered socially indispensable. A woman with a child and no husband is an incomplete and anomalous group. The disapproval of an illegitimate child and of its mother is a particular instance of the general disapproval of everything which does not conform to custom, and runs counter to the accepted social pattern and traditional tribal organization. The family, consisting of husband, wife, and children, is the standard set down by tribal law, which also defines the functions of its component parts. It is therefore not right that one. of the members of this group should be missing.

Thus, though the natives are ignorant of any physiological need for a male in the constitution of the family, they regard him as indispensable socially. This is very important. Paternity, unknown in the full biological meaning so familiar to us, is yet maintained by a social dogma which declares : " Every family must have a father ; a woman must marry before she may have children ; there must be a male to every household."

The institution of the individual family is thus firmly established on a strong feeling of its necessity, quite compatible with an absolute ignorance of its biological foundations. The sociological rôle of the father is established and defined without any recognition of his physiological nature.

6

THE SINGULAR CLAIMS OF SOCIOLOGICAL PATERNITY

The interesting duality between matrilineal and patriarchal influences, represented by the mother's brother and the father respectively, is one of the Leitmotivs of the first act of Trobriand tribal life. Here we have come to the very core of the problem : for we see within this social scheme, with its rigid brother-sister taboo and its ignorance of physical fatherhood, two natural spheres of influence to be exercised over a woman by a man (see ch. i, secs. 1 and 2) : the one, that of sex, from which the brother is absolutely debarred and where the husband's influence is paramount ; the other, that in which the natural interests of blood relationship can be safeguarded properly only by one who is of the same blood. This is the sphere of the woman's brother.

By the brother's inability to control or to approach, even as a distant spectator, the principal theme in a woman's life—her sex—a wide breach is left in the system of matriliny. Through this breach the husband enters into the closed circle of family and household, and once there makes himself thoroughly at home. To his children he becomes bound by the strongest ties of personal attachment, over his wife he assumes exclusive sexual rights, and shares with her the greater part of domestic and economic concerns.

On the apparently unpropitious soil of strict matriliny, with its denial of any paternal bond through procreation and its declaration of the father's extraneousness to progeny, there spring up certain beliefs, ideas and customary rules, which smuggle extreme patrilineal principles into the stronghold of mother-right. One of these ideas is of the kind which figures so largely in sensational amateur records of savage life, and it strikes us at first as savage indeed, so lop-sided, distorted and quaint does it appear. I refer to their idea about the similarity between parents and offspring. That this is a favourite topic of nursery gossip in civilized communities needs no special comment. In a matrilineal society, such as the Trobriands, where all maternal relatives are considered to be of the " same body ", and the father to be a " stranger ", we would have no doubt in anticipating that facial and bodily similarity would be traced in the mother's family alone. The contrary is the case, however, and this is affirmed with extremely strong social emphasis. Not only is it a household dogma, so to speak, that a child never resembles its mother, or any of its brothers and sisters, or any of its maternal kinsmen, but it is extremely bad form and a great offence to hint at any such similarity. To resemble one's father, on the other hand, is the natural, right, and proper thing for a man or woman to do.

I was introduced to this rule of *savoir vivre* in the usual way, by making a *faux pas*. One of my bodyguard in Omarakana, named Moradeda, was endowed with a peculiar cast of features which had struck me at first sight and fascinated me, for it had a strange similarity to the Australian aboriginal type—wavy hair, broad face, low forehead, extremely broad nose, with a much depressed bridge, wide mouth with protruding lips, and a prognathous chin. One day I was struck by the appearance of an exact counterpart to Moradeda, and asked his name and whereabouts. When I was told that he was my friend's elder brother, living in a distant village, I exclaimed : " Ah, truly ! I asked about you because your face is alike—alike to that of Moradeda." There came such a hush over all the assembly that I was startled by it at once. The man turned round and left us ; while part of the company present, after averting their faces in a manner half-embarrassed, half-offended, soon dispersed. I was then told by my confidential informants that I had committed a breach of custom ; that I had perpetrated what is called *taputaki migila*, a technical expression referring only to this act which might be translated : " To-defile-by-comparing-to-a-kins-man-his-face " (see ch. xiii, sec. 4). What astonished me in this discussion was that, in spite of the striking resemblance between the two brothers, my informants refused to admit it. In fact, they treated the question as if no one could possibly ever resemble his brother, or, for the matter of that, any maternal kinsman. I made my informants quite angry and displeased with me by arguing the point, and even more so by quoting cases of such obvious similarity between two brothers as that which obtained between Namwana Guya'u and Yobukwa'u (pl. 40).

This incident taught me never to hint at such a resemblance in the presence of the people concerned. But I thrashed the matter out with many natives subsequently in the course of general conversation. I found that everyone in the Trobriands will, in the teeth of all the evidence, stoutly deny that similarity can exist between matrilineal kinsmen. A Trobriander is simply irritated and insulted if striking instances are pointed out to him, in exactly the same way as, in our own society, we irritate our next-door neighbour by bringing before him a glaring truth which contradicts some cherished opinion, political, religious, or moral, or which, still worse, runs counter to his personal interests.

The Trobrianders maintain that mention of such likenesses can only be made to insult a man. It is, in fact, a technical phrase in serious bad language to say *migim lumuta*, " Thy face thy sister's," which, by the way, is the worst combination of kinship similarity. This expression is considered quite as bad as " have intercourse with thy sister ! " But, according to a Trobriander, no sane and decent man can possibly entertain in a sober dispassionate mood such an outrageous thought as that anyone should in the slightest degree resemble his sister (see ch. xiii, sec. 4).

Still more remarkable is the counterpart to this social dogma ; namely, that every child resembles its father. Such similarity is always assumed and affirmed to exist. Where it is really found, even to a small degree, constant attention is drawn to it as to a thing which is nice, good and right. It was often pointed out to me how strongly one or other of the sons of To'uluwa, the chief of Omarakana, resembled

his father, and the old man was especially proud
of the more or less imaginary resemblance between
himself and his youngest son, Dipapa (see pl. 41).
Especially were the five favourite sons of himself and
Kadamwasila each said to be exactly like his
father. When I pointed out that this similarity to
the father implied similarity to each other, such a
heresy was indignantly repudiated. There are also
definite customs which embody this dogma of
patrilineal similarity. Thus, after a man's death,
his kinsmen and friends will come from time to
time to visit his children in order to " see his face
in theirs ". They will give them presents, and sit
looking at them and wailing. This is said to soothe
their insides because they have seen once more the
likeness of the dead.

How do the natives reconcile the inconsistency
of this dogma with the matrilineal system ? When
questioned they will say : " Yes, maternal kinsmen
are the same flesh, but similar faces they have not."
When you inquire again why it is that people
resemble their father, who is a stranger and has
nothing to do with the formation of their body, they
have a stereotyped answer : " It coagulates the
face of the child ; for always he lies with her, they
sit together." The expression *kuli*, to coagulate,
to mould, was used over and over again in the
answers which I received. This is a statement of the
social doctrine concerning the influence of the father
over the physique of the child, and not merely the
personal opinion of my informants. One of my
informants explained it to me more exactly, turning
his open hands to me palm upwards : " Put some
soft mash (*sesa*) on it, and it will mould like the hand.
In the same manner, the husband remains with the
woman and the child is moulded." Another man
told me : " Always we give food from our hand to
the child to eat, we give fruit and dainties, we give
betel nut. This makes the child as it is."

I also discussed the existence of half-castes with
my informants, children of white traders married to

native women. I pointed out that some look much more like natives than like Europeans. This, again, they simply denied, maintaining stoutly that all these children have white man's faces, and giving this as another proof of their doctrine. There was no way of shaking their conviction, or of diminishing their dislike of the idea that anyone can resemble his mother or her people, an idea condemned by the tradition and the good manners of the tribe.

Thus we see that an artificial physical link between father and child has been introduced, and that on one important point it has overshadowed the matrilineal bond. For physical resemblance is a very strong emotional tie between two people, and its strength is hardly reduced by its being ascribed, not to a physiological, but to a sociological cause—that of continued association between husband and wife.

I have to record one more important assertion of father-right in this matrilineal society, one of a purely social and economic nature. That there is a compromise between the two principles of matriliny and paternal influence in social and economic matters, we have already seen ; but it is worth while to restate this briefly here, and to mention its most peculiar feature.

The matrilineal principle is maintained by the more rigid rules of tribal law. These rules decree absolutely that a child must belong to the family, sub-clan, and clan of its mother. Less absolutely but still very strictly, they regulate the membership of a village community and the office of magician. They also assign all inheritance of land, privileges and material goods to mother-line. But here a number of customs and usages allow, if not an evasion, at least a compromise and modification of tribal law. By these usages, a father can, for his own lifetime, grant the right of citizenship in his village to his son and bestow upon him the usufruct of canoes, lands, ceremonial privileges, and magic. By cross-cousin marriage, combined with matrilocal residence, he can even secure all these things to his son for life.

All this we know already, but here we have to note one more important difference in the transmission of material goods and privileges, as from maternal uncle to a nephew on the one hand, and a father to a son on the other. A man is obliged to relinquish all his possessions and offices to his younger brother or maternal nephew at death. But usually the younger man wants to possess some of these things during his senior's lifetime ; and it is customary for a maternal uncle to part with a portion of his gardens or some of his magic while he is still living. But in such cases he has to be paid for it, and the payment is often quite substantial. It is called by the special technical name *pokala*.[1]

When a man gives any of these things to his son, on the other hand, he does it of his free will, and quite gratuitously. Thus, a maternal nephew, or younger brother, has the right to claim his share, and always receives it if he gives the first instalment of the *pokala*. The son relies on his father's goodwill, which, as a rule, works very effectively on his behalf, and he receives all the gifts for nothing. The man who has the right to the things has to pay for them, while the man who receives them without the sanction of tribal law gets them gratis. Of course he has to return them, at least in part, after his father's death ; but the use and enjoyment he has had of material benefits remain his, while the magic he cannot return.

The natives explain this anomalous state of things by the father's partiality to his children, which, in its turn, is accounted for by his relation to their mother. The natives say that his free gifts to the children are a reward for the free cohabitation which he enjoys with his wife.[2]

---

[1] This word has more than one meaning : it denotes several types of economic transaction. Compare *Argonauts of the Western Pacific*, index s.v. *pokala*.

[2] I have dealt with the relation between tribal law and the usages which are formed in reaction to it in *Crime and Custom*, esp. pt. ii, ch. iii.

CHAPTER VIII

PREGNANCY AND CHILDBIRTH

WE had to make a digression into the domain of
sociology, led thereto by the Trobriand beliefs concerning procreation and spiritual incarnation and the
great influence which these exert upon family and
kinship. Let us now resume our consecutive account
by considering the course of pregnancy and childbirth. In the first two sections of this chapter I shall
describe one observance which is of outstanding
interest to the ethnologist : the special public
ceremonial performed when a woman is passing
through her first pregnancy. The succeeding two
sections will be devoted to the customs associated
with childbirth and maternity in general.

I

PREPARATION FOR THE FIRST PREGNANCY RITES

Pregnancy is first diagnosed by the swelling of
the breasts and the darkening of the nipples. At
this time a woman may dream that the spirit of one
of her kinswomen brings her the child from the
other world to be reincarnated. If during the next
two or three moons her menstrual flow makes no
appearance, then, say the natives, it is certain that
she has become pregnant (*isuma*). Native embryology
teaches that four moons after the appearance of the
baloma in the dream the abdomen begins to swell ;
and when this stage in a first pregnancy is reached,
the relatives of the mother-to-be take steps to provide
her with certain ceremonial garments prescribed
by custom ; a plain white fibre petticoat, and a long

cloak (*saykeulo*) of the same material (pl. 42). These will be given to her in about the fifth moon of her pregnancy with a great deal of ceremony, and she will wear them on that occasion for a month or two and also after she has given birth to the child. This ceremony is never performed for an *igamugwa*, a woman who has already been pregnant, but only for an *igava'u*, a woman who conceives for the first time.

As with every other ceremonial occasion in the Trobriands, this presentation of the fibre cloak has its place in a definite sociological scheme. The duties connected with it are distributed among certain relatives who subsequently receive an appropriate payment. The task of making the robes and of offering them to the *igava'u* falls to the female relatives of the girl's father—the women whom she calls generically *tabugu*—and the lead is taken by the father's own sister. We have already seen on an earlier occasion of great importance in the life of a girl, namely when her marriage is about to be concluded, that it is the father, and not her official guardian, the mother's brother, whose consent is decisive and who has to supervise the whole affair. Again, in this later crisis, it is the father and his matrilineal kinswomen who take the active part. The father summons his sister, his mother, and his niece, and says to them : " Well, come to my house and cut the *saykeulo* for your niece, my daughter." The father's sister then takes the lead, and rouses as many of her kinswomen as possible to help in the work. They come together, talk the matter over, and arrange when they will begin. The *saykeulo* is always made in front of the father's house, or, if he be a chief, on the central place of his village. The women sit down in a wide circle round a heap of banana leaves to which every worker has contributed several bundles, frayed ready for use. Then the pieces are bound together, amid continuous chatter and a hubbub of voices and laughter. It is an exclusively female gathering, and no man with any sense of decency and etiquette would come near. Four garments have to be made : two long mantles and two skirts. One of the mantles is to be worn at the initial celebration of first pregnancy and the second when the mother first appears in public after her confinement ; the two skirts are also for use after the birth. The four garments can be easily finished at one sitting, though a second is sometimes necessary when there are too many gossips present for the work to go quickly. When the garments are finished, usually in the afternoon, the workers pass to the magical part of the performance. For, as always in the making of a really important object, or one which has to be endowed with definite properties and powers, magic is an essential part of the process of production.

I had good opportunities for studying the magic of pregnancy robes. I observed and photographed the rites in progress at the village of Tukwa'ukwa, and in the same village I obtained the formula of *saykeulo* magic, as it was then recited, also I discussed the ceremonial with the actual performers, as well as with women in other localities.

The rite is simple, but interesting, for it reveals the native ideas of the nature of magical force and of the way in which it operates. A mat is spread on the ground and the four pregnancy garments are placed upon it (pl. 43). The women have brought with them the fleshy lower parts of certain creamy white leaves, which come from a lily plant bearing a snow-white flower. These are cut into pieces (pl. 44) and strewn over the robes. Those among the robe-makers who know the formula—and there are always several of them—kneel round the bundle, and, bending over it, thrust their faces right into the fibre stuff (pl. 43), so that it may be well permeated with the breath which carries the magic words :

" Oh *bwaytuva* (a bird similar to the reef heron but with quite white plumage), hover over Waybeva (the creek of Tukwa'ukwa village), swoop down to Mkikiya (the waterhole of the village) ! O *bwaytuva*, hover over Mkikiya, swoop down to Waybeva ! "

This is the exordium(*u'ula*),the opening part of the magical formula, in which, as we see, a white bird is invited to hover over the bathing place and the principal water supply of the village.[1] Then follows the main part (*tapwana*) of the spell. In this the phrase *bwaytuva ikata*—" the *bwaytuva* bird sharpens " (i.e. makes brilliant or resplendent) is repeated with various words, each of which describes a part of the pregnancy robe. In the Trobriands, as no doubt in every other society, each detail of a lady's garment is carefully defined and has its specific name. These are enumerated and coupled one by one with the leading phrase. Thus the formula contains a series of such incantations as " the *bwaytuva* bird makes resplendent the top hem of the robe," " the *bwaytuva* bird makes resplendent the fringe of the robe ", and so on. Then the same phrase is repeated with various words describing parts of the body: " the *bwaytuva* bird makes resplendent the head of my *tabu* (my brother's child) ", " the *bwaytuva* makes resplendent the nose of my brother's child " ; and so on to the cheeks, the chest, the belly, the groins, the buttocks, the thighs, the knees, the calves, and the feet. The formula thus enumerates every part of the body with a consistent pedantry characteristic of Trobriand magic. The end-part (*dogina*) runs thus : " No more is it her head, her head is like the pallor before dawn ; no more is it her face, her face is like the white sprouts of a young leaf of the areca plant ; praise her by robbing her house ! praise her by demanding a *tilewa'i* (flattery gift) ! "

This formula expresses, in terms of magic, a wish to improve the personal appearance of the wearer of the robes, and it is especially associated

---

[1] For the structure and general characteristics of the Trobriand spells see *Argonauts of the Western Pacific*, ch. xviii.

with the whiteness of her skin. A bird of beautiful form and of brilliantly white plumage is invoked at the beginning, and its name acts as the most powerful charm in the principal part of the formula. Its association with the names of the creek and the waterhole in which the pregnant woman has to bathe and wash, may possess the power to whiten her skin.

The conclusion anticipates the result, a form very common in the Trobriand spells : the face of the pregnant woman becomes pallid like the white sky before dawn, and like the young sprouts of areca. The last two sentences of the formula refer to the curious custom which allows anyone who gives flattery or praise after a remarkable achievement or performance and removes a piece of decoration as a pledge, to demand a special gift, *tilewa'i*. In the case of a still more remarkable achievement, the lucky man who is to gain by it may have to see all his belongings on which the members of the community can lay hand *kwaykwaya*—that is, " taken away as expression of admiration ". The remarkable achievement thus foreshadowed in the first pregnancy rites is the resplendent whiteness of the pregnant woman's skin.

From another village—Omarakana—I obtained the initial fragment of the magic used there by certain women. In this formula also a bird is addressed :

" O white pigeon, come, lull our pregnancy cloak to sleep. I shall go and lull your egg to sleep."

The pigeon invoked is notable for the whiteness of its plumage and of its eggs' shell. The " lulling " of the pregnancy cloak refers, it is said, to the child to be born, whose skin should also be made white. We shall have to speak at some length about this fundamental idea of whitening the skin which underlies the pregnancy ceremonial.

In their general character, the proceedings are similar to most rites in the Trobriands. The women finish the robe and then, in very much the same business-like manner, go on to the magic. The white lily leaves are cut by one of them immediately after the robe is finished (pl. 44), and the garment is spread on the mat by another. While the magic is being recited (pl. 43), no disturbing noises are allowed, but neither is anyone excluded; the onlookers adopt no special attitude, nor have they any observances to keep. After the women have impregnated the robes with the magical virtues of the spell, they beat the bundle with their palms. This increases the garments' power of imparting whiteness to the wearer. The tapping is conceived as the " waking up of the garment ". The rite is called *yuvisila saykeulo*, the breathing over of the pregnancy robe. The four robes, together with the white cut leaves strewn over them, are now covered with another mat, so that the magic may not evaporate, and the whole bundle is placed in the house of the principal *tabula*, the father's sister.

2

CEREMONIAL OF FIRST PREGNANCY

On the day following the making and charming of the robe, the actual investment of the pregnant woman takes place. With this is associated her public bathing and washing and her magical adornment. I shall describe the ceremony as I saw it in the village of Tukwa'ukwa, where, in May, 1918, I and my friend, the late Mr. B. Hancock, were able to take photographs of it (pls. 43, 44, 45, 46, 49, and 50). My friend had also photographed and recorded the ceremony about a year before when it had taken place in the same village (pls. 42, 47, and 48). In the course of my narrative, I shall indicate such local differences as obtain between the coastal villages, of which Tukwa'ukwa is one, and the inland settlements, distant from the seashore.

Very early in the morning, the whole village, or at least all its female inhabitants, are astir and preparing for the spectacle. The *tabula* (father's sister and other paternal relatives) foregather in the father's hut, where the pregnant woman awaits them. When all is ready, the prospective mother proceeds to the seashore, walking between two of her *tabula*.

From the inland villages not too far distant from the sea, the procession would also go down to the beach ; but those villages far enough away to consider themselves " inland people " perform the pregnancy bath at the waterhole where they usually wash. If the woman is of high rank, she will be carried all the way to the shore or to the waterhole. In the ceremony, only women take an active part.

Tukwa'ukwa lies right on a tidal inlet of the lagoon, and the woman was carried to the beach by her female *tabula*. Since this is a purely female ceremony, good manners indicate that no man should participate, and men would not enter the water to look at the performance. There is no specific taboo, however, nor were any objections raised to my presence.

Arrived at the water's edge, the women arrange themselves in two rows, facing each other, and join hands with their opposite partners crosswise, in the manner called by children " queen's chair ". Over this living bridge the pregnant woman walks, holding on by the women's heads, and as she advances, the rear couple move to the front, constantly extending the bridge. Thus they go some distance into the water, the pregnant woman walking dry foot on the arms of her companions (pl. 45). At a certain point she is allowed to jump into the water. Then they all begin to play with one another, the prospective mother being always the centre of the game. Her companions splash water over her, and duck and drench her to the utmost, all in a spirit of exuberant good-natured playfulness (pl. 46). It is the duty of the *tabula* to see that the woman is well washed during the ceremonial bath. " We rub her skin with our hands, we rub her surface, we cleanse her."

The drenching and washing being thoroughly done, she is brought on to the shore and placed on a mat. Although on most occasions she is carried by her relatives to the beach, from this moment she has to be completely isolated from the earth, and must not touch the soil with her feet. She is placed on a coco-nut mat and her *tabula* (father's maternal relatives) proceed to make her toilet very carefully and with an elaborate magic ritual. This magic of beauty has certain affinities with the ceremonial performed by men during the *kula* expeditions (see *Argonauts of the Western Pacific*, ch. xiii, sec. 1), though the spells of men and women differ.[1] It is, on the other hand, identical in spell and rite with the beauty magic performed by women on men at great dancing festivals ; in fact, the spells which I obtained at the pregnancy rites and which are given later in this book, are used on either occasion (see ch. xi, secs. 2-4).

After her bath, the pregnant woman has first to be rubbed and dried. This is done ritually. Some coco-nut husk fibre, which is kept ready at hand, is charmed over with the *kaykakaya* spell by the *tabula* (father's sister) and the skin of the young

---

[1] I have stated in the above-mentioned work, on p. 336, that " This branch of Kula magic has two counterparts in the other magical lore of the Trobrianders. One of them is the love magic, through which people are rendered attractive and irresistible. Their belief in these spells is such that a man would always attribute all his success in love to their efficiency. Another type closely analogous to the beauty magic of the Kula is the specific beauty magic practised before big dances and festivities." This statement is slipshod, in that the real counterparts of *mwasila* (*kula* magic) of beauty are the magic performed on dancers and described here in ch. xi, and the magic of pregnancy with which we are dealing just now. The three forms, *mwasila*, pregnancy rites and festive beauty magic are, in fact, akin to each other, though only pregnancy magic and the festive ritual are the same in spell and rite, while the *mwasila* resembles both only in aim and doctrine. Love magic, though presenting some similarities, not only differs profoundly in rite and spell, but is based on a special native doctrine. (Cf. below, ch. xi.)

woman is rubbed.[1] Then some of the soft spongy
leaves of the *wageva* plant, which usually serve the
native as a natural towel, are charmed with another
formula and the woman is rubbed again. After her
skin has been thoroughly dried, the pregnant woman
is anointed with charmed coco-nut oil, and the
attendants put a new brightly coloured fibre skirt
on her, while the wet bathing skirt is removed from
underneath. This festive skirt is not one of those
recently made for the pregnancy, nor is its putting
on associated with any magical rite. But a purely
magical action follows: the face of the young
woman is stroked with a mother-of-pearl shell
while one of the *tabula* mutters a spell of beauty
(see ch. xi, sec. 4). The three acts of the
ceremonial so far described are supposed to make
her skin smooth, clear, and soft, and her appearance
generally beautiful. Several successive stages of
personal decoration follow, each performed in a
ritual manner. First, muttering a magical formula,
a *tabula* decorates the prospective mother's mouth
and face with red paint. After that black paint is
applied to the face with another spell. Then the
hair is combed while yet another formula is recited.
Red hibiscus flowers are fastened in her hair, and
aromatic leaves with charms breathed into them
thrust into her armlets. After this the young woman
is considered to be fully arrayed.

All this ritual dressing and adornment is
associated with beauty magic, which custom and
tradition impose at this stage but which stands in
no direct connection with pregnancy or the
pregnancy robes. Only when this beauty magic
has been performed may the proper pregnancy
rite, the investment with the long robe, be carried
out. The *tabula* place one of the two *saykeulo*
(pregnancy robes) on the young woman's shoulders,

---

[1] For the text of this and the subsequent spells here mentioned, see
below, ch. xi, sec. 3 and 4. The spells of *mwasila*, quoted on pp. 337-
342 of *Argonauts*, should also be consulted.

and once more recite the formula used in the making of it, breathing the charm right into the robe (see pl. 47). It is also customary at this point, though not imperative, to recite over her some magic against the dangers of pregnancy and childbirth, a magic prophylactic against the special evil of sorcery, which is always dreaded at a confinement (see next section).

Throughout this ritual the prospective mother has been standing on a mat, for, as we have already said, her bare feet must not touch the soil after the bath. Now, dressed in full dress and covered with the long fibre mantle, she is lifted up by two of her *tabula* (pls. 48 and 49) and carried to her father's house, where a small platform has been erected on which she is set down (pl. 50). It is customary for a woman of chieftain's rank to go, not to her father's, but to her maternal uncle's house, and there to remain seated on a high platform.

Upon this platform the woman has to stay for the rest of the day. During that time she must remain practically motionless, she must not speak except to ask for food or drink, and even this she ought if possible to do by signs. She must not touch food with her hands; it is put into her mouth by her *tabula*. Her immobility is only broken from time to time that she may wash her face, her arms and shoulders, and rub her skin. For this purpose water is either brought to her in a wooden basin by her husband, or she is carried by two women back to the water's edge, and there she washes standing on a mat. After sunset she is allowed to retire to her father's house to rest, but the next day she has to return to the platform and there resume her seated immobility, and observe all her taboos as on the first day. This is repeated for from three to five days, according to the rank and importance of the woman and of her husband. Nowadays, with the relaxation of all customs, one day is often considered long enough.

When the ceremonial vigil on the platform is over, the woman may return for a few more months to her husband's house ; or she may go to the house of her father or of her maternal uncle. To one of these she must in any case repair for her confinement. She dresses in the *saykeulo* (pregnancy mantle) until it is worn out. As a rule it lasts for about two months, so that it has to be discarded some two months before confinement.

There is more than one important feature associated with the first pregnancy ritual. As always in the Trobriands, ceremonial services rendered by a certain class of relative must be repaid by the actual, that is maternal, kinsmen of the person served. In this case the work, the magic, and the ritual are performed by the female relatives of the father. In the distribution of food (*sagali*), which immediately follows the ceremony, it is the mother's brother, the brother, and the other maternal kinsmen of the young woman, who do the distributing. If she is a woman of small importance, this distribution takes place before her father's house. But if she, or her father or husband be a person of high rank, it is carried out on the central place of the village. The procedure is the same as in the mortuary and other ceremonial distributions.[1] The food is divided into heaps and every heap is allotted to a single person, his or her name being called out in a loud voice. After the first pregnancy rites, each one of the *tabula* who has been working at the robe and taking part in the ceremony receives a heap of food. Besides this, the givers of the *sagali* (distribution) usually select some specially large and fine yams, or a bunch of bananas or areca nut, and carry the gift to the house of the paternal aunt, and perhaps to those of one or two other relatives as well. Such additional payment is called *pemkwala*.

A minor but very interesting ceremonial is

---

[1] See *Argonauts of the Western Pacific*, pp. 182-3, and references in Index, s.v. *sagali*, and below, ch. xi, sec. 2.

associated with this distribution. The father of the pregnant woman—who has nothing to do with the *sagali*—chooses some specially good food and carries it, on his own account, to certain women who are known to possess a form of black magic of which pregnant women stand in great fear. " Black " this magic is, literally as well as metaphorically, for by addressing the *mwanita* (black millepede), the sorceress is able to make a pregnant woman's skin black, as black as the worm itself. The father's gift, which is brought to the house door and belongs to the class called *katubwadela bwala* (house-closing-gift), is intended to forestall and arrest any evil intentions which the sorceress might harbour. As one of my informants put it : " That their anger might come to an end, that they might not perform the evil magic that blackens the skin of that woman, that pregnant one."

This brings us back to the question of the idea underlying the first pregnancy ceremony, and of its aims and purpose. If the average Trobriander is asked the reason or cause, *u'ula*, of a custom, the usual ready answer is one of the stereotyped phrases, *tokunabogwo ayguri* (" of old it has been ordained "), *Laba'i layma* (" it came from Laba'i," the mythological centre of the district), *tomwaya, tomwaya, ivagise* (" the ancients have arranged it "). In other words, the custom has in their eyes a traditional sanction ; and every respectable person among savages, as well as among ourselves, has, of course, to do a thing because it is done and because it always has been done. But I obtained a certain number of special reasons for this particular usage besides the general one. Some maintain that the ceremony makes for a quick and easy birth ; " for," as they say, " the playing about in the water loosens the child in the womb." Some say that it assures the health of the mother and of the baby ; and yet others that it is necessary for the proper formation of the fœtus. One woman gave as the reason for the ceremony, that the spirit child was said to enter the woman while she was in the ritual bath, but her statement was not confirmed by anyone else, and I consider it spurious.

But the prevalent opinion of the natives is that the ceremony is to whiten the skin of the woman. This opinion was expressed to me by my best informants among the men, as well as by several women with whom I discussed the matter. It is also in harmony with the text of the magical formula and with the ritual actions, as well as with the nature of the central symbol, the pregnancy mantle. The use of the *saykeulo*, as my informants pointed out, is to keep the sun off the skin. The woman has to wear it after the ceremonial bathing, and when she has had to discard it she should keep indoors as much as possible until the confinement. This idea of whiteness as a thing to be desired is also expressed in the main ceremony of first bathing, and in the subsequent ritual washings, which the pregnant woman continues until her confinement and after it.

It is impossible to get beyond the idea that whiteness as such is desirable. One thing is clear, however. Although whiteness of the skin is usually regarded as a personal attraction, in this case the woman is not made white in order to be erotically seductive. When I asked why a pregnant woman must try to make her skin white, I received the answer: " If a woman does not wash and anoint, and if her skin is black, people will say this woman is very bad, she has men in her mind, she does not look after her confinement." Again they would say, explaining the motive for the whole ceremony: " This is done to prepare her skin for the confinement washings ; and to make her desire to be white. Thus we see when her skin is white that she does not think about adultery." From another informant I received the statement : " The *saykeulo* covers her up completely : breasts, legs, back ; only her face you see. It makes her skin white, it shows she does not have connection with men." Thus the woman is made white and beautiful by all this magic. Yet she must hide her charms, she must not attract other men, and she has to keep more stringently faithful than at any other time of her wedded life. Nay, as will be seen, she must even abstain from lawful intercourse with her husband.

3

CUSTOMS OF PREGNANCY AND CONFINEMENT

In the foregoing section the ceremony of first pregnancy was described. Now we proceed to the customs of pregnancy and confinement in general. The ritual bathing, the ceremonial investment with the pregnancy mantle, the magic of whiteness and of beauty, are only performed before the first child is born. But making the skin as white as possible by ordinary means, including the use of the mantle, is a feature of every pregnancy. On subsequent occasions the mantle is made by the woman herself or it may be given by a *tabula* and repaid by her, but as a private transaction only.

Some five months after conception, that is at the time of the ritual bathing in a first pregnancy, the prospective mother begins to observe certain food restrictions. She must abstain from what the natives call *kavaylu'a* (delicacies which consist mainly of fruit). The banana, the mango, the malay apple, the South Sea almond, the pawpaw, the bread-fruit, and the *natu* fruit are forbidden to her. This taboo has reference to the future health of the child. " If she eat *kavaylu'a*, the child will have a big belly ; it will be full of excrement and will soon die." The diet of a pregnant woman is henceforth reduced to the staple vegetable food (*kaulo*), that is yams, taro, native peas, sweet potatoes, and other produce of the garden. She is also allowed to eat meat and fish, but she must abstain from certain kinds of the latter. The fish which she is forbidden to eat are such species as live in the submarine holes of the coral. The natives say that just as it is difficult to haul these fish out of their hiding places, so the baby would not easily be brought forth. Fish with sharp, pointed and poisonous fins, which are on that account dangerous to the fishermen, are taboo to the pregnant woman. If she were to eat any of them the child would be ill-tempered and constantly wailing. As pregnancy progresses and the woman becomes big, sexual intercourse must be abandoned, for, as the natives say, " the penis would kill the child." This taboo is rigorously observed.

Otherwise the pregnant woman leads a normal life almost up to the time of her confinement. She works in the garden, fetches water and firewood, and cooks the food for the household. She has but to shield herself from the sun by wearing the *saykeulo* (pregnancy mantle), wash frequently, and anoint herself with coco-nut oil. Only towards the close of pregnancy when the first *saykeulo* is worn out and discarded, must she keep out of the sun and therefore abandon some of the heavier work.

As in a first pregnancy, so in all the subsequent ones, the woman, about the fifth month, has to take up her abode in her father's house and she may remain there or she may return again to her husband's house until some time before the confinement, when she invariably goes to the house of her parents or maternal uncle. This removal to the father's or mother's brother's house is a rule observed in every childbirth, the woman leaving her husband's house in about the seventh or eighth month of her pregnancy.

This custom is associated with the strong fear of the dangers which surround a woman in childbed, and which are conceived to be due to a form of evil magic, which is called *vatula bam* (the chilling or paralysing of the uterus). And again, in the face of this great danger, we see once more the interesting recrystallization of kinship ties, the shifting of responsibility and solidarity. Here, again, only the actual maternal kinsmen and kinswomen are, in the eyes of custom and tribal law, regarded as reliable. The woman has to go to her father's house, for that is also her mother's home, and her mother is the proper person to look after her and the baby. The mother also is concerned in warding off danger with the help of her male relatives, who foregather at the house of the birth and see to it that a proper watch (*yausa*) is kept over the lying-in. Such a watch, kept by men armed with spears who sit all the night long over fires and guard the house and its every approach, is considered the main defence and precaution against sorcerers who, surrounded by nocturnal birds, are supposed to prowl about, attempting to cast the *vatula bam* magic. Primarily, it is the duty of the husband to carry out the *yausa*, but in this he is never trusted alone, and the male relatives of the pregnant woman not only assist but also control him. The interesting thing about this form of sorcery is that it does not only exist in the fear and superstition of the natives, but that it is actually attempted and carried out by male sorcerers. The formula is recited, the house approached, and the evil charm cast according to the prescribed rites.[1] I have even obtained the spells of this magic and the curative counter spells, but as this question essentially belongs to the subject of sorcery, I shall reserve it for a future publication.

When her time approaches, the parental house is made ready. The father and all the male inmates have to leave, while some female kinswomen come in to assist the mother. When the first pains are felt, the woman is made to squat on the raised

---

[1] Cf. the difference between the purely imaginary witchcraft of the flying women (*yoyova*) and the sorcery really carried out by the male wizards (*bwaga'u*), *Argonauts of the Western Pacific*, ch. ii, sec. vii, and ch. x, sec. i; and ch. ii of this book.

bedstead with a small fire burning under it. This is done " to make her blood liquid ", " to make the blood flow ". At the critical moment the woman in labour and her attendants may repair to the bush, where confinement is sometimes allowed to take place, but more usually they remain in the house.

About the actual travail, I have been able to obtain only the following information. The woman in labour is seated on a mat placed on the ground, with her legs apart and her knees raised. Leaning back, with her hands on the ground behind her, she rests her weight on her arms. At her back stands her sister or some other close maternal relative, who bears heavily on the labouring woman's shoulders, pressing down and even thumping her vigorously. As the natives say : " This woman presses on the parturient one so that the baby may fall out quickly." The mother of the woman in travail waits to receive the baby. Sometimes she catches hold of her daughter's knees. A mat is placed in position, and on this the newly born is received. I was told that the baby is allowed to come to birth by means of natural efforts only, and that it is never pulled out or manipulated. " The child will fall on to the mat, there it lies, then we take it. We do not take hold of it before." The parturient woman tries to help on the process by stopping her breath and so bearing down on the abdomen.

If the labour is very hard they ascribe the fact, of course, to the evil magic of the *vatula bam* and they summon someone who knows the *vivisa* (curative formula) to counteract this evil. This is recited over the aromatic leaves of the *kwebila* plant, and the body of the woman is rubbed with them. Or else the charmed leaves are placed on her head and then thumped with the fist. Only in the most difficult cases and when the *vivisa* has proved ineffective would the child be manipulated, and even then, from what I gathered, very timidly and incompetently. If the afterbirth does not come out in due course, a stone is tied to the mother's end of the navel string. The *vivisa* (curative formula) is then recited over it, and the woman made to stand up. If that does not help, they are at their wits' end, and the woman is doomed, as they do not know how to extract the afterbirth by manipulation. The natives were very much astonished when they saw how Dr. Bellamy, who for several years had been medical officer in the Trobriands, used to remove the afterbirth.[1]

Some three days after the birth, one of the *tabula* (paternal kinswomen) of the mother of the new-born child heats her fingers at a fire and kneads off the remaining piece of the navel string near to the baby's abdomen. This and the afterbirth are buried in the ground within the garden enclosure. Underlying the custom is a vague idea that it will make the new-born a good gardener, that it will " keep his mind in the garden ". After the removal of the umbilical cord, the child may, though it need not, be carried out of the house. The mother has to remain for a month or so confined within the parental hut. Soon after the delivery, a string is twisted by the *tabula* and tied round the mother's chest. Some magic is associated with this, but unfortunately I never learnt what it was nor ascertained the meaning of the ceremony.

4

MOTHER AND CHILD

Mother and baby spend the greater part of their time during the first month on one of the raised bedsteads with a small fire underneath. This is a matter of hygiene, as the natives consider such baking and smoking to be very beneficial for the health, and a sort of prophylactic against black

[1] This information I received independently from Dr. Bellamy, at that time Assistant Resident Magistrate and Medical Officer of the district, and from the natives.

magic. No men are allowed into the house, for, since the woman baked over the fire is usually naked, no male should enter; but there are no supernatural sanctions for the custom, nor is any serious harm done if the taboo should be broken. After a month or so a magic is performed called *vageda kaypwakova*; flowers of the white lily are burned with some dry wood, while the charm is spoken, and the woman is covered with the smoke of the smouldering faggot. This is done on two days in succession, and is supposed to make her skin still whiter. I did not obtain the formula of this magic. On the third day, the *tabula* ritually wash the young mother, and rub her skin with leaves charmed by the beauty spell used in the corresponding rite during the first pregnancy ceremony.

The woman then goes out with the baby and makes the round of the village, receiving from friends and her father's relatives small gifts of food called *va'otu*. After she has finished the round, there is a mimic driving home (*ibutusi*) of her by the *tabula* (her maternal aunt and other relatives of the same class), and here she has to remain for another month in seclusion.

During this time husband and wife may only speak together through the door and glance at each other now and then. On no account must they eat together or even partake of the same food. Sexual intercourse between them is strictly taboo for a much longer time, at the least until the child can walk. But the stricter rule is to abstain from intercourse until it is weaned—that is, some two years after its birth—and this stricter rule is said always to be observed by men in polygamous households. The husband, even one who has several wives, must abstain from all conjugal or extra-conjugal intercourse until the baby and its mother go out for the first time. A breach of any of these rules is said to bring about the death of the child.

In the case of illegitimate children also, if the mother copulates too soon, the child is sure to die.

After the second seclusion, mother and child return to their own household, and the mother resumes her normal life, although much of her time is taken up with the baby. She wears a plain fibre skirt, two of which have been made for her by her *tabula* if this has been her first pregnancy. She also now wears the long mantle, *saykeulo*, the second of the two made for her by the *tabula* before the first pregnancy (pl. 51). If it is a second pregnancy, or if the baby is illegitimate, the skirt and the mantles are made by herself or privately by a relative, and are as a rule much shorter (see pl. 90). Also a young mother frequently wears a sort of maternity cap, called *togebi*, which is often made by twisting a small grass fibre petticoat into a sort of turban.[1] Into her armlets she must insert a bundle of aromatic herbs (*vaːna*).

The most important of the cares bestowed on the child is, of course, concerned with its feeding. Besides the mother's breast which, as I was told, but very seldom fails, the child is given other food almost from the first days. Taro, well boiled, is chewed by the mother or by some of her relatives, and the mash, called *memema*, is given to the infant. The natives think that the child would be too weak if it were restricted to its mother's milk. Chewed yams and fish are not given till much later, when the child is almost a year old. The child's head is smeared with coco-nut oil mixed with charcoal " to make the head strong " as the natives say. One measure of cleanliness is observed day after day from the first hours of the baby's life : it is bathed regularly in warm water, with which the mother also washes her own skin. A specially deep wooden platter, called *kaykwaywosi*, is used for this purpose.

---

[1] *Togebi* is the general name for plaited discs or folded petticoats worn on the head as a support for baskets and other loads carried by women (cf. ch. i, sec. 3, and pl. 6).

The water is warmed by throwing stones heated in the ashes into the platter. Thus a hot and somewhat alkaline water is prepared, and this daily washing, followed by an anointing with coco-nut oil, is said to keep the skin of the mother and child white. The weaning of the child takes place long after birth, usually some two years or, as the natives put it, " when it is able to say clearly *bakam bamom* (I want to eat, I want to drink)."

During the weaning the child is separated from the mother, and sleeps with its father or with its paternal grandmother. When it cries at night a dry breast is given to it, or some coco-nut milk. If it is fretful and loses condition, it is taken to some distant village where it has relatives, or from inland villages to the seaside, so that it may regain its normal health and good spirits.

We have now brought the child up to the time when he will shortly join his playmates in the small children's world of the village. In a few years he will begin his own amorous life. Thus we have closed the cycle which runs through infantile love-making, youthful intrigues, settled liaison, marriage, and its results in the production and rearing of children. This cycle I have described in its main outline, giving special consideration to the sociological aspects as seen in prenuptial intercourse, marriage, kinship ideas, and the interplay of mother-right and paternal influence. In the following chapters it will be necessary to describe certain side-issues and psychological aspects, concerned more particularly with the erotic life before marriage.

CHAPTER IX

CUSTOMARY FORMS OF LICENCE

WE must now return to certain aspects of love making, which had to be left out or barely touched upon in relating the life history of the native. The facts described in chapter iii have shown us that, subject to certain restrictions, everyone has a great deal of freedom and many opportunities for sexual experience. Not only need no one live with impulses unsatisfied, but there is also a wide range of choice and opportunity.

But wide as are the opportunities of ordinary love making for a Trobriander, they do not exhaust all the possibilities of erotic life. In addition, seasonal changes in village life and festive gatherings stimulate sexual interest and provide for its satisfaction. Such occasions, as a rule, lead to intrigues beyond the limits of the village community ; they loosen old ties and establish new acquaintanceships ; they bring about short passionate affairs, which sometimes develop into more stable attachments.

Traditional usage allows, and even encourages, such extensions of ordinary erotic life. And yet we shall see that, though countenanced by custom and public opinion, they are felt to be an excess, to be something anomalous. Usually they produce a reaction, not in the community as a whole, but in the individuals offended by them.[1] Some excesses—those, that is, which really deserve the name of orgiastic licence—are limited to one district alone, and are viewed by the other natives as quaint local anomalies ; while those who practise

[1] For a discussion of such licensed yet resented usages, see *Crime and Custom*, part ii.

them are proud, and at the same time ashamed of them. Even the common and outwardly decorous relaxations are considered as escapades and adventures, always to be planned in the penumbra of secrecy, and often resented, if not avenged, by the regular partners.

It has seemed best to divide the description of native sexual life into two parts, and to treat these separately. The normal maturing of the sexual impulse and its issue in matrimony had to be dealt with first. The facts which illustrate how the impulse is given a wider range, how it strays beyond the local group of every-day acquaintances and leads athwart home-made intrigues, will be given in this and the following chapters.

This division corresponds to the native point of view, and makes it possible to present the facts in a far truer perspective than if they were lumped together. But the two parts are closely connected, and the way in which they fit into each other will be evident in the account which follows.

I shall begin with a description of those occasions which regularly, in the course of each year, stimulate erotic interest, and at the same time provide wider opportunities for its satisfaction. There are certain seasonal and periodical games ; there are arrangements for picnics, excursions, and bathing parties ; there are customary festivities associated with the economic cycle, and finally there is the annual season of festivities.

I

The Erotic Element in Games

Throughout the year, there is a periodic increase in play and pleasure-seeking at full moon. When the two elements so desirable in the tropics, soft light and bracing freshness are combined, the natives fully respond : they stay up longer to talk, or to walk to other villages, or to undertake such enterprises as can be carried out by moonlight. Celebrations connected with travel, fishing, or harvesting, as well as all games and festivals are held at the full moon. In the ordinary course of tribal life, as the moon waxes, the children, who always play in the evening, sit up later and band together to amuse themselves on the central place of the village. Soon the young boys and girls join them, and, as the moon grows fuller, the maturer youth, male and female, is drawn into the circle of players. Gradually the smaller children are squeezed out ; and the round games and competitive sports are carried on by youths and grown-ups. On specially fine and cool nights of full moon, I have seen the whole population of a large village gathered on the central place, the active members taking part in the games, with the old people as spectators.

The younger men and women, however, are the main players, and the games are associated with sex in more than one way. The close bodily contact, the influence of moonlight and shadow, the intoxication of rhythmic movement, the mirth and frivolity of play and ditty—all tend to relax constraint, and give opportunity for an exchange of declarations and for the arrangement of trysts. In this book we are chiefly concerned with the erotic element in games, but in order not to lose the right perspective, it must be realized that this is but one aspect of them. Children's play and adult games often contain no such element, and in none of them is it the only interest, or even the chief inducement to participation. Love of athletics, the need for exercise, competition, display of skill and daring, æsthetic satisfaction and a sense of fun, are each quite as important as the sexual element.

The games which are played on moonlit evenings on the central place of the village are perhaps the most important of all. They usually begin with a round game of " ring-a-ring-a-roses " type, called

Kasaysuya (pl. 52).[1] Boys and girls join hands and sing, while they move first slowly and then, with the quickening rhythm of the chant, spin round faster and faster, until, tired out and giddy, they stop, rest, and begin again in the reverse direction. As the game progresses, and one ditty follows another, the excitement grows. The first ditty is one which begins with the words, " *kasaysuya, saysuya,*" referring to a bush after which the game is named. Each time they start on a new round, a new ditty is chanted. The rhythm in song and step is at first slow, grows rapidly quicker, and ends in a swift staccato repetition of the last syllables as the players whirl round and round. Towards the end of the game usually the rhymes become rather ribald.

These are examples of such *kasaysuya* ditties with sexual allusions :—

I

Taytulaviya, viya, taytulabeula, beula (repeated)
furious taytu,   stout taytu
Kavakayviyaka, kwisi tau'a'u
Enormous   penis (of) men
Isisuse   *wa bwayma.*
They sit   in   food-house.
Toyatalaga   *popu*
Fornicator   excrement.

Free Translation

O, the rapidly growing taytu yams, O, the stout
    taytu yams.
Men with enormous penises sit on the food-house
    platforms
(i.e. keep away from women)—they are pederasts !

[1] This and the following illustrations (pls. 52–6) were taken whilst the children and youths were demonstrating the details of the games. The actual performances take place always after nightfall, and could not be photographed. The difference consists mainly in the presence of spectators, who are not to be seen in these illustrations.

II

Imayase   *la*   *kaykivi*
They bring   his   soliciting message (of)

tokaka'u (repeated).
widower.

Ipayki   *nakaka'u.*
He [she] declines widow.

Ikaraboywa   *kwila*   *tokaka'u.*
It remains idle   penis (of)   widower.

Free Translation

They brought her the invitation to lie with him from
    the widower—
But the widow refused.
So the widower's penis had to remain idle !

    This ditty, I was told, would be sung if a widower
were present, especially if he were too enterprising
in his amorous offers, or if he misdirected them.
It would also be sung if a woman wanted to
stimulate his interest and encourage him.

III

Yokwamiga   *tau'a'u miyawimi*   *sayduwaku.*
You indeed   men   your pubic leaves duwaku piece.
Saydukupi, kupi.
Short piece, short.
Galaga   *takakaya*   *kukupi.*
No indeed we fornicate short (things).

Free Translation

O men you use *duwaku* strips for your pubic leaves :
They are short strips, far too short !
Nothing so short will induce us to fornicate with
    you !

IV

Yokwamiga vivilaga   *midabemi siginanabu,*
You indeed women indeed your skirts (a flimsy leaf),

Siginapatu,   *patu.*
(Flimsy leaf) narrow,   narrow.

Galaga,   *takakaya*   *patu.*
No indeed   we fornicate   narrow (holes).

Free Translation

O women, you use the *siginanabu* leaves for your
     skirts :
They are narrow leaves.
Nothing so narrow will induce us to penetrate you.

    The two chants are counterparts of one another,
and show the typical kind of joke made about the
dress of the other sex. My informant stated
emphatically that they mean simply : " *Gala
takayta kaykukupi kwila—gala takayta kwaypatu
wila,*" " We do not copulate (with one having)
a short penis, we do not copulate (with one having,
a narrow cunnus."

V

Yokwamiga giyovila   *kaynupisi nunimiga.*
You indeed   women of rank   small   your breasts
                                     indeed.

Kaykawala   *mitasiga gweguyaga.*
Impressionable   their eyes men of rank indeed.

Kamilogi   *babawa,*
Your copulating support   earthen mound,

kamiyaguma
your lime pots

       kwe, kwe, kwe.
(make) kwe, kwe, kwe.

Free Translation

O women of rank, your breasts are small indeed,
But the eyes of men of rank are lecherous.
You copulate on the ground, and while you do that,
    your limepots produce a rattling sound *kwe,*
    kwe, kwe.

Social games always begin with this rhythmic running in a circle. Other figure games follow, in several of which only two people participate. Thus, a boy will put his feet on one of the thighs of another boy or man, who, standing up and holding him by the hands, swings in a circle (pl. 53); or two boys sit facing each other with the soles of their feet together, get a good grip on a stick, held between them, and try to lift each other off the ground. This is a form of " cock-fighting ". Most of the games, however, are played by many people; sometimes they are very conventionalized and remote imitations of serious pursuits, and sometimes they represent the behaviour of animals. Thus in " Dog's Tail ", two rows of boys face each other, and move to left and right; in " Rats " a row of boys squat and hop one after the other (pl. 54); in " Cooking Pot ", boys in the same position move slowly from one foot to the other; in " Fishing of Kuboya ", boys advance in single file, the last one being caught by two who stand on either side with raised arms and let the others pass (pl. 55). In this last we find the elements of our " Oranges and Lemons ". More elaborate figures are enacted in " Stealing of the Bananas ", " The Parrot ", and " The Fire ". All these games without exception are accompanied by rhymes which are sung sometimes at the beginning, sometimes right through the game, and sometimes, as in " Bananas", at appropriate moments in the action. In none of these games is there any direct erotic element, but they all provide opportunities for contact and for the handling of one another, for teasing and an exchange of jokes. In contest games, such as "Rats", "Dog's Tail", and "Fishing", only boys take part as a rule. In the more elaborate games, such as "Fire", "Bananas", and "Parrot", both sexes participate.

2

GAMES INVOLVING PHYSICAL CONTACT

This, also, is the invariable rule in the following games, which admit of even more intimate physical contact. The *sina* game forms part of the bathing ritual in the pregnancy ceremony, and has been described in the previous chapter. In the village, boys and girls play it together. There is also a game in which the players stand in a long chain holding hands, and then walk, reciting a chant, round the person who stands at one end. This end remains immovable and the person at the other end leads the chain round in gradually narrowing circles until the whole group is pressed together into a tight knot. The fun of the game consists in squeezing the knot very tightly. It is then unrolled gradually by reversing the motion faster and faster, till at the end the others run round and round the fixed end until the chain breaks. Another game begins by two of the players sitting back to back ; two more sit between the legs of each, serving as a support, and then two more between the legs of the second pair, and so on ; and so seated they sing and begin to push backwards ; the row which pushes the other one out of position wins. In both these games, close proximity lends itself to the preliminaries of love making.

The favourite and most important game is a tug-of-war, *bi'u* (literally pulling). A long stout creeper is cut and an equal number of players, each standing behind the other, take hold of either half of the creeper ; usually the game starts somewhere

in the middle of the village place (*baku*). When all
are in position, one side recites half the ditty, the
other responds with the second half, and as the
recital ends they begin to tug. Sometimes it is men
against women ; sometimes by accident or preference, the sides are mixed. Never is there any
division according to clan, though kinship taboos
between men and women are always observed,
so that brother and sister, for instance, never stand
near each other. Each side strives to " get the other
going ", and the real fun begins when one side
proves itself the stronger and drags the other. A
great deal of roughness is displayed in this game,
also a considerable amount of disregard for any
damage done to houses, young trees, or domestic
objects lying about. When it is played in the form
of a *kayasa*, a competitive arrangement of which we
shall speak presently, houses, yam stores, and young
trees are said to be destroyed and people are
sometimes injured.

The main interest in these competitive games of
strength and skill lies in the game itself ; but many
of the players make use of them for erotic purposes.
Not only does physical proximity allow of certain
intimacies not otherwise possible, but, as we shall
see later, it is indispensable for the exercise of some
forms of love-magic.

Late at night, usually as a climax to the other
games, the natives play " Hide and Seek " (*supeponi*).
When this game is played on a large scale, the sides
start from the central place, but hide outside in
the *weyka*, the village grove (pl. 56). As a rule
the sexes divide, women and men hiding alternately.
When one player finds another he has to chant a
ditty in a loud voice. Those who are not found for
a long time, return by themselves, each singing a
special phrase, as he or she arrives at the meeting-
place. As with the tug-of-war, this game is extremely
popular, and the sexual motive is without doubt
partly responsible for this. Couples will arrange to

look for each other or to meet at some particular place, and it is easy to see how well this game is designed for trysts, though probably such are mainly of a preliminary nature. It is accordingly not considered proper for married women to join in " Hide and Seek ".

On fine days the boys and girls will often arrange an excursion to some favourite spot. Usually they take food and cook it on a beach, or among the coastal rocks, or at some specially attractive waterhole. Sometimes they combine the excursion with fruit-gathering, fishing, or bird-trapping. At such times lovers will walk apart for greater intimacy. In the season of sweet flowering plants and trees they gather blossoms, adorn each other with garlands, and even with paint, and thus æsthetically celebrate the occasion.

On hot days in the season of calm weather, boys and girls repair to the beach, to waterholes, and to creeks, where they engage in bathing games. Each game has its stereotyped action and its special name ; and most of them are accompanied by a chant. The players swim and dive in groups ; or stand in a row, chanting a ditty, and, as it ends, fall backwards into the water and swim away on their backs. Again, they stand in a ring, facing inwards, sing a few words, and then splash one another. There is a game which commemorates an old legend about the change of a man into a dugong. They also know the use of the surfboard and amuse themselves with it on the open sea-beach.

It is difficult to say exactly how far an erotic interest enters into these games. As in all the other games, so far described, the observer can see nothing in the slightest degree indecorous, but from conversations with natives and from their personal confidences, it is clear that amorous intrigues frequently start on such occasions. The splashing often passes into wrestling, and water games present the human body in a fresh and stimulating light.

3

Seasons of Love and Festivity

The games on the central village place are played, for the most part, between May and September, the cool season of the trade winds. There are no bathing games in these months, as a strong wind blows during the midday hours. Water games are most popular in the hot seasons between the dry and the rainy weather, from February to May, and during October and November. These latter months—the spring of the Southern Hemisphere, and, in the Trobriands, the calm season following the dry months of the trade winds—are also the time of harvest celebrations.

Harvest time is one of joy and social activity, of constant visits between the communities, of competition, display, and mutual admiration. Each village must send out its parties of boys and girls, with gifts of food. They wear a special dress, put aromatic leaves into their armlets and flowers into their hair, and a few lines of paint upon their faces. The girls put on a new fibre petticoat (pl. 61), the boys a fresh pubic leaf. At times the central place is crowded with such harvest carriers (pl. 57). Such festive visits are an occasion for making new acquaintances and for a display of personal beauty, and thus lead to intrigues between members of different communities.[1] All the harvest customs favour erotic pursuits—visits to other villages and the added freedom, the gay mood and the care taken in personal adornment. After sunset, on the pretext of visiting the gardens, parties of boys and girls amuse themselves in other villages, returning home late at night. The fervour of these activities increases towards the full moon.

[1] For the sociological and economic systems which underlie the distribution of the crops at harvest and the gifts between villages, see my article in *The Economic Journal*, March, 1921, and ch. vi of *Argonauts of the Western Pacific*.

The harvest period is directly followed by the *milamala*, the annual feast associated with the return of ancestral spirits to the village.[1] The inaugural ceremony is held at a certain full moon, and is followed by a month of dancing which reaches its climax at the next full moon. On the last few days before full moon, certain solemn celebrations are held, dances in full dress are performed, and offerings made to the spirits of the departed. The whole interest of the community is concentrated on these final celebrations. Men and women are intent on producing an effect of lavishness, on doing honour to their ancestral spirits and thus to themselves, and in general on achieving that renown (*butura*) so dear to the heart of the Trobriander. The dances during this time are never directly associated with sex, but they serve to establish the fame of good dancers and thus to add to their personal charm. On the night after the full moon, the spirits are ceremonially driven away from the villages, and all dancing stops.

A period of quieter festivity follows the *milamala*, that of the *karibom*. After the evening meal, the village drummers, standing in the centre of the village place (*baku*), beat out a slow rhythm. Soon children, old men and women, youths and maidens, assemble in the central place and begin to walk round it. There is no special step, no complicated rhythm; only a slow, regular, monotonous walk. Such *karibom* walking takes place also in the earlier stages of the *milamala* month, to be replaced towards its end by regular dancing.

The slow rhythmic walk of the *karibom* is to a great extent a social promenade. In place of the single file of the ordinary dance, two or three people walk abreast; conversation is allowed and free

---

[1] For a detailed description of beliefs and practices associated with the *milamala* see my articles, " Baloma, the Spirits of the Dead in the Trobriand Islands", in *Journal R. Anthrop. Inst.*, 1916, and " Lunar and Seasonal Calendar," *ibid.*, 1927. Cf. also ch. xi, sec. 2, of this book.

choice in the matter of partners. An old man or woman will be seen leading a grandchild by the hand or carrying it. Women, sometimes with babies at the breast, gossip together, and lovers walk arm-in-arm. Since the *karibom* usually falls on dark, moonless evenings, it lends itself to erotic approaches even more than the ordinary games, and considerably more than the regular dancing. There are a number of modes of erotic attack which can be practised during the *karibom* by a boy walking immediately behind the object of his fancy. From this position he can clasp her breasts, a proceeding which, as the natives say, is useful in stimulating her erotic interest, and is also a condition of certain forms of love-magic. Or else he may hold certain aromatic herbs under her nose, the smell of which, by its own virtue alone or by this enhanced with magic, exercises a powerful erotogenous effect. Or, if he be enterprising and his desire strong, he may, parting the fringe of her grass skirt, insert a finger in her vulva.

During the whole period of this festival, but more especially during the first part, the *milamala*, visits between communities take place. Sometimes these visits are official and ceremonial, as when one community is invited by another to admire a newly acquired dance, or to sell one of their own to it. A special term *laga* is applied to the sale of dances and one or two other privileges and titles.[1] For such an occasion, the whole community, with its headman and best dancers, moves in a body to the other village and there ceremonially performs the dance, instructing the purchasers in its intricacies (pl. 58). The visit is always returned. Large gifts (*va'otu*) are associated with such visits, and have, as always, to be returned in an equivalent form. But sometimes groups of youths and maidens, boys and girls, will go from one village to another for their private pleasure, and join in the local *karibom* (slow

[1] Cf. *Argonauts*, p. 186.

rhythmic walking). In this way new acquaintances are made and more or less temporary intrigues begun, distance and strangeness adding spice to the adventure.

Thus, in normal years, the festive mood of the *milamala* spreads itself through the dull round of the *karibom*. But if the food be plentiful and the festive mood exuberant ; if there are special reasons for celebration or some need to comfort the spirits of the people, as after a defeat in war or an unsuccessful *kula* expedition, then the period of dancing is deliberately prolonged. Such an extension is called *usigola*, "together for a dance " (*usi* from *wosi* = dance, *gola* = to accumulate or foregather). It may last one, two, or even three months. Like the *milamala*, this extension has its inaugural ceremony, its intermediate feasts, and its climax in an orgy of feasting and dancing which may last for several days. People from friendly villages are invited ; they arrive with presents and return home laden with counter-gifts. All that has been previously said with reference to the sexual opportunities offered by the main festival period obviously applies also to the *usigola*.

4

CEREMONIAL GATHERINGS : KAYASA

The *usigola* (extension of dancing period) is only one type of the festivities into which the *milamala* may be extended. The generic name for such periods of competitive obligatory dancing, amusement or other activity is *kayasa*. A *kayasa* is always organized upon a definite pattern, with a ceremonial according to its kind ; and it has, in some aspects, the binding force of law. A *kayasa* need not be specially a period of amusement. There are *kayasa* of economic activities, such as gardening, fishing or the production of shell ornaments. But although the *usigola* belongs to this type of communal activity, it is never called *kayasa*; nor is this term applied to competitive ceremonial and obligatory expeditions of the *kula* type. Such special *kula* expeditions are always called *uvalaku*.[1]

In certain cases the activity round which a *kayasa* centres is an exclusive privilege of the community or clan; but whatever its kind, initiative must always be taken by the headman, who acts as *tolikayasa* (master of the *kayasa*). It is he who, with the assistance of his clansmen and kinsmen, has to provide the wherewithal for the big feast or, rather, the ceremonial distribution of food (*sagali*) which inaugurates the proceedings. Those who partake of this—and practially all the community have to do so—are under a formal obligation to exert themselves for the whole period, so that the *kayasa* may be a success; and, at times, when their zeal in work or amusement shows signs of flagging, a new feast is given to revive enthusiasm. There is a reason behind this fiction of a legal obligation towards the leader on account of food and gifts received: for the glory of a successful *kayasa* devolves principally upon the *tolikayasa* (the leader or owner of the *kayasa*). But, as we know already, there is also scope for the ambition of any participant, and the element of emulation is very strong in all *kayasa*. Each of them includes some form of competitive display or contest, and there is always a pronouncement of public opinion on the result. So that the most successful or energetic participants also receive an individual share of glory.

Among the *kayasa* of pure amusement, we may mention first the tug-of-war game, already described in this section. When played as a *kayasa* it is inaugurated ceremonially by a big distribution of food (*sagali*, see ch. xi, sec. 2). After that it has

---

[1] For a description of the *uvalaku*, cf. *Argonauts of the Western Pacific*, *passim*. The place of the *kayasa* in economic life has been indicated in my article on the "Primitive Economics of the Trobriand Islanders", *Economic Journal*, March, 1921. Its legal aspect has been referred to in *Crime and Custom in Savage Society*, p. 61.

to be continued night after night in full force, with
utter disregard of personal inclination, comfort,
or even property, which, as mentioned already, is
often damaged. The community divides regularly
into two parts; especially good tuggers acquire
renown, and the stories of extraordinary feats, of
special havoc wrought, or of long and arduous
deadlocks, fill the whole district with the fame
(*butura*) of leader and participants. There is a
sporting *kayasa*, specially popular in the southern
part of the district, in which miniature canoes are
sailed competitively. Another type of *kayasa*,
called *kamroru*, is performed exclusively by women,
and consists of communal singing. This is regarded
as a counterpart of the ceremonial dancing, in
which, with very rare exceptions, only men take
part. In the *kamroru kayasa*, women, in full dress,
seat themselves on new mats spread on the central
place and, swaying rhythmically, sing certain songs
in unison. The men look on from the platforms of
the storehouses and admire the most beautiful
figures and the finest voices.

There is a more direct erotic appeal in the
festivities connected with the sweet-smelling *butia*.
The flowering season of the *butia* tree coincides with
the *milamala* period (annual feast of the returning
spirits), and the flower *kayasa* is therefore only held
in those years when owing to mourning there can
be no dances in the village. Otherwise the season is
always devoted to dancing. The flowers are collected
in the jungle, made into wreaths and garlands, and
exchanged with a blowing of conch-shells. As the
natives put it: "We make *kula* (ceremonial
exchange) with *butia* wreaths." In fact, whoever
initiates an exchange has to say, as he offers
the wreath: *um'maygu'a* (thy valuable present).
A small return gift of food or betel-nut is then made,
with the words: *kam kwaypolu* (thy preliminary
return). Finally a counterpart of the first present
is returned to the donor with the words: *um*

yotile (thy return gift). Thus the exact terminology of the *kula* is followed in these transactions.[1] A festive character is given to the whole
proceedings by the groups of people walking about
and singing ; by the gaily dressed boys and girls
taking part in the ceremonial far into the night ;
and by the sound of the conch-shells, blown as
each gift is presented.

The competitive element in the *butia* festival
lies in the quality and quantity of the presents
received and given, and, as in all forms of such
exchange, to give or to receive a magnificent gift
contributes to the glory of either side. This
kayasa provides opportunities for courtship and for
the expression of mutual admiration ; a would-be
lover can display his appreciation of a girl in the
magnitude of his gifts, and at the same time flatter
her vanity and satisfy her ambition. Thus beauty,
erotic interest, ambition, and vanity are the chief
interests in this *kayasa*.

A more pronounced part is played by vanity in
the festivals of hair-dressing (*waypulu*) and of
ornamental shell discs (*kaloma*). The *waypulu* is
confined to the islands of Kitava and Vakuta. After
a long period during which no deaths have occurred
so that the people have been able to grow long hair,
a display of this highly-valued natural beauty is
held (see ch. x, sec. 3). Only men take part in
this *kayasa*. They adorn themselves, spread mats
on the central place, and, teasing out their hair with
the long-pronged Melanesian comb, they sing
and display its charm. The women admire and
pronounce judgment on the quality and beauty of
the hair. The *kayasa* of shell ornaments is held in
the villages of Sinaketa and Vakuta. When a large
number of these discs have been produced, the men
adorn themselves, and day after day, evening after
evening, parade the central place.

To a European observer the proceedings of a

[1] Cf. *Argonauts of the Western Pacific*, pp. 352–7.

kayasa appear unspeakably monotonous and point-
less. The repetition for weeks on end of exactly the
same procedure prevents even an ethnographer from
regular attendance at any *kayasa*. But, for the
native, apart from any feeling of duty, the whole
affair has an intense interest and considerable
attraction. In this, sex plays a considerable
part. For the desire to show off, to produce a
personal effect, to achieve *butura* (renown) in its
most valued form, that of irresistible charm,
contains a pronounced erotic element.

5

ORGIASTIC FESTIVALS

There is, or, at least, used to be till the
missionaries came, one *kayasa* which centred round
erotic dalliance satisfied in public and that very
thoroughly. This *kayasa* was never practised in
the northern and central parts of the district, but
only by a few villages in the extreme south end of the
island of Vakuta. It was called *kamali*, a dialectic
variation of the word *kimali*, the erotic scratching,
which symbolizes the erotic approach, as does
kissing with us. It is a general rule in all districts
of the Trobriands that, when a boy and girl are
strongly attracted to each other, and especially before
their passion is satisfied, the girl is allowed to inflict
considerable bodily pain on her lover by scratching,
beating, thrashing, or even wounding with a sharp
instrument. However severely he is handled, such
treatment is accepted in good part by the boy, as a
sign of love and a symptom of temperament in his
sweetheart. On one occasion, during the harvest
festivities, I had to dress the wound of a boy who
came to me with a deep cut in the muscles right
across the back under his shoulder-blades. The girl
who had made it hovered near in deep concern. I
was told that she struck too hard without realizing

it. The boy did not appear to mind, though he was evidently in pain, and (so I heard) he reaped his reward that same night. This case was typical. The *kimali* or *kamali* is a form of feminine wooing, a compliment and an invitation, which in the *kamali kayasa* was systematized and carried out on a large scale. Boys in gala dress would walk round the central place singing : girls would come up to them and teasing jokes and repartee would be exchanged, very much as in other *kayasa*. But things were allowed to go very much further. Women, who were expected on such occasions to be much more forward than usual, would pass from teasing to scratching, and attack the boys with mussel-shells and bamboo-knives, or with a piece of obsidian or a small sharp axe. A boy was allowed to run away, and would do so if his assailant were not attractive to him. But it was a sign of manliness and a proof of success to be properly slashed about. Also, when a boy was attracted by a girl, he would, naturally, not run away, but take her attack as an invitation. The ambition of a woman was successively to slash as many men as she could ; the ambition of a man to carry away as many cuts as he could stand, and to reap the reward in each case.

I have never assisted at such a *kayasa*. As far as I could find out, through the interference of the white missionaries and officials, not one had occurred within twenty years of my arrival. So that data collected about this *kayasa* are what might be called " hearsay documents ". The account of scratching and cutting, however, tallies so well with facts observed by myself that I have not the slightest reason to doubt its accuracy. What follows is given with due reservation, though it agrees with the reports about some other Melanesian and Polynesian natives. I was told by several independent informants, both from the districts concerned and from the north, that the relaxation of all control was complete during that *kayasa*. Sexual acts would be carried out in public on the central place ; married people would participate in the orgy, man or wife behaving without restraint, even though within hail of each other. This licence would be carried so far that copulation would take place within sight of the *luleta* (sister, man speaking ; brother, woman speaking) : the person with regard to whom the strictest sexual taboos are always observed (see chs. xiii and xiv). The trustworthiness of these statements is confirmed by the fact that I was told several times, when discussing other forms of *kayasa* in the north, that all of them were carried out in a much more orgiastic manner in the south. Thus at a tug-of-war *kayasa* in the south, men and women would always be on opposite sides. The winning side would ceremonially deride the vanquished with the typical ululating scream (*katugogova*), and then assail their prostrate opponents, and the sexual act would be carried out in public. On one occasion when I discussed this matter with a mixed crowd from the north and the south, both sides categorically confirmed the correctness of this statement.

In this context two occasional forms of customary intercourse may be mentioned. During the mortuary wake (*yawali*), which takes place immediately after a man's death, people from all the surrounding communities congregate and take part in the songs and ceremonies which last for the best part of the night. When, far into the night, the visitors return home, it is the custom for some of the girls to remain behind to sleep with certain boys of the bereaved village. Their regular lovers must not, and do not, interfere.

Another type of sexual latitude is associated with hospitality given to strangers ; but this obligation was more strictly observed in former times when, owing to the greater fear and mistrust of strangers, the visitors were fewer and better chosen. I am told that it was then considered the duty of a girl from the village to act as the stranger's partner for the night. Hospitality, curiosity, and the charm of novelty would make this duty perhaps not very arduous.

The only overseas strangers, who, in olden days, used to voyage regularly, were those who came to the Trobriands on the *kula* trading expeditions. When the ceremonial stages of the visit were over and some exchange of goods had taken place, the visitors would enter the village and hold friendly converse with the inhabitants. It was also the duty of the hosts to provide the guests with food ; but this could never be given in the village, since it was against all etiquette to eat within a strange community. Therefore it was taken to the beach where the canoes were moored. Thither the village beauties would carry it on platters, and wait till these were emptied. Friendly talk would ripen into intimacy, presents would be offered by the strangers to the girls, and their acceptance was a sign that the girl was willing. It was considered right, and sanctioned by custom, that the local girls should sleep with the visitors ; and for this, also, accepted lovers had not the right to punish or reprimand them.

This holds good especially about the northern half of the island, visited by men from Kitava and the other Marshall Bennet Islands. In the southern villages, visited by the foreign speaking Dobuans and Amphlettans, the strangers also sometimes slept with the local girls. But this was not so usual, as the Dobuans never reciprocated or allowed their women folk to grant any favours to visiting Trobrianders.

The customs and arrangements so far considered are partly seasonal, partly dependent on special circumstances. The games described at the beginning of this chapter, which take place by moonlight on the central place, are mostly played during the trade-wind season, from May to September. The harvest activities and festivals

begin in June and last into August. The *milamala*
begins in September and ends in October. Its date
is fixed by the appearance of the *palolo* worm, which
comes up regularly at a certain full moon. The name
for this worm is also *milamala*, and it is sometimes
mystically connected with the arrival of the spirits.
The *kayasa* is sometimes held during the *milamala*
season, but usually it occurs immediately afterwards
as an extension of the festival. During the full rainy
season which follows, January, February, and March,
the telling of fairy tales and gardening are the main
social occupations. We shall have to touch upon
these presently. Bathing games take place in April
and May, October and November, between the
dry and wet seasons.

What is the relation of these customs to the normal
course of courtship described in chapter iii ? They
give opportunities for strangers to meet and for
erotic interest to pass beyond the confines of the
village. This may lead merely to romantic escapades
which enrich experience and guide maturer choice
within the community. But sometimes such intrigues
end in marriage, and then the woman always
follows her husband since, as we know, marriage is
patrilocal.

6

ULATILE—YOUTH IN SEARCH OF AMOROUS ADVENTURE

The periodical rise and fall of erotic life in the
Trobriands might be represented by a curve determined by tribal festivals, ceremonial customs, and
economic activities. These, in turn, follow the moon
and seasons in their courses. The curve rises
regularly at full moon and its highest point occurs
at and immediately after harvest. The drops in the
curve are associated with absorbing economic
pursuits and sports, with gardening and overseas

expeditions. Certain of the festivals favour an over-flow of erotic interest beyond the boundaries of a village community.

A liaison between two people who live at a distance from one another, is not too easy. Many special customs of assignation, visit, and tryst, which the natives comprehensively call *ulatile*, tend to assist separated lovers. Such visiting when done by men is called *ulatile*, which means literally " male youth ", and describes the group of adolescent boys and young men who often act in a body in work or play (pl. 59). By an extension of meaning, the noun *ulatile* is used to describe " youthful exuberance ", or even, more specifically, " sexual activity." We have met with this term already (ch. iii, sec. 2) in the compound *to'ulatile* (young man). Pronounced with a certain intonation, this term conveys the meaning of " gay dog ", or even " fornicator ". Applied to a woman, it assumes the form *naka'ulatile*, and is used only with the derogatory meaning, " wanton woman ", or more precisely, " a woman who desires more than she is desired ". In its original etymological implication, it probably means " forward like a man " (see ch. xiii, sec. 4). Used as a verb, the root *ulatile* is applied primarily to males, and it signifies " to go on a love-making expedition ", " to have success with women ", " to indulge in excessive sexual intercourse ". It can be used by extension about women, except when it is applied to an expedition outside the village, in which case it refers only to men.

There are two forms of *ulatile* expedition to which the word applies in a somewhat technical sense. The first is a matter of necessity : a lover must visit his sweetheart in her own village. If, on one of the several occasions described in the previous section, two people from different communities have become strongly attracted by each other, they will arrange a meeting. As a rule the boy has some intimate friend in the girl's village, and this makes things easier, since this friend will help him. It is a matter of etiquette for the lover to adorn himself for the tryst, and this compels him to observe a certain measure of secrecy. He will not walk on the main road, but surreptitiously steal through the bush. " Like a sorcerer he will go ; stop and listen ; go sideways and push through the jungle ; no one must see him." Thus one of my informants likened such *ulatile* to the clandestine expeditions of sorcerers who, on their nocturnal expeditions, must not be seen by anybody.

As he approaches the village he has to be specially careful. In his own village such a passing intrigue, if discovered, would only arouse the jealousy of the accredited lover and start a minor quarrel. But an erotic poacher caught in another community might be seriously mishandled, not only by the jealous lover, but by all the other boys. He might also bring upon his sweetheart the reproaches of her regular lover. However, the main reason for secrecy is that it is enjoined by custom as a rule of the game. The two usually arrange to meet in the jungle near the girl's village. Sometimes the girl guides her lover to the chosen place by lighting a fire ; sometimes they agree to imitate the call of a bird ; sometimes she marks the way into the chosen spot of the jungle by tearing the leaves in a pattern or by placing leaves on the road.

If the passion stands the test of time and difficulty and ripens into affection, steps are taken to make the liaison permanent and official. The boy may join his friend in the village, and remain there under some pretext as a temporary citizen. Or else the girl will be accepted in his village and come to live there. When taking a village census, I often came across a girl who was staying in the community because she was living with some boy belonging to it. The two would sleep together in a *bukumatula* (unmarried boys' and girls' house) in the same way as an ordinary affianced couple (see ch. iii, sec. 4), and if the liaison went well, it ended naturally in marriage.

Another technical use of the word *ulatile* applies to an entirely different type of love-making expedition. Sometimes a group of boys, who have brought away specially pleasant memories of another community from some festive gathering, will decide to go there in a body, on a regular *ulatile* expedition. Here secrecy is necessary, too. For though such expeditions are customary and, in a way, lawful, they constitute an encroachment on the rights of two other groups, the ordinary sweethearts of the *ulatile* boys, and the youths of the other village. If caught by either party the adventurers would have to face a volley of abuse, or even of blows; for girls in the Trobriands can defend their rights by force, and the boys in each community regard their womenfolk as their own preserve. The adventurers would, therefore, usually steal out at night and put on their ornaments outside their village. But once on the main road, they become boisterous and defiant, for this is the proper behaviour on such an occasion. There are even some special bawdy songs, called *lo'uwa*, to which they keep time as they go along.

LO'UWA SONG (I)

Aramwaye!   *Bagigido'u!*   *Bagiwawela!*
Hoho!   Fine necklace!   Necklace of Wawela!
  Sayam, Rapa'odi.
  Sayam, Rapa'odi.

Bakwatega   *Kadiratume,*
I anchor indeed (on) Kadiratume (beach),
Isideli   *uni'unatine;*   *itolala.*
He sits by her   young man;   she stands up.
Waydesi!   *kapukapugula*   *Kalamwaya!*
Hallo!   young woman.   Hoho!
Agudeydesi!   *Kalamwaya!*
Hollay!   Hoho!

Free Translation

" Hoho—(I come adorned with) a fine necklace,
The necklace of Wawela, like Sayam with the armshell Rapa'odi,
I anchor on a beach in Gawa, a boy sits by his girl,
She stands near him. Hallo! Young woman.
Hurray, hoho, hurray."

Sayam is said to be a man celebrated for beauty; and famous ornaments, such as the Rapa'odi armshell, are associated with attraction, success and love magic. He appears here adorned with a famous armshell named Rapa'odi, which, as indicated in the free translation, means that the " I " of the song also wears a fine necklace. In the reduplicated form *uni'unatine*, the *n* is a dialectic equivalent of the *l* of *ulatile*.

LO'UWA SONG (II)

Aramwaye!   *Bamasisi,*   *bamamata;*
Hoho!   I'll sleep,   I'll wake;

balage   *kupira*   *saygwa'u.*
I'll hear   drum his (of)   festival skirts.

Raytagine   *layma'i*
It throbs (with dance music) it fetches (attracts)

        karisaygwa'u,   *okuvalila.*
        their festival skirts,   on their flanks.

Kala wosi owadola,   *lakatunenia*   *oyamala.*
His song on mouth,   his small drum   in hand.

Gigiremutu   *kudula*
Blackened   his teeth

Tokivina   *yamtu*   *Wavivi*
Tokivina   treads (village of)   Wavivi

Yamtumutu   *Wavivi.*
He treads and treads (through the village of) Wavivi.

Free Translation

Hoho! I awake from my sleep, I hear the festive beat of the drums, as they throb with dance music—attracting women with full-dress

skirts, with festive skirts on their flanks. With
his song on his mouth, with his small drum in
his hand, his teeth blackened, Tokivina
rhythmically treads in the village of Wavivi, he
walks in dancing rhythm through the village of
Wavivi.

In this short song we have a condensed picture of
a *ulatile* situation—the awakening at night, the
sound of a distant drum announcing great festivities
in a neighbouring village. And here, again, there is a
legendary person moving in the background, partly
as a good augury, partly as an ideal. The psychology
of this traditional worship of personal beauty and
charm will be discussed later on.

Such songs, I am told, were also sung in olden
days to indicate that the party was neither on the
warpath nor on a sorcery expedition, nor bent on any
any other real mischief. As they approach their
goal they become quiet again, for they must not be
seen by the village youths. The girls, of course,
know when the expedition is drawing near, for
everything has been previously arranged in detail.
The visitor most familiar with the village creeps near
and gives the agreed signal. One by one the girls
sneak out of the houses and meet their lovers in the
bush. Sometimes the girls are already awaiting
them at some pre-arranged meeting place outside.
Should this gathering of lovers be detected, a fight
might ensue, leading, in former times, even to war
between the two communities.

Such *ulatile* expeditions are definite deviations
from the regular course of tribal life.[1] They lead
invariably to lovers' quarrels in both villages, and
to serious differences between the two communities.
They were an important feature of love life in former
days when armed expeditions for purposes of love-
making were more usual than an individual *ulatile*.

[1] For a discussion of the customary abrogations of law and conflicts
between various classes of custom, see *Crime and Custom*, part ii.

Nowadays, however, when it is so much easier and safer for a man or woman to walk alone even at night, the trysting of one boy with one girl is much more common.

To preserve perspective and to place the *ulatile* expeditions correctly in their context of tribal life, it must be realized that there are various occasions, apart from courtship, on which the youth of the village would visit other communities in a body. At harvest and during the dancing season (see pls. 57 and 58), for common games and mortuary feasts, groups of young men, more or less dressed up, can be met on the road or seen paddling along in the large fishing canoes. As a matter of fact, the love-making expeditions from the lagoon villages of the west coast would also be made by water (see pl. 60). Thus a party of boys on the road, decorated and singing, may be either bent on a real *ulatile* expedition, or else on some ordinary inter-village business or amusement; and it is difficult on surface evidence to draw any sharp distinction between erotic and other expeditions.

It is easy to see how inter-village intrigues fit into the general scheme of courtship described in chapter iii. The childish erotic experiences with which the sexual life history of an individual begins always take place within the community; the *ulatile* is one among the customs which carries erotic interest and those transitory affairs, which are the next stage in development, beyond the village. Such intrigues may become permanent and thus the *ulatile* is one of the ways in which matrimonial choice is extended beyond a single village.

7

KATUYAUSI—A CEREMONIAL ESCAPADE OF GIRLS

In matters of love the Trobriand woman does not consider herself man's inferior, nor does she lag behind him in initiative and self-assertion. The *ulatile* have their counterpart in the *katuyausi*, amorous expeditions of village girls to other communities.

Sometimes these expeditions are simply to avenge too much *ulatile* on the part of the boys. Or, as happens in coastal villages, the men are long absent fishing, trading, or sailing, and the girls seek consolation in another village. At times the incentive is more directly feminine. The girls have equipped themselves with a specially brilliant supply of grass petticoats, and want to display them on a wider stage than their own village. Some of my cynical informants affirmed that a *katuyausi* expedition is the girls' best means of replenishing their store of betel-nut and tobacco and of collecting an armlet or a comb, a pleasing handbag or a new supply of beads.

I am also under the impression that on each occasion the *katuyausi* party offer some pretext for their visit, such as the desire to see the crops, or to admire a new construction, a chief's house or yam-house, or else they pretend to be hawking some object for sale.

Whatever the chief incentive, and the pretext, as soon as their decision is taken the girls will choose an intermediary to arrange the date and conditions of their prospective visit to the boys of the other village. The procedure of a *katuyausi* expedition differs greatly from that of a *ulatile*. The boys leave after sunset under cover of night, whereas the girls start as a rule early in the afternoon. The boys creep out of the village, but once fairly on the road, sing and behave boisterously. The girls also steal quietly away, but their behaviour is decorous throughout the journey. Near the other village the boys have to hide, but the girls enter the village grove openly, sit down there and put the finishing touches to their toilet. They paint their lips red with betel-nut, draw decorative lines on their faces, and fill their armlets with aromatic herbs (pl. 61). It is etiquette

for the local boys to allow them to remain alone on
the outskirts of the village until they give the sign
for the boys to approach. During this time the
girls may sing, play the native (now the imported)
jew's harp, and chew betel-nut ; when they are
ready to receive, they sing the song which is the
previously arranged signal for the boys to come
nearer. The latter have, of course, been expecting
them, and now approach in groups. Soon the whole
village community is seated facing the girls, with
the exception of their local rivals, who resent the
intrusion and sulk, though custom does not allow
them actively to interfere with the proceedings.

It is evening by now, and the interesting stage
of the visit is approaching. The *katuyausi* party have
remained seated, nonchalant and detached (pl. 62).
The youths and older men stand facing them,
pursuing their own conversations with apparent
unconcern. Then banter and jokes begin to pass
from one side to the other ; the boys come nearer
the girls and the ceremony of choice begins.
According to custom, the initiative in pairing off
should come from the hosts, and each guest has
to accept any offer made to her as a matter of
etiquette. But, of course, definite preferences
between the outstanding individuals of each group
exist and are known. An unimportant boy would
not dare interfere with the pleasure of his stronger,
elder, and more influential comrade, so that in
reality the choice is largely based on anterior
intrigues and attachments. Each boy then
ceremonially offers a small gift to the girl of his
choice—a comb, a necklet, a nose stick, a bunch of
betel-nut. If she accepts the gift she accepts the
boy for that night as her lover. When the boy
knows the girl well he presents the gift himself. If
he does not, or if he feels too shy, he will ask
help of an older man, who hands over the offering
with the words, " *kam va'otu* " (*va'otu*—visiting
present, present of inducement), " So-and-so gives

it to you; you are his sweetheart." Very rarely does a girl refuse or ignore such a present; if she did, she would greatly offend and mortify the man.

After the boys and girls have thus been allotted in pairs, they all, as a rule, go to some spot in the jungle, where they spend the best part of the night chewing, smoking, and singing, each couple keeping to themselves. At times a boy and a girl will leave the main group without any attention being paid to them. Some of the boys may invite their sweethearts to spend the rest of the night in a *bukumatula* of the village, but usually this presents difficulties. All the arrangements associated with the *katuyausi*, as well as with the *ulatile*, are distinguished by complete decorum, and by the absence of all orgiastic elements. They are carried out, no doubt, in a less delicate manner in the southern villages than in the north, but even in the south they essentially differ from such orgiastic customs as the *kamali*, the *bi'u*, and the custom of the *yausa*, which will be described in the next section.

As far as I could gather, in former times no year would pass without some two, three or four *katuyausi* parties visiting a community. The first missionary had to ask for a special regulation in order to put down this " abominable abuse ". At present, as a result of the white man's interference with local custom, combined with his introduction of much worse immorality, the regulated and decorous custom of the *katuyausi* has fallen into decay. But even while I was in the Trobriands, parties of girls from Okaykoda visited Omarakana, and from Kaybola went to Kwaybwaga; also the Kwaybwaga girls avenged themselves on their lovers by going on *katuyausi* to Vilaylima. Early in my stay at Omarakana in 1918, a number of such guests came, at harvest time and ostensibly to admire the yams, and I was even able to photograph them and to watch the earlier part of the proceedings.

The return of a *katuyausi* party to their own village

is often a sad epilogue to a gay night. The girls try to enter the village and regain their houses unobserved. But they are not always successful. If the whole party is waylaid and caught, the reckoning takes place then and there. The culprits are abused, beaten, and, as I was told by several of my informants, sometimes actually violated by their own lovers in public. Several boys would hold a girl, while the rightful owner exercised his prerogative as a punishment. If this be true it is the only exception to that rule of strict decorum in public which is observed by all Trobrianders, with the exception of the people of Vakuta, Okayaulo, and some others of the southern villages.

8

YAUSA—ORGIASTIC ASSAULTS BY WOMEN

We now turn to the extreme south of the main island, and the adjoining island of Vakuta. We have already mentioned these districts, not very honourably, several times. They are in general distinguished ethnologically by a certain coarseness of character and habit which is displayed in many aspects of their life. In sexual matters they are undoubtedly much more crude than the northerners, and have practices which would offend the finer feeling for etiquette and decorum, if not for morals, of the latter. Also, in the past, these villages were on hostile terms with most of their neighbours.

The data which we have given above as to the orgiastic character of one or two forms of *kayasa* receive additional confirmation from another custom which used to be in vogue among these natives. The exact nature of the custom, its full details and its correct perspective, must unfortunately remain obscure. All I know about it is from hearsay, and the custom is so unlike anything which I have seen myself, that I am unable to add those necessary touches of life which depend on actual observation.

All districts in the Trobriands have the economic custom of female communal labour in the weeding of gardens. Since it is a tedious, monotonous activity, which requires little skill and not much attention, and can be best enlivened by gossip and company, the women work together at each garden in turn, until all the village plots are weeded over. As in all other exclusively feminine occupations, it is bad form for any man to come near them while they are working, or to pay any attention to them save on a matter of business.

Now this communal weeding when practised by women of the villages of Okayaulo, Bwaga, Kumilabwaga, Louya, Bwadela, or by the villages of Vakuta, gives the weeders a curious privilege.[1] If they perceive a stranger, a man from any village but their own, passing within sight, they have the customary right to attack him, a right which by all accounts they exercise with zeal and energy.

The man is the fair game of the women for all that sexual violence, obscene cruelty, filthy pollution, and rough handling can do to him. Thus first they pull off and tear up his pubic leaf, the protection of his modesty and, to a native, the symbol of his manly dignity. Then, by masturbatory practices and exhibitionism, they try to produce an erection in their victim and, when their manœuvres have brought about the desired result, one of them squats over him and inserts his penis into her vagina. After the first ejaculation he may be treated in the same manner by another woman. Worse things are to follow. Some of the women will defecate and micturate all over his body, paying special attention to his face, which they pollute as thoroughly as they can. " A man will vomit, and vomit, and vomit," said a sympathetic informant. Sometimes these furies rub their genitals against his nose and mouth, and use his fingers and toes, in fact any projecting part of his body, for lascivious purposes.

[1] Compare map.

The natives from the north are very much amused by this custom, which they despise or affect to despise. They love to enter into details, and to demonstrate by convincing mimicry. Local informants from the south confirmed this account in all essentials. They were by no means ashamed of their custom, regarding it rather as a sign of the general virility of the district, and passing on any possible opprobrium to the stranger-victims. Some of my local informants added that at the *yausa*, as this custom is called, women would throw off their fibre skirts, and naked "like a band of *tauva'u*" (evil spirits) pounce upon the man. He also added that hair would be torn from the man's head, and that he would be lacerated and beaten till he was too weak to get up and move away.

9
ACTUALITY OF ORGIASTIC LICENCE

Such is the natives' account of the *yausa*. What are the facts ? I never observed them at first hand ; partly because I was never able to go south at the time of weeding, partly because I was told that, even now, no stranger to the district would dream of going there at that season. Had I gone there in person, the negative result would have been ethnologically disappointing, the positive distinctly unpleasant ; so I abstained. When I tried, as always in such cases, to test the general statement by historical fact ; to find out how many people had been thus ill-treated—who, when and on what occasion—I invariably drew a blank. I always received the same answer : "Oh, people are so afraid that no one would dare to come near." The only concrete argument in support of its truth was that Misipelosi and Misimoytena (the Rev. S. B. Fellowes, the first Missionary, and the Hon. M. H. Moreton, the first Resident Magistrate) had been afraid to face the *yausa*, and that no *gumanuma* (white man) had ever dared to do so. I also was begged not to make any attempt to go south in the *yausa* season, and I obeyed the advice. And I thus became another proof of the reality of this custom to the natives.

So I was left with the principal question unanswered : is this custom, so exactly and minutely described, so prominent in the native interest, a fact in the sense that it has been really practised ? Or only in so far that it would be practised should occasion arise ? Or is it merely one of those customs which only exist in belief and in legend, and have never had any basis in actual occurrence ?

The most that can be said with certainty is that the *yausa*, if it happened at all, happened extremely rarely ; for even less in the olden days than now would a stranger have occasion to visit those inhospitable regions, which were on a hostile footing with all their neighbours and always ready to harm a stranger in one way or another. Taking the tradition at its lowest value, it is a standing myth, backed up by lively interest and a strong belief. It gives the women of the region a bellicose attitude, it surrounds them at weeding time with an absolute taboo, and gives their communal work in the garden the character of a sex privilege. The only parallel for the custom in folk-lore is the legend about Kaytalugi, the land of the sexually insatiable women (see ch. xii, 4) ; and in actual fact, the orgiastic nature, in the south, of the *kayasa* of the tug-of-war and of the erotic scratching, and the greater sexual coarseness to be found there.[1]

[1] In this matter parallels might be found perhaps among tribes further south on the d'Entrecasteaux Archipelago, and on the mainland of New Guinea. I was told by a white trader that on the southern shore of Normanby Island there are several orgiastic performances and festivities. On certain occasions a small hut with a very high front gable is constructed and passes under the name of " the entrance of the body ". In this hut a girl will remain during the festivity, boys will visit her semi-publicly, and have intercourse with her one after the other. Again, among the natives of the south coast, east of Crangerie Bay (the Da'ui and Su'au), several boys sometimes cohabit with one girl, each in the presence of the other ; a procedure which would be repugnant to the Trobriander's finer sensibilities. On the other hand, such tribes, for

It is characteristic that all the natives are interested in this custom and amused by it. Whenever any cognate or associated subject is discussed—gardens, communal work, the position of women, fighting or sex—the *yausa* is dragged in, and the natives embark on detailed and graphic descriptions, until it becomes the anthropologist's bugbear. Only once did I find it really useful. In one of the surly, reticent and coarse communities on the lagoon, there was special difficulty in finding suitable informants. One afternoon I was working with a group of unwilling informants, seated under a large banyan tree on the shore of the lagoon. It was one of those slack and sterile periods so well-known to the fieldworker, when he discovers only gaps and inconsistencies in his information, becomes cross and bored with his native instructors, and they with him ; when the imprisonment in a profoundly alien and emotionally meaningless cultural atmosphere weighs heavily and everything tempts to desertion at any cost. In such moods the lagoon landscape, so charming and so monotonous, symbolized this temptation, luring my eyes towards the dimly visible Koya, the southern mountains of the Amphlett and d'Entrecasteaux archipelagoes—where lay my road back to civilization. I looked at the scene on the beach (pl. 63) and envied some visitors from the south, who were due to sail home in a day or two. Conversation was flagging, and I could get nothing out of my informants, until we happened on the subject of the *yausa*. Immediately the natives became voluble and dramatic ; their laughter and animation attracted other people, and soon I was surrounded by a group of men, among whom I was

instance, as the Dobuans of the d'Entrecasteaux Archipelago and the Mailu, are considerably more restrained in sexual matters than either the Trobrianders or the other Southern Massim. Compare C. G. Seligman, op. cit., on the Southern Massim, chap. xxxviii, " Courtship, Betrothal, and Marriage," and chap. xliii, " Morals." Compare also my account of the Mailu in the " Natives of Mailu ", *Transactions of the Royal Society of South Australia*, 1915.

able to find some tolerably good informants for my future work. At the same time, I had a practical demonstration of the contrast between the way in which such a custom is represented by those who have it, and by those who do not. By the local men it was obviously caricatured as a shameful and savage habit ; the men's derisive laughter and amused exaggerations were a clear indication of how superior they felt to the benighted heathen who practised it. But the southern visitors, some of whom had come from Okayaulo and Bwadela, the home of the *yausa*, took, in a later conversation, a different view, showing no embarrassment whatever. They told me boastfully that no stranger ever dared to enter their district at that time, that they themselves were the only people free to walk about, that their women were the best garden-weeders and the most powerful people in the island. The two districts have been in contact for centuries, they speak the same language and have an identical culture. Yet neither the custom of *yausa* nor the mental attitude which characterizes it have begun to diffuse. The mental attitudes are correlated and fit into each other, but each district adheres to its own prerogative of superiority, which consists in contradicting the other's point of view.

CHAPTER X

LOVE MAKING AND THE PSYCHOLOGY OF EROTIC LIFE

IN the course of this inquiry we have been gradually approaching our main interest, and taking an increasingly detailed view of native love making. At first we merely made a general survey of the social organization and economic activities of the natives, in so far as they affect the relative positions of man and woman in the community. We studied their associations and their diversions, in private and in public, at work and at play, in magical and religious pursuits, as well as in everyday life.

Then coming nearer to our special subject we followed the typical progress of courtship, and found it leading to marriage and parenthood. In the last chapter we described certain customs which enrich and diversify the normal course of courtship.

In this chapter it will be necessary to observe the dalliance of lovers at still closer quarters. We have to learn the nature of their love interest and of the bonds which unite them.

Throughout my exposition, I have always attempted not only to state the norm, but to indicate the exceptions, to trace what might be called the amplitude of deviation, the margin within which people usually try, and sometimes succeed in circumventing the strict rule. As we proceed now to the study of more intimate behaviour, the elasticity of the rules becomes greater, and it grows more imperative to give a dynamic description of how a rule or an institution works, rather than how, in native theory, law and morality is supposed or desired to work.

In general, as the ethnographer moves away from the big fundamental, well-defined institutions—such as family, marriage, kinship organization, the clan, exogamy, the rules of courtship—towards the manifold details of personal life, his methods of observation must become more complex and his results less reliable. This cannot be remedied and, for our comfort, it may be remembered that, even in the most exact fields of human thought and experience, a theoretical result can only be verified within certain limits. The most exact of human observations is only approximate, and all that even the chemist or physicist can do is to state the limits within which his error is encompassed. When investigating integral institutions, such as marriage or the family, the ethnographer should, if he be doing competent and intensive field-work, rely on observation rather than on what the native informants tell him. But when dealing with the subtler phases of behaviour, this rule cannot, unfortunately, always be followed. In the study of sexual attraction and the growth of a passion, direct observation is always difficult, and at times impossible, and a great deal of information has to be collected from confidences and gossip.

The ethnographer must be alert to all that happens round him. He must patiently win his way into village life and make such personal friend-ships as encourage spontaneous confidences and the repetition of intimate gossip. He must check *ad hoc* statements by remarks dropped in more unguarded moments, explicating the implied and estimating the importance of reservations and reticences. For these are everywhere apt to be more illuminating than direct affirmations, and are especially so among these natives, whose keen sense of delicacy makes the roundabout and allusive way the natural approach to such subjects. It is possible to force them into speaking directly, but this always produces an artificial and false mental attitude, and exclusive reliance on such a method would lead to results which lack entirely the colour of real life.

Thus in the most delicate subjects the ethnographer is bound to a large extent to depend on hearsay. Yet if he resides for a long time among the natives, speaks their language and makes close personal acquaintances, he will be provided with sufficiently useful information. His material will be certainly better than if it had been obtained through the mechanical pumping of informants by the question-and-answer method at so many sticks of tobacco an hour.

Love is a passion to the Melanesian as to the European, and torments mind and body to a greater or lesser extent ; it leads to many an *impasse*, scandal, or tragedy ; more rarely, it illuminates life and makes the heart expand and overflow with joy. " Out of a full heart the mouth speaketh," and the cold ethnographer must industriously jot down confidences poured out under the stress of strong personal emotion. Also the gossip of those not directly affected by the event, yet sufficiently interested in it to talk, especially if it be untoward— *puisqu'il y a quelque chose dans les malheurs de nos amis qui ne nous déplaît pas*—is scarcely less valuable material for the investigator.

Spontaneous outpourings and village gossip dictated by genuine interest, records of past tragedies, and stories of erotic adventure, have yielded most of the raw material for the descriptions given in this chapter. And the direct knowledge of personal histories and interests made it possible for me to get a true perspective, to look at matters from the native point of view. I was even often able to go behind the explicit statements of the natives, observing, as sometimes happened, that their actions and feelings belied their words, and following up the clue thus given me.

The reader will remember the misadventures of Bagido'u, one of my best friends and informants (see pl. 64, and ch. vi, sec. 1), the animosities and quarrels between Namwana Guya'u and Mitakata (see pl. 3 and ch. i, sec. 2), the boasting Gomaya and his relations to Ilamweria (see pl. 39 and ch. vii, sec. 4). It would have been impossible for me to ascertain the rules of custom and the moral ideas of the natives without the subjective out-pourings of these friends of mine.

Side by side with such live material, I naturally always endeavoured to collect objective " documents " : records of historical events, samples of tradition, folk-lore and magic. Thus my general impressions, and strong but somewhat vague intuitions, were constantly checked and confirmed by data drawn from every sphere of tribal life. In fact, chronologically, the " documents " are usually obtained first, but their real comprehension can be gained only from the knowledge of real life.

The reader interested in methodology will realize that this exposition by cumulative versions—passing from institutions through the general record of a life history to the detailed and intimate analysis which follows—does justice not only to the nature of the material, but also to the manner of its collection.

After this digression on the method of collecting data and of their presentation, let us return once more to a Trobriand village and approach a group of young people playing in the moonlight, in festive mood and dress ; let us try to see them as they see each other ; follow up their attractions and repulsions. So far we have kept at a discreet distance from the intimate behaviour, the motives and feelings of lovers. More especially we have never attempted to spy upon their passionate caresses. Now we must try to reconstruct the history of a personal intrigue, to understand the first impressions made by beauty and charm, and to follow the development of a passion to its end.

I

EROTIC ATTRACTION

What is it that makes the boys look with entranced attention at one among a group of girls, moving rhythmically in a game or carrying baskets at harvest ; or that fascinates the girls in one of the dancers who lead the ring of swift runners in a *kaydebu* dance ? (See pl. 65.)   Is it possible for us to find out why a member of either sex is almost universally rejected and why another is sought after ; why one category is labelled as plain or unattractive and the other as fascinating and beautiful ? The European observer soon finds that his standard of personal charm does not essentially differ from that of the natives, when he has once become accustomed to the physical type and to the mannerisms of the Melanesians. Thus, for instance, the girl on plate 66 is universally regarded as a beauty, the one on plate 67 as a plain woman ; and with this opinion the reader will not disagree. And yet the latter is a well-built woman and of a pronounced Melanesian type.   But it would be perhaps difficult and certainly useless to convey native standards of beauty by means of European phrases and comparisons. Fortunately there are a number of native expressions, descriptions and categories which furnish some sort of objective material, and together with the ethnographer's commentary, may convey a fairly adequate idea of the Trobriander's ideal of beauty.

It must be understood that the problem of erotic charm with which we are now engaged, is different from that discussed in chapter iv, which was concerned with the motives which lead a Trobriand man or woman to enter upon matrimony.   In this connection, we found that personal preference, though a powerful inducement to marriage, was only one among others, some social, some economic and some domestic.   And even in the matter of personal preference, the erotic motive is not exclusive. A man or woman of mature age will choose a domestic partner quite different from the paramour who occupied the best part of his or her youth. Marriage is often determined by the attraction of character and personality rather than by sexual adaptation or erotic seduction. This fact, which has been already mentioned, I found confirmed in many concrete cases and in a hundred details. Only in the passing intrigues is simple bodily charm the principal attraction. Let us return then to our imaginary pair and try to find out what it is that they see in each other, as lovers.

When treating of love in fiction or anthropology, it is easier and more pleasant to imagine objects really worthy of admiration. In the Trobriands it would not be difficult to find them, even for one equipped with European taste and Nordic race prejudices; for, within a considerable variety of types, there are to be found men and women with regular delicate features, well-built lithe bodies, clear skins, and that personal charm which predisposes us towards a man, a nationality, or a race.

Verbal descriptions of a racial type are always weak and unconvincing. They may be couched in anthropometric terms and backed by numerical data, but these give little help to the imagination and could only stimulate a physical anthropologist. It is better for the reader to look at pictures, in this book and in other works where the Trobrianders have been described,[1] and to hear what the natives themselves have to say on the subject of beauty and its opposite.

The natives are never at a loss when asked what elements go to the making of personal beauty in man or woman. The subject is not only interesting to

[1] As, for instance, in C. G. Seligman, op. cit., and in *Argonauts of the Western Pacific.* For comparative anthropometric data concerning Melanesians and Papuans, cf. " A Classification of the Natives of British New Guinea ", *Journ. R. Anthrop. Inst.*, vol. xxxix, 1909, by C. G. Seligman.

them as to all other human beings, but it is surrounded by a rich folk-lore and therefore commands an extensive vocabulary. Many of their legends and songs have been specially composed to exalt some famous dancer or singer, and in such texts there are descriptions of ornament and dress, and expressive phrases referring to personal appearance. The charms used in beauty magic give instructive indications of the Trobriander's desires and ideals as do also the laments for the dead, and descriptions of the blissful life in Tuma, the land of the departed.

But although the renown and tradition of famous beauties is handed down for generations with rich descriptive details, it is difficult for the ethnographer to find a living model for his inquiry. Whenever I asked any of the old, and therefore expert, connoisseurs of beauty whether any living woman could match the radiant divinities drawn from their own and their father's memories, the answer was always in the negative. The Golden Age of real beauty seems to be quite over!

2

REPULSION BY UGLINESS, AGE, AND DISEASE

Let us approach the ideal of beauty by way of its negation, and see what, for the native, makes a person ugly and repulsive, and therefore impossible from the erotic standpoint. Deformity and disease in mind or body, old age and albinism, all, according to native statements, put a person beyond the pale of erotic interest. The expressions *migila gaga* (his face bad), or *tomigaga* (ugly man, literally man—face—ugly) are frequently in use, and often with the added comment: " No one would sleep with such an one."

Malformations are rare, and I myself cannot recall a single hunchback or congenitally deformed person. Through accident men may lose a limb :

kaykela ipwase (his leg has rotted away) ; *yamala ipwase* (his arm has rotted away) ; but the most frequent congenital defect is that of speech, which the natives describe by the same word, *tonagowa*, as is applied to idiocy and feeble-mindedness.

The bad or repulsive characters of folk-lore are also endowed with bodily deformities or abnormalities. Dokonikan, the most prominent ogre of Kiriwinian folk-lore, has several rows of teeth and cannot speak properly. Women covered with hair and men with disgusting bodies figure in some fairy tales.

As regards disease: sores, ulcers, and skin eruptions are naturally held to be specially repulsive from the viewpoint of erotic contact. Also to be so afflicted is the usual punishment for breaking certain taboos. Indeed, a number of such taboos are only observed by young men, and have no other *raison d'être* than to prevent their skins from being covered with sores. They might be called specific beauty taboos. Thus, it is dangerous to eat fish which is not quite fresh, or fish which has a very strong flavour. Some kinds of fish are covered with unseemly scales or spots, and these also are forbidden to young men and women. Young people must abstain from yams or fish which have been cut with a sharp instrument. Similar taboos have to be kept by men about to sail on an overseas expedition ; they will say that they must only eat " good fish " so that their faces may be beautiful.[1]

The unpleasant disease, tropical ring-worm, covering the skin with perpetually pealing scales, and very prevalent among Melanesians, is said to be a definite drawback, and persons with this disease would not be reckoned among the beauties even if their faces were fine. But it does not seem to form a positive bar to love-making, any more than to other pursuits. On the other hand, this repulsive and contagious affliction is a real inconvenience to

[1] Cf. *Argonauts of the Western Pacific*, p. 336.

the field-worker, who has constantly to deal with afflicted natives and takes a long time to become accustomed to it.

Old age is felt to be a serious handicap in affairs of gallantry. The contrast between repulsive old age and attractive youth is brought out clearly in myth. A hero, who is unsuccessful because of his elderly appearance, becomes rejuvenated and gets everything that he wants. First the marks scored upon him by the hand of time are ruthlessly enumerated : a wrinkled skin, white hair, and toothless jaws. Then the magical change is described : his rounded face, the smooth full lines of his body, his sleek, glossy skin, the thick black hair covering his head, the beautiful black teeth shining between vermillion lips. Now he can win the favours of desirable women, and impose his wishes on men and Fate. Such pictures are drawn in two of the chief myths of the *kula* (the ceremonial exchange), which plays such a great part in tribal life, and shows so many psychological affinities to their erotic interests. Similar pictures are also to be found in the myth of rejuvenation, in the ideas of the natives concerning a future life, and in one or two fairy tales.[1]

Obesity is extremely rare, and in its more pronounced forms is classed as a disease. Baldness is not infrequent. It is considered a blemish, and a certain amount of criticism is contained in the word *tokulubakana* (bald man, literally man-occiput empty-space). To a Kiriwinian, however, it is not so fatal as it is to his European contemporary, for wigs are still used in that happy island (pl. 68). Either a narrow band of hair is tied just above the forehead—a sort of fuzzy wreath—or a wig covering the whole head is worn. The wig is made by sewing tufts of hair on to a skull cap made of plaited fibre or string. The hair is easily obtained, for

[1] For the *kula* myth cf. *Argonauts*, pp. 307–10 and 322–4, and *Myth in Primitive Psychology*, 1926.

mourning customs demand that every member of the afflicted community, with the exception of the deceased's clansmen, shall shave off his beautiful mop of hair.

Cutting off the hair is not the only mourning custom which aims at the reduction of personal charm. The transformation in appearance imposed by mourning embodies, to a certain extent, the native idea of what is ugly. The shaven head, the body blackened with a thick layer of mixed grease and charcoal, colourless and purposely soiled dress, no ornaments and no scents—these are the outward signs of bereavement. The transformation undergone by a woman in mourning is shown in the frontispiece, where two girls, equally pretty under normal conditions, can be contrasted. In fact, the idea that the chief mourner, especially the widow, should be made ugly so that she may not attract other men, is explicitly stated by natives, and is also implied in the whole scheme of mortuary proceedings, apart from the alteration in appearance (see ch. vi).

The essential conditions of personal charm are now obvious : normal bodily build, health, absence of mental and functional disorders, strong growth of hair, sound teeth, and a smooth skin—all signs of vigour and of a good constitution.

But an important caution must here be entered. Natives speak with such horror about the various forms of ugliness, and repulsion is so clearly discernible in their behaviour that there is no temptation to doubt their word. In fact, in games and amusements, an albino, an idiot, or a man afflicted with skin disease is so completely left out of the fun that his loneliness and isolation wake pity even in the frigid heart of an ethnographer. Thus observation fully confirmed the verbal proposition in which all the natives are agreed, that all such people are absolutely debarred from sexual intercourse and that they have to resort to solitary means

of satisfaction. Nevertheless, I began to doubt its
validity, when, in the course of my field-work, this
very proposition was adduced as proof, with many
illustrative examples, that a woman can have children
without sexual intercourse (see ch. vii, 3 and 4).
Tilapo'i (to quote cases already mentioned) had one
child, Kurayana as many as six ; while a few albino
girls have been blessed with numerous offspring ;
yet : " No man would approach them, they are so
repulsive " was made the major premise of the
syllogism—though many of my informants must
have known better !

The more thorough research which followed
my realization of this discrepancy revealed the
astonishing fact that strong and, no doubt, genuine
physical repulsion does not prevent a Melanesian
from the sexual act. This probably has some connection with their manner of carrying out this
physiological activity. I was able to ascertain that
the ugliest and most repulsive people have, not only
sporadic, but regular intercourse. Orato'u, a
tonagowa—meaning in this case, not an idiot but
one afflicted with defective speech and a repulsively
deformed face—can always obtain favours from the
village beauties of Omarakana, the residence of the
paramount chief, whose henchman he is and whose
wives he is said to know intimately enough. The
albino seen on pl. 38 has had several notorious
love affairs. In most of the villages where I worked
I could mention a few old and thoroughly repulsive
women who were able, especially if they or their
husbands were of high rank, to obtain young and
attractive boys as lovers.

When I discussed this with my friend, the late
Billy Hancock of Gusaweta—a trader of exceptional
intelligence and one of the finest men I have known—
he told me that he had long ago arrived at the same
conclusion independently, and quoted from memory
a number of striking instances, in some of which
the women were repugnant, as he said, " far beyond

the toleration of a drunken sailor." He also mentioned the experience of a medical officer, especially appointed in the Trobriands for the treatment of venereal disease. This official was once baffled by finding all the boys in a community afflicted with very virulent and obviously recent gonorrhea, while all the women to be considered in this connection were as yet quite healthy. Finally he obtained a confession from one of his patients that he and his companions had copulated among others with a woman so old, decrepit, and ugly, that the medical officer had thankfully and unhesitatingly omitted her in his several inspections. It was found that she was the source of infection, and that she had for a long time been active in persuading boys to copulation. The boys, on discovery, tried to belittle the fact and to present the whole matter as a joke, but they were in reality rather mortified. The attitude of my informants when I confronted them with such and similar facts was also " ambivalent ". They had to admit that some people will copulate with repulsive women, but they treated it simply as the sign that such people are of unsound mind.

This was one more of the several cases in which I found how strongly convention (ideals of behaviour) obsesses the mind of the natives, but only on the surface and controlling their statements rather than their behaviour. Things about which he would not like even to speak, much less admit to having done, a native simply denies with consistency and vigour, although he is perfectly aware that they do happen, perhaps even under his own roof. *Tout comme chez nous !*

3

BEAUTY OF THE HUMAN FACE AND BODY

Vigour, vitality, and strength, a well proportioned body, a smooth and properly pigmented, but not too dark skin are the basis of physical beauty for

the native. In all the phases of village life I have
seen admiration drawn and held by a graceful, agile
and well-balanced person. The same generalization
can be inductively drawn from what we shall say
here of the native canons of perfection in form and
colour, bodily smell, quality of voice, and grace of
movement.

Since the natives have an extended view of each
other's bodies, there is no artificial barrier to their
æsthetic interest in them; nor are the various
elements in erotic fascination placed in the false
perspective which makes our full European clothing
the instrument of artificial modesty as well as of
disguised allurement, so that an estimation of erotic
values is difficult and complex, and is based on fashions
in dress as well as on the appreciation of physical
beauty. With this advantage over us, it is a notable
fact that their main erotic interest is focussed on the
human head and face. In the formulæ of beauty
magic, in the vocabulary of human attractions, as
well as in the arsenal of ornament and decoration,
the human face—eyes, mouth, nose, teeth, and
hair—takes precedence. It must be observed that
the head plays an important part in magic as an
object for admiration, and not as the seat of the
erotic emotions, for these are placed in the lower
part of the belly. For the rest of the body, the
breasts in the woman and build and size in the man
are most important, with the colour and the quality
of their skins. In certain magical formulæ, all the
limbs and portions of the human torso are
enumerated, besides the features of the face and
head. In others, however, only the latter are
mentioned.

The outline of the face is very important; it
should be full and well rounded. The phrases
imiliyapila (like the full moon); *imilibwata* (like the
round moon); *kalububovatu* (its roundness), appear
frequently in magical formulæ. The forehead must
be small and smooth. The word *talisalisa* (to

smooth) recurs in beauty charms. Full cheeks, a chin neither protruding nor too small, a complete absence of hair on the face, but the scalp hair descending well on to the forehead, are all *desiderata* of beauty.

Cosmetics are used on the face more than on any other part of the body. Facial painting (*soba*) is done in black, red, and white (pl. 76). For the red, either a compound of betel nut and lime is used or red ochre. Certain forms of clay, sometimes mixed with crushed coral, were formerly used to produce white; but nowadays European white lead has taken the place of this, though red is still usually made with native pigments. Black can be put on, either with simple charred coco-nut fibre or some other form of charcoal, or else with a mixture of this and an aromatic oil, prepared by cutting aromatic wood into small pieces and boiling it in coco-nut oil. The wood preferred in this preparation is called *sayaku*, and it is, I think, sandal wood imported from the eastern islands (Woodlark and Marshall Bennet). A similar though less appreciated wood, *kadikoko*, is found in the Trobriands and can be used for the same purpose. The strongly scented mixture is kept in coco-nut oil bottles and used for the tracing of fine lines on the face. The natives make a clear distinction between decorative painting (*soba*), which enhances their beauty, and smothering themselves in soot (*koulo*) in order to extinguish all their attractions in sign of mourning.

Having indicated the general character of facial beauty, let us proceed to the details. The eyes, as we know, are to the natives the gateways of erotic desire (ch. vii, 1); they are also, in themselves, a centre of erotic interest. Biting off the eyelashes, the custom of *mitakuku* as it is called, plays an important part in love-making. The expression *agu mitakuku* ("my bitten-off eyelashes") is a term of endearment. The eyes are frequently referred to in the magic of beauty : *mitayari* (shining eyes) ; *mitubwoyili* (lovely eyes) ; *mitapwa'i* (bright eyes). Eyes should be shining, but they should be small. On this point the natives are quite decided. Large eyes, *puyna-puyna*, are ugly. There is no special beauty treatment for the eyes, except, of course, shaving the eyebrows which, together with the biting off of eyelashes, leaves them singularly naked to European taste. Neither is any magic specifically devoted to their lustre and other charms.

Next to the eyes, the mouth is, perhaps, the most important feature. It plays a conspicuous part in love making, and its beauty is highly esteemed in native æsthetics. It should be very full, but well cut. Protruding lips (*ka'uvala'u wadola*) are considered as unattractive as pinched or thin ones (*kaywoya wadola*). Very ugly, I was told, is a hanging lower lip. There is a special magic of beauty associated with the mouth. It is the magic of *talo*, the red paint made of betel-nut, which is used to redden the lips.

The nose should be full and fleshy, but not too large. A nose, which the natives call *kapatata*, that is long, narrow and sharp, in short aquiline, is ugly. A beautiful nose is called *kabulitoto* (standing up nose), for too flat a one is also a serious blemish, and men or women so handicapped are called *tonapa'i* or *nanapa'i* according to sex. A nose-stick used to be considered æsthetically indispensable, but it is now gradually going out of fashion, and there is no magic associated with this ornament or its organ.

The ears must be neither too small nor too large— a safe rule to follow for all parts of the body, whether in the Trobriands or elsewhere. Ears that stand out from the head (*tiginaya*) are distinctly ugly. Every ear must be pierced at the lobe and ornamented with ear-rings. The hole is made early in childhood by placing on the ear a turtle shell ring which has been cut and the ends sharpened, so that the points gradually work their way through the gristle. The resultant small hole is then gradually enlarged until a considerable opening surrounded by a pendulous ring is formed in the lobe. This is filled with ear-rings of turtle shell and other ornaments, especially red discs made of spondylus shell. Such treatment of the ear is *de rigeur*, otherwise a man or woman would be said to have *tegibwalodila* (ears like a bush pig).

Teeth, in order to be really attractive, have to be blackened (*kudubwa'u*: literally black teeth, or *gigiremutu*: an expression for the process). This blackening is done by placing a piece of a special mangrove root against the teeth overnight and repeating the process over a long period. The majority of the Trobrianders do not, however, blacken their teeth.

Hair in its proper place is considered a great beauty, but, as we know, it must not be allowed to grow anywhere except on the scalp. Eyebrows are shaved off, the beard is never allowed to grow except by old men " who do not wish to have anything to do with women ". Hair is never pulled out; it is always shaved, in the old days with obsidian, at present with bottle glass. The hair on the head is admired when it is very full, and then it is allowed to grow into a thick mop of which almost every hair radiates from the scalp, in the manner so characteristic of Melanesia.

The natives distinguish black, light and grey hair (*yabwabwa'u*, *yadidaydaya* and *yasoso'u*). The albino is called *topwaka'u*, " man with white hair ", or *tososo'u*, " man with grey hair ". They further classify it as straight-to-wavy (*yasinare'i* or *yasisiye'i*) curly (*yasusaybulu*); thick and moppy (*yamtumwatu*); tangled and almost matted (*yakulupaki* or *yatutuya*). The two middle qualities are considered beautiful; but the straight-to-wavy and the matted kinds are not. As to the trimming and dressing of it, the really typical Melanesian mop, *gugwapo'u*, is the favourite mode. When it is cut round the sides and back and left long on top, giving the head an elongated cylindrical form, it is called *bobobu*. Sometimes when a man comes out of mourning, the hair is allowed to grow in the middle of the head, while the edges are kept shaved ; this is called *takwadoya*. Hair which is growing after mourning is called *sayva'u* while it is still short. Persons of rank in mourning have the privilege of leaving some hair at the back of the head near the nape of the neck (pl. 25). This grows into long strands which are plaited sometimes and are called *saysuya* (literally, " ringlets ").

Body hair (*unu'unu*—a word also given to the growth on yam tubers, on the backs of leaves and so forth) is regarded as ugly and is kept shaven. Only in myth and in fairy tale do certain people appear who are covered with *unu'unu* ; to the natives a grotesque and at the same time a perverse characteristic.

Hair dressing plays a great part in the personal toilet. Trimming is done by means of a sharpened mussel shell (*kaniku*) and the hair is cut off in tufts against a piece of wood. It is combed or teased with a long-pronged wooden comb (*sinata*) ; and one of the most important types of beauty magic is done over the comb. We have seen that teasing out the hair (*pulupulu*, *waypulu* or *waynoku*) is the centre of certain festivals (*kayasa*), which are really organized solely for the display of this beauty. Nails are cut and trimmed with sharpened mussel shell.

A slim, straight, tall body is much admired in a man. *Kaysaki*, like a " swift long canoe ", *kuytubo*, like a rounded tree, are both terms of praise, of which the latter shows that emaciation is not an asset. *Kaylobu*—well adorned, well trimmed—expresses the same idea. All three words occur in the lament of a widow for her young husband.

In women, also, a slim body without excessive abdominal development is considered desirable.

Kaygumita (slim), *nasasaka* (small-bellied), are words of praise. *Napopoma* (pot-bellied), *nasoka* (with the body like a globe-fish), on the contrary, express disapproval.

A woman's breasts are of special importance. The same word *nunu* is used to describe the female breast, the nipple in man or woman, the central portion of the male chest, and milk. There are a number of partly metaphorical, partly specific expressions to describe the æsthetic appearance of the female breasts. *Nutaviya* (like the *taviya*, a small round fruit) describes a full, round, firm formation ; and *nupiyakwa*, a word the etymology of which I was unable to trace, has the same connotation. *Nupipisiga* or *nupisiga* is applied to small, undeveloped, girlish breasts, which are considered less attractive than the first category. For flabby breasts the word *nusawewo* is used, a compound of the specific prefix *nu* and the word *sawewo*, to hang limply down, as, for instance, a ripe fruit hangs. Another apt simile is contained in the word *nukaybwibwi*, in which long, thin, pendant breasts are compared to the aerial roots of the pandanus tree. Breasts wrinkled and flabby with age are called *pwanunu*, the prefix *pwa* meaning deterioration and *nunu* being the specific noun. The meaning of this word has become extended to describe wrinkled skin in general.

Firm, well-developed breasts are admirable in a woman. Adolescent girls massage (*i'uwoli*) their breasts, which then may also be called *nu'ulawolu* (literally, massaged breasts). When a lover prefers his girl with small breasts, he will say, *yōku tage kuwoli nunum ; kwunupisiga* (" Do not thou massage thy breasts, remain with girlish breasts ").

Returning to physical beauty in general, it has already been mentioned that smoothness of skin and a full brown colour are much sought after. In magical formulæ, smooth objects with a pleasant surface are often mentioned in this connection :

fish without scales, trees with smooth bark, smooth, rounded shells. As to the colour, dark brown is decidedly a disadvantage. In the magic of washing and in other beauty formulæ, a desirable skin is compared with white flowers, moonlight, and the morning star. Pregnancy magic has already given us an example of this ideal of bodily perfection. But deficient pigmentation is not admired; and the insipid, pale yellowish-brown which is sometimes found, is as unpleasant to the Trobriander as to the European. Albinos, with their flaxen hair and long golden body fluff, their enormous freckles, as if something dirty and brown had been splashed over them, produce an unpleasant impression on European and native alike (pl. 38).

4

THE CARE OF THE BODY

The main care of the body is directed to cleanliness. The natives have an extreme sensitiveness to smell and to bodily dirt. *Kakaya* (bathing, or washing all over with plenty of water) is the first act in all ceremonial ornamentation, and is a frequent one at other times. The natives often rinse their hands and wash their faces, such minor ablutions being called *wini*. Washing before a grand toilet is always followed by anointing (*putuma*) with coco-nut oil, which gives a fine lustre to the skin and is also a strong and lasting deodorizer. If possible, some perfume is added to the oil: pandanus flower, *gayewo*, the aromatic *butia* blossom, and other scented flowers and herbs according to the season, are used for this purpose; as is the aromatic paint, *sayaku*, which has already been mentioned.

Dried and bleached leaves are the material for native dress, the men using the pandanus—or, to produce a garment of a finer quality, the areca palm—and the women, banana leaves (see pl. 69). Their dress is of the slightest, especially for men, who only wear a pubic leaf. This is a narrow band which covers the pubic regions, the lower part of the abdomen, and the back up to the first lumbar vertebræ. The band is attached, front and back, to a belt. Usually above this support the man wears another ornamental belt, made sometimes of valuable material. The pubic leaf is very carefully adjusted, so that the limited area which modesty demands should be hidden remains always precisely and carefully covered. Men very seldom take off their pubic leaf, except in the intimacy of their sleeping place. Only when fishing or bathing with other men is it removed. The word *yavi-* (pubic leaf) takes the same suffixed possessive pronouns as are only otherwise used with parts of the human body (*yavigu*, my leaf; *yavim*, thy leaf; *yavila*, his leaf; and so on). This gives a grammatical expression to the intimate union of this garment with the male body.

Women wear skirts made of narrow strips of vegetable fibre, variously prepared and coloured. A full description of the technology of Trobriand " models " and of feminine psychology in the always important matter of dress would lead to a voluminous dissertation. To be brief : women wear an underskirt and a top skirt. At home and among intimate friends and when at work, the top skirt is taken off, and only the petticoat remains (see pls. 9, 18, 21). This is usually shabby and always scanty ; but it adequately fulfils all the demands of modesty. The overskirts are full and sometimes very thick. At ordinary seasons and for ordinary purposes they are not artificially stained and show only their natural rich gold-and-silver colour of dried coco-nut or banana leaf. In times of mourning and during menstruation, slightly longer skirts are worn. For bathing or during rain, coco-nut fibre is preferred to other materials. The greatest variety of colour and form is seen in the gala skirts worn during harvest and at festitivies (pls. 13, 61, 69). These display radiant combinations of colour, all the range of materials available and great ingenuity in " cut ". The word for the female garment is *doba*, also used with affixes of nearest possession. In its compound form it changes some of its vowels, as *dabegu*, my skirt, *dabem*, *dabela*, and so forth.

The more important ornaments have already been mentioned incidentally. The natives adorn themselves with wreaths of aromatic blossom ; put flowers, especially the red hibiscus, in their hair, and aromatic herbs or long leaves and streamers into their armlets. Necklaces of shell and wild banana seed are worn, and armlets on the upper arm. All men and women wear ear-rings and belts.

The body, as distinguished from the face, is very seldom painted, and no tattoo markings are ever visible. I am told that girls at the time of their first menstruation are tattooed round the vagina. This tattooing is called *ki'uki'u*, and is done, according to my informants, for æsthetic purposes. Also men and women burn marks on their forearms, as an adornment.

One more personal charm must be mentioned— the voice. The good singer is only second in renown to the good dancer. The power of a beautiful voice is known and praised far and wide, and many instances of seduction by song are quoted. Perhaps the most notorious is that of Mokadayu, whose success with the fair sex culminated in an incestuous liaison with his own sister, one of the most beautiful girls in the village.[1]

As a background to Trobriand ideals of beauty, it may be interesting to hear the natives' comments on other racial types. Though other natives are generally considered less attractive than one's own tribe, distinctions are made and degrees of ugliness

[1] Compare *Sex and Repression*, 1927, part ii, ch. iv, and ch. xiv, 3, of this work, where the story of Mokadayu is given

gradated. The pure Papuan type from the Papuan Gulf and from the northern coast, who are now frequently seen in the Trobriands with white men, are undoubtedly classed as the least attractive. Their ugliness is chiefly ascribed to their dark skin ; it is, in fact, much darker than the Trobriander's, and has a characteristic chocolate tinge. Their pronouncedly frizzy hair and their strange manner of dressing it in plaits and fringes is also regarded as very unbecoming. Unattractive, too, are their prominent thin lips and their large, aquiline, almost Jewish noses, set in a long narrow face. These criticisms were made to me on the occasion of a series of dances performed by Papuan Gulf natives who had been employed on one of the plantations. Their dancing was genuinely admired, but not their physical appearance. The Dobuans with their dark skin, their thick-set build, and their short necks, are often made fun of by the Trobrianders. The more distant natives from the Eastern Archipelagos, the Southern Massim, receive much higher marks for beauty. In spite of the fact that they are more distant strangers to the Trobrianders than are the Dobuans, the natives realize that they are racially akin and say : " They are like us, fine looking."

Europeans, the natives frankly say, are not good-looking. The straight hair " coming round the heads of women like threads of *im* " (coarse pandanus fibre used for making strings) ; the nose, " sharp like an axe blade " ; the thin lips ; the big eyes, " like water puddles " ; the white skin with spots on it like those of an albino—all these the natives say (and no doubt feel) are ugly. It is only fair to observe, in justice to their good manners and personal urbanity, that they were quick to add that the Ethnographer was a meritorious exception to the rule. They always told me that I looked much more like a Melanesian than like an ordinary white man. They even fortified this compliment by specific documentation : thick lips, small eyes, absence of any sharp outline in the nose, were credited to me as assets. The only points on which they were discreet and honest enough not to compliment me were my forehead and my hair. I am afraid, however, that the Trobrianders are more polite than truthful, and it must be remembered that personal praise is by right of custom always repaid with a suitable gift of tobacco or betel-nut, which, rather than æsthetic conviction, may have been the motive of the compliment (see, however, pl. 68).

It is clear, then, that the Trobrianders prefer their own racial type, and that this is not mere parochial conceit, since they make reasoned distinctions between other types and give praise where it is due. Thus the Southern Massim they regard as their equals ; and are even ready to admit that the Eastern portion of the Northern Massim, the natives of Woodlark Island and the Marshall Bennet group, are their superiors in personal appearance. I may add that, in common with all strangers, I was less susceptible at first to individual differences and more impressed by the general type. But with greater familiarity, I also came to feel that too dark or too yellow a skin, too straight or too frizzy hair, a mouth as thin as that of a European, or an aquiline nose were features unpleasant in a Melanesian. At the same time I became able to appreciate beauty within the racial type and *de facto* always knew more or less who would be attractive to a native, and who not. Even the artificial transformations—shiny black teeth in thick vermillion lips, graceful scrolls painted in three colours over the face, flaming hibiscus blossoms in the thick black mop of hair, golden brown skins, glossy with coco-nut oil—ceased to impress me as mere grotesque masquerade, and I saw them as becoming adjuvants to personal beauty. After all, it takes us some time to become accustomed to the changing fashions of our own race and to detect beauty where at first we were only able to see caricature.

I still remember the feeling of slight surprise at the formula of beauty with which the old chief To'uluwa started my first discussion of the subject:

"*Migila* *bubowatu* ; *matala* *kuvikekita*;
"Face his (hers) rounded; eye his (hers) small ;

kabulula *kaykekita* ; *kudula* *sene*
nose his (hers) small ; tooth his (hers) very

kobwabwa'u ; *kulula* *sene* *kobubowatu*."
blackened ; hair his (hers) very · rounded off."

This terse sentence roughly summarizes the results of our study, and gives an approximate standard of personal beauty. It presents a blend of cultural values, biological impulses and racial preferences. The point of view can be understood by a European ; that is, if he can maintain the feeling of human or biological solidarity across racial and cultural differences, and a sufficient mental plasticity to become thoroughly familiar with the cultural and æsthetic standards of another people.

5

THE COURSE OF AN INTRIGUE

To understand the effect of personal charm on the native, it may be helpful to present a typical Trobriand love affair against the background of Western romance.

Love is precipitated with them, as with us, by the first shock received from beauty and personality ; but a world of customary and cultural differences divides the after-effects of this. The initial barriers preventing a rapid sexual intimacy between two people in love, which are so characteristic of all higher civilizations, for us endow the beloved with inestimable virtues and enclose him or her

in an aura of holy and mysterious desirability.
In men whose creative imagination is developed
beyond their practical sense of the realities, such
passionate attachments may lead simply to day-
dreaming and excessive shyness in the romantic
relation, or to such outpourings as we find in
Vita Nuova or Petrarch's Sonnets. This shy,
self-centred adoration, this extreme creative exaltation of the eternal-feminine—of the Beatrice or
Gretchen leading man into the presence of God—is
a real type of Western romance, standardized in some
of the highest works of art, but existing also in
many not gifted with the power of self-expression.
The reaction against this same artificially-fostered
mystery and the consequent idealization of woman,
is seen with opposite results in the invective and
indictment of Schopenhauer and Nietzsche.

The man in the street, who sustains the same
shock, does not write sonnets, but none the less he
surrounds the object of his serious affection with
a more temperate exaltation and worship. At
the same time his emotion finds practical expression,
and he seeks every opportunity for closer
acquaintance. If liking ripens into mutual love,
the affair will follow the customary course of courtship, engagement, and marriage. A man and
woman may be driven by natural passion to the final
consummation, athwart all social or moral rules,
but it is none the less true that real love leads men
and women of our culture, not to the direct satisfaction of the sexual urge, but to a gradual blending
of sensuous elements with the general spiritual
attraction. Personal intimacy in a full common
life, legally sanctioned, is the direct goal of our
romantic ideology, and the rest, including sexual
relations, follows as a tacit implication.

Let us turn to an average Melanesian youth
attracted by a girl who is not put beyond his reach
by the taboos of kinship, social standing, or too great
a difference in personal charm. In him, also, the

first impression produces an æsthetic and sensuous reaction which transforms its cause into something desirable, valuable, and worthy of strenuous effort. But the feeling of mystery, the desire to worship at a distance or merely to be admitted into her presence, is not there. The Trobriand boy has had many sexual experiences with girls of the same type as his new ideal; and, from childhood, the attraction of beauty and direct erotic approach have been intimately associated in his experience. He has not to stumble upon the final fulfilment of erotic desire, he immediately anticipates it. All the customs, arrangements, and codes of behaviour dictate simple, direct approach, as we shall see in the following description.

An interesting sidelight is thrown upon Trobriand courtship by the customs in other Melanesian communities, where sexual freedom is much more restricted, and where the gradual approach and something of romantic love exist. In the nearest ethnographic region to the south, the Amphletts, and in the next one to this, which is inhabited by the Dobuan tribe, prenuptial intercourse is regarded as reprehensible, and custom does not encourage the free mixing of children in erotic games nor open untrammelled intercourse between boys and girls, nor institutions such as the *bukumatula* (bachelors' and girls' house). From a limited experience in the Amphletts, I received the impression that pre-nuptial intercourse hardly exists at all, and in Dobu it is certainly much more restricted than in the Trobriands. Correlated with this, we find a number of arrangements which allow of a prolonged courtship and which are symptomatic of a love not specifically directed towards sexual intercourse. I was told that both districts have love songs and that the boys court by playing on pan-pipes or on a jews'-harp; also that boys and girls meet at games and in amusements for the sake of personal acquaintance and social intercourse only. During the later stages of courtship and before marriage, a boy is allowed to visit his betrothed at her parents' house, but there is no cohabitation, and only conversation and caresses pass between them. A similar state of affairs exists with the Western Papuo-Melanesian tribes, among several of whom I conducted more or less prolonged investigations. These data, however, I submit with caution, and they are in no way comparable to my observations among the Trobrianders. They are based entirely on statements obtained from informants *ad hoc*, and not on the spontaneous material which comes to hand with long residence in a country.[1]

The love-sick Trobriander, however, taught by custom to be direct in amorous pursuits, proceeds at once to the approved methods of approach.

The simplest of these is direct personal solicitation. From previous descriptions of sexual licence, we know that there are numerous opportunities for a boy to express his desire, or for a girl to induce him to do so (see ch. ix). This is perfectly easy within the same village community. When the two belong to different villages, certain festivals bring them together; they can speak to each other, and indulge in the preliminaries of love during games and dances, and in crowds; also they can arrange a future meeting. After that, by the *ulatile* and *katuyausi* customs, the meetings can be repeated, or one of the lovers may move to the other's village.

Another method is that of solicitation by an intermediary (*kaykivi*). This is used when the two communities are distant and, owing to the season, no personal approach is possible. A mutual friend, male or female, is begged to express the boy's admiration and to arrange for a rendezvous. The *kaykivi* is not, as a rule, lightly set in motion, for

---

[1] With regard to the Western Papuo-Melanesians, see my monograph on " The Natives of Mailu ", in *Transactions of the Royal Society of South Australia*, 1915, pp. 559–64, and the references there given to Professor Seligman, op. cit.

its failure, if this becomes public, draws down considerable ridicule on the solicitor. But if direct approach and the *kaykivi* are both for some reason impossible, the lover uses the most powerful way of wooing, that of magic, as the first step in his attack. It is sufficient to say in this place that almost all final success in love is attributed to magic, that both men and women believe in it deeply and trust it completely, and that, because of this psychological attitude, it is very efficacious. But a full account of love magic will be given in the following chapter.

Thus there is nothing roundabout in a Trobriand wooing; nor do they seek full personal relations, with sexual possession only as a consequence. Simply and directly a meeting is asked for with the avowed intention of sexual gratification. If the invitation is accepted, the satisfaction of the boy's desire eliminates the romantic frame of mind, the craving for the unattainable and mysterious. If he is rejected, there is not much room for personal tragedy, for he is accustomed from childhood to have his sexual impulses thwarted by some girls, and he knows that another intrigue cures this type of ill surely and swiftly.

6

Cases of Personal Attachment

Though the social code does not favour romance, romantic elements and imaginative personal attachments are not altogether absent in Trobriand courtship and marriage. This will become clear if we review the three phases of the love life of an individual discussed in chapter iii. In the easy erotic play of children, sympathies and antipathies arise, and personal preferences declare themselves. Such early sympathetic attractions sometimes strike quite deep. From several of my friends I learned that their marriage had its roots in a childish affection. Tokulubakiki and his wife knew and liked one another as children. Toyodala, whom I saw in despair after his wife's death, had been a friend of hers in childhood (see ch. vi, sec. 4). Similar conclusions can be drawn from observation of children and stories of their behaviour. In a small way they try to win, to impress, and to catch the imagination of their playmates. Thus even at this stage some elements of romance are mixed with the direct sexuality of their playing.

At the second stage, when boys and girls amuse themselves freely with love - making, personal preferences are even more pronounced. They change frequently, but their imagination and feelings are unquestionably engaged for the time being. It is not difficult to overhear boys discussing the beautiful girls by whom they are attracted. One boy will praise his fancy while another disputes her supremacy ; and, in this argument, the amorous yearnings of each will find expression.

As to concrete instances, it was rather difficult for me to collect any circumstantial data either about children or adolescent boys or girls. But at the later stage, where attraction ripens into desire for marriage and matters are treated much more seriously, I had several opportunities for observation. The case of Mekala'i, a boy temporarily in my service, has already been mentioned (see ch. iv, sec. 2). He was seriously in love with Bodulela, of whom it was notorious that she slept with her step-father. The boy was very deeply attached to her, and though there was no chance for him to possess her in the immediate future, and he was not even allowed to visit her, for months he nourished hopes and plans for ultimately winning her. He was also obviously concerned to appear before her as a man of importance and influence. Another boy, Monakewo, had a liaison with Dabugera, who belonged to the highest rank. He often bewailed his low rank, which he knew would prevent his marriage with her (see ch. iv, sec. 1). This disability he tried to write off by personal achievement. He boasted of his fine voice, his skill in dancing, his many abilities—some of which really existed—and how Dabugera valued these. When for a few days she was unfaithful to him, he would be evidently mortified; and on each of these occasions he wanted to persuade me to sail away from the island and take him with me, at the same time dwelling in imagination on how greatly she would be impressed by this decisive step, and on the fine presents he would bring back to her.

There are also cases on record where a man wants to marry a girl, does not at first succeed, but after a long period of yearning, wins his first choice. Sayabiya, a rather good-looking girl, had a lover from her own village, Yalaka, whom she was going to marry. Tomeda, a handsome man from Kasana'i, famous for his strength, his efficiency in gardening and his skill in dancing, made an impression on her and finally persuaded her to marry him. On my first visit to the Trobriands, I used to see a great deal of both of them, and found her one of the really attractive women, and him a very good informant. When I returned, two years later, he was living alone, for she had gone back to her former lover and married him (see ch. v, sec. I). Magic, of course, was blamed, but unquestionably it was a return to the first love. My friend Tomeda was extremely depressed for a long time, and used often to speak to me about his lost lady with obvious longing. I left the district and did not see him for some six months, but a few days before sailing from the Trobriands I met him, painted and adorned on his way to another village—obviously in the rôle of a hopeful suitor, a *to'ulatile*. When I chaffed him, he confessed smiling that he had a new girl whom he was hoping to marry soon.

Another tangled amour was that of Yobukwa'u, a son of the chief To'uluwa (see ch. iv, sec. I, and ch. v, sec. 5). His sweetheart, Ilaka'ise, was married, for reasons of state, to his father, as the youngest of some twenty-four wives. After this the young man took another girl, Isepuna, whom he meant to marry. But he was unable to withstand the proximity of his former sweetheart, and it became notorious throughout Omarakana, the chief's residence, that he slept regularly with his father's youngest wife. This deeply offended his betrothed. At the same time Yobukwa'u's younger brother, Kalogusa, returned from a year's service on an overseas plantation. He was struck by his elder brother's betrothed, Isepuna, and an attachment sprang up between them. The situation was very difficult, for it is an extremely bad thing to take away a brother's betrothed from him. But love was stronger than moral considerations. Isepuna broke with Yobukwa'u and became engaged to Kalogusa. They were married a few months after my arrival in Omarakana. It may be added that in the meantime, Yobukwa'u married a very unattractive girl, Losa, but gossip has it that he and Ilaka'isi are still lovers.

Almost identical was the story of Gilayviyaka, an elder brother of Yobukwa'u (see ch. v, sec. 5). He also had slept with Nabwoyuma before her marriage to his father. Subsequently he married Bulubwaloga, a really attractive lightly pigmented brown-haired woman from Yalumugwa, to whom he was deeply attached. This, however, did not prevent his nightly visits to Nabwoyuma. His wife did not relish these, and spied on him ; and he was caught one night *in flagrante delicto*, with the result that a very big public scandal quite overwhelmed him. He had to leave the village for some time, and his wife returned to her people. During my stay in the village, a couple of years after the event, he made several attempts to get his wife back, and was obviously feeling his loss keenly. On my last return to the Trobriands, I learned that he had signed on as a plantation hand, come home after a year, and died a few months before my arrival. The hopeless attachment of Ulo Kadala has already been mentioned (ch. iv, sec. 1). One case at least of suicide because of an unhappy love affair has been given to me by the natives.[1]

In these examples we find elements of what we ourselves mean by love : imagination and an attempt to woo the heart through the imagination rather than by a direct appeal to the senses ; steadfast preference, and repeated attempts at possession. In many of them, there is a pronounced appreciation of the personality loved and of its power to enrich life or leave it empty. These elements certainly appear in unfamiliar combinations and in a perspective strange to us. The attitude to sex is different, and therefore certain characteristic elements of the Western sentiment are absent. A platonic attachment would be impossible. Above all most of the personal initiative in wooing is replaced to a considerable extent by the practice of magic. Such generalizations can only be approximate, but the facts given in this chapter and incidentally throughout the book, will enable the careful reader to gauge the differences between love and love making in the Trobriands and in our culture.

7

THE COMMERCIAL ASPECT OF LOVE

There is an interesting side to Trobriand love that might either escape the attention of the superficial observer, or give rise to many misunderstandings. In the course of every love affair the man has constantly to give small presents to the woman. To the natives the need of one-sided payment is self-evident. This custom implies that sexual intercourse, even where there is mutual

[1] Cf. *Crime and Custom*, p. 95.

attachment, is a service rendered by the female to the male. As such it has to be repaid in accordance with the rule of reciprocity or give-and-take, which pervades tribal life, so that every gift, every service and every favour must be paid by something of equivalent value. The reward for sexual favours is called *buwa*, and the word is used with the suffix of nearest possession (*buwagu buwam, buwala*, etc.). This is perhaps merely a grammatical archaism. If not, it expresses an extremely close relation between the gift and both the giver and the receiver : in other words, that the gift is an essential part of the transaction, as indeed it is.

This rule is by no means logical or self-evident. Considering the great freedom of women and their equality with men in all matters, especially that of sex, considering also that the natives fully realize that women are as inclined to intercourse as men, one would expect the sexual relation to be regarded as an exchange of services in itself reciprocal. But custom, arbitrary and inconsequent here as elsewhere, decrees that it is a service from women to men, and men have to pay.

As to the size and nature of the gift, this varies with the type of sexual relationship. As we have seen, even small boys, imitating their elders in every detail, will give their sweethearts some small gift : a pinch of tobacco, a shell, or simply a blossom. Boys of riper years have to give a more substantial present : half a stick of tobacco, a betel-nut or two, and, from time to time, a turtle-shell ring, a shell disc, or even an armlet. Otherwise a girl would object : *Gala buwam, apayki,* " You have no payment to give me—I refuse." And his reputation for meanness would spread, and interfere with his future conquests. In the later and more permanent intrigues, especially when they grow towards marriage, it is usual to give substantial presents from time to time rather than small gifts every morning.

When marriage is concluded, payment for sexual intercourse becomes the complicated family affair described in chapter v, in which husband and wife, their household and the wife's family, father and children, children and maternal uncle are all involved. The personal account between husband and wife consists in her offering him permanent sexual accommodation, which he repays by all he gives to the children in love, care, and goods. The children, as we know, are regarded as legally hers, and not his. The early cares he bestows on the children, their education, and even his love for them are accounted for by this obligation. "The payment for sleeping with the mother," "the payment for sexual services of the mother" and similar phrases are repeated when the subject is discussed. Thus the commercial aspect of love also, and very definitely, obtains in marriage.[1]

It must, however, be clearly understood that the word "commercial" is merely used to describe the give-and-take principle in erotic relations, and that this principle is here, as in all other social relations, but one, and that not the most significant, aspect of them. Above all, it would be entirely erroneous to draw any parallel with forms of prostitution in higher cultures. The essence of prostitution is that payment is the woman's motive for surrender. In the Trobriands, love-making is as spontaneous on the part of the girl as on the part of the boy. The gift is a custom, not a motive. The institution is much more akin to our custom of giving presents to a fiancée or to someone whom we merely admire than to the institution of purely commercialized sexual services, which are the essence of prostitution.

[1] Cf. *Argonauts*, pp. 177, 178, where I have *incorrectly* classed the father's gifts to his children as "free gifts". The rectification of this error will be found in *Crime and Custom*, pp. 40, 41.

8

JEALOUSY

One more question intimately concerned with the problem of personal attraction remains to be discussed. Love strives not only for possession but for monopoly ; hence the strong emotional reaction of jealousy. It has been affirmed by several ethnographers of tribes with great sexual freedom, that jealousy does not exist among them. In support of this, nothing more is adduced than the simple fact of licence. But the connection between licence and the absence of jealousy is by no means self-evident.

In the Trobriands, in spite of considerable licence, jealousy certainly exists. A man who desires a girl will not easily give way to a rival, as the frequent quarrels and fights occasioned by sexual rivalry bear witness. Nor will a man who has established some rights over a woman, whether of marriage or of engagement, or merely of a liaison, tolerate any infringement of these. There exists among them, in fact, both the jealousy of passion and that colder type based on ambition, power, and possession. As we know, relations within the *bukumatula* (bachelors' and unmarried girls' house) are subject to a definite code, and the infringement of individual rights is deeply resented and considered reprehensible. As we also know, adultery is a grave offence, punishable even by death. Among young boys and girls serious enmities and fights have been known to arise from one encroaching on the preserves of another, and even among children, fights are occasioned by jealousy.

This passion, however, is, as are all others, susceptible to social influence. When custom demands that a man should surrender his sweetheart, and this can be honourably done, he will submit. This happens, as we know, in the case of visiting *kula* strangers, and of youths who are guests in a village where a death has recently occurred. Also, there are occasions, less readily condoned, where girls go on a *katayausi* or steal out of the village to meet an *ulatile* party.

I was impressed by what might be called the reverse side of jealousy. The way in which boys would complain to me about such custom-sanctioned defection; the way in which they dwelt on the subject and described it with apparent depression, but not without some morbid curiosity; and the insistence with which they would return to it; gave me the impression that there was for them some element of pleasurable excitement in the situation. Whether jealousy among the Trobrianders is an emotion with two almost directly contradictory feeling-tones which alternate, the one strongly unpleasant, and the other somewhat pleasurable and sexually stimulating, it is difficult to say. But one or two facts as to the relation between native women and white men throw additional light on the subject.

Thus it is a notorious fact that Sinakadi, an important but impecunious chief of Sinaketa, prostitutes his wives to white men. He is old now, and is said to have married a young girl specially for this purpose; but he began the practice long ago, according to common report, even before a government station was established on the Trobriands. One of his sons, now a young man, is doing exactly the same thing. A white trader told me that he knew a native who seemed very much attached to and extremely jealous of his comely young wife. This native used to procure girls for the trader. On one occasion when he was unable to find anyone else, he brought his wife, and waited for her on the doorstep. Such facts throw an interesting side-light on the working of jealousy in these natives.

The social, cultural, and directly emotional motives in jealousy will be more easily isolated by

distinguishing its several types with their corresponding sanctions. In the first place there is jealousy
which springs from infringement of rights rather
than from thwarted instincts or wounded feeling.
The taboo on the chief's wives is an example, and
in former times was extremely strict. Even in the
case of a very old man, who was neither attached
to his young wives nor even living with them,
adultery would constitute a capital offence. The
misconduct of To'uluwa's wives with his sons, a
case in point already quoted, and the adultery of the
wife of M'tabalu, would never have been condoned
in the old days. But even the wife of a commoner,
if caught *in flagrante*, might have been killed with
her lover. This kind of jealousy, arising from
purely social considerations, is also expressed in the
close watch kept over the widow by the dead man's
relatives.

In the second place there is the jealous resentment of infidelities which interfere with a permanent
relation. This emotional reaction is present, together
with the social one, in the concrete instances quoted
in the foregoing paragraph.

Finally there is the pure sexual jealousy from
thwarted impulse or desire which will impel a man
or a boy to violent and vindictive actions.

9

BEAUTY, COLOUR, AND SCENT IN LOVE-MAKING

We know by now how a Trobriand girl and boy
are first attracted to each other, how they come
together, how their intrigue develops, leading to
separation or marriage ; but we know little as yet
of the way in which two lovers spend their time
together and enjoy each other's presence.

In this as in all other aspects of Melanesian tribal
life, custom and convention dictate to a large extent
even the details of behaviour. Individual deviations
always exist, but they fall within a relatively narrow

range ; much narrower unquestionably than at our own culture level. A lover does not expect from his or her partner the improvisation of a love rhapsody, but rather a properly executed repetition of traditional routine. The places in which it is desirable to make love, the manner of making it, the very types of caress, are defined by tradition. Independent informants would describe exactly the same procedure almost in the same words.

The word *kwakwadu* is a technical term which signifies something like " amorous transactions " or " being together for purposes of love ". It would be easier perhaps to express it in German, as *erotisches Beisammensein*, or by the American colloquialism " petting party " or " petting session ". English speech habits are, unfortunately, refractory to stereotyped terminology, except in matters of morality. The *kwakwadu* has a wide meaning. It signifies a collective excursion, or party of several couples setting out on a love picnic ; the being together of two people who are in love with each other—a sort of erotic *tête-à-tète* ; the caresses and approaches before the final union. It is never used euphemistically to designate the sexual act. At a collective picnic some of the games described in the previous chapter are first played in common, and afterwards the lovers seek solitude two by two. We shall attempt to reconstruct the behaviour of a pair who have left such a party, or else started off alone in order to enjoy each other's company in some favourite spot.

The scrub surrounding the village, which is periodically cut for gardens, grows in a dense underbush and does not everywhere offer a desirable resting place. Here and there, however, a large tree, such as the *butia*, is left behind for the sake of its perfumed flowers, or there may be a group of pandanus trees. Pleasant shady places, too, can be found under an old tree in one of the groves which often mark the site of a deserted village, whose fruit trees, coco-nut-palms, and big banyans make an oasis within the stunted tropical undergrowth of recent cultivation. On the coral ridge (*raybwag*) many spots invite a picnic party. Cavities and hollows in the coral, rocks of queer or attractive shape, giant trees, thickets of fern, flowering hibiscus make the *raybwag* a mysterious and attractive region. Especially delightful is the part which overlooks the open sea towards the east, towards the islands of Kitava, Iwa, and Gawa. The roar of the breakers on the fringing reef, the dazzling sand and foam and the blue sea, provide the favourite surroundings for native love making, and also constitute the scene in which the mythical drama of incestuous love has been laid by native imagination (see ch. xiv).

In such places the lovers enjoy the scent and colour of the flowers, they watch the birds and insects, and go down to the beach to bathe. In the heat of the day, or during the hot seasons, they search for shady spots on the coral ridge, for water-holes and for bathing places. As the cool of the evening approaches they warm themselves on the hot sand, or kindle a fire, or find shelter in some nook among the coral rocks. They amuse themselves by collecting shells and picking flowers or scented herbs, to adorn themselves. Also they smoke tobacco, chew betel-nut, and, when they are thirsty, look for a coco-nut-palm, the green nut of which yields a cooling drink. They inspect each other's hair for lice and eat them—a practice disgusting to us and ill-associated with love making, but to the natives a natural and pleasant occupation between two who are fond of each other, and a favourite pastime with children (pl. 70). On the other hand, they would never eat heavy food on such occasions and especially would never carry it with them from the village. To them the idea of European boys and girls going out for a picnic with a knapsack full of eatables is as disgusting and indecent as their *kwakwadu* would be to a Puritan in our society (see also ch. iii, sec. 4).

All such pleasures—the enjoyment of landscape, of colour and scent in the open air, of wide views and of intimate corners of nature—are essential features in their love making. For hours, sometimes for days, lovers will go out together gathering fruits and berries for food and enjoying each other's company in beautiful surroundings. I made a point of confirming these particulars from a number of concrete instances; for, in connection with the question of romantic love already discussed, I was interested to know whether love making had direct satisfaction only for its object, or whether it embraced a wider sensory and æsthetic enjoyment. Many of the pleasures which enter into general games, amusements, and festivities, also form part of personal *kwakwadu*.

Of course, love is not made only in the open air; there are also special occasions for bringing lovers together in the village. In chapter iii, the special institution of the *bukumatula* and the more provisional arrangements of younger people have been mentioned. In the village, however, privacy is almost impossible except at night, and the activities of lovers are much more curtailed. They lie next to each other on a bunk and talk, and when they are tired of this, proceed to make love.

10

THE CONVERSATION OF TWO LOVERS

It is not easy to reconstruct personal conversations which in their nature take place under very intimate conditions and without witnesses. A question couched in such general terms as " What do a boy and a girl talk to each other about at a *kwakwadu* ? " is likely to be answered by a grin, or, if the man is familiar with the ethnographer, by the standard reply

to all difficult questions : *Tonagowa yoku,* " you
fool " ; in other words, " Don't ask silly questions."

From the spontaneous confidences of some of
my friends, however, I obtained some glimpses into
what passes during these *tête-à-têtes.* A boy would
often repeat, for the sake of impressing me or just
to give me some definite news, what a girl told him
and what he replied, or vice versa. There is no doubt
that the Trobriand lover boasts freely to his sweetheart and expects a sympathetic listener and an
enthusiastic response. I have already mentioned
how Monakewo used to tell me of the great
impression he had made on Dabugera and how
greatly she admired his exploits and virtues. Mekala'i
was equally certain that Bodulela was deeply
impressed by any achievements which he related to
her. Gomaya, a young chief of Sinaketa and an
incurable braggart, would tell me how his betrothed,
to whom he was plighted in infancy, would wonder
at his stories of personal excellence, of magical
knowledge and of overseas adventure. In fact,
whenever a Trobriander went into details about
his love affairs, the impression made on his mistress
would never be absent from his account, and would
be related to me, in native fashion, as fragments of
an actual conversation.

Gossip about other people's business, and
especially about their love affairs, is also a common
subject of conversation between two lovers ; and
on many occasions much of it ultimately came my
way, in that a boy would repeat what he had heard
from his sweetheart. For the rest, they talk of what
they are doing at that moment, the beauties of nature,
and of the things they like or do not like. Sometimes, too, a boy will vaunt his exploits in those
pursuits in which women do not usually participate,
such as *kula* expeditions, fishing, bird-snaring, or
hunting.

Thus a love affair may be set in a rich context of
general interest, both as regards mutual activity and

conversation ; but this varies with the intelligence and the personality of the partners. Ambitious, imaginative people would not be content with mere sensuous pleasure ; but the obtuse and limited would proceed no doubt, directly to the cruder stages—the usual caresses and the sexual act.

II

EROTIC APPROACHES

The place occupied by the kiss in South Sea communities is of general and perennial interest. It is a widely prevalent opinion that kissing is not practised outside the Indo-European horizon. Students of anthropology, as well as frequenters of comic opera, know that even in such high civilizations as those of China and Japan the kiss as a gesture in the art of love is unknown. A European shudders at the idea of such cultural deficiency. For his comfort, it may be said at once that things are not so black as they look.

To get at the facts and to see these in their right perspective, the question must first be put more precisely. If we ask whether lip-activities play any part in love making, the answer is that they certainly do. As we shall see, both in the preliminary caresses and in the later stages, the mouth is busy. On the other hand, if we define kissing more precisely as a prolonged pressing of mouth against mouth with slight intermittent movements—and I think that all competent authorities would agree with such a definition and with the proposition that this is the main erotic preliminary in Europe and the United States—then the kiss is not used in Trobriand love making. Certainly it never forms a self-contained independent source of pleasure, nor is it a definite preliminary stage of love making, as is the case with us. This caress was never spontaneously mentioned by the natives, and, to direct inquiries, I always received a negative answer. The natives know, however, that white people " will sit, will press mouth against mouth—they are pleased with it ". But they regard it as a rather insipid and silly form of amusement.

Kissing in the narrow sense is also absent as a cultural symbol, whether as a greeting, an expression of affection, or a magical or ritual act. The rubbing of noses (*vayauli*) as an act of greeting is rare, and never done except between very near relatives ; it is said that parents and children or husband and wife would thus celebrate their reunion after long separation. A mother who is constantly petting her small child, will frequently touch it with her cheek or her lips ; she will breathe upon it, or, putting her open mouth against its skin, caress it gently. But the exact technique of kissing is not used between mother and child, and in no form is it so conspicuous with them as with us.

The absence of kissing in the narrower sense brings us to a deeper difference in love making. The natives, I am convinced, never indulge in erotic caresses as a self-sufficient activity ; that is, as a stage in love making which covers a long period of time before full bodily union is accomplished. This is a local and not a racial character, for I am equally convinced (see above) that among other Melanesians, in Dobu and probably among the Motu, in the Sinaugolo and Mailu tribes, engaged couples do meet, lie together, and caress each other without cohabitation.

The comparison, however, cannot be satisfactory, for my knowledge of the latter tribes is much less complete than in the case of the Trobriands, and so I can only suggest a subject for further research. It is extremely important to know whether the nature of preliminary love is correlated with the level of culture, or with the social regulation of it—above all, with the moral restrictions condemning prenuptial intercourse.

We have spoken rather fully about kissing, to

satisfy a general curiosity on this point. Let us now observe the behaviour of two lovers alone on their bunk in the *bukumatula*, or in a secluded spot in the *raybwag* or jungle. A mat is usually spread on the boards or on the earth, and, when they are sure of not being observed, skirt and pubic leaf are removed. They may at first sit or lie side by side, caressing each other, their hands roaming over the surface of the skin. Sometimes they will lie close together, their arms and legs enlaced. In such a position they may talk for a long time, confessing their love with endearing phrases, or teasing each other (*katudabuma*). So near to each other, they will rub noses. But though there is a good deal of nose-rubbing, cheek is also rubbed against cheek, and mouth against mouth. Gradually the caress becomes more passionate, and then the mouth is predominantly active ; the tongue is sucked, and tongue is rubbed against tongue ; they suck each other's lower lips, and the lips will be bitten till blood comes ; the saliva is allowed to flow from mouth to mouth. The teeth are used freely, to bite the cheek, to snap at the nose and chin. Or the lovers plunge their hands into the thick mop of each other's hair and tease it or even tear it. In the formulæ of love magic, which here as elsewhere abound in over-graphic exaggeration, the expressions, " drink my blood " and " pull out my hair " are frequently used (see next chapter). This sentence, volunteered by a girl's sweetheart, describes his erotic passion :

Binunu   vivila   dubilibaloda,   bigadi ;
She sucks woman lower lip (ours), she bites ;

tagiyu   bimwam.
we spit, she drinks.

Erotic scratches are an even more direct way of hurting and of drawing blood. We have already spoken of these as the conventional invitation of a girl to a boy. We also described their place in tribal festivities (ch. ix, sec. 5). But they are also a part of intimate love making, and a mutual expression of passion :

Tayobobu,	*tavayauli,*		*takenu deli* ;

We embrace, we rub noses, we lie together ;

bikimali	*vivila*	*otubwaloda,*	*ovilavada*

she scratches woman on back (ours), on shoulders
　　　　　　　　　　　　　　　　　　　　　(ours) ;

sene	*bwoyna,*	*tanukwali,*	*bitagwalayda*

very much good, we know, she loves us

senela.

very much indeed.

On the whole, I think that in the rough usage of passion the woman is the more active. I have seen far larger scratches and marks on men than on women ; and only women may actually lacerate their lovers as in the case mentioned in chapter ix, section 5. The scratching is carried even into the passionate phases of intercourse. It is a great jest in the Trobriands to look at the back of a man or a girl for the hall-marks of success in amorous life. Nor have I ever seen a comely girl or boy without some traces of *kimali* in the proper places. Subject to general rules of good taste and specific taboo (see ch. xiii), the *kimali* marks are a favourite subject for jokes ; but there is also much secret pride in their possession.

Another element in love making, for which the average European would show even less understanding than for the *kimali,* is the *mitakuku,* the biting off of eyelashes. As far as I could judge from descriptions and demonstrations, a lover will tenderly or passionately bend over his mistress's eyes and bite off the tip of her eyelashes. This, I was told, is done in orgasm as well as in the less passionate preliminary stages. I was never quite able to grasp either the mechanism or the sensuous value of this caress. I have no doubt, however, as to its reality, for I have not seen one boy or girl in the Trobriands with the long eyelashes to which they are entitled by nature. In any case, it shows that the eye to them is an object of active bodily interest. Still less enthusiasm will probably be felt by the romantic European towards the already mentioned custom of catching each other's lice and eating them. To the natives, however, it is a pastime, which, while pleasant in itself, also establishes an exquisite sense of intimacy.

12

THE ACT OF SEX

The following is a condensed description of the whole process of love making, with several characteristic incidents, given me by my friend Monakewo :

Takwakwadu : *dakova,* *kadiyaguma,*
We make love : our fire, our lime gourd,

kaditapwaki : *kada* *gala, mwasila. Bitala,*
our tobacco ; food (ours) no, shame. We go,

tala *kaytala* *ka'i kayviava* ; *tasisu,*
we go (for) one (wood) tree tree big ; we sit,

takakakutu ; *taluki* *vivila* :
we louse and eat ; we tell to woman :

" *takayta.*" *Biwokwo,*
" we copulate " (let us copulate). It is finished,

bitala ovalu ; *ovalu* *tala* *obukumatula,*
we go to village ; in village we go to bachelors' house,

takenu tabigatona. *Kidama* *kadumwaleta,*
we lie, we chatter. Supposing we are alone,

taliku *yavida,* *biliku* *dabela*
we undo pubic leaf ours she undoes skirt (hers)

tamasisi.
we sleep.

This may be freely rendered : " When we go on a love making expedition we light our fire ; we take

our lime gourd (and chew betel-nut), we take our
tobacco (and smoke it). Food we do not take, we
would be ashamed to do so. We walk, we arrive at
a large tree, we sit down, we search each other's heads
and consume the lice, we tell the woman that we
want to copulate. After it is over we return to the
village. In the village we go to the bachelors' house,
lie down, and chatter. When we are alone he takes
off the pubic leaf, she takes off her fibre skirt : we
go to sleep."

With regard to the act itself, perhaps the most
noteworthy feature is the position.

The woman lies on her back, the legs spread and
raised, and the knees flexed. The man kneels
against her buttocks, her legs resting on his hips.
The more usual position, however, is for the man
to squat in front of the woman and, with his hands
resting on the ground, to move towards her or, taking
hold of her legs, to pull her towards him. When
the sexual organs are close to each other the insertion
takes place. Again the woman may stretch her legs
and place them directly on the man's hips, with his
arms outside them, but the far more usual position
is with her legs embracing the man's arms, and
resting on the elbows.

An interesting text gives the description of both
methods :

Kidama	*vivila*	*sitana*	*ikanupwagega* ;
Supposing	woman	a little bit	she lies open-(legged) ;

kaykela	*bima*	*ogipomada.*
legs hers	it comes	on our hips.

Kidama	*ikanupwagega*	*senela,*
Supposing	she lies open (-legged)	very much indeed,

ikanubeyaya,	*kaykela*	*bima*	*o*
she lies right open,	leg hers	it comes	on

mitutugu	*kaylavasi.*
end	mine elbow.

Which may be rendered :

" When the woman opens her legs only a little, her legs come (i.e. rest) on my hips ; when she lies with legs spread out very much, lies right open, her legs rest on my elbows."

Congress is sometimes effected in a reclining position. Lying side by side, with the lower limbs pressed against each other, the woman places her upper leg on top of the man, and the insertion is made. This mode, which is less popular, is used at night in the *bukumatula* (bachelors' house). It is less noisy, as the natives say, and requires less space ; and is done in order not to wake up the other inmates of the house (see ch. iii, sec. 4).

No other positions are used. Above all, the natives despise the European position and consider it unpractical and improper. The natives, of course, know it, because white men frequently cohabit with native women, some even being married to them. But, as they say : " The man overlies heavily the woman ; he presses her heavily downwards, she cannot respond (*ibilamapu*)."

Altogether the natives are certain that white men do not know how to carry out intercourse effectively. As a matter of fact, it is one of the special accomplishments of native cook-boys and servants who have been for some time in the employ of white traders, planters, or officials, to imitate the copulatory methods of their masters. In the Trobriands, Gomaya was perhaps the best actor in this respect. He still remembered a famous Greek buccaneer (Nicholas Minister was the name he went by among other beachcombers), who had lived in the islands even before the establishment of the government station. Gomaya's performance consisted in the imitation of a very clumsy reclining position, and in the execution of a few sketchy and flabby movements. In this the brevity and lack of vigour of the European performance were caricatured. Indeed, to the native idea, the white man achieves orgasm far too quickly ; and there seems to be no doubt that the Melanesian takes a much longer time and employs a much greater amount of mechanical energy to reach the same result. This, together with the handicap of the unfamiliar position, probably accounts for the complaints of white men that native girls are not responsive. Many a white informant has spoken to me about perhaps the only word in the native language which he ever learned, *kubilabala* (" move on horizontally "), repeated to him with some intensity during the sexual act. This verb defines the horizontal motion during sexual intercourse, which should be mutual. The noun *bilabala*, originally means a horizontally lying log; and *bala* as a root or prefix, conveys a general sense of the horizontal. But the verb, *bilabala*, does not convey the immobility of a log; on the contrary, it gives the idea of horizontal motion. The natives regard the squatting position as more advantageous, both because the man is freer to move than when kneeling, and because the woman is less hampered in her responsive movements—*bilamapu*—a compound of *bila*, from *bala*, horizontal, and *mapu*, repay or respond. Also in the squatting position the man can perform the treading motion (*mtumuta*), which is a useful dynamic element in successful copulation. Another word, *korikikila*, implies at the same time rubbing and pushing, a copulatory motion.

As the act proceeds and the movements become more energetic, the man, I was told, waits until the woman is ready for orgasm. Then he presses his face to the woman's, embraces her body and raises it towards him, she putting her arms round him at the same time and, as a rule, digging her nails into his skin. The expression for orgasm is *ipipisi momona* = the seminal fluid discharges. The word *momona* signifies both the male and female discharge; as we know, the natives do not make any sharp distinction between male semen and the glandular secretions of a woman, at least, not as regards their respective functions. The same expression *ipisi momona* is also applied to (male or female) nocturnal pollution. The word for onanistic ejaculation is *isulumomoni*, "it boils over sexual fluid." Male masturbation is called *ikivayli kwila*—"he manipulates penis"; female masturbation is described in concrete phrases and has no specific name.

An interesting personal account was given to me by Monakewo and illustrates some of the points just mentioned. It was hardly discreet of him to speak of his mistress by name; but the ethnographer's love for the concrete instance may excuse my not emending it.

Bamasisi deli   Dabugera ;   bayobobu,
I   sleep   together   Dabugera ;   I embrace,

bavakayla,   bavayauli. Tanunu dubilibaloda,
I hug all length, I rub noses. We suck lower   lips
                                                    ours,

pela   bi'ulugwalayda ;   mayela   tanunu ;
because we feel excited ;   tongue his we suck ;

tagadi kabulula ; tagadi kala gabula ; tagadi
we bite nose his ;   we bite   his   chin ;   we bite

kimwala ;   takabi   posigala,
jaw (cheek) his ; we take hold (caress) armpit his,

visiyala. Bilivala minana :   " O didakwani,
groin his. She says this woman : " O it itches,

lubaygu,   senela ;   kworikikila
lover mine,   very much indeed ; rub and push

tuvayla,   bilukwali   wowogu—
again,   it feels pleasant   body mine—

kwopinaviyaka,   nanakwa   bipipisi
do it vigorously, quick   (so that) it squirts

momona :—   kwalimtumutu tuvayla bilukwali
sexual fluid :— tread   again   it feels pleasant

wowogu.
body mine.

THE ACT OF SEX

Free Translation

" When I sleep with Dabugera I embrace her,
I hug her with my whole body, I rub noses with
her. We suck each other's lower lip, so that we are
stirred to passion. We suck each other's tongues,
we bite each other's noses, we bite each other's
chins, we bite cheeks and caress the armpit and the
groin. Then she will say : ' O my lover, it itches very
much . . . push on again, my whole body melts with
pleasure . . . do it vigorously, be quick, so that the
fluids may discharge . . . tread on again, my body
feels so pleasant.' "

The same informant gave me the following samples
of a conversation which would occur after the act,
when the two rested in each other's arms :

" *Kayne*   *tombwaylim*   *yaygu ?* "
" Whether sweetheart thine I ? "

" *Mtage !*   *nabwayligu*   *yoku—* *sene*
" Yes !   sweetheart mine thou— very much

magigu ;   *tuta, tuta, bitakayta* ;   *sene*
desire mine ; time, time, we copulate ; very much

migimbwayligu   *migim*   *tabuda !* "
face yours beloved by me face thine cross-cousins ! "

" *Gala* *magigu*   *bukuyousi*   *nata* *vivila*
" No   desire mine   you get hold   one   woman

nava'u ;   *yoku wala,*   *yaygu.*"
new woman ; thou indeed,   I."

" Am I thy sweetheart ? " " Yes, thou art my
sweetheart ; I love thee very much ; always,
always we shall cohabit. I love thy face very much ;
it is that of a cross-cousin (the right woman for me)."
" I do not desire that thou shouldest take a new
woman ; just thou and I."

I was informed that sexual relations between
married people would be on the same lines, but, from
the following text, it is clear that passion ebbs with
time.

Vigilava'u   *imasisisi*   *kwaytanidesi*
Married newly   they sleep   single one

kabasi ;   *bimugo*   *vayva'i*   *bikwaybogwo,*
bed theirs ;   it matures   matrimony   it is old,

kwayta kabala,   *kwayta kabada.*   *Bisala'u*
one   bed her,   one   bed ours.   It is energetic

uwasi,   *magisi*   *bikaytasi,*   *bikenusi*
body theirs,   desire theirs   they copulate,   they lie

deli   *bikamitakukusi*   *bivayaulasi,*
together   they bite eyelashes   they rub noses,

bigedasi.
they bite.

" Newly married people sleep together in one bed. When matrimony has matured, when it has become old, she sleeps in one bed, and we (i.e. the husband) sleep in another. When they feel sexually vigorous they want to cohabit ; then they lie together, they bite their eyelashes, they rub their noses, they bite each other."

Here my informant, Tokulubakiki, a married man, tries to convey the idea that even long-married persons can behave at times as lovers.

In conclusion,[1] I should like to draw the attention of the reader to the data supplied by Dr W. E. Roth and other informants concerning the sexual life of the aborigines of Australia.[2] The subject is of considerable importance as the mechanism is very characteristic of the whole nature of erotic approach. The manner in which the Queensland aborigines copulate closely resembles that described in this chapter. In both regions the act can be so carried out that there is the minimum of bodily contact. I think that this to a

[1] Compare also what has been said about native ideas concerning the anatomy and physiology of procreation and the psycho-physiological mechanism of falling in love, chapter vii.
[2] Dr W. E. Roth, *Ethnological Studies among the North-West Central Queensland Aborigines*, 1897, and H. Basedow, in *J.R.A.I.*, 1927, on "Subincision and Kindred Rites of the Australian Aboriginal," pp. 151–156.

great extent accounts for the undiscriminating way in which young and handsome boys will sometimes fornicate with old and repulsive women. On the other hand, where love exists, the man can bend over the woman or the woman raise herself to meet him and contact can be as full and intimate as is desired.

CHAPTER XI

THE MAGIC OF LOVE AND BEAUTY

PERHAPS nothing is so akin to the mysterious and stirring condition which we call falling in love, as that mystic expectancy of miraculous intervention and of benevolent and unexpected happenings which comes to all men at certain psychological moments and forms the foundation of the human belief in magic. There is a desire in every one of us to escape from routine and certainty, and it can be said, without exaggeration, that to most men nothing is more cheerless and oppressive than the rigidity and determination with which the world runs; and nothing more repugnant than the cold truths of science, which express and emphasize the determination of reality. Even the most sceptical at times rebel against the inevitable causal chain, which excludes the supernatural and, with it, all the gifts of chance and good fortune. Love, gambling and magic have a great deal in common.

In a primitive community, not yet in bond to science, magic lies at the root of innumerable beliefs and practices. *Megwa*, which may be almost exactly rendered by our word " magic ", is, to the Trobriander, a force residing in man, transmitted to him from generation to generation through the medium of tradition. This force can only become active by the performance of a ritual appropriate to the occasion, by the recital of proper incantations, and by the observance of specific taboos. In all matters relating to love, it is of fundamental importance. Magic can endow with charm and engender love; magic can alienate affection in consort or lover; and magic can produce or enhance personal beauty.

I

THE IMPORTANCE OF BEAUTY

The magic of which the purpose is so to increase personal attractiveness that the performer may become erotically irresistible to some one member of the opposite sex, is but one among several kinds of beauty magic. Personal appearance and charm are not valued on amorous grounds only. A woman in her first pregnancy, as we know, is subject to an elaborate ritual, with spells to enhance her bodily beauty, which is in no way intended to make her attractive to men. She is sexually taboo to her own husband ; and the idea of adultery under such circumstances is, without exaggeration, morally repulsive to the natives. Again, a beauty magic has been described elsewhere which is performed at a certain stage in an overseas expedition.[1] This has no erotic reference—indeed love making, on such occasions, is often taboo—but its purpose is to make the personal charm of the visitors so irresistible that they will be offered many gifts of valuable ornaments. The heroes of ancestral days, who make themselves beautiful for reasons which have nothing to do with sex, figure in the mythology of the *kula* (*Argonauts*, ch. xii). It is important that the practice of beauty magic to a directly sexual end should be placed in its proper setting in this general and intense interest in personal charm.

2

CEREMONIAL OCCASIONS OF BEAUTY MAGIC

In our description of the opportunities given by festive occasions for mutual admiration and contact, the importance of beauty and skill in dancing, and of " deportment " was made clear. Beauty magic

---

[1] See *Argonauts of the Western Pacific*, ch. xiii, sec. 1, and especially pp. 335–6. Compare also footnote on p. 186 of the present volume.

is a part of the personal preparation for all big
festivals; special charms are recited over certain
parts of the body during the care and cleansing of
them, and during ornamentation. This is always
done on the last and culminating day of the period
of festival dancing (*usigola*) or of competitive games
(*kayasa*), during the third feast in which they
terminate (ch. ix, secs. 3 and 4). The tension,
interest and personal animosities characteristic of
these competitive displays must be realized before
we can understand the nature and importance of
the beauty ceremonial; and we shall, therefore,
give a short account of the proceedings as ritual
observances, but without returning to the games
and amusements round which they centre (see
above, ch. ix, sec. 2).

The festive period, which lasts twenty-eight days,
always begins, as we know, at the full moon after
the return of the ancestral spirits. It is opened by
a ceremonial distribution of food (*sagali*) (pls. 71
and 72). A *sagali* is a very important institution
in the Trobriands; it accompanies most ceremonial
occasions, such as mortuary rites, commemoration
feasts, competitive enterprises and the annual season
of amusement. The mortuary *sagali* (distributions),
which are the most important, are based upon the
division into clans and sub-clans (see ch. vi,
sec. 4, and ch. xiii, sec. 5), since members of only
one clan always act as distributors, men of the
remaining clans receiving the food. At other times
the apportionment of the food follows some other
sociological principle. In all cases, however, it
is the headman of the local community who officiates
as " master of the distribution " (*tolisagali*). He
and his kinsmen arrange the allotment of each heap
of yams, moving among them, discussing and
memorizing (pl. 71). After that the same committee
slowly walk from one heap to the other and the
master or his spokesman calls out the name or
description of the recipient. When this has been

done, the men move away from the place and, after a time, the women belonging to each recipient collect the yams in baskets and carry them to their store houses (pl. 72). In a small *sagali*, such as is held within the community at the beginning of a dancing or playing season, the duty of providing the food invariably falls on the master and his kinsmen, while the renown (*butura*) of the distribution goes to their credit, and those who receive food are responsible to them for the success of the entertainments which follow.

The distribution in fact imposes an obligation on all participants to go on steadily with the dance, game, or whatever special display has been chosen, for the whole period. In an *usigola* (dancing period) each heap of food would be allotted according to its size, and be given to a special class of performer. One of the largest would go to the leaders of the round dance (*tokolimatala*). The three men who perform the complicated figure dance, the solemn *kasawaga*, receive an equally big portion. The singers (*tokwaypo'u*), a body of no mean importance, also have their special place in the distribution. Smaller heaps of different sizes are given to the drummers, the mutes in the figure dance, the boys who catch the iguana for the drumskin, and to all the rest of the villagers, according to the part they play in the proceedings. In a *sagali* (distribution), therefore, the respective importance of each group is emphasized and this causes a certain amount of tension and jealousy, and some little boasting.

On the first day, magic is performed over a conch-shell and over food. The conch-shell is blown on that day and also during the dance ; the food is buried wherever a road enters the village. Both rites are meant magically to enhance the splendour of the performance. The charmed conch-shell announces the coming display with the thrilling ostentation of magical power. The burial of the food expresses the desire for plenty within the village, is a symbol of it, and is believed to effect it. I was unable to obtain the formula of this magic, so my information is but approximate.

After these ceremonies, the dancing period begins. At first, there is much to do in the way of learning, training, and preliminary contests. In the middle of the month a second *sagali* (distribution of food) is held, called *katumwalela kasakasa* (the priming of the rank and file). There is a special dance on such a day, but no other rites are performed.

Finally, at the next full moon, there comes the *kovayse* (the winding up), which lasts for three days, and is the main festivity of the period. Two days before the full moon, there is a great communal eating of sago or taro pudding (see pls. 5 and 86). This day is called *itavakayse kaydebu* (" preparing of the dancing shield "), or *itavakayse bisila* (" preparing of the pandanus streamer "), in reference to the shield and streamer which are both used in dancing. On the next day, which is called *itokolukwa'i*, the same proceedings are repeated. On both days ceremonial dancing takes place

The third day is called *luvayam*, " the day of consummation," or *lapula*, " the rounding off day," and is a great occasion. People from many villages are invited, and begin to arrive in the morning, soon filling the village street and surrounding spaces. Each community sits in a group, camping on mats, surrounded with baskets and children. Those on more intimate terms with their hosts assist them in the preparations. The villagers, with serious set faces, move quickly to and fro among the guests, in gala dress, some already adorned for the dance— the men perhaps in female grass petticoats with the whole body decked out in valuable ornaments and flowers.

In the morning, the performance begins with an inaugural round dance, the *mweli* (as on pls. 58, 65, 82). The *mweli* is followed at about noon by the

ceremonial figure dance (*kasawaga*) (pl. 73). All
is done in full dress and with great display, to
the attentive observation of the onlookers. But this
is only a preparation for what will follow.

After midday, the real ceremonial begins. The
performers have now ritually to wash, dress, and
ornament themselves. The visitors and the rest of
the villagers are in the meantime engaged in a
distribution of food and in feasting. Early in the
afternoon, platters of baked yams, bananas, and
coco-nut, and sometimes of fish as well, are brought
to the guests and distributed to each community
as *mitalela valu* (" eye of the village "—a metaphor
which I was unable to elucidate). This is usually an
occasion for much merriment and some horseplay,
the givers and receivers exchanging appropriate
jokes. Then each group sets to work on their portion,
sitting round the platter with backs turned to the
people from other village communities, as is required
by good manners.

To complete our account of food distributions:
there follows another *sagali*, in which the performers,
now fully dressed and adorned, give presents to their
tabusia (father's sisters, and their daughters). This
is a repayment for the beauty magic which the
women have performed upon them, to the
description of which we now proceed.

3

BEAUTY MAGIC : THE RITUAL OF WASHING

The ceremonial washing and decoration of the
dancers is undertaken on this occasion by women
of a special class, namely those who stand to them
in the relation of *tabu*. We shall have to discuss
the *tabu* and their place in the social scheme more
fully in the chapters which follow (ch. xiii, sec. 6 ;
see also ch. viii, sec. 2). In this place we need
only mention that they are the approved and suitable
partners for passing intrigues, for more stable

liaisons or for marriage (see also ch. iv, sec. 4). It is their duty now to prepare the men for the dance, to deck them out with ornaments, with flowers and with paint, and to perform the magic incidental to each stage of the proceedings. In this, the ritual differs from the beauty magic in the *kula*, where each man makes his own magic and adorns himself. It is, on the other hand, similar in every respect to the beauty magic performed in the first pregnancy ceremony (see above, ch. viii, sec. 2).

The ceremonial dressing must, as always, be preceded by a ritual washing and cleansing, conducted to a running accompaniment of appropriate spells. The dancers and their attendants have now assembled outside the village in the grove, usually at a place not far from the waterhole (pl. 74). While the boys wait, their *tabula* recite a spell over some coco-nut fibre, with which the skin is to be rubbed as with a sponge ; and over some soft leaves (usually of the *wageva* shrub), with which the skin will be dried as with a towel. This is, in free translation, a *kaykakaya* (ablution) formula for the charming of the coco-nut fibre [1] :

> Polishing, polishing off,
> Cleansing, cleansing off,
> There is one piece of fibre,
> My own, a keen fibre, a buoyant fibre,
> One which is as the morning star,
> Which is as the full moon.
> I cleanse his chest, I improve his head,
> I improve his chest, I cleanse his head,
> They climb up a pole (to admire),
> They bind a flattery-bond round his knees.

This formula needs hardly any comment. It contains, as with most magic, the affirmation of the desired effect. It begins with a simple statement of the action of cleansing, and then extols the value of the coco-nut, comparing it to the morning star and to the full moon. The quality thus charmed into the coco-nut fibre will, it must be remembered, be

[1] For information as to the linguistic plan adopted in the translation of this and other native texts, see ch. xviii, "The Power of Words in Magic," in my *Argonauts of the Western Pacific*.

later on transferred by friction to the skin of the bather. The idea of a light colour as an attribute of beauty is clearly expressed. The formula closes with an exaggerated statement of the effect to be produced by the magic. It is a custom to remove a piece of decoration from the body of a dancer or, in the case of people of high rank, to tie a string round his leg or arm, in order to express admiration. This is done with the words : *Agu tilewa'i* " my flattery-bond ", and has to be redeemed by the admired dancer with a suitable present, which is also called *tilewa'i*—flattery-gift.

The following formula is spoken over the leaves used for drying the skin :—

> I pull and pull, I pull hither and thither,
> I pull my leaves of drying.
> There is one kind of towel leaves,
> The leaves of my companions;
> Sere, parched leaves they are.
> There is another kind of leaves, my towel leaves.
> The leaves of me, of Ibo'umli,
> They are keen buoyant flashing leaves.

Here again we find the usual affirmation, but the three middle lines are very interesting, for they show what might be called a typical case of magical relativity. The magic of the speaker, who in such cases always mentions his or her own name, is extolled at the expense of the magic of his or her companions. This type of phrasing is prevalent in magic applied in competitive activities.[1] The pulling of the leaves mentioned in the first line refers to the act of breaking them from the tree, and is a typical magical expression.

After the coco-nut fibre and the leaves have been charmed, each man takes his sponge and towel from his *tabula* and wraps it up in leaves, so that no magic virtue shall evaporate, even during the short passage from the spot where they are assembled to the water-hole, whither the men presently repair, leaving the

---

[1] Compare, for instance, the formula referring to the speed of the canoe, *Argonauts of the Western Pacific*, p. 130.

women behind. Arrived there, the men remove all dress and ornament, and begin to wash, scraping off any paint which still remains from the morning. The coco-nut fibre is first unwrapped from its covering, and with this they rub their skin. They rub carefully and earnestly and with a scrupulous minuteness, so that no part of the skin shall remain untouched. The face and the chest are perhaps most thoroughly scrubbed. With the same meticulous attention to detail, the skin is dried with the soft, spongy leaves. Then they return to their female magicians who are awaiting them.

4

BEAUTY MAGIC: THE RITUAL OF ADORNMENT

In the meantime, the women have been preparing various cosmetic substances. Each boy, before the washing, has taken off his most precious ornaments, such as shell-belt, armshells, and valuable necklaces, and left them with his *tabula*; so now the toilet can begin. First comes the anointing with charmed coco-nut oil, always the next stage after washing (I failed to obtain the magical formula of coco-nut oil). When this has been well rubbed all over the skin, by the man himself and not by the women, the latter proceed to stroke the skin with a mother-of-pearl shell (*kayeki* or *kaydobu*) (pl. 75). Slowly and gently each *tabula* presses the smooth shell up and down over his cheeks, his arms and his chest, and laterally across his forehead; reciting a formula, as she does so, in a clear audible voice. The words must always be spoken towards the boy's face which she is stroking.

> Who makes the beauty magic ?—
> To heighten the beauty, to make it come out.
> Who makes it on the slopes of Obukula ?—
> I, Tabalu, and my mate Kwaywaya.
> We make the beauty magic.

I smooth out, I improve, I whiten !
Thy head I smooth out, I improve, I whiten !
Thy cheeks I smooth out, I improve, I whiten !
Thy nose I smooth out, I improve, I whiten !
Thy throat I smooth out, I improve, I whiten !
Thy neck I smooth out, I improve, I whiten !
Thy shoulders I smooth out, I improve, I whiten
Thy breast I smooth out, I improve, I whiten !
Bright skin, bright ; glowing skin, glowing.

The opening sentences of the formula again present a typical pattern of Trobriand magic. They express the traditional filiation of the actual performer. By reciting them, the magician charms, not in his own name, but as a representative, so to speak, of the original source of the magic. He— or in this case she—is even projected to the spot from whence the magic came ; in the present rites on the slopes of Obukula, where the primeval grotto lies, near the village of Laba'i.[1] From this grotto, according to tradition, the earliest clan-ancestors emerged. There, also, the culture hero Tudava was raised and lived with his mother. It is the centre of traditional magic, of custom and of law. The formula identifies the speaker with two ancestors of the highest sub-clan, which takes its name from one of them, Tabalu. In the form given in this charm, the names can be either male or female. In practice, the masculine prefix Mo- or the feminine prefix Bo- is usually added to indicate whether a man or a woman is named. Thus, the old chief of Kasana'i, who was still alive on my first visit to the Trobriands, was called M'tabalu, and one of his nephews, Kwaywaya. The feminine forms would be Botabalu and Bokwaywaya respectively. The rest of the formula is typical of all the longer spells and follows, step by step, the ritual applications to the object charmed. This is the longest formula and the most circumstantial act of beauty magic.

After the body has been anointed and smoothed

[1] For details of these legendary places and persons, see *Myth in Primitive Psychology*.

with the pearl shell, the cosmetics are ceremonially applied. The mouth is painted with crushed betel-nut, while the following words are chanted :

> Red paint, red paint thither.
> Red paint, red paint hither.
> One red paint of my companions,
> It is sere, it is parched.
> One red paint, my red paint
> Of me, of Ibo'umli;
> It is keen, it is buoyant, it is flashing :
> My red paint.

This charm is similar in form to that of the *wageva* leaves.

When the mouth has been painted red, and perhaps a few lines in the same colour on the face, ornamental spirals are painted on the cheeks and forehead with *sayaku* (pl. 76), an aromatic black cosmetic, while the following words are recited :

> O black paint, O buoyant black paint !
> O black paint, O decorative black paint !
> O black paint, O comely black paint !
> Glowing eyes, glowing, bright eyes, bright.
> For this is my *sayaku*.
> The ornamenting, the alluring black paint indeed.

Then the hair is teased out with a comb to the accompaniment of this spell :

> Who makes the beauty magic—
> To heighten the beauty, to make it come out ?
> Who makes it on the slopes of Kituma ?
> I, Ibo'umli, make the beauty magic
> To heighten the beauty, to make it come out.
> I make it on the slopes of Kituma.
> Keen is my comb, buoyant is my comb,
> My comb is like the full moon,
> My comb is like the morning star.
> For this is my comb,
> It will adorn me,
> It will make me beloved indeed.

The name, Ibo'umli, occurring in this and one or two of the previous formulæ, is that of my informant. The place, Kituma, seems to be somewhere in the eastern archipelago, but my informant could not locate it exactly.

The toilet is now almost complete. The dancers

are adorned with red flowers, aromatic herbs (*vana*),
and garlands of the *butia*, which always blooms at
this season (pl. 77). Appropriate incantations are
said, but I shall not here cite them, for, although I
obtained them, I cannot translate them satis-
factorily. Finally, and with no adjuvant magic,
such valuable ornaments as belts, armshells, necklaces, and last, but not least, the feather ornaments
for the head, are put on the dancers. This last part
of the toilet is done by men (pl. 78).

5

THE MAGIC OF SAFETY AND RENOWN AT FESTIVITIES

The elaborate ritual preparation of the dancers
gives some indication of the tense emotional atmosphere which is characteristic of these big festive
assemblies. The whole complex of dangerous
passions, which, at the same time, spring from and
generate the spirit of emulation, is wrought upon
by such a culminating occasion for personal display.
·While charms are being said over the dancers in
the grove to give them added beauty, strength, and
skill, two other kinds of magic are being prepared
in the village, one of which is a measure of protection. There is a deep belief and a strong
apprehension among the natives that black magic
is being used against the dancers by the enemies of
the village. Excellence in dancing is, indeed, one
of those dangerous accomplishments which arouse
great envy, and against which many an evil magician
directs his powers. In fact, among the symptoms
by which the wizard murderer is identified on the
corpse of his victim an important place is occupied
by marks which signify : " This man was killed
for his excellence in dancing." [1]

There is a special evil magic called *kaygiauri*,
which is practised against the dancers, and indeed

[1] Cf. *Crime and Custom*, part ii, ch. ii, p. 89.

against all the bystanders except the sorcerer himself and his friends. I was not able to find out any details about this magic, how it is performed, or how it is supposed to act. But I have myself seen men preparing an antidote and making the counter-magic over the dancers. When the ritual toilet had been completed, small parcels were produced, containing magically treated wild ginger-root hermetically wrapped up in leaves. These were chewed by the magician, who then spat over the skin of the dancer. Next he took some aromatic leaves (*kwebila*); over these he muttered a short formula, and then put them into the armlets of the dancers.

The operation of these evil passions is not, in fact, wholly confined to the realm of idea and belief. The danger of a fight during the culminating day of a *kayasa* is even now not quite excluded. I was never present when feeling ran high enough to develop into a brawl, but, even so, I was strongly aware of a violence and ruthlessness in the behaviour of the performers and of the crowd, of a certain nervous mistrust and clinging together of each group, which confirmed the direct statements of the natives and my general information as to the conduct of such affairs in former times. Then the natives would come fully armed, with spears, wooden sword clubs, throwing sticks, and shields ; each community would stand in a group with every man on his guard, suspicious of all strangers and on the look-out for possible trouble. When interest in the performance was at its height, people would push forward, the closer physical contact would cause suspicion of sorcery, and anything might be the signal for a fight. The presence of women in the various groups was another important source of danger, because of sexual rivalry.

To the envy and jealousy and mutual mistrust must be added an ardent desire for renown (*butura*). This finds full and independent expression in a further type of magic, which, with that of beauty and the specific against hostile sorcery, is launched into the exalted atmosphere of the village. This is the magic of *uributu*, " spreading of renown " (*uri*, from " *wori* ", to strike, to flick, to spray ; *butu*, root of renown "). While the dancers are being made ready under the trees of the village grove ; while a distribution of food is in progress on the central place, the magician of glory, the *to'uributu*, proceeds in his own house to manufacture fame for his community. He is the same man who, on the first day of the festivities, a month ago, has performed the important magic of the conch-shells and the buried food. In the morning he has also prepared the scene of the dances by ritual sweeping of the *baku* (central place) with a charmed broom. Now comes his most important performance. On a large mat, folded over so that it encloses them, he places a drum, a conch-shell, and a few pieces of reed (*dadam*). Into the open mouth of this improvised magic bag he then chants his spells. The formula unfortunately I was not able to obtain.

His task is completed as the dancers are ready, fully dressed and waiting to start (pl. 79) the *lapula* or final dance. He gives one of the drummers the magic drum, and another man takes the charmed conch-shell.

The dancers, the singers, and the drummers now put themselves into position, ready for the signal. This is given by the magician of glory and one or two assistants. They run from the village street into the central place with the magic reed in their hands. Each of them must have both his hands upon the reed, which is pointing towards the ground. They strike the ground at intervals with the reed, while they utter a high-pitched scream (*igovasi*). Arrived at the opposite end of the place, they turn about and throw the reed into the air. The man who catches the reed scores a point in this contest for renown, and will be spoken of all over the district when the feast is gossiped about and its heroes mentioned. Then the men of the reed utter another very loud cry and this gives the signal for the drummers to beat, for the conch-shells to blow, and for the dancers to begin their final performance.

6

THE MAGIC OF LOVE

We now pass to the most important system of magic connected with erotic life in the Trobriands, the magic of love. While the magic of beauty is always associated with ceremonial events, such as the *kula* (ceremonial exchange), first pregnancy celebrations, a *kayasa* (period of competitive activity), or an *usigola*, the magic of love is performed whenever occasion arises. While the magic of beauty, again, is always done openly and in public, that of love is a private matter and carried out on the individual's own initiative. This, of course, does not mean that there is anything illicit or clandestine about the magic of love. People who possess it boast about it, and talk about having put it in operation. Nor, from the nature of the rites, would it be possible to conceal it completely from its object. The magic of love becomes illicit only in so far as the love itself is illicit ; as, for instance, when it is directed towards a chief's wife, or towards some other tabooed person.

It has been mentioned that this magic belongs to a *system*. A system of magic in the Trobriands is a series of spells, which accompany some chain of linked activities and are performed in a fixed order following the development of the chain. In economic pursuits such as gardening, fishing, the construction of a canoe, or a *kula* expedition, or, again, in the magic of beauty just described, the rites accompany each successive stage of the enterprise, which naturally proceeds in a definite order.

But there are other spheres of magic where the system possesses a slightly different character. For instance, sorcery is believed to be the real cause of disease. Indeed, black magic must be effective and finally fatal, *provided* that it is properly carried out with due observance of all conditions, and *provided* that it is not met by a stronger counter-magic. The sorcerer opens the attack, the victim defends himself by securing counter-magic, and by making use of every factor which could counteract the full efficiency of black magic. Even if the sorcerer is successful, or partially so, the resultant illness does not develop along fixed lines as does the growth of a garden. Hence this system cannot follow a fixed sequence of events. Instead, a system of black magic consists of a succession of spells and rites which gradually increase in strength. When the sorcerer is successful, the increasing strength of his spells produces the more rapid decline of his victim until death supervenes. If the sorcerer is being thwarted, he launches increasingly strong formulæ in order to get at his victim through the barrier of precautions, adverse conditions, and counter-magic with which the latter has protected himself.

Let us examine black magic, not from the native, but from the ethnographer's point of view. A sorcerer is either paid to remove a victim or does so from personal motives. It may happen, by a mere coincidence, that the victim falls more or less seriously ill within a few weeks of the initial operations. As black magic is often advertised and always suspected, the illness is put down to its influence. If it be known that a powerful sorcerer, in the pay of a chief, is at work, suggestion may have a serious effect on the victim. It does not follow that he gives in utterly and dies, but I suspect that this occasionally happens.[1]   As a rule, however,

---

[1] I have no well-attested instance in my notes, but several cases of rapid wasting disease have appeared to me to belong to this category. Examples of people dying from sheer conviction that a broken taboo

if pressed hard, the victim will mobilize all the forces of defence. He will put counter-magic in operation ; set armed watches at night around him ; move away to another place, change his diet, and observe all the taboos and other conditions of recovery. Thus we have the interplay of two forces in the imagination of the patient, corresponding to the interplay of the two real forces in his organism : resistance and disease. The progress of the system of magic, accompanied by the progress of the system of counter-magic, proceed side by side with the struggle between the organism and the invading forces of bacteria or malignant changes. Once the sorcerer has determined on black magic, or has received payment for it, he has to go through the whole repertory from the initial formula to the final pointing of the bone—even if he has to admit failure in the end. An unwittingly broken taboo is perhaps an important sorcerer's best excuse for unsuccess ; but bad luck in the final application of charmed substances and powerful counter-magic also serve to account for the impotence of his magic. After such failure, the sorcerer bides his time and awaits a suitable opportunity—such, for instance, as his victim actually falling ill. Then he sets to work again. For though the natives believe that real illness (*silami*) can only be produced by magic, they are perfectly well aware that an indisposition (*katoulo*) which may be natural forms an excellent soil for the operations of sorcery.

It was necessary to enlarge on the general character of magical systems, and on the distinction between the system which follows the naturally

---

has a lethal influence, or that black magic, too powerful to be counter-acted, has been set in motion against them, are numerous in ethnographic literature. The argument in the text does not rest on the assumption, however, that what might be called psychological death from sorcery is inevitable. It rests rather on the principle which we can regard as established by modern psycho-therapy that a conviction of good and bad influences working upon the patient's health is a most powerful element in the treatment. Cf. P. Janet, *Les Médications Psychologiques*, 1920.

determined progress of activity or enterprise, on the one hand, and the system which follows a course determined by the chance play of unknown factors on the other, in order to lay bare the essential character of love magic. This type also deals with a configuration of chances and elements which do not follow a definite natural course. Here also the belief is very strong that love-magic, properly executed and not counteracted, is infallible. The *nanola* (mind and emotional centre) of man or woman cannot resist the complete consecutive series of rites and spells; even if it were no more than strongly affected by the initial steps, it must succumb to the cumulative ritual—that is if the magic be not magically counteracted. For here also there are causes which account for failure; the performer may not have the words accurately or he may have broken a conditional taboo; or a counter-magic may frustrate his almost successful attempts. As in all supernatural control of chance, magical infallibility is absolute only under absolutely perfect conditions; that is to say, it is never attained in practice, though it may be claimed in theory.

7

THE RITE AND THE SPELL IN LOVE MAGIC

In following the practice of love magic through its successive stages, we must have in mind the setting of a Trobriand love story, in ordinary village life and among the customary forms of communication between the sexes. Although girls are said to practise this magic, it is more usual for the man to take the initiative. The story begins in the ordinary way; a boy is fascinated by a girl. If there be no response and he does not win her favours immediately, he resorts to the most potent way of courting her, that is by magic.

As in ordinary beauty magic, he must first wash

or bathe in the sea. Thus he makes himself handsome and attractive ; in the same rite he also charms a responsive affection into the loved one's heart. Let us suppose our hero to live near the sea. On his way to the shore, he gathers in the bush some of the soft spongy leaves of the *wageva, silasila*, or *ponatile* shrubs, and also some leaves from a tree with a specially smooth and clean bark—preferably from the *reyava* and *gatumwalila*. He puts the whole bundle into some large leaf and chants the special washing formula over it. This corresponds to analogous spells in the *kula* beauty magic and in the beauty magic described in the previous sections.

One of the *kaykakaya* spells of love magic, which I obtained, may be freely rendered thus :

THE KAYKAKAYA SPELL

Leaves of dirt and leaves of cleansing,
Leaves of dirt and leaves of cleansing,
Smooth as the bark of the *reyava* tree
As the tail of the oppossum.
My face shines in beauty ;
I cleanse it with leaves ;
My face, I cleanse it with leaves,
My eyebrows I cleanse them with leaves.

And so on.

The boy then has to name various parts of the head and of the body, adding after each the word *ayolise*, which has been translated here : " I cleanse with leaves." These were the parts named by the informant who gave me the charm : head, face, eyebrows, nose, cheek, chin, jaws, throat, shoulders, larynx, breasts, flanks, armpits, buttocks, thighs, knees, calves, and feet. The formula then proceeds :

Beautiful will my face remain,
Flashing will my face remain,
Buoyant will my face remain !
No more it is my face,
My face is as the full moon.
No more it is my face,
My face is as the round moon.
I pierce through,
As the creamy shoot of the areca leaf,
I come out,
As a bud of the white lily.

Then the charmed leaves are carefully wrapped up, lest the magic virtue should evaporate (*kayawa*), and the boy washes himself in water. When he is thoroughly cleansed, the wrapping is opened, and the skin rubbed all over and dried with the charmed leaves. At this point the rite takes on its specific character as part of a system of love magic; for the leaves that have been thus used are thrown into the sea, with the words : "*Kirisana akaykakaya, kula kworisaki matana* . . ." (here the girl's personal name is mentioned). The word *kirisana*, also known in the forms *kirisala* or *karisala*, signifies the influence which a dream induced by magic may exercise over the seat of the emotions—the heart, as we would say—the belly, as the natives put it.[1] The word might be rendered : " The spell or the influence of a magical act in inducing a dream." The verbal form is *korisaki* with the active suffix *-ki*. The translation of the sentence would, therefore, run as follows : " Dream-spell of my *kaykakaya* charm ; go and effectively influence the eye of So-and-so."

Thus the rite has a twofold effect : it makes a man beautiful, as does all washing magic, and it carries sweet dreams about him into the mind of the girl. As the natives put it, referring to the ritual casting of the herbs into the sea : " As the leaves will be tossed by the waves, and as they move with the sea up and down, so the inside of the girl will heave."

What follows depends, as in sorcery, upon the effect of what has already been accomplished. If the loved one surrenders easily, perhaps one more formula will be recited, to attach her affections the more securely. But if the washing magic fails completely, another attack is made on the beleagured heart by means of a stronger magic called the *kasina*. This has to be administered through the mouth. A piece of food or betel-nut—or, to-day, some tobacco—is charmed and given to the girl. The

[1] Cf. below, ch. xii, sec. 1.

washing magic has already made her more interested in her suitor and, though she is not yet prepared to yield, she will probably ask for some such small gift. In any case, she will not refuse such an offering, even though she suspects that it is given with an ulterior motive.

THE KASINA SPELL

My flashing decoration, my white skin !
I shall take the faces of my companions and rivals
I shall make them be cast off.
I shall take my face, the face of me (personal name),
And I shall get a flattery-bond for it
For my beautiful full-moon face.

The simile in the last line would not perhaps send a thrill to the heart of a white girl, but the full-moon, for the Trobriander, is a symbol of colour and of roundness in a more emotionally appealing sense than it is with us. The " flattery-bond " (*tilewa'i*) has already been explained above (sec. 3).

When the girl has eaten this little *douceur*, the magic enters into her inside and moves her mind. There is a fair chance already that her affections are favourably inclined, but a still more potent magic remains. The first attack, as we saw, was through the ethereal medium of dreams ; the second, by the very material way of eating ; there remain the two senses of touch and smell. These are considered the most susceptible in love-magic.

The next rite, therefore, centres round an aromatic herb called *kwoyawaga*, which grows only in the eastern islands and has to be traded mainly from Kitava. This herb is put into a receptacle with coco-nut oil, and the following spell is chanted over it :

THE KWOYAWAGA SPELL

Spread out, fold up,
Spread out, fold up,
I cut off, I cut, I cut.
A bait for a bird, for a small fish-hawk,
Uve, uvegu-guyo, o !

> My *kayro'iwa* love charm remains,
> My *kayro'iwa* love charm weeps,
> My *kayro'iwa* love charm pulls,
> My *kayro'iwa* love charm spills over.
> Press down, press upon thy bed ;
> Smooth out, smooth your pillow-mat ;
> Enter my house and tread upon my floor.
> Tease out and tear out my hair ;
> Drink my blood and take hold of my penis ;
> *Apicem penis suge,* for my guts are moved.

This formula is much more obscure than the previous ones. The first sentence, " spread out, fold up," may refer, as my informants told me, to the mat on which a boy and girl recline in amorous embrace. The cutting, by analogy with similar formulæ, is of the plants to be used in the magic. In the next phrase, the magic is likened to a bait for a bird and the girl to a fish-hawk which hovers over the trap. One sentence I was unable to translate even approximately, and it is therefore given in native. What follows is less cryptic. *Kayro'iwa* is the name of one of the systems of love magic, with which we shall become more intimately acquainted in connection with the native myth of incest (ch. xiv). The last part is typical of the more passionate forms of love magic. I have obtained several formulæ with similar endings.

I may add that, for every formula which I was able to write down, to check after a few weeks' interval, to get a commentary upon, and to translate into anything like sense, I had to reject several as spurious, fragmentary or not understood by the natives. I was always able to distinguish the genuine archaic formulæ from the corrupt, by the method of checking and re-checking them with my original informant, after having allowed an interval of time to elapse between each repetition.

Returning to the magic of the *kwoyawaga* herbs, this charmed and prepared aromatic substance can only be used at close quarters. An even more intimate approach to the desired girl has to be effected than is possible with the piece of betel-nut or tobacco of the previous ritual. For some of the aromatic oil must be smeared upon her body, or poured on to her face, or, best of all, applied to her breasts. Thus close physical contact is needed, and for this, opportunities are given in games, in dances, in tribal festivities, and in the rythmic round called the *karibom*. Only when a boy is very clumsy or shy, or has no opportunity for intimate approach, would he put the oil on a piece of cigarette paper, or, in olden days, on a flower, so that the smoke or scent may enter her nostrils.

There remains still one rite—that of the all-powerful *sulumwoya*, the mint plant, which is the symbol of charm and seduction, the main instru-ment of attraction in the *kula* (ceremonial exchange), the herb which plays the central part in the myth of the origins of love, and which figures also in the culminating act of love magic. This ritual would still be performed, even if the magic had been successful at an earlier stage. For *sulumwoya* gives a full and undivided sway over the loved one's heart. *Boge bipayki kumaydona, magila yakida*, "Already she will refuse all others ; her desire is only for us." This is the formula of the *sulumwoya* magic in the *kayro'iwa* system.

SULUMWOYA SPELL

O, her sensual excitement !
O, her erotic swoon !
O, desire, O feminine swoon !
My clasping, thy clasping kindle our erotic swooning !
My embraces, thy embraces kindle our erotic swooning !
My copulation, thy copulation kindle our erotic swooning !

The same complicated phrasing is repeated with a number of words inserted instead of clasping, embracing and so forth. The words are : horizontal motion (*bilabala*), horizontal response (*bilamapu*), erotic scratching (*kimali*), erotic biting (*kayalu*), nose rubbing (*vayaulo*), and eyelash biting (*mitakuku*), lousing (*kopokutu*), rubbing each other's lips (*kawidova*). Then come the following sentences :

> My going first, thy following, kindle our erotic swooning,
> My waiting, thy waiting, kindle our erotic swooning.

and finally :

> Thou goest my way, crying for me,
> Thou enterest my house, smiling at me.
> The house is shaken with joy, as thou treadest my floor.
> Tease and tear out my hair,
> Drink my blood,
> So that my feelings are glad.

This is a long formula—the longer since, as in all Trobriand magical spells, the middle part, the litany, is always repeated over and over aga'n, and not necessarily in the same order. It is chanted over a mint plant boiled in coco-nut oil. If the magic is practised on someone whose love has already been captured, there is no difficulty in spilling the scented and charmed oil over her, or anointing her with it. If she is not yet subdued, the problem remains of entering her hut at night, and spilling some of it below her nostrils, so that she may dream of the magic maker. But if this is achieved the spell is irresistible.

Less certain methods are to smear the oil over her hands, or bring some of it near to her face ; or to take a sweet smelling sprig of herbs, dip it in the oil and flick it under her nose. These three methods obviously make her cognizant that love magic is being employed ; and this produces the desired effect—psychologically at least, if not magically !

As an additional charm, the same formula may be recited over the long spine of a fish called *umlaybasi*, a prick from which inflicts a lasting and smarting pain. Holding it in the hollow of his hand, the boy brings his lips close to his hand and chants the spell into it, after which the spine may be put into the stopper of the coco-nut bottle in which the oil is being kept. Or else, holding it in the hollow of his hand, the boy may stab the girl with

his finger in the ribs or thereabouts ; or, during the
karibom, he may make one of those even more
intimate insertions already mentioned (ch. ix, sec. 3).

8

THE REALITIES OF LOVE MAGIC

A direct and consecutive statement of a complex
and somewhat chaotic subject such as that of love
magic inevitably suggests more precision and
system than actually exists, especially when the
component parts hang together, at least in theory.
And it is well to realize that actual proceedings are
never as complete and well defined as might appear
from native statements.

A certain amount of complication is introduced
by the fact that there are a number of different
systems. The most famous one is that of *Kayro'iwa*.
But the systems of *Kwoygapani* and *Libomatu*, from
the islands of Vakuta and of Kayleula respectively
are also prominent. These systems, being perhaps
the most widely known and practised, have now
become mixed up and few natives have a complete
set of formulæ belonging to the same system. As a
matter of fact, only a few of my informants, even
among those who boasted of having a powerful set
of formulæ, could go through a full set satis-
factorily. Each knew two or three or only one
spell. I may add that perhaps no native in the
Trobriands would be able to judge magical texts
as well as myself. For no human memory is a match
for a written comparative collection. Towards the
end of my field-work, I found little difficulty in
deciding whether a spell recited to me was genuine
or corrupt ; and, in the latter case, whether it was
deliberate deception, self-deception, or deception
on the part of my informant's predecessor, or just
lack of memory.

What matters to us is that few natives are in

possession of a full system in an unadulterated form. A youth who knows his spell or two—sometimes only a fragment—will as a rule genuinely believe that there is a great deal of virtue in it ; very often experience strengthens his belief. He will recite his fragment or his full charm over the *kaykakaya* leaves, and if unsuccessful he will try his formula over the other herbs.

Each rite has a certain positive effect on him and usually also on his sweetheart. The washing magic gives him the conviction of increased strength and power to attract, an attitude very favourable to his enterprise. The same magic makes him hope that the girl has dreamed of him, and that she is ready to receive his advances. He approaches her with confidence, and jokes with her without embarrassment.

The other rites afford a still more material help in love-making. All of them imply a direct contact ; a gift, an erotic touch, the wafting of some scent. Thus not only does he believe in his magical powers, but she also is made aware that he is working on her heart. And she also is susceptible to the influence of belief and tradition. If he is hopelessly repulsive to her, this need not shatter her belief in love magic. She concludes that his rites are spurious and his formulæ badly recited. But if he has the least attraction for her, it is easy to see how magic will do its work.

These conclusions are based on observation of native behaviour, on statements of natives, and on the actual working of love magic in cases analysed to me by my friends as they were proceeding.

The deep conviction of the natives in the virtue of love magic and their belief that it is the only means of wooing, have already been mentioned. All a man's hopes of success, his boasting and his anticipations are based on confidence in his magical equipment, exactly as all failure is attributed to lack or impotence in this respect. I have already several times alluded to Gomaya ; vain, arrogant, and wilful, yet with remarkable personality. He always used to vaunt his success with women, and invariably in terms of magic. He would say : " I am ugly, my face is not good-looking. But I have magic, and therefore all women like me." He would then boast of his intrigues with Ilamweria, of the attachment that his cross-cousins had for him, and of other amorous successes, some of which have already been mentioned in this volume. My other informants were one and all agreed in their conviction of the potency of love magic. To a direct question I would always receive the same answer : " If one man is good-looking, a good dancer, and a good singer, and he has no magic ; while the other man is ugly, lame, and dark-skinned, but has good magic ; the first will be rejected, the second will be loved by women."

This, of course, is exaggeration for the sake of emphasis, typical of a Melanesian's way of presenting matters. All natives know the magic, yet not all by any means have the same success. Met by such an argument, the natives will say that the man who has success has it because his magic is " keen and strong ". And here the fiction of native belief comes nearer to reality. A man of intelligence, of strong will, personality, and temperament, will have greater success with women than a beautiful but soulless dullard—in Melanesia as in Europe. A man who is convinced that he is going the right way to work ; a man who has the energy to find out who has the best magic and the industry to acquire and learn it, such a man will be good at love making as well as at magic. The native belief thus expresses some truth, though it is psychological rather than physical or occult, and refers to results rather than to mechanism.

Gomaya was a case in point. The five sons of To'uluwa and Kadamwasila were all pleasant and clever, attractive and enterprising, and were all renowned for their love-magic. As a matter of fact, the first and last of the formulæ here given I received from Yobukwa'u who, knowing only two out of the four charms, yet achieved an incestuous love-affair with his father's youngest wife, several adulteries, and two engagements one after the other. All these affairs were attributed to love magic; as was the case with Kalogusa, his younger brother, who subdued Yobukwa'u's fiancée, Isepuna. Another of the five brothers, Gilayviyaka, with whose intrigues too we are already acquainted, was also reputed to be an expert at love magic. Many more examples could be adduced, but it is better to keep to the more notorious cases.

Bagido'u, the nephew and heir-apparent of the principal chief, an extremely intelligent and pleasant informant, was ill of some internal wasting sickness, probably tuberculosis. We have already heard of his domestic mishaps, the defection of his handsome wife, who left him in order to join her late sister's husband, Manimuwa, a young, healthy and handsome man of Wakayse (see ch. vi, sec. 1). She often visited her sister, and during the latter's last illness she stayed for a long time with her brother-in-law. The issue was obvious: Manimuwa and Dakiya formed an attachment and entered upon an illicit intrigue, which ended in her joining him. Magic was blamed for all the trouble. Even Bagido'u himself, the deserted husband, would say that she was a good woman, but that this bad man had first performed evil magic to estrange her from her husband, and afterwards love magic to seduce her. Dakiya, in fact, was quoted as the classical instance of the power of magic. "Magic made the mind of Dakiya; Manimuwa only remains in her mind." The comic side of this otherwise sad story was that Bagido'u had the reputation of being the greatest expert in the magic of love. Of course, my informants were ready with explanations of the theoretical conundrums involved.

Finally to return once more to a story which is a case in point: the tragedy of Namwana Guya'u's expulsion from the village by the kinsmen of Mitakata (see ch. i, sec. 2). On my return after more than a year's absence from the Trobriands, I met Namwana Guya'u in one of the southern villages. His hatred of Mitakata was as implacable as ever. When I asked him what had happened to his enemy, he told me that the wife of Mitakata, Orayayse, had rejected him (see pl. 25). She was, as a matter of fact, the first cousin of her husband's enemy, and I knew that her husband had sent her away for political reasons. But Namwana Guya'u hinted that he had estranged her feelings from her husband by magic. Then he enlarged on the bad habits of his enemy. " He tries to get hold of girls and they refuse him " ; yet he had to inform me that Mitakata had married Ge'umwala, a young and pretty girl. " *Boge, ivakome minana ; magila imasisi deli ; m'tage biva'i, ipayki — matauna ibi'a.*" " Already he gave magic to her to eat ; her desire to sleep together ; but to marry she refused—he took her by force." Here then the value of the success was actually minimized by its attribution to love magic ; and the consent to marriage, which cannot be won by any such impersonal means, was denied to his enemy by Namwana Guya'u !

9

THE MAGIC OF OBLIVION

In the Trobriands all positive magic has a negative counterpart, in belief and theory at least, if not always in reality. The magic of health and disease is the clearest example, for, against every rite and spell which produces disease, there is a counter-magic which cures it. The positive magic of success, which accompanies each economic enterprise, always implies the existence of a negative preventive rite, which accounts for the possibility of failure in positive magic.

So it is not surprising to find that love-charms have to contend with a magic which acts in the opposite direction. This is the magic of estrangement and oblivion, a department of black magic, generically called *bulubwalata*, though in its narrower meaning this term designates just this magic. The root *bulu* on which the word is built is also the formative element " pig " (*bulukwa*). Whether this means that the prototype of all this magic consists of the rites which aim at the dispersion of pigs by malicious magic, I was unable to decide. The fact is, however, that this magic is used for sending away pigs into the bush as well as for estranging wives and sweet-hearts.

Whenever a man has reasons for hating a girl or, even more often, her paramour or her husband, he will practise this magic. It acts upon her mind, and turns away her affections from her husband or lover. She leaves his house, leaves her village, and wanders away. The informant who gave me the following spells told me that when the magic is administered in a mild form, the girl will leave her husband or lover, but return to her own village and her own people ; but if it is given in a large quantity, and properly, with minute observation of accuracy in spell and rite and in the taboos, she will run away to the bush, lose her road, and maybe disappear for ever. In this, as in other types of magic, the man might recite the initial spell only in order to produce a partial effect, that is to alienate the girl's feelings from her sweetheart or husband.

The following formula has to be said over a piece of food, or some tobacco, or some betel-nut, which is then given to the victim. It is called *kabisilova* (literally " causing to reject "), and may be freely translated as follows :.

His name be extinguished, his name be rejected ;
Extinguished at sunset, rejected at sunrise ;
Rejected at sunset, extinguished at sunrise.
A bird is on the *baku*,
A bird which is dainty about its food.
I make it rejected !
His mint-magic, I make it rejected.
His *kayro'iwa* magic, I make it rejected.
His *libomatu* magic   ,,   ,,   ,,
His copulation magic ,,   ,,   ,,
His horizontal magic   ,,   ,,   ,,
His horizontal movement   ,,   ,,
His answering movement   ,,   ,,
His love dalliance   ,,   ,,   ,
His erotic scratching   ,,   ,,   ,,
His caresses of love   ,,   ,,   ,,
His love embraces   ,,   ,,   ,,
His bodily embracing ,,   ,,   ,,
My Kabisilova spell,
It worms its way within you,
The way of the earth heap in the bush gapes open
The way of the refuse heap in the village is closed.

In the opening lines there is a play upon two words, both of which contain the root of the verbs " to extinguish " and " to reject ". The spell begins, therefore, with an anticipation of its primary effect. It goes on to invoke oblivion openly and in detail : all caresses are to be forgotten. Two lines follow to give power to the spell, that it may insinuate itself into the mind of the girl, and worm its way into all her thoughts. Finally the jungle is opened to the girl and the way to the village closed.

The following spell, obtained from the same informant, was said to be a stronger instalment of this magic. It is administered in the same way, or else it is said over some leaves and coco-nut husk, which are then burnt above a fire, so that the evil-smelling smoke may enter the nostrils of the girl to be bewitched. Freely translated it runs :

Woman, woman repelled,
Man, man repelled,
Woman, woman refusing,
Man, man refusing.
She is repelled, she refuses.
Thy man, thy sweetheart, startles and frightens you,
Swear at him, by his sister ;
Tell him, " Eat thy filth."
Thy road is behind the houses
His face disappears.

> The way of the earth heap in the bush gapes open,
> The way of the refuse heap in the village is closed.
> His face disappears ;
> His face vanishes ;
> His face gets out of the way ;
> His face becomes like that of a wood-spirit ;
> His face becomes as that of the ogre Dokonikan.
>
> There falls, forsooth, a veil over thy eyes
> The evil magic comes,
> It covers completely the pupils of the eyes.
> His mint-magic is as nought,
> His love-magic is as nought,
> His erotic scratchings are as nought,
> His love caresses are as nought,
> His copulations are as nought,
> His horizontal movement is as nought,
> His movement in response is as nought,
> His bodily relaxing is as nought.

The first period of the spell is then repeated up to the words " she is repelled, she refuses ", and it then concludes :

> Thy sun is westering, thy sun goes down.
> Thy sun is westering, thy sun shines aslant.
> She is cut off, she goes far away,
> She goes far away, she is cut off.

The only point in this formula which may need explanation is the sentence inviting the girl to swear by his sister at her husband. Such abuse is one of the deadliest offences, and especially so between husband and wife. We shall speak about it in chapter XIII.

Although the magic of the *bulubwalata* is negative in regard to love-magic, yet the evil done by it cannot be undone by love formulæ. But if a man, in passing anger, should have done great injury to a home by practising this evil magic, there is, within its own system, a possible remedy in the " fetching back " formula, the *katuyumayamila* (*katuyumali*—an archaic form of *ka'imali*, the ordinary form for " return, give back "). This formula has to be spoken in the open, *owadola wala* (" just in the mouth "), as the natives say. But the magician has to recite it towards the various points of the compass successively, so that the magical virtue may reach the woman wherever she may be wandering in the bush. This formula also begins by a play on words containing the formative roots of the verbs " to make up " and " to attract ". Then follows :—

> May my *bulubwalata* be blunt !
> May my fetching magic be keen !
> I am fetching back !
> From the north-eastern quarter, I am fetching back
> From the south-eastern quarter, I am fetching back ;
> From the jungle of Ulawola, I am fetching back ;
> From the jungle of Tepila, I am fetching back ;
> The one who is like a woodsprite, I am fetching back ;
> From the stone heaps, I am fetching back ;
> From the boundary stone walls, I am fetching back ;
> From the fern thickets, I am fetching back ;
> With the smell of mint magic, I am fetching back ;
> I am fetching back thy mind, O woman !
> Come back to us-thy-mother.
> Come back to us-thy-father.
> Tear open the house,
> Tease and tear off my hair,
> Tread on my floor,
> And lie on my bed,
> Come and pass over the threshhold,
> Come and remain at thy dung-heap,
> Let us continue to dwell together,
> Within our house.

Here the intention of the opening sentences is clear, the evil magic is to be impotent, the good magic effective. The truant is called back from the several points of the compass and from the two parts of the jungle (Ulawola and Tepila), one in the North and the other in the Sout , which, surrounded by marches (*dumia*), are perhaps the most inaccessible spots in the main island of the Trobriands, and are regarded as the home of the bush pig. The last part, as the reader has probably noticed, is built on the same pattern as the formula of the love magic. The compound words " us-thy-mother ", " us-thy-father " are constructed with the inclusive dual possessive *ma*. Thus by the magical virtue of this charm the man and woman should not only be as husband and wife should be to one another in the conjugal house, but as the father and mother in the parental home also.

This formula is said to be very powerful, and to have restored married happiness to scores of broken households.

With the pious hope that this is true we may conclude the present chapter.

CHAPTER XII

Erotic Dreams and Fantasies

So far we have studied the psychology of sex as it is embodied in stereotyped behaviour; that is, in customs, institutions, and in magic. In short, in order to gauge his attitude towards sex, we have studied how a Trobriander acts. Now we must turn to such manifestations of sexual ideas and feelings as are to be found in dreams, day-dreams, and folk-tales; that is, in his free and set fantasies about the past, about the future, about distant countries, and above all about his life in the next world.

This chapter will be simply a record of collected data, but even such records are inevitably made with certain problems in view and are influenced by the mental attitude of the recorder. Some academic pedants are apt to contemn any signs of a wider knowledge or of intelligence on the part of an observer of fact. Theory should be eliminated from field-work, so they say; but to my mind this is mere intellectual hypocrisy, under the cloak of purism. The observations which I have made were not recorded by some mechanical device or apparatus, but were made with my own eyes and ears, and controlled by my own brain. The trick of relevant observation consists, in fact, in this very control. It is quite inevitable that my field-work should have been affected by my ideas, interests, and even prejudices. The honest way is to state them so that they may be more easily detected and, if it appears necessary, discounted and eliminated. The other way is to conceal them as skilfully as possible.

The observations to be recorded in this chapter

were mostly done before my psycho-analytic interest was stimulated. In my earlier work, I looked upon folk-lore as a direct expression of social and cultural conditions. When I found a certain motive, such as that of incest or breach of exogamy, in folk-lore, I felt that it was puzzling, but I did not see that it was significant. I treated it as an exception which confirms the rule, rather than as a clue to further inquiry into typical social taboos and repressions. I paid little attention to the investigation of dreams, of day-dreams, and of free fantasies. It did not take me long to see that dreams did not play the part among the Trobrianders ascribed to them by Tylor and others, and after that I did not trouble much more about them.

Later only, stimulated by some literature sent to me by Dr. C. G. Seligman and by his advice, did I begin to test Freud's theory of dreams as the expression of " repressed " wishes and of the " unconscious ", as the *negative* of acknowledged and official principle and morality. In doing this, I came upon important correlations between folk-lore and fancy on the one hand, and social organization on the other ; and was able to discover certain undercurrents of desire and inclination running counter to the established order of ideas and sentiments, which appear, on the surface, insignificant and capricious, but which are in reality of great sociological importance.[1] That in the course of my inquiry I had to reject far more of psycho-analytic doctrine than I could accept does not in any way diminish my obligation ; and my results showed beyond all doubt how even a theory which has, in the light of investigation, to be partly rejected can stimulate and inspire.

The source of illicit feelings and inclinations is to be found in the social taboos of a community. And the failure, indeed the explicit disinclination,

---

[1] Part of my results I have published in the two books on *Crime and Custom* and *Sex and Repression*.

of psycho-analysts to take social organization seriously, stultifies almost completely their own application of their doctrine to anthropology.[1]

Though no reference will be made to these points in what follows, it was fairer to indicate them at the start, as they have played some part in the discovery and a considerable part in the presentation of the material given in this and in the following chapters.

I

DREAMS

Spontaneous dreams are not of any great importance in the life of the Trobrianders. On the whole the natives appear to dream but seldom, have little interest in their dreams, and do not often tell their experiences on waking or refer to dreams in order to explain a belief or justify a line of conduct. No prophetic meaning is ascribed to ordinary dreams, nor is there any system or code for their symbolic interpretation.

Our interest is mainly in sexual and erotic dreams ; but, in order to understand these, it is necessary to form some idea of the native's attitude to dreams in general. And at the outset it must be understood that by " ordinary " or " free " dreams, I mean spontaneous visions arising in sleep, in response to physiological stimuli, to moods and emotional experiences, to memories of the day and of the past. Such is the material of the dreams which come to every human being, and they play, as I have said, a small part in Trobriand culture, and are apparently rare and easily forgotten.

Quite another class of dreams are those which are prescribed and defined by custom. These are expected of certain people by virtue of their position or of some task that they have undertaken, as a consequence of magic which they have performed,

---

[1] The reader will find this argument substantiated in my *Sex and Repression*.

or which has been performed upon them, or of the influence of spiritual beings. Such stereotyped or standardized dreams are expected, hoped for, and awaited ; and this might easily account for the frequency of their occurrence and for the ease with which they are remembered.

It should be noted that the distinction between free and standardized dreams is not made in native terminology nor even formulated in native doctrine. But as will presently be seen, it is embodied in behaviour and in the general attitude towards dreams.

In standardized dreams, a prominent part is played by visions of departed spirits. They appear to people in sleep under appropriate circumstances and at certain seasons. This is in fact one of the chief ways in which they manifest their existence to the living. But not all dreams about the departed are regarded as true. The appearance may be either a *sasopa* (lie, illusion) or a real *baloma* (spirit). Real spirits always come with a purpose and under conditions in which they can properly be expected. Thus if a recently dead person appears in sleep to a surviving relative, giving him some important message or announcing his death at a distance—such a dream is true. Or when a well-known seer or spiritistic medium is visited in his sleep and next day announces the message he has received, no one doubts the reality of his vision. Or when people go to the island of Tuma and there dream of dead relatives, no doubt exists in the native mind that these really have appeared to them. Or again, in the moon of *milamala*, when the spirits of the dead return to the villages, they will appear to the headman, or to some other notable person, in his sleep and convey to him their wishes. Several such nocturnal visits occurred during my residence in the Trobriands.[1] At times a substitution will

[1] Cf. my article in the *Journ. of the R. Anthrop. Inst.*, 1916, sec. 3, pp. 362 *sq*.

take place, as when an old woman appeared to her son and told him that she was dead, while, in reality, it was the mother of another boy working on the same plantation who had died in the distant Trobriands. But there are also visions of dead friends and relatives who tell untrue things, announce events which never happened, or behave in an unseemly manner. Such dreams are not caused by spirits who, say the natives, have nothing to do with them ; and they are not true.

Another important type of dream in which spirits play a part are those which are initiated by some condition in the dreamer. Whereas in visitations at the *milamala*, or from the spirit island of Tuma, or directly after the death of some person, it is the recently deceased who are seen, in this other class of dreams ancestral spirits of old standing are active. Thus when a child is to be born (see ch. viii), the spirit of an ancestress appears and announces the coming incarnation. More important are the visits of ancestral spirits associated with the art of magic, in which spirits play a considerable part. Many spells begin with a list of persons who have at one time wielded this magic. Such lists of ancestral names are perhaps the most universal feature of Trobriand spells. In certain magical rites, spirits receive offerings of food with a short invocation ; in return they show some concern for the aims of the rite and communicate with the magician, thus affecting not only the ritual but also the practical activity which goes with it. For a magician has in most cases not merely to utter the spell and perform the ritual, but also comprehensively to control the practical activity with which his magic is connected.

To put it more concretely : the *ex officio* leader of a *kula* expedition, the traditional organizer of fishing and hunting, the hereditary master-in-charge of the gardens, invariably wields the magic proper to these pursuits. In virtue of both offices, he is

credited with deeper knowledge and greater fore-
sight than his associates. For one thing, he
is liable, under the control of ancestral spirits,
to dream about his enterprise. Thus the master of
the gardens, in dreams inspired by his predecessors
in office, will learn of impending drought. or rain,
and he will give advice and orders accordingly.
The fishing magician hears from his ancestral spirit
of shoals coming through this or that passage in the
reef, or swimming along a certain channel on the
lagoon, and he will order his team to set out in the
morning and to cast their nets at the appropriate
spot and hour.[1]

A cynical ethnographer might be tempted to
suspect that such prophetic dreams are double-
edged : when they come true, this is not only
practically useful, but proves the goodwill of
ancestors and the validity of magic ; when they do
not come true, it is a sign that the spirits are angry
and that they are punishing the community for
some reason, and still the truth of magical tradition
is upheld. The dream in any case serves its purpose
to the magician. And indeed, in these latter days
of disbelief and decay of custom, the spirits have
frequent occasion to become angry, and the magician
needs all the means at his disposal to vindicate his
personal authority and to maintain belief in his
powers. But in the old days, as even now in
districts with an unimpaired tradition, there was
no question of made-up dreams. In any case they
were not born of anxiety for his own position, but of
care for the success of the enterprise he was controlling. The garden magician, the head fisherman,

[1] Compare the more detailed descriptions of these facts given in
other places : for the part played by ancestral spirits in magic, article
on " Baloma : The Spirits of the Dead in the Trobriand Islands ",
Journal of the Royal Anthropological Institute, 1916, pp. 384-482 ;
for prophetic dreams, p. 366 ; for *milamala* dreams, p. 379 ; for
pregnancy dreams, chap. vii of this book and " Baloma ", pp. 406-18 ;
for the psychology of magical filiation and the relation between
magic and myth, *Myth in Primitive Psychology*, and chap. xii of
Argonauts of the Western Pacific.

the leader of an expedition, identifies himself to a great extent in ambition, in hope, and in effort, with the communal interest. He is extremely keen that all should go well, that his village should surpass all others, that his ambition and pride should be justified and win the day.

There are also dream revelations connected with the black magic by which disease and death are produced. Here it is the victim who has the vision, and, in fact, this is one of the ways of detecting which sorcerer, by evil spells and rites, has caused his illness. Since the sick man always suspects one or other among his enemies of practising or of purchasing sorcery, it is no wonder that such dreams reveal a culprit. However, they are naturally not regarded as " subjective ", but as a by-product of the evil magic.

Yet another class of dreams, to which allusion has already been made (ch. xi, sec. 7), is the dream induced by magic not indirectly and secondarily, but as its main effect. The natives have a definite theory of magic acting through dreams upon the human mind. In connection with the half-commercial, half-ceremonial exchange of the *kula*, the magic of compulsion to generosity (the *mwasila*) will be performed, and this acts upon the mind of the other party to the transaction. Although distant hundreds of miles and separated by stormy seas and reefs, the latter will be visited by the " dream response " (*kirisala*) of this magic. He will dream agreeably and benevolently of the magic maker, his mind (*nanola*) will soften towards him, and he will be generous in his preparation of gifts.[1]

Some forms of love magic described in the previous chapter are based on the same assumption. Erotic dreams (*kirisala*) are the response to certain

---

[1] I am afraid I have not made this point quite clear in *Argonauts of the Western Pacific* (cf., however, pp. 102, 202, 203, 360, and 361). Most spells of the *kula* magic act at a distance upon the partner's mind, even as they are recited at home.

charms. Dreams of a sexual or erotic nature are in fact always attributed to magic. A boy or girl dreams of a person of the opposite sex ; this means that this person has performed love magic. A boy dreams that a certain girl enters his house, speaks to him, approaches him, lies beside him on the mat, though before she had been unwilling to talk to him or even to look at him. Her shyness has been only pretence. All the time she was preparing or even performing magic. In the dream, she is loving and submissive ; she permits all caresses and the most intimate approach. The boy wakes up : " It is all an illusion (*sasopa*, literally, a lie) ", he thinks. " But no, there is seminal fluid spilt over the mat." The girl, in her dream-form has been there. He knows that she makes magic for him and already is half-inclined to pursue her. This is an account, noted down partly in native as it was given to me, from the man's point of view ; but an analogous dream would come to a girl. It is characteristic that the dream takes place, not in the mind of the performer, but in that of his victim.

A married man would try to conceal such visitations from his wife, for she would be angry because he had had congress in dreams with another woman. Also she would know that the other woman had made magic and would be specially watchful, so that the man would find it difficult to follow up the dream intrigue.

One very important class of erotic dreams are those of an incestuous nature. There are, however, serious difficulties in the way of any inquiry about them. Free and easy as these natives are, by custom and convention, in most sexual matters, they become extremely sensitive and prudish whenever their specific sexual taboos are touched upon. This is especially true of incest taboos, and above all of that one concerning the brother-sister relation. It would have been quite impossible for me to inquire directly into the incestuous dream experiences of any of my informants ; but even the general question, whether incestuous dreams occurred, would be met with indignation or vehement denial. Only by dint of very gradual and guarded inquiry among my most trustworthy informants, was I able to find out that such dreams do occur and that, in fact, they are a well-known nuisance. " A man is sometimes sad, ashamed and ill-tempered. Why ? Because he has dreamed that he had connection with his sister ", and " This made me feel ashamed," such a man would say. The fact that the incestuous dream, especially as between brother and sister, occurs frequently and disturbs the mind of the natives considerably, accounts in part for the strong emotional reaction to any inquiry into the subject. The lure of " forbidden fruit ", which everywhere haunts men in dreams and day-dreams, suggests incestuous motives in Trobriand folk-tales and has for ever associated love and the magic of love with the myth of incest (ch. xiv).

It is important to note that, as we shall see presently, even incestuous erotic dreams are excused on the ground that some magic has been misapplied, accidentally mis-directed, or wrongly performed with regard to the dreamer.

We are now in a position to formulate more precisely the native attitude towards dreams. All true dreams are in response to magic or to spiritual influence, and are not spontaneous. The distinction between free or spontaneous dreams on the one hand and stereotyped dreams on the other, corresponds roughly to the native distinction between dreams which are *sasopa* (a lie or illusion), and those which are induced by magic or spirits—that is, are true, relevant and prophetic ; or again to the difference between dreams which come without, and those which come with an *u'ula* (cause or reason). While the natives do not attach much importance to spontaneous dreams, they regard the others as of the same substance as magical influence and as possessing a reality comparable to that of the spirit world. The inconsistencies and lacunæ in their beliefs about dreams are similar to those found in their ideas of an after-life in a disembodied state. Most conspicuous in their belief, perhaps, is the view that magic first realizes its effect in dreams which, by influencing the mind, can thus bring about objective changes and events. Thus all "true" dreams may be actually prophetic.

Another interesting link between dreams and the mystical doctrine of the Trobriander is the recurrence of clairvoyant visions in myths and folk-tales—a subject only to be touched on here. Thus we shall see in the myth of the origins of love, that the man from Iwa is led to discover the tragic double suicide and the magical spray of mint by a dream of what has occurred in the grotto. In a myth about the origins of sorcery, a brother sees in a dream that his sister has been killed by the primeval crab-wizard. In a folk-tale to be related presently, about the snake and the two women, a man from Wawela dreams of the distressed maiden and comes to her rescue. In other folk-tales, events happening in a different place are visualized, or a rhyme sung at a distance acts as a spell and produces day-dreams.

It is clear that dream, day-dream, magical incantation, realization by ritual and mythological precedent are welded into an interlocking system of self-confirmatory realities. Dreaming is conceived as one of the real manifestations of magic, and, as it is a definite personal experience, it brings home the efficacy of the specific magic employed. It is thus an important empirical link in the doctrine of magical efficiency and of mythological reality, one which should not be overlooked if we want to understand the psychology of belief among the Trobrianders.

The subject of dreams in general, and erotic dreams in particular, throws valuable light on the natives' flow of imagination and desire. The psychology of their dreams is closely parallel to that of romantic love and of " falling in love ". In native tradition and official doctrine we find a distrust of spontaneous and free elements, of untrammelled and unprescribed impulses in conduct. Similarly we find that the legitimate and true in dreams is always due to some definite motive, once for all laid down by tradition ; and among the motives by far the most important is magic.

That this official view does not cover the facts, that it is not completely true to them, is obvious. In dreams as in romantic love and love impulse, human nature breaks through and flatly contradicts dogma, doctrine, and tradition. Incestuous dreams are the best example of this. Established doctrine in the Trobriands as elsewhere makes use of man's susceptibility to authoritative suggestion, and of his tendency to be impressed by positive instances and to forget negative ones. It first makes the distinction between true and false dreams ; then minimizes, explains away, or forgets contradictory instances, while using all confirmatory ones as further proof of its validity. Thus incest, whether in myth, reality, or dream, is always explained by an accidental misuse of magic. This motive is as clear and prominent in the Trobriand story of incest as in our own myth of Tristan and Isolde.

2

SEX IN FOLK-LORE—STRING FIGURES

IN passing to the expression of sex in folk-lore, we must bear in mind that Trobriand manners do not ban sex as a subject for conversation, save in the presence of certain tabooed relatives, and Trobriand morals do not condemn extra-marital intercourse, except·in the forms of adultery and incest. The attraction of the subject and its piquancy is not due, therefore, to the feeling that it is socially and artificially forbidden. And yet there is no doubt that the natives regard bawdiness as " improper " ; that there is a certain strain about it, barriers to be broken and a shyness to overcome and a corresponding enjoyment in getting rid of the strain, breaking the barriers and overcoming the shyness.

It follows from this emotional attitude that sex is seldom treated crudely and brutally ; that there is a considerable difference in the manner and tone adopted towards it by, for instance, a coarse fellow of low rank who has no social dignity to maintain, and the descendant of chieftains who touches sexual subjects, but touches them lightly, with refinement, subtlety, or wit. In short, manners exist in this matter and are socially valued and graded according to rank. Sex, like excretory functions and nudity, is not felt or regarded as " natural ", but rather as naturally to be avoided in public and open conversation, and always to be concealed from others in behaviour ; hence, to repeat, the " improper " interest in occasional infringements.

Folk-lore, the systematized forms of oral and intellectual tradition, includes significant games and sports, carving and decorative art, folk-tales, typical sayings, jokes, and swearing. In the Trobriands, representations of sexual matters are completely absent from decorative art and from dancing. The only exceptions to this rule are to be found in certain artistically inferior modern productions, invented under the decomposing influence of European culture, though not in any way influenced by European patterns. Dancing and decorative art, therefore, do not fall within our scope. For the rest, sexual elements in games and sports have already been discussed, sex in joking and swearing will be dealt with in the next

chapter, and there remain, for our present consideration, sexual folk-tales and the bawdy figures
and sayings connected with " cat's-cradles ".

String figures or cat's-cradles (*ninikula*) are
played by children and adults in the day time during
the rainy months from November till January,
that is, in the season when the evenings are passed
in reciting folk-tales. On a wet day, a group of
people will sit under the overhanging roof of a
yam house or on a covered platform and one will
display his skill to an admiring audience. Each
set of figures has a name, a story, and an interpretation. Some also have a ditty (*vinavina*),
which is chanted while the artist evolves and
manipulates the figure. Many sets are completely
devoid of sex interest. Among the dozen or so
which I have recorded the following ones show
pornographic details.[1]

In *kala kasesa Ba'u* (the clitoris of Ba'u) the
performer, after preliminary manipulations, produces
a design (Diagr. A, in Fig. 3) in which two large loops
are formed in the main plane of the figure, while at
the bottom of each, a smaller loop sticks out at right
angles to the main plane. The large loops each
represent a vulva and the smaller ones a clitoris.
There is obviously a little anatomical inaccuracy
in this arrangement, since in nature there is only
one organ and in this the clitoris is placed at the
top and not at the bottom of the vulva. But, no
doubt, Ba'u was an anomaly.

The figure complete, the artist skilfully wriggles
his fingers, producing a movement first in one and
then in the other of the clitoris loops. While thus
engaged, he recites rythmically, but not without
jocular inflections, the following words :

---

[1] I did not make any attempt to record the technique of cat's-
cradles. In each set I merely recorded the significant figure or figures,
the meaning and the psychology

Kala kasesa   Ba'u (repeated)
Her   clitoris of Ba'u (repeated)
Kam kasesam, kam kasesam, etc.
Thy   clitoris, thine, etc.

which might be freely rendered : " Look, that is
the clitoris of Ba'u, that is her clitoris. O Ba'u,
thy clitoris, O thy clitoris ! " The movements
and song are repeated a number of times, to the
great amusement of both onlookers and artist ;
then the figure is undone, to a repetition of the
words :

Syagara dyaytu dyaytu, Syagara dyaytu dyaytu, etc.

These words are merely onomatopoetic, imitating
the rythmic beat of the drums in dance music.
Ba'u is obviously a female personality, but nothing
is known of her besides what we learn from this
performance. The clitoris is a favourite subject
for jokes, stories, and allusions. It is often used
in *pars pro toto* figures of speech and is regarded
as a specially attractive and funny detail in the
female organism.

A short set, entitled with some directness and
simplicity " copulation " (*kayta*), represents this
function in a naturally somewhat conventionalized
manner. The strings (Diagr. B, in Fig. 3) are made
to form a double cross, in which the horizontal arm
represents the woman and the vertical the man.
The strings are then pulled so that the centre loop,
which represents the genitals, moves rapidly, up
and down, and right and left, and this, to the
imagination of the amused onlookers, stands for
the characteristic motion in sexual congress. There
is no ditty to this set.

Tokaylasi, the adulterer (C, in Fig. 3), is a
more complicated set and requires both hands, the
two big toes and the heels for its composition. The
accompanying commentary is just spoken in ordinary
prose. The first figure (C, 1) is formed, in its
significant section, of two isosceles triangles, one

337

above the other and touching by the apex. These triangles represent the adulterer and the wife engaged in the act of copulation. To indicate this, strings are manipulated so that the point of contact moves up and down, while each triangle in turn increases and decreases in size. At the same time the artist declares in unambiguous language : " This is the adulterer ; this is the wife ; they copulate." The figure will not be devoid of significance to those acquainted with the native method of copulation described above (ch. x, sec. 12).

The figure is then dissolved to the artist's comment : *tokaylasi bila wa bagula*, " the adulterer goes to the garden." He then adds : *layla la mwala*, " the husband comes "—and by that time the strings form a figure consisting of two loops placed at an angle (C, 2). As these loops begin to move in their turn, each shrinking and expanding (C, 3 and 4), he says placidly : *Ikayta la kwava*, " he has intercourse with his wife." Thus adultery in the Trobriands is represented by two triangles instead of one.

One more cat's-cradle of a purely anatomical character has still to be mentioned. It is named after the hero Sikwemtuya, though this personality has no other claim to fame than his cat's-cradle. Four loops symmetrically disposed around the central point (D, in Fig. 3) represent the head, the legs and the two testicles of Sikwemtuya. Then this duologue is sung :

" *Sikwemtuya, Sikwemtuya avaka kuvagi?* "
" Sikwemtuya, Sikwemtuya what art thou doing? "
" *Bayamata la kaybaba guya'u.*"
" I guard the decorated food of the chief."
" *Bagise puwam?* "
" May I see your testicles ? "

With the last words, one of the testicles begins to enlarge and to move slowly, while Sikwemtuya,

338

through the mouth of the artist, utters a self-satisfied grunting noise, somewhat like *ka ka ka ka* . . . He is then requested to show the other one.

" *Tagise   piliyuwela.*"
" Let's see the other one."

and answers with the same words, *ka ka ka ka* . . . and a similar exhibition of his second testicle.

I should like to add that the comical effect of the grunting noises, *ka, ka, ka, ka,* is irresistible, and would be as much envied by a modern (and somewhat *risqué*) cabaret artist, as Melanesian or West African carvings and modellings are admired by modern sculptors. But it is very difficult to render linguistic effects and a sense of fun and ribaldry embodied in speech through the medium of another tongue, whereas decorative art, sculpture, and music speak their own universal language.

3

SEX IN FOLKLORE : FACETIÆ

In the matter of stories, we will begin with the amusing folk-tales (*kukwanebu*) told during the evenings of the rainy season for the entertainment of young and old. They contain accounts of avowedly fantastic and unbelievable events ; they are meant to stir the imagination, to pass the time pleasantly, and, above all, to raise a laugh—at times a very ribald laugh.[1] A few of them are entirely devoid of sexual or scatological motives, and can only be touched on here. There is the tale about fire and water, in which fire threatens to burn water, but water touches it and quenches it. There is one in which a greedy crab wants to catch the fruit collected by a grasshopper, but the fruit falls on him and he

---

[1] For a more detailed account of the sociological and cultural character of these stories and their relation to other types of folk-lore cf. *Myth in Primitive Psychology.*

is killed. A pretty story is told of a beautiful girl who is wooed by the birds. She finds fault with one after another, and finally accepts the smallest and most modest among them. A tale is told of the legendary ogre Dokonikan; his gardens are robbed by a girl who is imprisoned by him and then set free by the youngest of her five brothers; and another describes a contest between the same ogre and a hero. The latter tale is told, in certain districts, not as a myth but as a funny story. A purely gustatory account of two brothers, who, after a time of starvation, over-ate to bursting point, provokes much laughter by its entirely innocent jokes.

Only in one story does the fun turn on defecation: a man sticks to a tree after he has relieved himself, and dies as his relatives try to pull him free. In the tale of the louse and the butterfly, the joke consists in the louse emitting a resounding noise from the rectum, by which explosion he is thrown off the butterfly's back and drowned in the sea.

I will now relate the stories with a sexual motive, giving them in order of increasing ribaldry.

The Snake and the Two Women.—Two sisters go in search of eggs. The younger, in spite of a warning, takes away the eggs of the snake. The mother snake chases the thief through all the villages, and finds her at last roasting the eggs in her own village of Kwabulo. To punish her, the snake enters her body through the vulva, coiling up inside it with only the tail and the nose sticking out. After which, as the natives put it:—

ivagi	*kirisala,*	*ikarisaki*	*matala*
it makes	dream response	it induces dream	eye his

Gumwawela.
man of Wawela.

In other words, this happening brought about a dream response, it induced a vision before the eyes

of a man of Wawela. This man comes to the rescue
and, by magic, induces the snake to creep out, when
he kills it.

The two Brothers and the Chief's Wife.—A younger
brother goes to a distant chief's garden, meets the
chief's wife there and they fornicate under a mango
tree. He is caught by the outraged husband, who
brings him to the village and places him on a high
platform, to await his death. However his brother
rescues him by magic, and makes all the men of that
village disappear by the same means ; after which
the two marry the women and settle down.

The Reef Heron and Ilakavetega.—Ilakavetega is
an old woman who lives with her granddaughters.
These go to the seashore, where they meet a reef
heron who inquires who they are. " We are the
granddaughters of Ilakavetega." " Tell her then,"
answers the bird, and intones :—

> *Kaypwada'u*   *wila,*
> Full of sores   cunnus hers,
> *kaypilipili*   *wila,*
> full of small sores   cunnus hers,
> *kaypwada'uyala*   *wila,*
> sore covered   cunnus hers,
> *kaykumikumi*   *wila :*
> eaten away by sores   cunnus hers :
> *ibusi*   *kalu*   *momona,*
> It flows down   her   discharge,
> *akanuwasi*   *yaegu*   *bo'i.*
> I lap it up   myself   reef heron.

This somewhat gratuitous insult is repeated in
full and with the same sing-song intonation to
the grandmother, who accompanies her granddaughters to the seashore next day, meets the reef
heron and hears what he has to say for herself ;
so that his song is chanted three times in the course
of the narrative. The heron unfortunately gets
entangled among the coral on the reef, and is caught,

killed, and eaten, but the interests of poetic justice
are served, for a sorcerer kills Ilakavetega and her
granddaughters to avenge the death of this amiable
and witty bird. Also the sorcerer copulates with
each·of his victims before killing them.

The Stingaree.—In this story the ribald and
dramatic interest are nicely balanced. In the village
of. Okayboma there lives a woman, mother of five
sons, who is endowed with the anatomical anomaly
of five clitorises.[1] In the tidal creek of that village
dwells a giant stingaree. One day when the boys are
out in the taro-garden, the stingaree flops up the
mangrove swamp, gets into the village, and enters
the house, intoning a ribald and cruel ditty :

> *O vavari, vavari, O varvari, vavari,*
> *Vari to'i, to'i.*
>
> *Apasisi,   apaneba,*
> I cut it sore, I scarify it,
>
> *magusisi,   magusike'i,*
> I want to cut it, I want to cut at it,
>
> *oritala wila   inumwaya'i,*
> one   cunnus hers   slackens,
>
> *bayadi kala kasesa,*
> I saw   her   clitoris,
>
> *ba'ilituli, bitotina, biwokwo.*
> I cut off, it snaps, it is over.

This may be rendered, the onomatopoetic words
being repeated as they occur : " *O vavari, vavari,
vari to'i, to'i*—I cut it and make a scar of it, I cut
it with a will, I like to cut at it, one part of her vulva
has got slack, I shall saw off one her clitorises,
I saw it off till it snaps and is gone."

The stingaree then proceeds to business, copulates
with the old woman and cuts off one of her multiple
appendages. My native informants, in their commentary, affirmed that the *va'i* had a penis ; but it
seems more likely that those who originally contributed to the making of the story were inspired

---

[1] The arithmetical expert will, no doubt, discover that the old lady
had six clitorises. I reproduce the native story as it was given me.

by the long, saw-edged dart in the middle of the stingaree's tail, which, were it used as a sexual instrument, would certainly have the baleful results described in the story.

The sons come back and the mother complains ; so the eldest one offers to protect her next day. But when the stingaree flops along into the village, and when he intones his sadistic ditty, and when this chant, like a magical spell, produces a portent (*kariyala*) in the form of lightning and thunder, the son runs away and the mother is deprived of another *kasesa* (clitoris). Nor do the second, third, and fourth brothers behave any better. Four times does the stingaree repeat every word of his ditty and every detail of his behaviour, until the mother is left with but one clitoris, and only the youngest son to defend it and to save her life. For the story assures us that she could not survive the loss of all the five *kasesa*.

The youngest son prepares a number of spears made of strong hardwood, places them all along the road which the cruel fish has to traverse from the creek-head to the house, and then waits in ambush.

When the stingaree appears, he sings his ditty for the last time. Now, however, he sings : " One only, a solitary one clitoris remains. I have come, I shall finish it off ; it will be over with her clitorises, she will die." I shall quote the end of the narrative in free translation.

" The stingaree imagines that he will enter the house. The son sits high up, on the raised platform in front of the house. He grasps the spear, he pierces the stingaree. This runs away ; the man, however, comes down. He takes the spear made of *se'ulawola* wood, which he had stuck in the areca palm. He throws it, and the impact causes the stingaree to stand up. The next spear has pierced it also. The man runs to the *natu* fruit tree, takes the spear made of *tawaga* wood and throws it. He runs to the mango tree and takes the spear of hard palm wood, he pierces the stingaree's eye. He takes a strong cudgel and hammers the stingaree till it dies." The story ends with the return of the elder brothers who disbelieve the young man's story, until they are convinced by the sight of the stingaree's corpse. Then the fish is cut up and distributed among those lagoon villages in which it is not, as is usual in the Trobriands, considered an abomination.

The Story of Digawina.—The heroine's name etymologically defines her anatomical peculiarities and her character. The root *diga* means "to fill out", "to pack into"; *wina* is the dialectic and archaic form of *wila*, cunnus. Digawina is endowed with very large and comprehensive genitals. It is her custom to attend the big distributions of food (*sagali*) made after a man has died, and to steal more than her share; packing coco-nuts, yams, taro, areca nuts, betel pods, large chunks of sugar cane, and whole bunches of bananas into her vagina. Thus things mysteriously disappear, to the great annoyance of all others present, and particularly of those who arrange the feast. Her practices are discovered at last. The master of the next distribution conceals a large black mangrove crab (*kaymagu*) among the food, who cuts through her *kasesa* (clitoris) and thus kills her. With this tragic event the story ends.

The White Cockatoo and the Clitoris.—A woman named Karawata gave birth to a white cockatoo, who flew away into the bush. One day Karawata went to the garden, telling her *kasesa* (clitoris) to look after the *kumkumuri* (earth baking oven). The *kasesa* replies confidently : *Kekekeke.* But the white cockatoo has seen everything from the bush ; he swoops down and strikes the clitoris, who cries out plaintively : *Kikikiki*, and topples over, while the cockatoo eats the contents of the oven. (It is necessary to imagine the big, flat mound-like earth oven, the tiny clitoris standing on guard, and the cruel white cockatoo watching sardonically for its chance. The absurdity of the situation appeals to the natives' sense of the ludicrous.)

Next day, Karawata says again to her *kasesa* : " Let us catch pig, get some yams, and bake it all in the earth." Again she takes off her *kasesa*, and leaves it to look after the oven, and the *kasesa* says confidently as before : *Kekekeke*. Again the white cockatoo descends from the branch, strikes the *kasesa*, who, with a plaintive *kikikiki*, topples over ; and again the cockatoo eats the contents of the oven. Next day the woman says : " I shall go to garden and you look properly after the food." *Kekekeke*, answers the *kasesa*, but all that happened on the two previous days is repeated, and Karawata and her *kasesa* die of hunger.

Mwoydakema.—This hero sees two women who are going to fetch salt water from the beach. He hails them :—

Wo !	*tayyu*	*vivila !*	*Wo !*	*mitakuku,*
Wo !	two	women !	Wo !	nibbled eyelashes,
	kada	*mitakuku*		*yoku.*
	our (dual)	nibbled eyelashes		thou.

This, in free translation, means :—

" Hullo ! two women are coming. Hullo ! Sweethearts, those with whom I would like to exchange nibbling of eyelashes."

The women answer :—

O.gala	*ikwani*
O not	it grips,

Which amounts more or less to our colloquial " nothing doing ".

Mwoydakema then exclaims :—

O ! kimali kadi kimali yoku,

which means : " Oh thou, erotic scratching " ; in other words : " You with whom I would like to exchange erotic scratches."

The women, however, walk on and leave him to the polishing of his stone axe. But he runs ahead of them to the beach and, by means of a magic ditty, moves the sea, which covers him and leaves him buried in the sand with only the penis sticking out.

The women come upon this solitary object on the beach, and begin to quarrel about to whom it belongs. Finally, one after the other, they bestride it, pulling each other off, and each wanting to enjoy it as long as possible. This to the natives is the most hilarious part of the narrative. After they have gone, Mwoydakema shakes off the sand, runs back to his axe, and hails the women again (almost in the same words) as they walk back from the beach. Next day the same events are repeated, and the women have three turns each at the " stick " (as they call it) on the beach. On the third day the same thing happens again, but after the women have enjoyed the " stick ", they conceive the idea of digging it up and taking it home. They gradually discover the various parts of Mwoydakema, till he jumps up and runs away. And when they go back to the village they have to pass him once more, and he teases them with their performances.

Momovala.—Momovala goes with his daughter to the garden and sends her up a tree. He looks up and sees her genitals, and emits the long-drawn *katugogova*. This is produced by giving voice on a high-pitched note, while the sound is interrupted by the rapid beating of the mouth with the hand. It is used to express intense emotional excitement of a pleasant kind. She asks him why he screamed. " I saw a green lorry," he answers. The same sequence is repeated, and he mentions another bird, and so on several times over. When she comes down from the tree, the father has already discarded his pubic leaf and is in a state of erection. She is very confused, and weeps. He, however, seizes her, and copulates and copulates. After all is over, she sings a ditty which may be rendered : " O *Momovala,*

Momovala ! Gut of my gut, father my father. Father by name, he seized me, he brought me, he wronged me." The mother hears her and guesses what has happened. "Already he has got hold of the girl and copulated. I shall go and see."

The mother meets them, the girl complains and the father denies. The girl goes to the seashore with all·her belongings, and sings to a shark to come and eat up, first her wooden board for the making of grass skirts, then her basket, then one arm, then the other arm, and so on, interminably singing the same ditty for each object. Finally she sings : " Eat me up altogether," and the shark does so.

At home Momovala asks the mother where the girl has gone, and learns of her tragic death. His answer is to ask the mother to take off her grass skirt and to copulate with him. The story describes his horizontal motions, which are so strong that his wife complains : *Yakay*, *yakay*, an expression of pain. But he only pushes deeper and deeper. She complains again to no purpose. She dies after the act.

Next day people ask him in the garden what has happened. He says that his wife has been speared. " Where ? " " In her vagina." Momovala then cuts off his penis and dies.

This is perhaps the cruellest story of my collection.

4

SEX IN FOLK-LORE : LEGEND AND MYTH

Passing from the purely narrative and entertaining fairy tales to more serious forms of folk-lore, we find, in Kwabulo, one of the lagoon villages, a local legend of a pronouncedly sexual character. The story is told in a manner half-way between the serious and the jocular. It is, indeed, a significant legend to the inhabitants, for it is embodied in a famous song, it is associated with the history of their village and it is believed to be true, since certain natural features in the locality witness to its authenticity. Also it contains elements of the tragic, especially in the self-castration of the hero and in his lyric yearning for his distant home. The central theme is ribald, however; and when telling it or referring to it, as they often do, the natives are by no means solemn, but delight to exaggerate and multiply unseemly similes about the crux of the tale, which is the long penis of the hero, the legendary headman of Kwabulo. I shall quote this story, keeping as closely as possible to the native style of narrative.

The Legend of Inuvayla'u

In the village of Kwabulo there lived Inuvayla'u the head of his clan, the Lukuba clan; the head of his village. He copulated with the wives of his younger brothers, of his maternal nephews.

When the men went out fishing, he would stand outside a house, and make a hole in the thatch; he then thrust his penis through the thatch and fornicated. His penis was very long; his penis was like a long snake. He would go into the garden when the women made *koumwala* (clearing the ground from debris preparatory to planting); or when they *pwakova* (weeded the ground). He would stand right away behind the fence, he stood in the uncut bush and his penis wriggled on the ground like a snake. The penis crept along all the way. The penis would approach a woman from behind as she was bending down to her task. It would strike her hard till she fell, and on all fours she would be fornicated with as the penis entered the vulva.

Or when women went to bathe in the lagoon the penis would go under the water like an eel and enter the vulva. Or when they went to collect shells, as women do on the western shore (pl. 80), wading and feeling for them with the toes in the mud of the lagoon, Inuvayla'u would fornicate with them. When the women went to the water-hole, he would smash

their coco-nut shell bottles and fornicate with them.
The men were then very angry for they had no water
to drink. They would abuse the women. The women
would be too ashamed to speak, for their bottles
had been broken. One day the men ordered, telling
their wives :

" Cook fish, cook *taytu*, make pudding of taro,
so that our revered old man eats his fill." " No,"
answered the women, " we shall not do it ; this man
does wrong by us ; when you go to fish, and we
remain in the village, when we work in the
garden, by the water-hole, in the lagoon, he does
violence to us."

Then the men watched him. They said they were
going to fish. They hid in the *weyka* (the thick
scrub surrounding the village), they saw : Inuvayla'u
stood outside a hut, he made a hole in the thatch ;
his penis sneaked on the ground, it crept through the
hole, it came in : he wronged the wife of his younger
brother. The men went to the garden . . . (here the
various conditions under which the hero plays his
foul pranks on the women are again enumerated,
in almost exactly the same words as before).

When his younger brothers, his maternal nephews,
saw this, they grew very angry. Next morning they
ducked him ; they ducked him in the head pool
of the tidal creek, which comes up to the village of
Kwabulo (pl. 81).

He came out of the water. He returned to his
house, his mind was full of shame and of sorrow.
He spoke to his mother Lidoya : " Bake some *taytu*
and fish. Bake it in the ground. Pack all our
belongings and the food in your big basket ; lift it
and put it on your head ; we shall go, we shall
leave this place."

When all was ready, he came out of his house,
which stood on the *baku* (central place of the village).
He wailed aloud, facing the *baku*. He took his
kema (axe), he cut at his penis. First he wailed and
wailed over it, holding it in his hands. Then he cut

off the point of his penis ; it came off on the *baku* in front of his house ; it was turned into stone. The stone is still there, on the *baku* of Kwabulo in front of the headman's house. He cried and wailed and went on. He stood outside the outer ring of houses, he looked back, he took his penis and wept over it. He struck again with his axe. The second bit fell off and was turned into stone. It can be seen still outside the village in Kwabulo. He cried and wailed and went on. Half-way between the village and the tidal pool of the creek he stopped. He looked back towards the houses. He took his penis into the palms of his hands, he wept over it and cut off another bit. It turned into stone, and can be seen there not far from Kwabulo. He came to the canoes ; he looked back towards the village, he wept over his genitals. He took the axe and cut off the remaining stump of his penis. It was turned into stone, and it lies now near where the Kwabulo men moor their canoes. He entered his canoe and punted along. Half-way down the creek he wept once more. He gripped his axe and cut off his testicles. Large white coral boulders (*vatu*) lie in the creek. They are the token : they show where Inuvayla'u cut off his testicles.

Inuvayla'u and Lidoya, his mother, went to Kavataria (to the north of Kwabulo, a village, from which overseas expeditions are made south). He stole a large *waga* (canoe), a *mwasawa* (sea-going canoe). But the owner caught him and chased them away. They went to Ba'u (a village further north). He took a sea-going canoe ; he told his mother Lidoya : " Put in your basket, we shall sail." They sailed, they came to I'uwaygili (a village on Kayleula). He told his mother . . . (here the same words as above are repeated ; then they sail again, arrive at another village and again he asks her to put in her basket ; and so on, through a monotonous enumeration of the villages along the lagoon and through the Amphlett Islands down to the *koya*, the high mountains on the D'Entrecasteaux Archipelago). Inuvayla'u arrived in the *koya*. There he settled, there he lived, and with him his mother, who helped him to make gardens and cooked his food for him. He went out to fish with a flying kite, and with the deep sea net which has to be sunk far under the water. His mother made gardens on the mountain slope and she made cooking pots for him.

One day he went high up the mountain slope. The day was clear. Far away among the *budibudi* (the small clouds that gather round the horizon in the monsoon season), he saw the large flat island of Kiriwina, he saw the wide lagoon. On its water he saw a canoe, a canoe of Kwabulo, his native village.[1] His inside grew soft (*inokapisi lopo'ula*). He wanted to see his village, he wanted to punt among the mangroves of Kwabulo.

They sailed. On the sea they met a boat from Kitava. He tells his mother: "Beg them for *sayaku* (aromatic black paint); beg them for *mulipwapwa* (ornaments of shell)." The mother offered herself to the Kitava men. They copulated with her on their canoe; they gave her some *sayaku* and a few shell ornaments. He had some red paint and some red shell ornament.

On the landing-place at the head of the creek he adorned himself. He went to the village. In his festival adornment he stood on the *baku* (central place), he sang the song which he had composed in the *koya* (southern mountains). He taught the song to the villagers, to his younger brothers, and maternal nephews. He gave them the song and the dance. For all time this has remained the dance and song of the people of Kwabulo. It is danced with the

---

[1] For the strange and impressive contrast between the green waters and white chalk of the Trobriands and the brown volcanic rock, high mountains and deep blue sea of the *koya*, compare *Argonauts of the Western Pacific*, *passim*. The reader will also find there accounts of the emotional attitude of the natives towards the landscape and further expressions of it in folk-lore.

kaydebu (dancing shield); (pl. 82). The men of Bwaytalu and of Suviyagila have purchased it and they dance it also. Inuvayla'u lived in his village till he died. This is the end of the story.

I obtained a few variants of this myth by hearing it told in several villages, and also some comments which may be added. The act of expiatory self-castration is sometimes made to take place on Inuvayla'u's return home. This, however, does not tally with the sequence of natural relics. All the stones described in the myth still exist, though the similarity to their anatomical prototypes has worn away with time, while their size must have enormously increased. I have seen the relics several times, but unfortunately I was always prevented by weather or the time of day or high tide from taking a photograph of the stones. Making the necessary allowances for imagination and latitude in exegesis, there can be no doubt that the testicles are in the creek—large, round boulders just awash at low tide ; while the *glans penis*, a pointed helmet-shaped piece of white coral, is in the central place of the village. This disposition confirms the version given in the text.

The etymology of the hero's name indicates his failing; the *inu* is unquestionably the feminine particle *ina*, woman, while the verb *vayla'u* means actually to rob or steal ; so that his name can be translated " the thief of woman ". To those who believe in the existence of an old-time gerontocracy in Melanesia this myth will be of special interest ; for in it we have the old (male) " matriarch " trespassing on the rights of the younger men of his clan and, by means of his enormous organ (the symbol of his greater generative power, a psycho-analyst would say), claiming all the women of the community. Some parts of the story show indisputable signs of greater antiquity, whereas others have obviously been modernized. The simple crudity of the first part and its association with natural features has all the interesting sociological significance of the genuine myth, gradually degenerated into mere legend. The second part, on the contrary, with the song which will be quoted presently, is set in modern and realistic conditions, and its lyrical narrative character stamps it as a tale of more recent origin.

It is characteristic also that, in the first part of the legend, the women are described as especially open to attack during their specific privileged occupations, when normally a taboo protects them and not only should a man never make love to them but should not even approach them (see chapter ii, male and female provinces in tribal life). It must be remembered that, while engaged in communal weeding, women are entitled in certain districts to attack any man who approaches them (ch. ix, sec. 8). This is certainly an interesting correlation and might, to an anthropologist endowed with some imagination and a faculty for hypothetical construction, serve as a proof of the antiquity of the myth and furnish a theory as to the custom of *yausa*. By outraging the women when engaged in such occupations as weeding and filling the water-bottles, Inuvayla'u adds insult to injury, and in the legend we see the women more ashamed for the manifest insult to female prerogatives in the broken water-bottles than for their abused chastity. Superficially this breaking of the bottles might appear merely an unpleasant sadistic trait in the otherwise amiable character of Inuvayla'u. In reality, however, all such details are sociologically very significant.

Another slight variant of the legend declares that Inuvayla'u was not allowed to return to his village, but was chased away immediately on his appearance. I prefer to discard this tragic version, partly because Anglo-Saxons do not like sad endings in fiction, partly because it does not harmonize well with the amiable and little vindictive character of the Trobrianders.

The song which is ascribed to the mutilated hero of Kwabulo is but loosely connected with the story of the myth. The first stanza alludes to his trespasses and their consequences, and the expiatory resolution to go away. The coral outcrop or coral ridge mentioned in the first stanza and the marshy ground through which the hero is made to wander, are poetical images of that part of the legend in which the wanderings of the hero and his mother are described.

The second and third stanza still follow the myth. The part of the mother, the sorrow of the son, and the first stages of the journey are common to both song and legend. But the song, neglecting completely the coarser and perhaps more archaic elements of the myth, does not mention castration. There is only the sorrow for the village left behind and the house abandoned.

To indulge in tentative speculation for another moment : may not the first and second parts of the myth be different stories altogether—the first part, a primitive myth with several interesting sociological hints and implications ; the second part and the song, a tale of a real or imaginary man, who, too amorous to be tolerated in the community, was banished from it, and, later, offered in expiation his song and his repentance ? In the course of time the two were amalgamated in the legend, but not in the song.

From the fourth stanza on, the song turns on the motives of decoration, of dancing, of personal renown, and of self-glorification ; of women admiring the singer's ornaments, of his wandering through the villages and his recurring nostaglia. In all this the song is typical of its kind in the Trobriands. I am giving only the first six stanzas because I was unable to translate the remaining ones as fully as these.

THE SONG OF INUVAYLA'U

I

One day they ducked Inuvayla'u.
The news of the fornication spread :
He was dipped, he went under, he came out of the water.
He turned and went to the sea—
Through the *raybwag*[1] and *dumia* he went to the sea.

II

" Our mother Lidoya get together the food,
I turn my eyes to Dugubakiki.[2]
My tears flow at the thought of the *bwaulo*[3] of my village.
My tears flow at the thought of Kwabulo, of the sweet air of Kwabulo.

III

" O mother Lidoya put your basket on your head."
She goes carefully, she stumbles along the creek.
She has left Kwabulo—the house is closed up.
Inuvayla'u will not fornicate any more.
Thy house is locked up—there is no more Inuvayla'u's house.

IV

" It is put up—the mast at the mouth of the creek.
I seek for my song—I am taking the road—I—Inuvayla'u.
My road is Gulagola which leads to Tuma,
And afterwards the Digidagala road which leads through Teyyava.

V

" Women of Kulumata, dance your dance !
Prepare for a round dance with the *tubuyavi*[5] on your faces !
A *tilewa'i*[6] for you—go then to my village,
Go to Oysayase—to Oburaku ! "[7]

VI

" It is the time for the journey, the journey to Kiriwila, usually
pronounced Kiriwina.[8]
The children tried to retain me.
I shall go my road and come to Yalumugwa.[9]
My *dala*[10]—the men ; my love—the women.
They admire my *paya*.[11]
When I come to Okaykoda, my friends will greet me.
My mind is sad.
I am a Luba man, my fish is *kaysipu*.
I have fallen on evil days."

[1] *Raybwag*—coral outcrop, coral ridge ; *dumia*—swamp marshes.
[2] The landing-place of Kwabulo on the lagoon.
[3] *Bwaulo*—cloud of smoke, surrounding a village.
[4] Both roads lead to the north-west district.
[5] Pattern of facial decoration.
[6] Flattery-bond (cf. ch. xi, sec. 3).
[7] Both southern villages.
[8] North-western district.
[9] Village due north of Kwabulo.
[10] Sub-clan.
[11] Turtle-shell ear-rings.

The Story of Kaytalugi

Besides legends of events in a distant epoch, the natives tell tales of far away places. At almost every point of the compass, if we were to believe the natives, some remarkable country is to be found if we travel far enough. One such place is of interest to us here because of the peculiarities of its inhabitants.

" Far away, beyond the open sea—*walum*, as the natives say—if you were to sail between Sim-sim and Muyuwa (i.e. in a northerly direction) you would come to a large island. It is called Kaytalugi. Its size is that of Boyowa (the name of the largest island in the Trobriand group). There are many villages. Only women live in them. They are all beautiful. They go about naked. They don't shave their pubic hair. It grows so long that it makes something like a *doba* (grass petticoat) in front of them.

" These women are very bad, very fierce. This is because of their insatiable desire. When sailors are stranded on the beach, the women see the canoes from afar. They stand on the beach awaiting them. The beach is dark with their bodies, they stand so thick. The men arrive, the women run towards them. They throw themselves upon them at once. The pubic leaf is torn off ; the women do violence to the men. It is like the *yausa* of the people in Okayaulo. The *yausa* has its season during the *pwakova*. When it is over, it is over. In Kaytalugi the women do it all the time. They never leave the men alone. There are many women there. When one has finished, another comes along. When they cannot have intercourse, they use the man's nose, his ears, his fingers, his toes—the man dies.

" Boys are born on the island. A boy never grows up. A small one is misused till he dies. The women abuse him. They use his penis, his fingers, his toes, his hands. He is very tired, he becomes sick and dies."

356

Such is the account given by the natives of the island with the significant name. *Kayta* means " to copulate " ; *lugi* is a suffix denoting complete satiation. Thus Kaytalugi means " the fill of copulation ". The natives believe absolutely in the reality of this island and in the truth of every detail of their account. They tell circumstantial stories of how sailors, driven towards the island by a strong wind, will land on desert reefs rather than risk making Kaytalugi. The distance to the island is about a night and a day's journey. If you set sail in the morning and go *obomatu* (due north), you will arrive next morning at the island.

There are also stories, believed to be true, about men who went there and succeeded in escaping. Thus, long ago, some men of Kaulagu were stranded on the island, driven off their course, according to some versions, during a *kula* expedition. But another story has it that they went there on purpose. It is a custom in the Trobriands, when work comes to a dead-lock, for one of the men to utter a challenge. Some extraordinary exploit, some diversion or festivity is proposed by him, which he always has to lead, usually to organize, and sometimes to finance. Those who are challenged have to follow him. On one occasion the men of Kaulagu were engaged in planting yams. The work was very hard, the yam supports refused to penetrate the stony soil. The headman cried out : *Uri yakala Kaytalugi* ! " My challenge Kaytalugi ! Let us go and see the women." The others agreed. " They filled their canoe with food, firewood, water bottles, and green coco-nuts. They sailed. One night they slept on the sea, the second night they slept on the sea, the third morning they made Kaytalugi. (This does not agree with the version of other informants, but perhaps the wind was not propitious !) The women assembled on the beach: ' *Wa* ! men are coming to our country ! ' They pulled the canoe to pieces, made a heap of the debris on the beach and sat on it. They copulated, copulated, copulated ; one month, month after month. The men were distributed, each man was married to one woman. They settled.

" They made gardens for months and then they spoke to their wives. ' Are there many fish in your sea ? ' The women answered : ' Very plentiful.' ' Let us repair our canoe,' said the men. ' We shall get some fish, we shall eat it all of us.' They repaired the canoe, they put leaves and food in it, they put in water-bottles and they went away. They sailed three days and came back to Kaulagu, their native village. Their wives, who had mourned them and then re-married, were glad to see them, and came back to them again. They brought home, among other things, a new kind of banana called *usikela*. You can see *usikela* growing in any village now, and eat them. They are very good." (pl. 83) And this is another proof that the story is true, and that Kaytalugi really exists.

When I asked my informants why it was that the men of Kaulagu not only survived but escaped, I was told that they were very strong and that no man allowed sexual access to more than one woman. And just as the women were beginning to get too much for them, they made their escape. It is an interesting example of how every dogmatic version relaxes when elaborated into actual examples, even though these are imaginary.

Another story is told about a man of Kaybola, a village on the northern shore. Fishing for shark, he sailed far away. He came to Kaytalugi and was married by one woman. Feeling tired of her too persistent embraces, he made holes in all the local canoes, overhauled his own, and then suggested to his wife that the fish were very good that morning. He put to sea and set sail. The women of Kaytalugi pushed their canoes into the water to pursue him. But the canoes were swamped and the man returned safely to Kaybola.

When I expressed my doubt as to the reality of this island, my informants suggested that it was all very well to be sceptical, but at the same time I must not try to go there on pain of never getting away again. They added that all *gumanuma* (white men) would like to go to Kaytalugi, but were afraid to do so. " Look, not one *gumanuma* has been to Kaytalugi ! "—another irrefutable proof of its existence.

So far we have been discussing the less sacred classes of folk-lore, and in these we have found the sexual motive predominant. The less the religious or moral significance of a story—the less " real " it is to the native—the more frivolous it becomes ; and the more frivolous it becomes, the more frequently, as in the fairy tales (*kukwanebu*), does it hinge on sex. But among legends, there is only one story which has sex as its principal motive, that of Inuvayla'u, and only one geographical account, that of Kaytalugi. The real myths (*lili'u*) hardly ever have a sex motive ; the myths of the origins of humanity and of the social order, for instance, are completely free of it. Again, in the cycle of stories about the hero Tudava, the only sexual reference occurs in the incident of the virgin birth, the mechanism of which is discreetly and chastely described : the hero's mother sleeps in a grotto, and the dripping water (*litukwa*) from the roof pierces her hymen, penetrates the vagina and thus " opens her " (*ikaripwala*), making it possible for her to conceive (see ch. vii).

No sexual elements are to be found in the several myths referring to the circular trade *kula* ; or in those of the origin of fishing, of canoes, and of diving for the spondylus shell. Nor are any to be found in the myth of old age, death, and the annual visit of the spirits.

Fire, according to legend, was brought forth by the same woman who produced the sun and the moon. The sun and moon wander away into the sky, but the mother keeps the fire, concealing it in her vagina. Whenever she needs it for cooking, she takes it out of its hiding place. But one day her younger brother discovers where she keeps it, steals it, and gives it to other people. This is the only genuine myth with a distinctly sexual element.

Sex does not play a very important part in beliefs about supernatural beings. The only exception to this rule is the idea that some witches (*yoyova*) have intercourse with *tauva'u* (malignant, anthropomorphic beings who come from the southern islands and cause epidemics). Thus Ipwaygana, a woman of the Malasi clan who was married, against all the rules of exogamy, to Modulabu, the Malasi headman of Obweria, has a familiar *tauva'u*, who visits her sexually and teaches her the arts of evil magic (she is to be seen on plates 77 and 78). Bomwaytani of Kaybola, the headman's wife and a notorious *yoyova*, is also known to have a liaison with such a malignant, super-human instructor.

But in the Trobriands such cases are sporadic. The belief in a witches' Sabbath which seems to obtain among the Southern Massim, is not found in the northern district. Informants from Normanby Island and from the islands of the east end told me that witches foregather at night and meet Ta'ukuripokapoka, a mythological personality and apparently an expert in evil craft. Dances and orgies take place, in which the witches copulate with male beings and even with Ta'ukuripokapoka himself.

5

THE EROTIC PARADISE OF THE TROBRIANDER

In the Trobriands, as in almost every culture, one of the most important dogmatic systems or mythologies is that referring to a future life.

The Trobrianders place the spirit world on a small island called Tuma lying to the north-west.

There, unseen by mortal eyes, undisturbed by the troubles of the world, the spirits lead an existence very much like that of ordinary Trobriand life only much more pleasant.[1] Let me quote a good description by one of my best informants, Tomwaya Lakwabulo (pl. 37), a famous seer, a spiritistic medium of no mean talent and imagination (also of no small cunning) and a frequent guest of the spirit world :

" In Tuma we are all like chiefs ; we are beautiful ; we have rich gardens and no work to do—the women do it all ; we have heaps of ornaments and we have many wives, all of them lovely." This summarizes the ideas and aspirations of the natives with regard to the spirit world—at least, as long as it remains a matter of remote speculation, for their attitude towards death and the desirability of an immediate move to Tuma remains unaffected by what they think of and hope for in the next world. On this point they are exactly like ourselves. Many a good Christian will grow enthusiastic about the joys and consolations of Heaven without showing, however, any alacrity to repair thither.

But in distant perspective and as a picture for dogmatic fantasy, the home of the spirits in Tuma remains a paradise, and above all an erotic paradise. When a native talks about it, when he grows eloquent and relates the traditional stories, filled out with scraps of information gathered from recent spiritistic mediums, and elaborates his personal hopes and anticipations—all other aspects soon fade into the background and sex comes to the fore ; sex primarily, but set about with its appropriate trappings of personal vanity, display, luxury, good food, and beautiful surroundings.

In their anticipations, Tuma is thronged with beautiful women, all ready to work hard by day

---

[1] Cf. " Baloma : The Spirits of the Dead in the Trobriand Islands," in *Journ. of the R. Anthrop. Institute*, 1916, for a preliminary account, based on my first year's investigations in the Archipelago.

and dance by night. The spirits enjoy a perpetual scented bacchanal of dancing and chanting on spacious village-places or on beaches of soft sand, amid a profusion of betel and of green coco-nut drinks, of aromatic leaves and magically potent decorations, of wealth and the insignia of honour. In Tuma each one becomes endowed with such beauty, dignity, and skill that he is the unique, the admired, the pampered protagonist of a never-ending feast. By some extraordinary sociological mechanism, all commoners become chiefs, while no chief believes that his relative rank is to be diminished or dimmed by the spirits of his inferiors.

Let us follow the adventures of a spirit as he enters his future home.

After certain preliminary formalities, the spirit comes face to face with Topileta, the guardian of the road to Tuma. This person, who belongs to the Lukuba clan, looks very much like a man and is essentially human in his appetites, tastes, and vanities. But he is of the consistency of a spirit, and his appearance is distinguished by very large ears which flop like the wings of a flying fox. He lives with a daughter or several daughters.

The spirit is well advised to address Topileta in a friendly fashion and to ask the road, at the same time presenting the valuables which were given to him for the journey to Tuma by his surviving relatives. These valuables, be it noted, are not buried with the body nor destroyed, only pressed and rubbed against it before death and afterwards placed on the corpse for a time (see ch. vi, sec. 3). Their spiritual counterparts are supposed to be taken by the spirit of the deceased on his journey to the next world, and then, according to one version, offered to Topileta, or, according to another, used to decorate the spirit's own person on his entrance into Tuma. No doubt an intelligent spirit finds a way to do justice to both requirements.

Topileta, however, is not satisfied with mere

gifts. His lust is equal to his greed, so that if the
spirit is a female he copulates with her, if a male he
hands him over to his daughter for the same purpose.
This accomplished, Topileta puts the stranger on
his way, and the spirit proceeds.

The spirits know that a newcomer is arriving
and throng to greet him. Then a rite is performed
which deeply affects his mind. The spirit arrives
filled with sorrow. He yearns for those left behind,
for his widow, his sweetheart, his children. He
longs to be surrounded with his family, and to
return to the bosom of his wife or of his earthly love.
But in Tuma there is an aromatic herb called *bubwayayta*. This is made into a *vana* (bundle) and magic
is spoken over it by a fair spirit-woman, immediately
before a male spirit appears upon the island. As
he approaches the group who stand awaiting him,
the most passionate, and, no doubt, the loveliest
of the spirit women runs towards him and waves
the scented herb before his face. The scent enters
his nostrils, carrying with it the magic of *bubwayayta*.
As with the first sip of the water of Lethe, so this
scent makes him forget all that he has left on earth,
and from that moment he thinks no more of his
wife, yearns no more for his children, desires no
more the embraces of earthly loves. His only wish
now is to remain in Tuma and to embrace the
beautiful though unsubstantial forms of spirit
women.

His passions will not remain long unsatisfied.
Spirit women, unfleshly though they appear to us
mortals, have fire and passion to a degree unknown
on earth. They crowd round the man, they caress
him, they pull him by force, they use violence on
him. Erotically inspired by the *bubwayayta* spell,
he yields and a scene is enacted, unseemly to those
unused to the ways of a spirit, but apparently quite
the thing in Paradise. The man submits to these
advances and copulates with the hostess-spirit in
the open, while the others look on, or, stimulated by

the sight, do likewise. Such promiscuous sexual orgies, in which male and female mix indiscriminately, congregate, change partners and reunite again, are frequent among the spirits. So at least I was told by several eyewitnesses, not from the world of spirits, but from that of mediums.

For I luckily had the privilege of discussing these matters with a number of seers who had actually been in Tuma, dwelled among the spirits, and returned to tell the tale. Most prominent among my informants was Tomwaya Lakwabulo, whose name had been mentioned to me and his exploits recorded with a mixture of respect and cynicism, before I actually met and worked with him.[1] I also had opportunities of speaking with Bwaylagesi, a woman medium, with Moniga'u, and with one or two other lesser mediums. The details of life in Tuma given so far are common property and form part of general folk-lore ; and my eyewitnesses only confirmed these, though they were able to add colour and concrete vividness to them. I shall now proceed to more esoteric information.

Tomwaya Lakwabulo was married on earth to a woman called Beyawa, who died about a year before I came to Oburaku. He has seen her since in Tuma, and, remarkably enough, she has remained faithful to him, regards herself as his wife over there, and will have nothing to do with anyone else. This is Tomwaya Lakwabulo's own version. He agrees, however, that in this respect the late Beyawa, or rather her spirit, is an unprecedented exception to all other spirit women. For they all, married and unmarried alike, are sexually accessible to anybody— to him, Tomwaya Lakwabulo, in any case. They

---

[1] Cf. " Baloma : The Spirits of the Dead " (*Journ. R. Anthr. Inst.*, 1916), published before my third expedition. During this expedition I lived for several months in Oburaku, saw Tomwaya Lakwabulo in trances and in his sober moods, and used him as a medium. I found that in spite of the unmasking of Tomwaya Lakwabulo, described in the article noted, he enjoyed an undiminished prestige in his own community and in the Trobriands universally. In this respect also, the Trobrianders do not greatly differ from ourselves.

all, with the exception of Beyawa, make *katuyausi* and receive *ulatile* visits.

It was long ago, when Beyawa was young and attractive, that Tomwaya Lakwabulo paid his first visit to Tuma. He then made the acquaintance of one of the most beautiful spirit girls, Namyobe'i, a daughter of Guyona Vabusi, headman of Vabusi, a large village on the shore of Tuma. She fell in love with him; and, as she was so very beautiful and moreover performed *bubwayayta* magic upon him, he succumbed to her charms and married her. Thus he became, so to speak, a bigamist, or at least a spiritual bigamist, having his wife on earth in Oburaku and his spiritual wife in Vabusi. Since that time, he has regularly frequented the land of spirits during trances, when he neither eats nor drinks nor moves for weeks. (At least, in theory: I visited Tomwaya Lakwabulo in one of these trances, and succeeded in insinuating a tin of bully beef and some lemon squash into him, and moved him to accept two sticks of tobacco.) These professional visits to Tuma, besides being agreeable on account of Namyobe'i, are profitable, for he carries rich presents to the spirits, entrusted to him by their surviving relatives. There is no reason to doubt that the spiritual part of the presents reaches the ghosts in Tuma.

It is to the credit both of Tomwaya Lakwabulo and of the late Beyawa that she knew and approved of his spiritual partnership, and even allowed her own daughter to be called Namyobe'i after the spirit wife. Now both wives have met in Tuma, but they inhabit different villages. This is in accordance with a general rule, for each earthly community has its spirit colony to which the deceased move after death. There are also a few villages *sui generis*, not recruited from this world and showing strange characteristics. One of them is inhabited by women who live in houses on piles as tall as coco-nut palms. No man is ever allowed to enter the village and no man has ever had intercourse with the women. They bring forth children, but exclusively of the female sex. Such female puritans are, however, happily the exception in Tuma, where love, enjoyment, and lazy pleasure enfold the happy spirits.

To enjoy life and love it is necessary to be young. Even in Tuma, old age—that is, wrinkles, grey hair, and feebleness—creeps upon the spirits. But in Tuma there exists a remedy, once accessible to all mankind, but now lost to this world.

For old age to the Trobrianders is not a natural state—it is an accident, a misadventure. Long ago, shortly after mankind had come upon earth from underground, human beings could rejuvenate at will by casting off the old withered skin ; just as crabs, snakes, and lizards, and those creatures that creep and burrow underground, will every now and then throw off the old covering and start life with a new and perfect one. Humanity unfortunately lost this art—through the folly of an ancestress, according to legend—but in Tuma the happy spirits have retained it.[1] When they find themselves old, they slough off the loose, wrinkled skin, and emerge with a smooth body, dark locks, sound teeth, and full of vigour. Thus life with them is an eternal recapitulation of youth with its accompaniment of love and pleasure.

So their time passes in dancing, singing, and all that goes with these—festive dressing, decoration, scents of aromatic oils and herbs. Every evening, in the cool season, when the persistent trade wind abates, or when the fresh sea breezes quicken the air during the sultry time of the monsoon, the spirits put on festive attire and repair to the *baku* of their village to dance, just as is done in the Trobriands. At times, departing from earthly

[1] For a fuller account see " Myths of Death and the Recurrent Cycle of Life ", on pp. 80–106 of *Myth in Primitive Psychology*.

usage, they will go to the beach and dance on firm cool sand beaten by breakers.

Many songs are composed by the spirits and some of these reach the earth, brought thither by mediums. In common with most such productions, these songs are a glorification of the composer. " The glory of their *butia* (flower wreath) they sing ; of their dancing ; of their *nabwoda'u* (ornamented basket) ; of their facial paintings and decoration." It was quite clear that skill in gardening or carving, outstanding achievements in war or in the *kula*, were no longer objects of ambition to the spirits. Instead we find dancing and personal beauty celebrated, and these mainly as a setting and a preliminary to sex enjoyment.

I will quote one example of such a song, entitled Usiyawenu ; it was composed by a ghost in Tuma, and brought to earth by Mitakayyo of Oburaku, a medium who was already permanently settled in Tuma when I came to the Trobriands.

I

I shall sing the song of idle enjoyment—
My mind boils over upon my lips—
They range themselves round a circle on the *baku*,
I shall join them on the *baku*—
The conch shell is blown—listen !
Look ! The flaming *butia* wreath,
The *butia* of my sweetheart.

II

My father weeps, they start the mortuary dance for me.
Come ! Let us chew betel-nut, let us throw the *bubwayayta*,
Let us break the pod of the betel-pepper,
The betel-nut—my mind becomes numb !

III

My friend, standing on the beach—he is full of passion.
He boils over, my friend on the northern shore of Tuma.
The red-haired man dreams of me,
He has an ornamental basket,
His face shines like the moon in its fullness.

* * * * *

IV

The white clouds gather low over the skyline,
I cry silently.

* * * * *

V

On a hill in Tuma, I rock my baby to sleep,
I shall go and look after my sister,
I shall put a *bagido'u* round my head,
I shall paint my mouth with crushed betel-nut,
I shall adorn myself with armshells on the western shore.

*   *   *   *   *

A Trobriand song is always full of omissions and of allusions to events well known to the listeners, and can never be quite intelligible to a stranger. Even my native informants, however, were not able fully to interpret this song.

After two introductory lines, the first stanza describes the preparations for a dance in Tuma. In the second stanza we have the sudden abandonment of earthly interests, brought about by *bubwayayta*. In the third, a woman sings of a man beloved by her. She is obviously still on earth, and her husband or sweetheart—the composer of the song apparently—has passed into Tuma. She looks to the north-west where monsoon clouds gather, and weeps for him (stanza iv). In the last of the translated stanzas she herself has entered Tuma and describes her attire which, as with all spirits, seems to have become her main concern. It is to her credit that she has not forgotten her baby, though how such a sentimental reminiscence fits into the frivolous atmosphere of Tuma none of my interpreters could explain.

CHAPTER XIII

MORALS AND MANNERS

THE sexual freedom which we find among the Trobriand Islanders must not be mis-called "immorality", and placed into a non-existent category. "Immorality," in the sense of an absence of all restraints, rules, and values, cannot exist in any culture, however debased or perverted it may be. "Immorality," on the other hand, in the sense of morals different from those which we pretend to practise, must be anticipated in every society other than our own or those which are under the influence of Christian and Western culture.

As a matter of fact, the Trobrianders have as many rules of decency and decorum as they have liberties and indulgences. Among all the customs of sexual liberty so far described, there is not one warrant of licence which does not imply definite limits ; not one concession to the sexual impulse but imposes new restrictions ; not one relaxation of the usual taboos but exacts compensation in one way or another.

All Trobriand institutions have their negative as well as their positive side : they bestow privileges but they also imply renunciations. Thus, marriage presents many legal, economic, and personal advantages, but it also means the exclusion of extra-matrimonial intercourse, especially for the wife, and a number of restrictions in manners and conduct. The institution of the *bukumatula* (bachelor's house) has its taboos as well as its privileges. Even such customs as *yausa*, *katuyausi*, and *ulatile*, all of which are especially constituted

369

for licence, are hedged round with conditions and limitations.

The reader who, after the perusal of the previous chapters, still retains a sense of moral superiority over the Trobrianders, will have to be told in the following pages directly and explicitly that the Trobriander has just as clear-cut a feeling for modesty in dress and in behaviour as we have, and that he would be as shocked by us on certain occasions, as we are shocked by him on others. In the matter of excretory functions, for instance, he shows far more delicacy than most Europeans of the lower classes, and certain " sanitary " arrangements current in the south of France and other Mediterranean countries would horrify and disgust him. His tolerance is certainly great as regards the natural forms of sexual intercourse, but to compensate for this, he is free from many aberrations of the sexual impulse. " Unnatural vice," on which we need to impose heavy penalties, has no place in his life, except as a subject for contemptuous amusement. He is shocked when he sees or hears about Europeans dancing pressed against each other ; or when he finds a white man jesting and unconstrained in his sister's company, or showing tenderness to his wife in public. In fact, his attitude to his moral rules is very much like our own, whether we call ourselves Christians or Agnostics : he believes in them firmly regards their infringement with disapproval, and even keeps to them, not perfectly and not without effort, but with a reasonable amount of earnestness and goodwill.

Many things which we regard as natural, proper, and moral are anathema to the Trobriander. And the *onus probandi* would rest on anyone who maintained that the Trobriander's morality is wrong and ours is right, that his limitations and barriers are inadequate and artificial while ours are sufficient and real. In some respects his moral regulations are biologically sounder than our own, in some more refined and subtle, in some a more efficient safe-guard for marriage and the family. In other matters again we might reasonably claim to be his moral superiors. The best way to approach sexual morality in an entirely different culture is to remember that the sexual impulse is never entirely free, neither can it ever be completely enslaved by social imperatives. The limits of freedom vary ; but there is always a sphere within which it is determined by biological and psychological motives only and also a sphere in which the control of custom and convention is paramount.

It was necessary to clear the ground before proceeding to the subject of this chapter, for there is no greater source of error in sociology than a false perspective in sexual morality ; and it is an error especially hard to confound, as it is based on ignorance which does not want to be enlightened and on intolerance which fears the wider charity of understanding.

I

DECENCY AND DECORUM

As we know, the natives not only have definite laws, stringent in their application and enforced by punishments, but also a sense of right and wrong and canons of correct behaviour not devoid of delicacy and refinement.

The forms and customs which are associated with the conduct of such elementary physiological functions as eating and drinking, defecation and micturition are a good illustration of this, and are also illuminating and relevant to our immediate subject, sexual manners.

Eating is not regarded as indispensable to life, nor is the value of food as a utility recognized and formulated by the natives. In fact, they have no idea that there is such a thing as a physiological need for alimentation, or that the body is built up

---

on food. According to them, one eats because one has appetite, because one is hungry or greedy. The act of eating is very pleasant, and it is a suitable expression of a joyful mood. Large accumulations of food (pl. 84), their formal distribution (*sagali*) and, at times, their immediate, though not public, consumption form the core of all native festivities and ceremonies. "We shall be glad, we shall eat till we vomit," say the natives, in anticipation of some tribal ceremony or festival. To give food is a virtuous act. The provider of food, the organizer of many big *sagali* (distributions) is a great man and a good man. Food is displayed in all forms and on all occasions, and they show great interest in new crops, in a rich yield of garden produce, and in a large catch of fish (see pl. 85).

Yet meals are never taken in public, and eating is altogether regarded as a rather dangerous and delicate act. Not only will people never eat in a strange village, but even within the same community the custom of eating in common is limited. After a big distribution, the people retire to their own fireplaces with their portion, each group turning its back on the rest. There is no actual conviviality on a large scale. Even when the big communal cooking of taro takes place, small groups of related people assemble round the pot which has been allotted to them, and which they have carried away to a secluded spot. There they eat rapidly, no one else witnessing the performance (pl. 86).

In fact, eating is rather a means of social division and discrimination than a way of bringing people together. To begin with, distinctions of rank are marked by food taboos. People of the highest rank are practically constrained to eat within their own circle, and those of a lower status have to forego part of their normal diet if they eat in the presence of their superiors, in order not to shock them. Table manners are thus a household affair and are not very polished. Food is eaten with the fingers ; and smacking of lips, noisy expressions of enjoyment and belching are not considered incorrect. To be intently concentrated on one's food and to eat voraciously is, however, thought to be ugly.

Plenty in the matter of food is good and honourable, scarcity is shameful and bad. But opulence in food is a matter of privilege, only to be enjoyed in safety by chiefs and people of higher rank. It is distinctly dangerous for a commoner to be too good a gardener, to have too big, too richly decorated and too well-filled yam houses. The chief distributes food in the form of gifts, he receives it in the form of tribute. He alone should have decorated yam houses ; he must surpass everybody in the display of food during the *milamala* (the return of the spirits), at ceremonial distributions and during the harvest.

Psychologically interesting is the magic called *vilamalia*. It is directed against the elementary impulse to eat and takes away appetite, so that the food remains in the yam houses until it rots. *Malia* (plenty) and *molu* (scarcity or hunger) are very important categories in native life.[1] *Molu* is bad and shameful. It is a terrible insult to tell a man he is hungry ; to say to him : *gala kam* (" no food thine "—" thou hast no food ") or *togalagala yoku* (" thou art a man of no substance "). The use of scarcity and hunger as means of insult is an illustration of the ways in which shortcomings can be brought home to the natives. A man will endure real hunger rather than expose himself to the sarcastic question : " Is there no food in thy village ? "

To sum up : the act of eating is regarded by the natives as an expression of a powerful impulse, of a strong passion. As such it is an important part of the ordinary routine of life ; the evening meal is

[1] Cf. my article, " The Lunar and Seasonal Calendar in the Trobriands," *Journal of the Royal Anthropological Institute*, 1927.

as indispensable a domestic event as rest after work and conversation with the neighbours. It also occupies an important place in every festival and within the realms of the sacred. Food is a means of emphasizing social distinctions, whether of rank or in tribal grouping, and thus indirectly provides a bond of social union. What happens in the alimentary duct after the food has been swallowed is not a matter of concern to the natives ; nor does metabolism influence cultural life again until the alimentary process is complete, when waste matters claim the native's attention and demand customs and cultural arrangements for the disguise of excretory processes. For, as we pointed out when describing the care of the body (see ch. x, sec. 4), the natives have a strong æsthetic feeling against uncleanliness, whether in their own persons or in their surroundings. Unpleasant smells and unclean matters disgust them, especially if they are of an excretory nature.

For this reason the greatest hardship of mourning lies, not in the covering of the body with soot or charcoal, but in the taboo on ablutions. Excretion within the house is quoted as a very heavy burden on those confined by mourning or disease and on their relatives who have to perform the necessary services. The duty of receiving the excreta of small children into receptacles, with the liability of becoming soiled and the necessity of carrying the dirty matter into the bush, is often mentioned as one of the hardships which give to parents, and especially to the father, a permanent claim on the gratitude of the child. It is also quoted as a reason why the child should look after the parents later on, and incidentally repay these particular services in kind should they fall ill.

The handling of the corpse and the operations upon it incidental to certain mortuary practices ; the ritual swallowing of putrid matter which is a duty of some of the survivors, are obligations which

involve heroic devotion on the part of the performers.

Good care is taken to prevent the accumulation
of dirt in the village, above all to prevent any
excretory matter from being deposited near the
settlement. Villages are always carefully swept, and
all refuse placed on the outskirts in large heaps
called *wawa*. Especially offensive matters, such
as decomposing fish, are usually covered with earth.

The sanitary arrangements consist of two reserves
in the bush at some distance from the village, the
one frequented by men and the other by women.
These reserves are scrupulously adhered to, and
the surroundings of a village in the Trobriands, as
well as the roads, would compare favourably with
those in most European countries, especially the
Latin ones.

Natives will never go to these reserves together,
nor will they ever defecate near one another. At
sea, a man will enter the water and ease himself
below the surface, supported by others in the canoe;
for defecation both sexes squat; for micturition
the women squat and men remain standing.

Certain villages, squeezed in between mangrove
swamp and lagoon, have little dry land outside the
settlement, and find it hard to satisfy the demands
of sanitation (pl. 87). In such a village each
sex repairs to one side of the beach and tries to
choose a spot which will be covered by the tide.
But even so they have an evil reputation, and often,
in passing through one, I have seen my native
companions close their nostrils and spit freely, and
have heard their outspoken comments upon its
dirt. And yet, in these fishing villages, even the
refuse of fish is carefully disposed of, and after
preparing fish for eating the people always wash
their hands carefully and anoint themselves with
coco-nut oil.

After excretion the parts are carefully cleansed
with soft leaves, called in this context *poyewesi*

(*po*, root of " excretion " ; *yewesi*, leaves). Children are taught to observe strict cleanliness in this respect, and a careless child is not infrequently shamed by its parents or elders :—

| *Mayna   popu* ! | *gala* | *kuvaysi* |
| Odour of excrement ! | Not | thou wipest |

| *kosiyam* | *mayna kasukwanise* ! |
| thy remnant of excrement, | odour we (excl.) smell ! |

Social distinctions influence considerably the way in which natives are allowed to speak about the subject. The ordinary name for excrement (*popu*), or the verb to defecate (*popu* or *pwaya*) are never used in the presence of a *guya'u* (chief, man of high rank). A special polite word, *solu* or *sola* (lit. : " descend "), is substituted, or else such euphemisms as to " go down " (*busi*), " go and return " (*bala baka'ita*). A man would never excuse himself from a chief's presence by saying " I have to go and defecate " (*bala bapopu*) ; he would say instead : *bala basolu*, or *bala babusi*, " I shall go down " ; or *bala baka'ita*, " I shall go and return."

The word " excrement " is also used in the typical form of bad language, " eat thy dirt " (*kumkwam popu* or *kukome kam popu*). This expression, if used good humouredly, might be taken as a joke and condoned, but it lies on the border-line between chaff and insult, and must never be said angrily. Above all, it must never be said in the presence of a chief, and to use it to him as an insult is an unpardonable offence.

The following incident, which took place during the last war between To'uluwa, high chief of Omarakana, and his traditional foe, the headman of Kabwaku, is a good illustration of the native attitude towards this insult when directed against a chief. During a lull in the fighting, when the two forces were facing each other, a Kabwaku man, Si'ulobubu, climbed a tree and addressed To'uluwa in a loud voice : " *Kukome kam popu, To'uluwa*."

Here was the insult delivered with every aggravating circumstance. It was addressed to a chief, it was said aloud and in public, and the personal name was added, the form in which the insult is deadliest. After the war, when peace was concluded and all other enmities forgotten, Si'ulobubu was openly speared in broad daylight by a few men sent by To'uluwa for that purpose. The victim's family and clansmen did not even raise a protest, still less did they ask for "blood money", or start a *lugwa* (vendetta). Everybody knew that the man had deserved this punishment and that his death was a just and adequate *mapula* (payment, retribution) for his crime. It is even an insult to make this remark to a chief's pig in his hearing, though it is permitted so to address his dog.[1]

The dissociation between sex and excretion, or the excretory processes, is very pronounced in native sentiment and idea. As we know, scrupulous cleanliness is an essential in the ideal of personal attraction. Sodomy is repugnant to natives, and their attitude to it is summed up in the phrase : *matauna ikaye popu* (" this man copulates excrement "). Fæces have no place in magic, custom, or ritual ; nor do they even play any part in sorcery.

In my own experience I have always found the natives very clean and never received any unpleasant olfactory impression in my various social contacts with them. Nor, by the consensus of opinion among white residents, is their bodily odour unpleasant to the European.

Intestinal gases are never released in the presence of other people. Such an act is considered very shameful, and would dishonour and mortify any one guilty of it. Even in a crowd where it can be committed anonymously, such a breach of etiquette

---

[1] Cf. the myth of the pig and the dog below in sec. 5, and in *Myth in Primitive Psychology*, 1926, where its historical importance is discussed.

never happens in Melanesia, so that a native crowd is considerably more pleasant in this respect than a gathering of European peasants.[1] If such a mishap befalls a man by accident, he feels the disgrace deeply and his reputation suffers. Also it will be remembered how quickly an explosive escape of intestinal gas was visited upon the unfortunate louse in one of the fireside stories told in the last chapter.

Scents are as much appreciated and sought after as bad smells are abhorred and avoided. We have seen what an important part is played in native toilet by the variously and exquisitely scented flowers of the Islands : the long white petals of the pandanus, the *butia* and a long list of aromatic herbs, in which the mint (*sulumwoya*) takes the lead ; and we have also seen the use made of oil perfumed with sandal wood. Pleasant smells are closely associated with magical influence ; and as we know already many charms in the magic of *kula*, of love, of beauty, and of success are made over mint, over the *butia* flower, and over several aromatic herbs used as *vana* (tuft placed in the armlet). Personal cleanliness is an essential in all these forms of magic, and charming the *kaykakaya* (washing leaves) is an important part of the ritual.[2]

Indeed, the sense of smell is the most important factor in the laying of spells on people; magic, in order to achieve its greatest potency, must enter through the nose. Love charms are borne into the victim on the scent of some spellbound aromatic substance. In the second and very dangerous stage of sorcery, the object or compound over which black magic has been done is burned, and the smoke enters through the nostrils into the body against which it is directed and causes disease (*silami*). For this reason, houses

---

[1] For some interesting sociology on this subject as among European peasants, cf. Zola's *La Terre.*

[2] Cf. chs. viii and xi of this book, and chs. xiii and xvii of *Argonauts of the Western Pacific.*

are never built on piles in the Trobriands, as it would greatly facilitate this stage in the sorcerer's work. Thus the idea of magical infection through the nose exercises a considerable influence on the culture of the natives.

The malignant witches (*mulukwausi*) are believed to emit a smell reminiscent of excrement. This smell is much feared, especially by people who are sailing, for witches are very dangerous on water. In general the smell of ordure and decomposing matter is thought to be noxious to human health. The natives believe that a special substance emanates from the corpse of a dead person. This, though invisible to the ordinary eye, can be seen by sorcerers, to whom it appears somewhat like the cloud of smoke (*bwaulo*) which hangs over a village. This emanation, which is also called *bwaulo*, is especially dangerous to the maternal kinsmen of the deceased, and because of it they must not approach the corpse, nor perform any of the mortuary duties (see ch. vi, sec. 2).

A few words will suffice to recapitulate here what we already know (see ch. x, sec. 4) about the conventions, manners, and morals of dress. The various functions of attire in enhancing personal beauty, in marking social distinctions, in expressing the character of the occasion on which they are worn do not concern us here, but a word must be added about dress in its relation to modesty. Modesty in the Trobriands requires only that the genitals and a small part of the adjacent areas should be covered, but the native has absolutely the same moral and psychological attitude towards any infringement of these demands as we have. It is bad, and shameful, and ludicrous in a degrading sense not to conceal, carefully and properly, those parts of the human body which should be covered by dress. Moreover there is a certain coquettish emphasis in the care and elegance with which women manipulate their fibre skirts whenever they fear that dress may fail in its duty, through wind or rapid movement.

The broad bleached leaf of the pandanus or areca palm which covers the male genitals is always put in place so precisely and securely that no instance of disarrangement has occurred within my knowledge. No person must ever touch it when it is in position. The word for it, *yavigu*, used with the pronoun of nearest possession, as if it were a part of the body, is also an improper word which must not be uttered save in intimacy. It is interesting, however, that when it is necessary for practical reasons for men to take off the pubic leaf, as during the fishing or diving activities, this is done without either false shame or the slightest symptom of improper interest. The natives convey clearly by behaviour and comment that nakedness is not shameful when it is necessary, but becomes so when due to carelessness or lewdness (see ch. iii, sec. 1, and secs. 3 and 4 of this chap.). Though the taboos surrounding female dress and its name are less stringent, it is just as carefully used as an instrument of modesty.

I have assembled these facts from certain aspects of intimate life, from the physiology of eating and excretion and from the treatment of anatomical aspects of the body, to illustrate native manners ; and to demonstrate that, in spite of certain things which shock us profoundly, the natives show a delicacy and restraint in others which is not only elaborate and well-defined, but is expressive of real moral attitudes : a substantial consideration for the feelings of others and certain sound biological principles. We may be shocked at a savage who tears his meat with his fingers, smacks his lips, grunts and belches in the enjoyment of his food ; while the custom of eating each other's lice is to us decidedly unappetizing. But the native is equally disgusted when the European gorges himself on stinking cheese, or consumes undefined abominations from tins ; or when he unashamedly eats stingaree, wild pig or any other matters permitted only to people of the lowest rank. He is also shocked at the white man's habit of making himself temporarily imbecile or violent with gin and whisky. If, to an uneducated white man, Melanesian dress may appear inadequate, the strange custom prevalent among white women of reducing instead of adding to their dress for festive occasions is upsetting and indecorous to the native who meets it on his travels to European settlements.

Even now, when a more liberal and instructed policy directs the relations between native and European, it is well to remember these things ; and to keep in mind that wisdom and good manners alike demand that we respect those feelings in other people which are dictated by their own cultural standards.

2

THE MORALS OF SEX

Before proceeding to a detailed consideration of the subject of this section, we will assemble and briefly restate the relevant facts already in our possession, so that they may be presented to the reader in their proper perspective. For the inter-relation of facts and the proportions they assume in native life are as important as, if not more so than, the isolated facts themselves, if we are to arrive at right conclusions and have a true picture of Trobriand communal life.

And to see the facts from the native point of view, that is, in their true relation to tribal life, we must again remind ourselves that sex as such is not tabooed. That is to say, the sexual act, provided that it is carried out in private and within certain sociological limits, is not regarded as reprehensible, even when it is not sanctioned by the bond of marriage. The barriers within which sexual freedom obtains, the methods by which these barriers are upheld and the penalties which fall upon the transgressor, can be classified broadly into two groups : the general taboos, which brand certain forms of sexual activity as objectionable, indecent, or contemptible ; and the sociological restrictions which debar certain individuals and groups from sexual access.

A. GENERAL TABOOS

1. *Byways and aberrations of the sexual impulse.*—Homosexual intercourse, bestiality, exhibitionism, oral and anal eroticism—to use psycho-analytic terminology—are, as we already know, regarded by the natives as inadequate and contemptible substitutes for the proper exercise of the sexual impulse. The natives achieve an almost complete freedom from perversion by means of what might be called psychological rather than social sanctions. Sexual aberrations are ridiculed, they are a subject for invective and comic anecdote, and thus treated, they are not only branded as improper but are effectively made undesirable.

2. *Publicity and lack of decorum in sexual matters.*—Public display of the sexual act or of erotic approaches is almost completely absent from tribal life. Lack of care in avoiding publicity, curiosity and any attempt to spy on other peoples' love-making are regarded as unseemly and contemptible. There are few occasions in tribal life when the sexual act could be carried on in public, nor does the *voyeur* figure even in their pornographic folk-lore. The only exception from this rule are the erotic competitive festivals (*kayasa*), described in chapter ix, section 5. From the taboo of publicity only the souls of the blessed in Tuma are permanently released, while in the legendary accounts of female assaults on men (in the custom of *yausa*, and on the Island of Kaytalugi), the openness with which copulation takes place is regarded as an

additional outrage on the passive victims. Thus sexual intercourse, to be in accordance with tribal sanctions, must be carried on within the strictest limits of privacy and decorum.

3. *Sexual Excess.*—The exhibition of sexual greed, or an unabashed forwardness in courting the favour of the other sex, is regarded as bad and despicable in either man or woman, but more especially in woman. This moral attitude should be strictly distinguished from the censure incurred by those people who are too successful in love, and who therefore arouse anger and jealousy.

4. *Lack of Taste.*—We have learned (ch. x, sec. 2) the forms of ugliness and repulsiveness which are regarded as deterrent to erotic interest and that the natives will even go so far as to affirm that no one could or would have intercourse with a person so afflicted. Behind this mere statement of fact there is a definite censure of a mixed moral and æsthetic character which is based on a real and lively sentiment, even though this fails occasionally in practice. It is bad, unbecoming, and worthy of contempt to have anything to do with a human being whose body arouses repugnance. This class of taboo has already been dealt with (in chap. x, sec. 2), and it will not be necessary to return to it.

5. *Miscellaneous and minor taboos.*—There are a number of pursuits which, while in progress, entail abstinence from sexual intercourse and all contact with women ; such, for example, are war, over-sea sailing expeditions, gardening and one or two magical rites. Again, in certain physiological crises, above all pregnancy and lactation, a woman must not be approached by man. The general principle which such taboos express is that sex is incompatible with certain conditions of the human body and with the nature and purpose of certain occupations ; and it must not be allowed to interfere with these.

B. SOCIOLOGICAL TABOOS

6. *Exogamy.*—Sexual intercourse and marriage are not allowed within the same totemic clan. They are more emphatically forbidden within a sub-division of the clan, common membership in which means real kinship. And the taboo is stricter yet between two people who can trace a common descent genealogically. Yet the natives have only one word, *suvasova*, to designate all these degrees of exogamous taboo. Also, in legal and formal fiction, the natives would maintain that all exogamous taboos, whether of clan, sub-clan or proven kinship, were equally binding. Thus, while an ethnographer would get one impression through conversation, he would get an entirely different one by observing the behaviour of the natives. In the more detailed examination of the subject which follows, we shall set practice and legal fiction side by side, and show how these work in together.

7. *Taboos within the family and household.*—The father is not a kinsman of his children, and therefore is not included in exogamous prohibitions. Nevertheless, intercourse between father and daughter is definitely and strongly forbidden. There is no doubt that the taboo which separates members of the same household is, in the reality of tribal life though not in legal theory, a distinct force which is superadded to the exogamous taboo. Not only do we find its influence in the separation of father and daughter, but also in the fact that incest with the own mother and with the own sister arouses incomparably greater moral indignation than incest with a cousin ; not to speak of incest with a " classificatory " mother or a " classificatory " sister, which is easily condoned.

8. *The taboo of adultery.*—This safeguard to the institution of marriage need only be mentioned here, as it has been fully dealt with in chapter v.

9. *The taboos of relationship in law.*—Although there is no formal avoidance, sexual intercourse

between a man and his mother-in-law is definitely wrong. Neither must a man have erotic relations with the sisters of his wife or with the wife of his brother. Marriage with a deceased's wife's sister, though not forbidden, is regarded with disfavour.

10. *Rules safeguarding the privileges of the chief.*— This type of restriction and those which follow are not of the same stringency as the foregoing taboos. They are rather vague rules of conduct, enforced by a general feeling for what is expedient and by somewhat diffuse social sanctions. It is unsafe to interfere with any woman in whom a man of high rank is interested. The ordinary prohibition of adultery becomes much more stringent when the woman concerned is married to a chief. The chief's wife, *giyovila*, is the subject of a special reverence and of a general taboo, which, however, is honoured as much in the breach as in the observance. For she is more desirable and generally no less willing to be desired ; and there is a touch of irony and mock respect in certain sayings and turns of speech in which the word *giyovila* figures.

11. *Barriers of rank.*—The distinction between high and low birth, which divides one sub-clan from another, applies to women as well as to men. It is a general principle that people of high rank (*guya'u*) shall not mate with commoners (*tokay*). In marriage, this rule is strictly kept only with regard to the pariah communities of Bwaytalu and Ba'u, which have had perforce to become endogamous, since no man or woman from another village likes to enter into permanent union with any of the inhabitants. The members of the highest sub-clan, the Tabalu of Omarakana (of the Malasi clan), find their most fitting consorts among two or three other *dala* (sub-clans) in the north-western district.

In prenuptial intercourse, also, there would be some show of discrimination. A girl of high rank would be ashamed of owning to an intrigue with a low class commoner. But the distinctions in rank are many and their interpretation not too rigid; and the rule is certainly not followed strictly where intrigues are concerned. Girls of high rank villages, such as Omarakana, Liluta, Osapola, or Kwaybwaga, do not visit the " impure " villages, Ba'u and Bwoytalu, on *katuyausi* expeditions.

12. *Restrictions as to number in intrigues.*—As we have already said, too open and too insistent an interest in sex, especially when exhibited by a woman, and too obvious and too general a success in love are both censured; but the kind of censure is entirely different in the two cases. In the latter, it is the male who incurs the disapproval of his less fortunate rivals. The great dancer, the famous love magician or charmer of his own beauty, is exposed to intense distrust and hatred, and to the dangers of sorcery. His conduct is considered " bad ", not as " shameful ", but rather as enviable and, at the same time, injurious to the interests of others.

This concludes the list of restrictions placed upon freedom in sexual intercourse. It is clear that moral indignation varies in kind and degree with the categories transgressed—whether these be perversion or incest, breach of exogamy or the infringement of matrimonial and other prerogatives. The last four categories—adultery, trespass on the chief's preserves, intercourse with social inferiors, and numerical excess of intrigues—embrace offences which arouse neither contempt nor moral indignation; they are enforced according to the power of the aggrieved party, backed by the passive support of communal opinion. An adulterer caught *in flagrante* may be killed, and this will be recognized as legal retribution, and not be followed up by a vendetta, especially if the adultery be with a chief's wife (see ch. v, sec. 2). The pre-eminently successful man—especially if of low rank and distinguished only by personal qualities—would be exposed to the danger of sorcery rather than to that of direct violence. And sorcery also would be used against a man suspected of adultery but not caught in the act.

An interesting ethnological document, which throws some light on the retributive use of sorcery, is provided by the specific signs found on a corpse at exhumation indicating the habit, the quality, or the misdeeds for which the man was killed by sorcery. The natives—in common with most primitive races—do not understand " death from natural causes ". When not the result of an obvious physical lesion, death is caused by black magic, practised by a sorcerer on his own account, or on behalf of some notable who pays him to bring about his enemy's death. On the body of the victim, when it is ritually taken out of the grave, are found signs (*kala wabu*) which show why he was killed and thus indicate on whose behalf it was done. Such signs may point to sexual jealousy, personal antagonism, political or economic envy as the motive ; and of frequent occurrence is the sign indicating that the victim's too pronounced erotic propensities were his undoing.

Thus marks are sometimes found on a corpse which resemble the erotic scratches (*kimali*) so characteristic of native love-making. Or the body when exhumed is found doubled up with the legs apart, an attitude taken during copulation by man as well as by woman. Or the mouth is pursed, as if to produce the loud smacking of the lips by which one sex invites the other into the darkness beyond the light of village fires. Or again the body swarms with lice, and, as we know, lousing each other and eating the catch is a tender occupation of lovers. All these signs indicate that the man was done to death by sorcery because he was too much addicted to sexual pleasures, or could boast of too many conquests and such as gave special offence to some powerful rival. There are also a number of standardized patterns which may be found on a corpse suggestive of dancing decoration. These indicate that jealousy of his personal appearance, of his renown as a dancer and as a seducer by the dance were the cause of his death.[1]

Such signs have to be noted by the deceased's own relatives, they are discussed freely—generally, however, without any mention of the suspected sorcerer's name or of his employer's—and no special shame attaches to them. This is note-worthy in connection with the native's attitude to the last few taboos, that is those which safeguard the rights of the husband, of the lover, and of the community. Success in love, personal beauty, and surpassing accomplishments are reprehensible because they appeal especially to women and always encroach upon the rights of someone who, if he can, will avenge the wrong by means of sorcery. But, unlike other sexual offences, adultery and success with women are not felt to be shameful or morally wrong. On the contrary, they are enviable, and surround the sinner with a halo of almost tragic glory.[2]

Perhaps the most important linguistic distinction which throws light upon the native psychology as regards taboos is furnished by the use of the word *bomala* (taboo). This noun takes the prenominal suffixes of nearest possession—*boma-gu* (my taboo), *boma-m* (thy taboo), *boma-la* (his taboo)—which signifies that a man's taboo, the things which he must not eat or touch or do, is linguistically classed

[1] Compare the writer's *Crime and Custom*, pp. 87 to 94, for a full list of sorcery signs and their significance in tribal law.

[2] It was necessary to classify taboos in some way, in order to present the material in a form in which it could be easily surveyed. Obviously my *fundamentum divisionis*—the type of action forbidden—is not the only possible basis for such a classification. The taboos could, for instance, be regrouped according to sanction, intensity of moral feeling, or the varying degree of general interest taken in the prohibition. These differentiating qualities, already indicated, will emerge even more clearly in the course of the descriptions which follow.

with those objects most intimately bound up with
his person : parts of his body, his kindred, and
such personal qualities as his mind (*nanola*), his
will (*magila*), and his inside (*lopoula*). Thus
bomala, those things from which a man must keep
away, is an integral part of his personality, something which enters into his moral make-up.

Not all the restrictions and prohibitions on our
list can be called by this name. And when it is
correctly used, its meaning is subject to many
subtle variations, indicated by tone and context,
according to its application. In its full and correct
meaning, the word *bomala* applies to all the acts
which are specifically called by the natives *suvasova*
—that is, to incest within the family and breach of
exogamy. In this context, the word *bomala* denotes
an act which must not be committed because it is
contrary to the traditional constitution of clan
and family ; and to all the inviolable laws which
have been laid down in old times (*tokunabogwo
ayguri*, " of old it was ordained "). Besides this
general sanction, which is felt to be rooted in the
primeval nature of things, the breach of the *suvasova*
taboo entails a supernatural penalty : an illness
which covers the skin with sores and produces pains
and discomfort throughout the body. (This supernatural penalty can, however, be evaded by the
performance of a specific magic which removes the
bad effects of endogamous intercourse.) In the case
of incest between brother and sister, a very strong
emotional tone enters into the attitude of the natives,
that is, into the significance of the word *bomala*,
endowing it with an unmistakable phonetic colouring
of horror and moral repugnance. Thus even in
their narrowest and most exclusive sense, the words
bomala and *suvasova* have various shades of meaning
and imply a complex system of traditional law and
of social mechanism.[1]

---

[1] Compare the detailed account of the various contraventions and
evasions of traditional law given in *Crime and Custom*.

The word *bomala* is also used in its legitimate sense of " taboo " for the several minor prohibitions, such as are inherent in a man's office, situation or activity, and in this application it still carries something of the idea of a peremptory traditional rule, maintained by supernatural sanctions. But though the only correct description for such taboos is the word *bomala*, it implies in this context a different emotional attitude, milder sanctions and a different type of rule.

In a less rigid sense *bomala* is used to denote the taboos of adultery, the inexpediency of meddling with what is sexually claimed by a chief, and the undesirability of mating outside one's own rank. In these contexts, however, the word covers only the idea and feeling of a definite rule. It entails neither supernatural sanctions nor the emotion of pronounced moral disapproval, nor even the feeling of a strong obligation. This application of the word is, in fact, not quite correct : the word *bubunela*, " custom, the things which are done," used with a negative, would be more accurate here.

Bomala could not be correctly used of actions felt to be shameful and unnatural, actions of which no sane and self-respecting person would be guilty. Neither does it apply to " lack of dignity and decorum ", nor to actions of hazardous enjoyment, nor to pre-eminent sexual success.

Thus, by the rules of usage, this word yields a native classification of taboos into three groups : the genuine taboos with supernatural sanction, the clear prohibitions without supernatural sanction, and prohibitions of acts which must not be done because they are shameful, disgusting, or else dangerous.

The widest linguistic instrument serving to express the distinction between lawful and forbidden, and applicable to all the restrictions of our twelve classes, is given by the pair of words *bwoyna* and *gaga* (good and bad). Such general terms are naturally of loose application, cover a wide range of meanings, and gain some precision only from the context in which they are used. Thus, acts as repugnant and unspeakable as brother-sister incest, and as desirably dangerous as adultery with a chief's wife, would be called *gaga* indiscriminately. *Gaga* means, in one context, " morally unpardonable and only to be atoned by suicide " ; in another, " against the law, against custom " ; in others, " indecorous," " unpleasant," " ugly," " disgusting," " shameful," " dangerous," " dangerously daring," " dangerous and thus admirable."

Analogously, the word *bwoyna* means everything from " palatable ", " pleasant ", " seductive ", " attractive because naughty " to " morally commendable because of the inherent hardships ". An action which is strongly flavoured with the tempting taste of forbidden fruit might, therefore, be plausibly labelled either *bwoyna* or *gaga*, according to the mood, context, situation, and emotional twist of the sentence. So that these words—taken as isolated fragments of vocabulary—afford only a vague index to the moral statements, and do not give us even as much help in defining native views and values as the word *bomala*.

There is, perhaps, no more dangerous instrument than a native vocabulary for the unwary ethnographer to handle, if he is not assisted by a thorough working knowledge of the native language, which alone enables him to control the meaning of his terms through their extensive usage in various contexts. To note down isolated terms with their translations into pidgin, and to parade such crude translations as " native categories of thought " is directly misleading. There has been no greater source of error in Anthropology than the use of misunderstood and misinterpreted fragments of a native vocabulary by observers not thoroughly conversant with native tongues and ignorant of the sociological nature of language. The misleading effects of this are most harmful in the faulty collection, in the field, of so-called systems of classificatory kinship terms, and in the reckless speculative use of such fragmentary linguistic material.[1]

To one who uses native speech freely, a clear indication of the shades of meaning implicit in the words *bwoyna* and *gaga* is given by their phonetic feeling-tone in actual utterance. This, together with the emotional inflexion of the whole sentence, the facial expression, the accompanying gestures and significant behaviour, gives a number of clearly marked distinctions in meaning. Thus, to repeat, *gaga* can express genuine moral indignation amounting to real horror, or serious considerations of a purely utilitarian nature, or, spoken with a smirk, a pleasant veniality. Such observations, however, though of the greatest value to the ethnographer for his own guidance, could be made into an unambiguous record only by means of a phonograph and cinematograph, which, again, by the nature of the subject, it would be difficult if not impossible to use.

Fortunately, once put on his guard and instructed by direct observation of expressive tone and gesture, the ethnographer can substantiate his results from other material more easily framed into convincing documents. There exist a number of circumlocutions and more explicit phrases, which the natives volunteer in elaborating the meaning of *bwoyna* and *gaga*. Such elaborations recur independently in the statements of different men from different villages and districts. They constitute a body of linguistic evidence coinciding with emotional distinctions, and expressing these in a more communicable manner.

When speaking of the most serious offences— the brother-sister incest, forbidden fornication within

[1] This thesis will be developed in my forthcoming work on *Psychology of Kinship*, announced in the *International Library of Psychology* (Kegan Paul).

the household, or open indecency between husband and wife—the natives say the word *gaga* very seriously, at times with real horror in their inflexion. Then an informant would be more explicit : *bayse sene gaga* ("this is very bad ") ; or *gaga, gaga*, a repetition which intensifies the sense of the word ; or *gaga mokita* ("truly bad "), and add : *sene mwa'u bayse, gala tavagi* ("this is very heavy, we do not do it."). Or, again, when pressed to say what a man would feel or do if he committed such a crime, the native would usually answer : *gala !— gala tavagi—taytala ta'u ivagi—nanola bigaga, binagowa, imamata, ilo'u* : "No, we don't do it. If a man did it, his mind having turned wrong and silly, he would wake up (i.e. become sober and realise his crime) and commit suicide." Or he might say more negatively : *gala tavagi—tanumwaylava*, or *gala tavagi—tamwasawa, bigagabile* : "We don't do it and then forget," or "we don't do it and then play round and remain light-hearted ". Sometimes an ordinary informant might refuse to discuss such matters at all : *bayse gaga, gala talivala, biga gaga* : "This is bad, we don't speak about it, it is bad talk." All these stock phrases spoken seriously, or with disgust and anger, express the strongest disapproval. Experience and tact teach the observer that such subjects must never be approached with direct reference to the informant, to his sister or to his wife. Even the friendliest native, if accidentally hurt by a tactless remark of this kind, immediately departs and remains away for days. All such sentences and types of behaviour define the first meaning of the word *gaga*.

Gaga in some contexts can, therefore, mean repugnant, horrible, unspeakable ; in others it refers to the naturally unpalatable and to contemptible actions which shock the natives' normal sexual impulse. Here the feeling-tone ranges from simple disgust to half-amused malice. The circumlocutions run as follows : *gala tavagi* ; *iminayna nanogu*; *balagoba*: "We don't do it; my mind turns sick (if I did it); I would vomit." *Tonagowa bayse si vavagi*: "These are the acts of a mentally deficient person." *Gala tavagi, kada mwasila*: "We don't do it, because we are ashamed." *Senegaga—makawala mayna popu*: "Very bad—smells like excrement." *Makawala ka'ukwa—tomwota gala*: "In the fashion of a dog—not of a man." That is, actions worthy of a dirty animal and not of a human being.

They can give definite reasons why sexual aberrations are *bad*: in sodomy, the disgusting nature of excrement; in exhibitionism, a contemptible lack of shame and dignity; in oral perversions, the unpleasant taste and smell. All these sayings express the second meaning of the word *gaga*, "unnatural, disgusting, not worthy of a sound human being." So used, it implies an æsthetic attitude as well as a moral one, and there is less feeling that a traditional commandment has been broken than that a natural law has been flouted.

Another class of sayings defines the word *gaga* as meaning *dangerous*. *Gaga—igiburu'a matauna*: *takokola bwaga'u, kidama igisayda, sene mwa'u—boge bikatumate*: "Bad—because that man (the aggrieved man) is angry; we are afraid of the sorcerer, if they see us (doing it), the punishment would be heavy—already we would be killed." Or again, *gala tavagi, pela guya'u*, or *pela la mwala*: "We don't do it because of the chief," or "because of the husband". Here bad means "dangerous, exposing to revenge, that which provokes the anger of the injured".

Finally, speaking of minor taboos we would be told: *Gaga pela bomala bagula*: "Bad because of the taboo of the garden." *Gaga pela kabilia*: *tavagi—boge iyousi kayala*: "Bad, because of war: if we do it—already the spear hits us." Here the word *gaga* qualifies a number of actions as undesirable and to be avoided, because of their specific consequences.

From this it can be seen that the classification of moral values indicated in the use of the words *bwoyna* and *gaga* roughly corresponds to that derived from the word *bomala*.

We will now give such details concerning the taboos on our list as have not been mentioned in this and the foregoing chapters, taking them in the following order : in the next two sections, the first group of our classification, general sexual prohibitions ; in sections five and six, sociological restrictions on sexual freedom.

3

THE CENSURE OF SEXUAL ABERRATIONS

The widest class of sexual activity excluded from native life is that comprising aberrations of the sexual impulse (No. 1 of the list in sec. 2). The natives regard such practices as bestiality, homosexual love and intercourse, fetishism, exhibitionism, and masturbation as but poor substitutes for the natural act, and therefore as bad and only worthy of fools. Such practices are a subject for derision, tolerant or scathing according to mood, for ribald jokes and for funny stories. Transgressions are rather whipped by public contempt than controlled by definite legal sanctions. No penalties are attached to them, nor are they believed to have any ill results on health. Nor would a native ever use the word taboo (*bomala*) when speaking of them, for it would be an insult thus to assume that any sane person would like to commit them. To ask a man seriously whether he had indulged in such practices would deeply wound his vanity and self-regard, as well as shock his natural inclination. Vanity would be especially wounded, by the implication that he must be unable to procure the full natural enjoyment of his impulse if he has to resort to such substitutes.

The Trobriander's contempt for any perversion is
similar to his contempt for the man who eats inferior
or impure things in place of good, clean food
or for one who suffers hunger because there is
nothing in his yamhouse.

The following are typical remarks on the subject
of perversions : " No man or woman in our village
does it." " No one likes to penetrate excrement."
" No one likes a dog better than a woman." " Only
a *tonagowa* (idiot) could do it." " Only a *tonagowa*
masturbates. It is a great shame ; we know then
that no woman wants to copulate with him ; a man
who does it, we know, cannot get hold of a woman."
In all native statements the unsatisfactory nature of
a substitute or makeshift is emphasized, and the
implication is of poverty as well as of mental and
sexual deficiency. The natives would also quote
instances such as that of Orato'u, the village clown
of Omarakana, deformed and defective in speech ;
the several albinos and a few specially ugly women ;
and say that such people, but not an ordinary man
or woman, might practise one perversion or another.

Of course, we know that such statements of a
general and absolute rule express a figment, an ideal,
which, in reality, is only imperfectly satisfied. Most
of these aberrations are practised, though to a very
limited extent, just as the deficient and ugly are
not entirely excluded from the normal exercise of
their sexual functions (see also ch. x, sec. 2).

Let us now consider different types of perversion.

Homosexuality.—This orientation of the sexual
impulse, if it exist at all among the Trobrianders,
can be found only in its more spiritual manifestation,
that is, in emotional and platonic friendships. It is
allowed by custom, and is, indeed, usual, for boy
friends to embrace one another, to sleep together on
the same couch, to walk enlaced or arm-in-arm. In the
personal friendships which to the natives naturally
express themselves by such bodily contacts, strong
preferences are displayed. Boys are often seen in

couples : Monakewo and Toviyamata, Mekala'i and Tobutusawa, Dipapa and Burayama, most of whom are now familiar to my readers, were constantly to be seen together. Sometimes such a friendship is just a passing whim, but it may survive and mature into a permanent relationship of mutual affection and assistance, as did that between Bagido'u and Yobukwa'u, and, I was told, between Mitakata and Namwana Guya'u before these two became implacable enemies. The word *lubaygu*, " my friend ", is used for such close alliances between man and man, and it is remarkable that this word also designates the love relation between man and woman. But it would be as erroneous to consider this identity in language as implying an identity in emotional content as it would be to assume that every time a Frenchman uses the word *ami*, a homosexual relation is implied, simply because of its connotation when used by one sex of another. In France, as in the Trobriands, context and situation distinguish the two uses of the word *ami* (*lubaygu*) and makes them into two semantically different words.

Difficult as it is exactly to draw the line between pure " friendship " and " homosexual relation " in any society—both because of laxity in definition and the difficulty of ascertaining the facts—it becomes almost impossible in a community such as the Trobriands. Personally I find it misleading to use the term " homosexuality " in the vague and almost intentionally all-embracing sense that is now fashionable under the influence of psychoanalysis and the apostles of " *Urning* " love. If inversion be defined as a relationship in which detumescence is regularly achieved by contact with a body of the same sex, then the male friendships in the Trobriands are not homosexual, nor is inversion extensively practised in the islands. For, as we know, the practice is really felt to be bad and unclean because it is associated with excreta, for which the natives feel a genuine disgust. And while the ordinary caresses of affection are approved as between members of the same sex, any erotic caresses, scratching, nibbling at eyelashes, or labial contact would be regarded as revolting.

As we have said, there is always some discrepancy between theory and practice ; but in estimating the importance of exceptions, we must allow for unnatural conditions of life and the influence of other civilizations. Many natives are, under the present rule of whites, cooped up in gaol, on mission stations, and in plantation barracks. Sexes are separated and normal intercourse made impossible ; yet an impulse trained to function regularly cannot be thwarted. The white man's influence and his morality, stupidly misapplied where there is no place for it, creates a setting favourable to homosexuality. The natives are perfectly well aware that venereal disease and homosexuality are among the benefits bestowed on them by Western culture.

Although it is impossible for me to quote any well authenticated instance of this perversion from the old times, I have no doubt that sporadic cases have always occurred. Indeed, the existence of such expressions as *ikaye popu* : " he copulates excrement," *ikaye pwala* : " he penetrates rectum," and the well-defined moral attitude towards it, are sufficient evidence of this. Some informants would go so far as to admit that homosexuality had been practised formerly, but they would always insist that it was only by mentally deficient people. On the whole, therefore, it is clear that this prohibition is not imposed upon an unwilling moral acceptance, but is well-entrenched in the feeling and natural impulse of the natives. How far this attitude is correlated with the wide and varied opportunities for normal intercourse ; how far it is true that homosexuality is more efficiently eradicated by derision than by heavy penalties, are questions which can only be submitted as a subject for further observations in the field.[1]

Bestiality.—This is derided as an unclean and unsatisfactory makeshift, even more incongruous and comical than inversion. It is remarkable that among a totemic people—who claim affinity with animals, and treat the pig as a member of the household—animal sodomy should still be regarded as a dirty and unnatural practice. The natives see no continuity or relation between totemic marriage and intercourse, on the one hand, as these took place in mythological times, and, on the other, what might be called totemic fornication at the present day.

A well-documented case of bestiality is on record, however, concerning a man who copulated with a dog. It is noteworthy that the case is famous throughout the district, that the name of the man, all the circumstances, and even the name of the dog " Jack " are household words in every village. It is also interesting that, while it is always described or alluded to with considerable amusement, there are clear indications that the matter would not be in the least amusing if it concerned oneself or a kinsman or friend. " If I did it, or anyone of my maternal kinsmen or friends, I would commit suicide." Yet the culprit, Moniyala, has lived down his shame. He leads a happy existence in Sinaketa, where I had the pleasure of meeting him, and having a long conversation with him. The subject of his past lapse, however, must never be mentioned in his presence, for, the natives say, if he heard anyone speaking about it he would commit *lo'u* (suicide by jumping from a tree).

The circumstances of this case were as follows : Moniyala was serving with a trader who owned a male dog called Jack. The two became friendly and, one day, a girl saw Moniyala sodomizing the dog on the beach. A scandal broke out, the native

[1] Cf. the writer's *Sex and Repression in Savage Societies*, 1927, where the problem has been discussed at length in part ii.

missionary preacher brought the matter before the white resident magistrate who placed Moniyala in gaol for six months. After his release Moniyala signed on for plantation work abroad and stayed on the mainland of New Guinea for several years. When he came back he was able to brazen it out ; but everybody seems to think that, in old days, he would have committed suicide. The natives agree that a dog is worse than a pig, the former being the uncleaner animal.

Sadism and Masochism.—Whether these complementary perversions play a large part in the sexual life of the natives I am unable to say. The cruel forms of caress—scratching, biting, spitting—to which a man has to submit to a greater extent even than the woman, show that, as elements in eroticism, they are not absent from native love making. On the other hand, flagellation as an erotic practice is entirely unknown ; and the idea that cruelty, actively given or passively accepted, could lead, of itself alone, to pleasant detumescence is incomprehensible, nay ludicrous, to the natives. I should say, therefore, that these perversions do not exist in a crystallized form.

Fellatio.—This is probably practised in the intimacy of love making (see above, ch. x, sec. 12). Receiving my information exclusively from men, I was told that no male would touch the female genitals in this manner, but, at the same time, I was assured that *penilinctus* was extensively practised. I do not feel convinced, however, of the truth of this masculine version. The expression, *ikanumwasi kalu momona*, " lapping up the sexual discharges," designates both forms of fellatio.

Masturbation (*ikivayni kwila* : " he manipulates penis," *isulumomoni* : " he makes semen boil over ") is a recognized practice often referred to in jokes. The natives maintain, however, that it would be done only by an idiot (*tonagowa*) or one of the unfortunate albinos, or one defective in speech ; in other words, only by those who cannot obtain favours from women. The practice is therefore regarded as undignified and unworthy of a man, but in a rather amused and entirely indulgent manner. Exactly the same attitude is adopted towards female masturbation (*ikivayni wila* : " she manipulates cunnus " ; *ibasi wila o yamala* : " she pierces vagina with her hand ").

Nocturnal pollutions and dreams have already been mentioned (see ch. xii, sec. 1). They are regarded, as we know, as the result of magic and a proof of its effectiveness.

Exhibitionism is regarded by the natives with genuine contempt and disgust : this has already been made clear in the above description of the manner of dressing and the careful adjustment of the male pubic leaf and feminine grass skirt.

In the treatment of these deviations of the sexual impulse, it is impossible to draw a rigid line between the use of certain practices—such as fellatio, passionate and exuberant caresses, interest in the genitals—when they are used as preliminary and preparatory sexual approaches on the one hand, and as definite perversions on the other. The best criterion is whether they function as a part of courting, leading up to normal copulation, or whether they are sufficient by themselves for the production of detumescence. It is well to remember in this context that the nervous excitability of the natives is much less than ours, and their sexual imagination is relatively very sluggish ; that excitation and tumescence are usually achieved only by the direct visual, olfactory, or tactual stimulus of the sexual organs ; and that orgasm, in man or woman, requires more bodily contact, erotic preliminaries, and, above all, direct friction of the mucous membranes for its production. It is, therefore, plausible to assume that preparatory erotic approaches with the natives would have less tendency to pass into autonomous acts, that is to develop into perversions, than is the case among nervously more excitable races.

4
MODESTY IN SPEECH AND BEHAVIOUR

On the subject of general decorum (No. 2 of the list in sec. 2) in sexual matters, there is little to add to the information given in previous chapters ; and a brief summary will suffice to bring the facts to mind. Decency in speech and behaviour varies according to the relation in which the members of any company stand to each other. The presence of a sister and brother imposes a rigid propriety in social tone and conversation ; and, to a lesser extent, so does that of maternal cousins and members of the same clan. Again, when a woman is accompanied by her husband, a strict etiquette must be observed. The wife's sister is also an embarrassing companion ; and in a lesser degree so is the wife's mother or any of her near maternal relatives. In the presence of a chief, commoners may not joke or use obscene expressions. The degree of verbal freedom permitted is determined by the degree of intimacy and length of acquaintance. Many a time have I seen my most ribald friends sit demure, polite, and dignified, discussing such subjects as weather, health, the amenities of travel, the welfare of mutual friends and other universal subjects of small talk, because of the presence of strangers from overseas or from some distant inland district. When these had gone away the conversation was apt to assume a specially hilarious tone to compensate for this polite reticence.

But though licence in speech is allowed and enjoyed in the right company, great restraint is always observed in public as regards action. In vain would one look in the Trobriands for traces and survivals of the untrammelled licence and lust alleged to have existed in primeval times. With the one possible exception of the Southern *kayasa* (chap. ix, sec. 5) there are no public orgies in which men and women would copulate in the sight of all present, orgies which have been reported from other parts of Melanesia. The myths and legendary customs which we have described are, of course, irrelevant, and even these are not really concerned with public orgies for the satisfaction of lust. To the natives sexual publicity is definitely objectionable. They will say that they are " ashamed to do or even to speak about such things ", that " such things are like those of a dog ". In the bachelors' house (see ch. iii, sec. 4) considerable attention is devoted to the maintenance of an exclusive privacy. All this is· in harmony with the natives' strict attention to modesty in dress.

Even courting is conducted most decorously. Scenes of frequent occurrence in any public park in Europe, after dark or even before, would never be seen in a Trobriand village. Holding hands, leaning against each other, embracing—gestures which, as we know, are not considered objectionable as between boys and are frequently seen between girls—are not permitted to lovers in public. I observed once or twice that Yobukwa'u and his betrothed used to lie together on a mat in broad daylight, decorously, but unmistakably leaning against each other and holding hands, in a manner which we would find perfectly natural in a pair of lovers soon to be married. But when I mentioned this in discussing the whole subject with some natives, I was told at once that it was a new fashion and not correct according to old custom. Tokolibeba, once a famous Don Juan, now a peppery old conservative and stickler for proprieties, insisted that this was *misinari si bubunela*, " missionary fashion," one of those novel immoralities intro-duced by Christianity. He spoke with as much feeling and righteous indignation as the late

Rev. C. M. Hyde of Honolulu might have used against heathen pruriency.

We can now understand better the value of erotic games to the native: The bodily contacts afforded by them are appreciated just because, under ordinary circumstances, they cannot be indulged. All preliminary erotic approaches must be carried out under cover of darkness. And since much of the love magic, with which they are so often fortified, requires close bodily contact (see chs. x and xi) the games are there to provide it. Nipples are touched with a magic-covered palm, a charmed finger is inserted into the vagina, or an enchanted perfume held below the nostrils, discreetly in the dark, as the game gives opportunity. It is always suspected but never seen ; even when quarrels and litigations arise because some such attempt to wile away affection is alleged, it is difficult to find a witness of the act.

This by-way of native practice gives incidentally a good illustration of the dangers which beset the ethnologist. In the early days of my field-work, my cook, Ubi'ubi, whom I had imported from the South Coast of New Guinea, was accused of digital insertion by the local natives. At this time I did most of my work in pidgin English, and I find in my notes that my interpreter informed me that his action had a special native name : " Boy he call him *kaynobasi wila*," that is to say : " The custom is named by the native the piercing through the vulva." I could not understand why among these easy-going people this action should arouse such strong moral feeling, and I made an entry in my notes : " The custom of inserting a finger into the vagina is morally very reprehensible to the natives." Thus, ignorance of the language and a superficial acquaintance with the natives led me completely astray. To put the whole incident in its proper perspective, it was necessary to understand the native attitude towards decorum in general and, in particular, their beliefs about erotic enchantment by magic. It was not so much that my cookboy allowed himself a somewhat unseemly gesture, but rather that he was suspected of exercising a powerful form of magic to alienate the girl's affections from her usual lover.

Thus behaviour between the sexes conforms to a definite standard of decorum, which, needless to say, is not the same as morality. Speech, on the other hand, is given a much more generous margin of freedom. Relative latitudes in speech and behaviour would make an interesting investigation for comparative ethnology, for they do not seem to develop along parallel lines. Indeed, greater freedom of speech, acting as a safety valve, may be associated with greater restraint in behaviour, and vice versa.[1]

In an appropriate social setting, sex is quite a favourite topic of conversation. Ribald jokes, indecent gossip and anecdotes are a recognized form of entertainment, as we saw in connection with sexual folk-lore. In this, as in everything else, I found considerable individual differences. Some natives were sober in speech and not much interested in sexual ribaldry; others specialized, so to speak, in obscene speech and doubtful jokes. The sense of humour, also, varied greatly from man to man, from the morose and unsmiling churl or the naïve good-natured simpleton, to the man with real wit and humour, always ready for a joke, able to tell a good story, and seldom taking offence unless it was meant. With Paluwa and his son Monakewo, with Tokulu-bakiki and Kayla'i, I could indulge in a considerable amount of mutual "ragging"; they would never misunderstand an allusion or a joke, and often they made me laugh with an apt observation, turned against myself and not always devoid of malice. Again there are the chartered village clowns, some of whom like Orato'u, the idiot of Omarakana, turn their speech impediment to advantage, while others

[1] Cf. *Sex and Repression*, part ii.

whose humour is of the crude and impudent kind, play practical jokes, shout out their witticisms, take liberties even with men of high rank, or imitate, sometimes quite cleverly, peculiarities of well-known persons.

But in all grades of humour, sexual jokes and allusions play an important part. When no people of the forbidden degrees are present, sexual matters are discussed without circumlocution; anatomical and physiological expressions, phrases denoting perversions and peculiarities are freely used.

I shall only quote a few typical sayings to indicate how this type of remark enters into daily conversation. In the excitement of games or of communal work, the native will express intense general enjoyment by exclaiming: *agudeydes, akay kwim!* " hullo, fornicate thy penis!" or, if addressing a female, *wim, kasesam!* " thy cunnus, thy clitoris!" A humorous expression is: *yakay, puwagu!* " oo, my testicles!" Exclamatory phrases referring to private parts with embellishments are often jocularly exchanged between friends, much as we might say: " damn your eyes!"

We have already met several such typical jesting allusions in the fairy tales, especially in the song of the reef heron to the old woman, Ilakavetega (see ch. xii, sec. 3). The interest taken in malformations of the private parts is to be found also in the story about the man with the long penis, the woman who stows away food in her vagina, and the old mother endowed with five clitorises. In actual life a native will say jocularly: *kwaypwase wim,* " decomposed thy cunnus "; or *wim ipwase,* " thy cunnus is decomposed "; or *kwaybulabola wim,* " enormously enlarged is thy cunnus "; or, for a change, *kwaypatu wim,* " contracted is thy cunnus." And to a man: *kaykukupi kwim,* " very small is thy penis "; *kaygatu kwim,* " dirty is thy penis "; *kalu nau'u kwim,* " covered with stale discharge is thy penis "; *kaypaki kwim,* " sore-

covered is thy penis." Apart from jokes, the natives
take a great interest in supposed malformations or
advantageous increments and developments of the
sexual organs. Thus, to a man of high rank and of
great reputation will be attributed an extraordinarily
long and stout organ. The late paramount chief,
Numakala, was credited with a penis which used
to grow in length during copulation and become
swollen and round like a ball at the end. This was
counted to his credit and treated seriously as an
enviable erotic asset.

Incongruity in sexual matters is a frequent
subject for jokes. Thus possible or imputed
copulation with women famed for their repulsiveness,
such as Tilapo'i or Kurayana, is, as we know, a
frequent form of jocular address. *Kwoy Tilapo'i* !
" copulate with Tilapo'i ! " is a very mild form of
abuse ; or a friend coming from the direction of her
village might be hailed, *Boge kukaye Tilapo'i* ? " Hast
thou already copulated with Tilapo'i ? " The
slightest inaccuracy or imagined inaccuracy in the
set of the pubic leaf is immediately seized upon :
Yavim boge ipwase—tagise puwam, " thy pubic leaf
is out of order—let us see thy testicles." Similar
jokes are made about insufficiently shaven pubic
hair and about alleged fornication with some old
woman or a chief's wife. Taunts implying intensity
or illicitness of copulation are frequent : *tokakayta
yoku, tokaylasi yoku, tosuvasova yoku*, " Thou
fornicator, thou adulterer, thou incest-committer."

All these remarks, however, are primarily used
in friendly banter from which serious and offensive
forms of abuse must be distinguished. Swearing
is used in the Trobriands, as with us, as a substitute
reaction to minor annoyances, and is so used against
things or people without giving serious offence.
The strongest forms of abusive language would
not, however, be used on such trivial occasions.
Swearing in anger may lead to serious consequences
when the temper of those concerned is not under

control. It may lead to a more or less prolonged breach of personal relations, to a fight, or even to a communal feud. Or, again, abuse can be used deliberately to shame or to startle people by putting their misdeeds before them in strong language. This is done when a grievance is real and serious enough to be brought up against the offender to check him, but not so grave and shameful as to entail such tragic consequences as a broken relationship or suicide. Thus a wife might shame a husband suspected of misconduct by using against him in public the various circumlocutions and direct expressions for adultery. She would only do so in a narrow circle of friends, breaking, for this moral purpose, the usual restraint which a woman has to observe with regard to her husband. Or, again, a matrilineal uncle might use this method to reprimand his nephew for minor cases of exogamous breach ; or a father might reprove his daughter for too indiscriminate or too aggressive fornication. Such reprimands would not be administered in the presence of many people, but, in their appropriate setting of friends or relatives, they play an important part in the regulation of tribal life. *Kakayuwa*, " to shame," " to startle," " to shake up," and *yakala*, " to have it out with someone," are the words used to describe such proceedings.[1]

In such admonitory accusations certain abusive terms are used, such as adulterer (*tokaylasi*), breaker of incest (*tosuvasova*) ; or, to a woman, wanton (*nakakayta*) or drab (*nakaytabwa*). The same terms can be used, not in well-meant and deliberate reprimand, but as abuse meant to hurt and to hurt only ; and if thus used they happen really to apply, the insult is doubly serious. For the truth, in the Trobriands as elsewhere, is the cruellest and most fatal instrument of malice.

---

[1] Compare *Crime and Custom*, ch. xii, for further data referring to *yakala* and the part played by verbal accusation in the regulation of tribal life, and *Sex and Repression*, part ii, ch. iv, on the subject of bad language.

Bad language is also used in certain expressions of specific abuse meant only to offend and not, as a rule, bearing any relation to fact, as they often refer to acts almost impracticable. Most such expressions begin with the characteristic imperative so widespread throughout swearing humanity: in this case, " Copulate with . . . ," followed by various unsuitable persons as putative objects for erotic approach—sometimes a repulsive person, sometimes a dog, sometimes an unattractive part of the body. This is the most innocuous form of this kind of abuse, and is only offensive if offence is intended. It becomes really serious when a sociologically forbidden person is inserted as object. The two incestuous imperatives *kwoy inam*, " copulate with thy mother," and *kwoy lumuta*, " copulate with thy sister," with *kwoy um kwava*, " copulate with thy wife," form the fundamental trio of this category. The first invitation can be merely a joke and is often used in good-natured abuse or at times sharply and with annoyance, but never implies serious offence. It is also a common impersonal expletive, such as our " bloody " or " damn ".

Used with reference to the sister, it is an unpardonable offence when addressed to a person, and is felt to be so pregnant with dangerous consequences that it is never used impersonally as a mere expletive. And when the real name of the sister or brother is inserted—for the word *lumuta* means thy sister when a man speaks and thy brother when a woman speaks—it is the second worst offence imaginable to a Trobriander. Remarkably enough, even stronger is the expression : " Copulate with thy wife." This is so unmentionable to the natives that, in spite of my scientific interest in bad language, I was very long without knowing that it existed and, even in telling me this expression, my informants were serious, subdued, and unwilling to dwell on the

subject. Their attitude to this phrase is correlated
with the rule that the erotic life of husband and wife
should always remain completely concealed, and
it has a special indecency in that it refers to an action
which does as a matter of fact take place.

Another form of typical abuse is : " Eat your
excrement ", with several variants which we have
already mentioned in this chapter. A third category,
also familiar to us (see ch. vii, sec. 6), is the assertion
of physical similarity to any maternal relative, and
worst of all, of course, to the sister. *Migim lumuta*,
" Thy face thy sister's," is one of the worst insults
possible.

Blasphemy, strictly speaking, does not exist,
although the natives say that they would not use
indecent expressions with regard to ancestral spirits
and that, both in this world and after they have left
it, they would use very guarded language about
Topileta (see ch. xii, sec. 5).

The native words for swearing or abuse are
kamtoki and *kayluki* used with reflective personal
plurals. Thus *ikaylukwaygu* or *ikamtokaygu* means
" he is abusing me ". Another expression *ikavitagi
yagagu* means literally : " He has fouled my name,"
or, when similarity with a maternal relative has been
referred to, *ikavitagi migigu*, " he has befouled
my face." ·In all swearing the addition of the name
of the person abused, and, when it is a sociological
insult, of the sister, wife or mother, adds considerably to the strength of the insult.

In this and in other contexts we find that whenever
the natives touch on something that has really
happened, greater restraint is necessary and allusions
and abuse become much more poignant. A man will
talk freely about himself and his own erotic affairs—
in fact the confidences of my various friends have
furnished the best material for the present book—
but even in this there were limits ; and of the
incestuous or adulterous or tabooed intrigues of
many of my acquaintances I had to learn, not from

them, but from their best friends. Here again, though such gossip would be retailed freely behind the man's back, it would never be spoken of, to his face. The incestuous affairs of the chief's sons in Omarakana, the hopeless matrimonial prospects of Monakewo or Mekala'i were never spoken about in their presence. Delicacy in touching upon the intimate concerns of those present is as great among the Trobrianders as among well-bred people in Europe.

We now pass to No. 3 in our classification of taboos, disapproval of sexual greed and lechery (see list in sec. 2). Inability to master desire, leading to insistent and aggressive sexuality, is regarded with contempt both in man and woman, though it is felt to be really repugnant only in women. Thus Yakalusa, a daughter of a chief of Kasana'i, was accused of spontaneously approaching men, talking to them, and inviting them to have intercourse with her. A similar reputation attached to several girls in Omarakana. Again there are clear cases on record of nymphomaniacs, who could not be satisfied with moderate sexual intercourse and required a number of men every night. There was a girl of Kitava who actually made the round of the main island in search of erotic diversion. While I was staying in Sinaketa she also was a visitor there and gossip was very active though not specially antagonistic. It was said that she would go out into the jungle with a group of boys and withdraw with one after another, spending days and nights in this occupation.

It must be made clear, exactly what it is that the natives find reprehensible about sexual greed in a woman. It is certainly not her interest in fornication, nor is it the fact that she initiates the intrigue; they object to direct invitation in place of the more seemly method of seduction by magic, and to the unsuccess and small sense of personal worth that such urgent solicitation implies.

The native term for such women is *nakaytabwa*
(drab) which was thus elaborated to me : *sene
bidubadu tomwota ikakayta ; gala ilukwali kalu
bulabola—sene nakaytabwa.* This might be rendered :
" Very many men she copulates with ; not satisfied
is ever her large orifice—such a one we call a drab."
Here we get a direct mention of sexual insatiability ;
in other words, an expression of the idea of
nymphomania.

Two alternative expressions for *nakaytabwa* are
nakakayta (literally, " female copulator "), and the
expression *naka'ulatile* (" wanton ") which was
explained to me as follows :

Kidama   tayta vivila   gala   imaymaysi tau'a'u,
supposing   one   woman no   they come men,

ilolo   wala   titolela imwayki   ta'u—
she goes indeed   herself   she comes   to man—

yagala   naka'ulatile.
her name wanton.

Or freely : " When a woman has no men who come
to her, and takes the initiative and goes herself
to a man, we call her a wanton." It is clear that
the moral censure incurred by such women is
founded on the shame that attaches to erotic
unsuccess.

Censure of lechery in a man has the same foundation. *Tokokolosi* is the word used to denote a man
who pursues women and inflicts his attentions on
them. An interesting instance occurred in my
own experience. After about eighteen months'
absence, I returned to Omarakana and resumed
my old acquaintance with Namwana Guya'u. He,
as we know, had been worsted by Mitakata and
hated him impotently, therefore he sought to
blacken him in my eyes, and brought the most
venomous possible charge against him :

Tokokolosi matauna ibia   vivila :   boge
A rutter   this man   he pulls women : already

ipakayse   kumaydona.   Minana   ipayki,
they refuse all.   This woman   refuses,

matauna   iyousi,   ibia.
this man   catches, pulls.

To make the picture really sinister Namwana Guya'u
added a touch of exhibitionism to it :

Iliku   yavila,   bitotona   kwila ;
He undoes pubic leaf his, it stands up penis his ;

iluki   vivila :   " *Kuma   kwabukwani*
he tells (to a) woman : " Come   get hold (of)

kwigu."   Boge   ipakayse   vivila,
penis mine."   Already   they refuse   women,

pela   tokokolosi   vivila.
because satyr (towards)   women.

In free translation : " He undoes his pubic
leaf, and allows his penis to become erect. He
then tells a woman : ' Come and caress my penis.'
Women already are disgusted with him because he
is such a satyr."

In this one text we find an expression of the native
contempt for exhibitionism, insistent pursuit of
women, and unsuccess in love ; and women's dislike
of too eager attentions. We have, also, the interesting
association between the removal of the pubic leaf
and erection.

The whole attitude of the Trobriander towards
sexual excess displays an appreciation of restraint and
dignity, and an admiration for success ; not only for
what it gives to a man, but because it means that he
is above any need for active aggression. The moral
command not to violate, solicit, or touch is founded
on a strong conviction that it is shameful ; and
shameful because real worth lies in being coveted,
in conquering by charm, by beauty and by magic.
Thus all the threads of our account weave into one
complex pattern ; manners, morals, and æsthetic
judgment fit into the psychology of love making
and of conquest by magic.

If I were allowed to go beyond the scope of the present study, I should like to demonstrate that the same pattern is also found in the psychology of economic and ceremonial give and take, and in the native views concerning reciprocity in legal obligation. Everywhere we find disapproval of direct solicitation, of covetousness and cupidity, and, above all, the dishonour attaching to real need and dearth. Plenty, on the other hand, and wealth, combined with a careless generosity in giving, are glorious.[1]

The only category of taboos in our general list which now remains is No. 5 of our list in section 2, that comprising miscellaneous prohibitions arising out of special occasions in tribal life. When engaged in warfare, men must abstain from sexual intercourse whether with wife or paramour. The taboo becomes operative from the day when, with a special ceremony called *vatula bulami*, the forces are mustered and war magic is set in motion. Not only must a man abstain from any sexual intercourse, but he is not allowed to sleep on the same mat or on the same bedstead with a woman. Certain houses are reserved for men, while the women and children congregate in others. Any amorous dalliance at such a time would be regarded as dangerous to the community's chances of winning the war, and therefore as shameful and unseemly. Further, there are definite penalties which would fall on the individual transgressor. Should he indulge in intercourse, a hostile spear would pierce his penis or his testicles. Should he sleep nose to nose with his sweetheart, he would be hit on the nose or thereabouts. Were he to sit even on the same mat with a girl, his buttocks would not be safe from attack. I had the impression from the way in which my informants spoke about the matter, that the war

---

[1] Cf. the analysis of economic psychology in *Argonauts of the Western Pacific*, chap. vi, and *passim*, and of the principle of reciprocity in *Crime and Custom*.

taboos were fully and rigorously observed. No doubt the men were far too engrossed in the excitement of the fighting to turn any attention to the more usual and therefore, perhaps, less absorbing sport of love.

The gardens should not be in any way associated with amorous advances. Neither within the enclosure proper nor anywhere near it, should a man and a woman be found love making. In the phrase for describing illicit love making the belt of bush adjoining the garden (*tokeda*) is specified (see pl. 88). To have intercourse in or near the gardens is called by the natives *isikayse tokeda*, " they sit down upon the belt of bush adjoining the garden." Particularly objectionable are any advances on the part of men during the garden work which is especially done by women : the *pwakova* (" weeding ") and the *koumwali* (" clearing of the ground before planting "). It will be remembered that the legendary fornicator, Inuvayla'u, was wont to approach the women when engaged on this and other specifically feminine occupations and that this was one of the worst traits in his character. It is improper for a man even to be present during any of these occupations : communal weeding or clearing, collecting shells, fetching water, gathering firewood from the bush, the ceremonial making of fibre petticoats. Intercourse in the gardens is punished by a special visitation : the bush pigs are attracted by the smell of seminal fluid, they break through the fences and destroy the gardens.

A special taboo enjoins chastity on women who remain at home while their husbands and lovers are away on a *kula* expedition. Any infidelity affects the speed of their husbands' canoes and causes them to move very slowly (see also above, chap. v, sec. 2). The taboos imposed during pregnancy and after childbirth have already been described in detail (see ch. viii), as well as the aversion (not fortified by supernatural penalties) from intercourse during menstruation. This concludes our survey of the general taboos, and we now proceed to special prohibitions associated with kinship and relationship by marriage.

5

EXOGAMY AND THE PROHIBITION OF INCEST

The sociological regulations which divide persons of the opposite sex into lawful and unlawful in relation to one another ; which restrain intercourse in virtue of the legal act of marriage and which discriminate between certain unions in respect of their desirability, have to be distinguished from the taboos of a general nature already described. In these we found expressions of disapproval, ranging from horror to distaste, of certain sexual acts and approaches, defined physiologically or by the occasion on which they occur. The rules to which we now proceed can only be stated with reference to social organization, and above all to the institution of family and the division into totemic clans.[1]

The totemic organization of the natives is simple and symmetrical in its general outline. Humanity is divided into four clans (*kumila*). Totemic nature is conceived to be as deeply ingrained in the substance of the individual as sex, colour, and stature. It can never be changed, and it transcends individual life, for it is carried over into the next world, and brought back unchanged into this one when the spirit returns by reincarnation. This fourfold totemic division is thought to be universal, embracing every section of mankind. When a European arrives in the Trobriands, the natives simply and sincerely ask to which of the four classes he belongs, and it is not easy to explain to the most

---

[1] The institution of marriage is inseparable from the family and will, therefore, be mentioned incidentally in what follows. It has already been treated in some detail with the taboos and regulations which it entails (cf. chs. iv, v, and vi, and the penultimate section of this chapter).

intelligent among them that the totemic four-fold
division is not universal and rooted in the nature of
man. The natives of neighbouring areas, where there
are more than four clans, are invariably and readily
made to conform to the fourfold scheme by
allocating several of the alien clans to each
one of the four Trobriand divisions. For such
subordination of minor groups to the larger divisions
there is a pattern in Trobriand culture, since each
of their big totemic clans comprises smaller groups
called *dala*, or, as we shall call them, " sub-clans."

The sub-clans are at least as important as the
clans, for the members of the same sub-clan regard
themselves as real kindred, claim the same rank, and
form the local unit in Trobriand society. Each local
community is composed of people belonging to one
sub-clan, and to one sub-clan only, who have joint
rights to the village site, to the surrounding garden-
lands, and to a number of local privileges. Large
villages are compounded of several minor local
units, but each unit has its own compact site within
the village and owns a large contiguous area of
garden-land. There are even different terms to
denote membership within the sub-clan and
membership in the clan. People of the same sub-
clan are real kinsmen, and call one another *veyogu*,
my kinsman. But a man will only apply this term
loosely and metaphorically to one who, though a
member of the same clan, belongs to a different
sub-clan, and will, if questioned directly, inform you
that the other man is only pseudo-kindred, using
the deprecatory term *kakaveyogu* (my spurious
kinsman).

Each of the four clans has its own name : Malasi,
Lukuba, Lukwasisiga, Lukulabuta. Such a clan
name is used by a man or a woman as a definition
of his or of her social identity : " My name is so-
and-so, and I am a Malasi." There are special
combinations of the clan names with formative
roots, to describe men and women and the mixed

plurality belonging to the same clan : Tomalasi—
a Malasi man ; Immalasi—a Malasi woman ;
Memalasi—the Malasi people ; Tolukuba—a
Lukuba man ; Imkuba—a Lukuba woman ;
Milukuba—the Lukuba people, and so on. When a
man says *Tomalasi yaygu*, he gives a sociological
definition of his place within the universal fourfold
division of mankind, and he also thereby settles his
associations in any community to which he has
recently arrived. To a native this statement indicates
a number of personal characteristics as well, or at
least potentialities : such as magical knowledge,
citizenship (when the sub-clan is also mentioned),
moral and intellectual propensities, historical
antecedents, relation to certain animals and plants
and also an indication of rank. Thus the
Malasi claim primacy among other totemic divisions,
though this is only very grudgingly granted by
members of other clans.

The Malasi have, however, a good piece of heraldic
evidence in their favour. Near the village of Laba'i,
on the northern shore of the main island, there is a
spot called Obukula, which is marked by a coral
outcrop. Obukula is, in fact, a " hole "
(*dubwadebula*), or " house " (*bwala*) ; that is to say,
one of the points from which the first ancestors
of a lineage emerged. For before they appeared on
this earth, human beings led a subterranean
existence similar in all respects to life in surface
Trobriand villages and organized on the same social
pattern. They dwelt in identical local communities,
were divided into clans and sub-clans, were grouped
into districts, and lived as good a family life as do
present-day natives. They also owned property—
that is *gugu'a*, the workaday implements and chattels,
and *vaygu'a*, " valuables," and houses, canoes, and
land. They practised arts and crafts and possessed
specific magic.

Now, when they decided to come up to the surface
of the earth, they collected all their belongings and

emerged in the locality of which they wanted to take possession. The spot of their emergence is usually marked by a grotto, a large boulder, a pool, the head of a tidal creek, or merely a large stone in the village centre or street (see pl. 89). In this way they established the traditional claim to owner-ship of the " hole " and its surroundings ; that is, of the village site, which often lies immediately round the hole, of the adjoining lands, and of the economic privileges and pursuits associated with the locality. It is the rule in Trobriand mythology that, originally, only one couple emerged from each such " hole ", a brother and a sister ; she to start the lineage, he to protect her and look after her affairs. Thus the rule is : one clan, one village, one portion of garden-land, one system of gardening and fishing magic, one pair of brother and sister ancestors, one rank and one pedigree. This latter can never be really traced, but it is firmly believed to go back to the original woman who came out of the hole.

To this " one-hole-one-line-one-sub-clan " rule there is only one exception, the hole of Obukula already mentioned. In this case we have one hole for the four main clans ; we have ancestors who are defined not by sub-clan but by their clan identity ; and we have an act of emergence which established not a special form of citizenship and ownership, not privileges for one sub-clan, but the respective position of the four clans in the scale of rank.

The myth of the hole of Obukula runs thus. First the representative of the Lukulabuta, its totemic animal the *Kaylavasi* (iguana or giant lizard), came to the surface, scratching away the earth as these animals will do. He ran up a tree and from this point of vantage waited for what should follow. Nor did he have to wait long. Through the hole he had made scrambled the dog, the animal of the Lukuba clan, who, the second on the scene, obtained the highest rank for the time being. His glory was short-lived, however, for soon afterwards came the pig: that noble animal, very close to man himself in rank, and representative of the Malasi. The last to appear was the animal of the Lukwasisiga clan, variously described as the snake, the opposum, or the crocodile. The myths disagree as to its identity and indeed this ambiguous animal plays the least important part in the story and in Trobriand totemism.

The pig and the dog played together; and the dog, running through the bush, saw the fruit of a plant called *noku*. This is considered by the natives a very inferior form of nourishment, and although it is not specifically forbidden to any clan or person, it is eaten only in times of greatest dearth and famine. The dog smelt it, licked it, and ate it. The pig seized his opportunity, and then and there laid down the charter of his rank, saying: " Thou eatest *noku*, thou eatest excrement; thou art a low bred com-moner. Henceforth I shall be the *guya'u*, the chief." From this incident dates the Malasi claim to rank higher than the other clans, and one of their sub-clans, the Tabalu, have, indeed, the highest position; they are the real chiefs, acknowledged to be of supreme rank, not by the Trobriands only, but by the adjoining areas as well.

Thus do the natives account for the difference in rank. The partaking of unclean food—the most important criterion of social inferiority—caused the downfall of the Lukuba, and the rise of the Malasi. But it must be remembered that this latter clan includes besides the highest sub-clan (the Tabalu), that one which is most despised, associated with the village of Bwaytalu. No respectable Lukuba man would marry a Malasi woman from that village; no Tabalu would claim kinship with anyone of its inhabitants, and he takes it very badly when it is pointed out that they are his *kakaveyola* (pseudo-kindred). The natives of the several local com-munities in the compound village of Bwaytalu,

Ba'u, and Suviyagila form, as we have already mentioned, a practically endogamous district in which the members of the various clans have to observe exogamy within their circle of villages, since they cannot mate outside it. We have thus an endogamous district within which totemic exogamy is observed.

Thus in respect of rank, it is the sub-clan rather than the clan that matters, and this holds good with regard to local rights and privileges. In a village community which belongs to the Lukwasisiga of the Kwaynama sub-clan, only members of the latter are citizens. Others of the Lukwasisiga clan, who do not belong to that sub-clan are no more at home there than the Malasi or the Lukuba would be. The clan, therefore, is primarily a social category rather than a group, a category into which a number of animals, plants, and other natural objects are placed. But the totemic nature of a clan is not of great importance, and its religious significance is very much overshadowed by its social functions. The clan as a whole is only to be seen at work in certain big ceremonies, when all the sub-clans of the Malasi or Lukuba or Lukwasisiga or Lukulabuta act together and support one another.

It was necessary to give a somewhat detailed and concrete account of clan and sub-clan, of their organization, mythology, and social functions, in order to present them as living and effective units rather than as a mere numerical scheme ornamented by native names. The aspect of clan organization, however, which interests us here primarily, is exogamy, that is the prohibition of sexual intercourse within the clan. All members of the same large group designate themselves, as we know, by the same name, and this, especially in the simpler cultures, is not merely a label but an indication of nature. A common name means, to a certain extent, an identity of personal substance, and kinship implies a bodily sameness.

The real importance of the clan in native imagination and society is illustrated by an interesting linguistic distinction. The native word for " friend " is *lubaygu*, signifying " the man with whom I associate from choice, because I like him ". A European who is learning the language invariably makes mistakes in using this word. Wherever he sees two men closely associated, getting on well together, and obviously on friendly terms, he describes their relationship by the word *lubayla* (his friend), without first finding out whether they are kindred. But this word may only be applied to a man's friend from another clan, and it is not only incorrect, but even improper, to use it of a kinsman. Whenever I used the expression *lubaym* (thy friend) to denote a man's close companion from the same clan, I was rather sharply corrected. *Gala! Veyogu matauna, veyoda—kumila taytanidesi!* (" No! this man is my kinsman; we're kinsmen—the clan is the same! ") Thus a twofold scheme in the relations between men is clearly defined linguistically by the two words for friend, one meaning " friend within the barrier ", the other " friend across the barrier ". This distinction shows how strong is the idea of clanship; it also corresponds to the classificatory use of kinship terms, and to the whole scheme of native relationship.

Needless to say, the same distinction is made when speaking or thinking of the relation between a man and a woman. The word *lubaygu*, meaning here " sweetheart or lover ", can never be applied to a woman of the same clan. In this context it is even more incompatible with the concept of *veyola* (kinship, that is the sameness of substance) than in the relation between two men. Women of the same clan can only be described as sisters (*ludaytasi*, our sisters; *luguta*, my sister; *lumuta*, thy sister; *luleta*, his sister). Women of other clans are described by the generic term *tabu-* (with affixed pronouns: *tubudayasi*, our cousins; *tabugu*, my cousin;

tabum, thy cousin, etc.). The primary meaning of this word is " father's sister ". It also embraces " father's sister's daughter " or " paternal cross-cousin ", or, by extension, " all the women of the father's clan "; and, in its widest sense, " all the women not of the same clan ".

In this, its most extensive application, the word stands for " lawful woman ", " woman with whom intercourse is possible ". For such a woman the term *lubaygu* (" my sweetheart ") may be correctly used; but this term is absolutely incompatible with the kinship designation, *luguta*, my sister. This linguistic use embodies, therefore, the rule of exogamy, and to a large extent it expresses the ideas underlying this. Two people of the opposite sex and standing in the relation of brother and sister in the widest sense, that is belonging to the same clan, must neither marry not cohabit, nor even show any sexual interest in one another. The native word for clan incest or breach of exogamy is, as we know already, *suvasova*.

As we know, the expressions *tosuvasova yoku* (thou incest committer), *kaysuvasova kwim* (thou incestuous penis), *kwaysuvasova wim* (thou incestuous cunnus) fall into the category of insults or accusations. They can, however, be used either lightly and without offence, or seriously as statements of fact with even tragic consequences. This double use of the expression corresponds to a deep-lying moral distinction between degrees of exogamous breach; a distinction which is not easily grasped save after prolonged field-work, as it is overlaid by an official and indoctrinated theory which the natives invariably retail to the unwary ethnographer. Let me first state this native theory of *suvasova* (as obtained by the question-and-answer method) which gives only the first approach to the true attitude of the natives.

If you inquire from intelligent and *bona fide* informants into the various aspects of exogamy and

423

clan organization point by point, and make a composite picture from their various statements, you will necessarily arrive at the conclusion that marriage and sex intercourse within the clan are neither allowed nor ever practised and that they do not even constitute a serious temptation to the natives. Marriage, anyone will tell you, is quite impossible between men and women of the same clan ; nor does it ever happen. As to intercourse, this would be most improper and would be censured by an indignant public opinion. A couple guilty of such an act would, if discovered, incur the anger of the whole community ; they would be deeply mortified and terribly ashamed. And to the question : " What would they do on discovery ? " the invariable answer is that they would commit suicide by jumping from a coco-nut palm.   This well-known method of escaping from an unpleasant situation is called *lo'u*.

" What would happen if they were not discovered ? " To this the usual answer is that a breach of exogamy entails by itself an unpleasant though not necessarily fatal disease. A swelling of the belly heralds the oncoming of this retributive ailment. Soon the skin becomes white, and then breaks out into small sores which grow gradually bigger, while the man fades away in a wasting sickness. A little insect, somewhat like a small spider or a fly, is to be found in such a diseased organism. This insect is spontaneously generated by the actual breach of exogamy. As the natives put it : " We find maggots in a corpse. How do they come ? *Ivagi wala*—it just makes them. In the same way the insect is made in the body of the *tosuvasova* (exogamy breaker). This insect wriggles round like a small snake ; it goes round and round ; it makes the eyes swollen, the face swollen, the belly swollen, like in *popoma* (dropsy, or any other pronounced bodily swelling), or in *kavatokulo* (wasting disease)." And examples are readily given of people who have had or are going through a similar disease.

Thus the native statements supply us with a consistent theory of incest and exogamy, which could be summarized so far by a conscientious ethnographer somewhat as follows : " Exogamy is an absolute taboo for the natives, both as regards marriage and sexual intercourse ; there is a strong moral disapproval of it which would provoke the anger of the community against delinquents and drive them, on discovery, to suicide. There is also a supernatural sanction against it, a dreadful disease culminating in death. Hence exogamy is strictly kept and breaches never occur."

To substantiate this statement an ethnographer would adduce linguistic testimony : there is only one word for the breach of exogamy, *suvasova*, whether this be incest with the nearest relative or merely intercourse with a woman of the same clan. The linguistic usage is, moreover, the typical expression of clan solidarity, of the so-called spontaneous obedience to law and custom. Clan solidarity is also expressed in the unity of names, in the unity of totemic animals, and in the many other forms of totemic identification. And, as an additional proof of its reality, there is the classificatory use of kinship terms.

And yet we have already had indications that neither the solidarity of clanship, nor the classificatory nature of kinship, nor the completeness of the exogamous taboo are absolutely maintained in real life. Not only does there exist a long scale of penalties and blame inflicted for the various degrees of exogamous breach, but marriages within the same clan are not unknown and even the most flagrant transgressions of the taboo allow of customary evasions and adjustments.

What I wish to make clear, by confronting the gist of native statements with the results of direct observation, is that there is a serious discrepancy between the two. The statements contain the ideal of tribal morality ; observation shows us how far real behaviour conforms to it. The statements show

us the polished surface of custom which is invariably
presented to the inquisitive stranger ; direct knowledge of native life reveals the underlying strata of
human conduct, moulded, it is true, by the rigid
surface of custom, but still more deeply influenced
by the smouldering fires of human nature. The
smoothness and uniformity, which the mere verbal
statements suggest as the only shape of human
conduct, disappears with a better knowledge of
cultural reality.

Since in this divergence between the hearsay
method of collecting evidence and first-hand
experience of savage life, we have a very important
source of ethnographic error, it must be made clear
that no blame can be laid on native informants,
but rather on the ethnographer's whole-hearted
reliance in the question-and-answer method. In
laying down the moral rule, in displaying its
stringency and perfection, the native is not trying
really to deceive the stranger. He simply does what
any self-respecting and conventional member of
a well-ordered society would do : he ignores the
seamy and ugly sides of human life, he overlooks
his own shortcomings and even those of his neighbours, he shuts his eyes to that which he does not
want to see. No gentleman wants to acknowledge
the existence of what is " not done ", what is
universally considered bad, and what is improper.
The conventional mind ignores such things, above
all when speaking to a stranger—since dirty linen
should not be washed in public.

The Melanesian is as sensitive to indelicacy and
as conventional in matters of decorum and propriety
as any mid-Victorian middle-aged gentleman or
spinster. Imagine an ethnographer from Mars
inquiring of our respectable gentleman (or spinster)
about matrimonial morals in England. He would be
told that monogamy is the one and only form of
marriage, that chastity is required of both parties
before marriage and that adultery is strictly forbidden

by law, morals, manners, and our code of honour. All this is, in a way, quite true: it embodies the authorized ideal of religion and morality. And if the Martian went on to inquire whether adultery occurs in practice, our gentleman (or spinster) would resent the question as an implied insult and would grow cold or hot over it. (For you must remember that he is no more accustomed to being used as an informant than is the Melanesian gentleman to whom you give a stick of tobacco for information received.)

If the Martian, versed in the modern method of field-work, as recommended by some schools of Anthropology, should proceed to the "concrete manner of questioning", he might really get into trouble. To the concrete inquiry: "How many times have you slept with your friend's wife, and how often has your wife slept with another man ? "— the answer would not be verbal but behaviouristic. And the Martian, if in a position to do so, would enter in his note-book: "The natives of the terrestrial planet never commit adultery; there is a powerful group sentiment, if not group instinct, preventing them from this crime; even the hypothetical mention of a possible transgression of this sacred law puts them into a singular mental state, accompanied by emotional discharges, explosive expressions, and those violent actions which make the term 'savage' so appropriate to the rude natives of the Earth."

This statement would be obviously one-sided, and yet the terrestrial informant was in no way trying to deceive the inquirer. In the case of our own society we know the answer to the riddle. The informant, though aware of possible breaches of marital fidelity, not only does not want to parade them before a stranger but is always ready to forget them himself under the influence of strong emotional attachment to an ideal. Now to a Melanesian the subject of possible incest with a near matrilineal relative is shocking in the highest degree; while

breach of exogamy is one of those subjects which
are to be discussed only in confidence and among
friends. A gentleman in the Trobriand Islands is
as ready as we are to deceive himself, when he
feels that tribal honour requires it. He is offered
a few sticks of tobacco, and told to speak about
intimate and delicate matters. The anthropologist
with his rapid and at times penetrating questions,
with his insistence on fact and on concrete detail,
arouses the same reactions as would the hypothetical
inquirer from Mars among us. The native may
feel hurt and refuse to discuss the matter, as happens
time after time to a field-worker in the earlier stages
of his ethnographic exploration. Or else he states
such ideal conditions as are demanded by his sense
of propriety, as do credit to himself and to his fellow-
tribesmen, and as do not compromise anybody or
any aspect of his communal life.

For besides the feeling of dignity and conventional
subservience to tribal honour, there is another grave
reason why the native does not want to introduce
any haphazard European talker to the seamy side
of his communal life. He is accustomed to find white
men nosing about his sexual affairs, some in order
to interfere with his women, others, and worse, to
moralize and to improve him ; and, most dangerous
of all, others to issue laws and regulations which
introduce difficulties, at times insurmountable, into
his tribal organization. Elementary caution, then,
tells him not to go beyond the most obvious
generalities and to state merely the bald outline of
his moral rules and regulations, such as seem
unassailable even by the most interfering missionary
or government official.

The upshot of all this is that the hasty field-worker,
who relies completely upon the question-and-
answer method, obtains at best that lifeless body of
laws, regulations, morals, and conventionalities
which *ought* to be obeyed, but in reality are often
only evaded. For in actual life rules are never

entirely conformed to, and it remains, as the most difficult but indispensable part of the ethnographer's work, to ascertain the extent and mechanism of the deviations.

In order, however, to penetrate to the exception, to the deviation, to the breach of custom, it is necessary to become acquainted directly with the behaviour of the native; and ,this can be done only through a knowledge of the language and through a prolonged residence among the people. But most modern scientific field-work has been accomplished by the rapid and precise, sometimes over-precise, methods built upon the technique of question-and-answer, and it suffers from over-simplifying and over-standardizing the legal constitution of native culture.[1] Such material again has -led unfortunately to the anthropological doctrine of the impeccability of native races, of their immanent legality, and inherent and automatic subservience to custom.

Returning now to our special problem of incest and exogamy and applying to it the methodological principles just discussed, we can ask what more there is to learn about these taboos and in what way it is possible to learn it. The same informant who at first supplied the rounded-off official version of them, who even indignantly repudiated any indiscreet suggestions, begins to know you better or finds that you have become acquainted with the real facts in some concrete incident. Then you can confront him with the contradiction, and he himself will very often put you on the scent of the truth and give you a correct account of the exceptions and contraventions which recur with regard to the rule.

A very capable and useful informant of mine, Gomaya, who has appeared several times in these

---

[1] This point has been elaborated as the main thesis in *Crime and Custom in Savage Society*, which should be read in connection with the above argument.

pages, was at first very touchy on the subject of incest and resented any suggestions as to its possibility. He was a valuable informant because of certain shortcomings in his character. Proud and sensitive on points of tribal honour, he was also very vain and inclined to boast. Moreover, he soon found that he could not conceal his own affairs from me as they were notorious through the district. His intrigue with Ilamweria, a girl of the same clan, was a subject for general gossip. So combining necessity with the satisfaction of his *amour propre*, Gomaya explained to me that a breach of clan exogamy— he and his sweetheart belonged to different sub-clans of the Malasi—is rather a desirable and interesting form of erotic experience.

He told me also that he would have married the girl, such marriages being possible though viewed with disfavour, had she not become pregnant, and he succumbed to the disease which follows upon breach of exogamous taboo. He then went off to his native village of Sinaketa where he grew worse and worse, until he was helped by an old man, a friend of his father's, who knew a very powerful magic against such disease. The old man chanted spells over some herbs and some water, and after the application of this remedy, Gomaya got gradually better. The old man then taught him how to perform the magic ; and ever after, Gomaya proudly added, he preferred to sleep with girls of the same clan, always using the prophylactic magic.

All his statements made it clear to me that breach of exogamy is rather an enviable achievement, because a man thus proves the strength of his love magic in that he is able to overcome, not merely the natural resistance of women but also their tribal morality. Thus even from one personal history it was possible to gather the main lines of practice and to understand certain complications and apparent contradictions of exogamous prohibitions. In further discussions with other natives, and above all by the collection of concrete material, I was able to supplement these earlier statements and to correct them. For Gomaya naturally exaggerated certain points in order to satisfy his vanity, and he thus put facts into a wrong perspective. He represented himself, for instance, as the one glorious exception to the rule ; gave me to understand that few people only knew the magic of incest, and that breach of exogamy was a singularly daring achievement. All of which was not true.

The fact is that the breach of exogamy within the clan, intrigues with what the natives call *kakaveyola* (kindred-in-clan or pseudo-kindred), though officially forbidden, ruled to be improper, and surrounded by supernatural sanctions, is yet everywhere committed. To use a somewhat loose comparison, it figures in the tribal life of the Trobrianders much in the same way as that in which adultery figures in French novels. There is no moral indignation or horror about it, but the transgression encroaches upon an important institution, and cannot be officially regarded as permissible.

Marriages—as distinct from intrigues—*within the clan* are definitely regarded as a serious breach of the rule. The one or two cases on record (see e.g. above, ch. xii, sec. 4) show that natives will not actively interfere with them, once they are contracted. But I found that it was not proper to mention the incestuousness of a marriage to any of the people concerned nor yet speak about it in the presence of their near relatives. Even general allusions to incest and exogamy have to be carefully avoided in the presence of such transgressors. As to the super-natural sanctions, the prophylactic magic already mentioned, performed over wild ginger root wrapped up in leaves, over water warmed by heated stones, and over dry banana leaf, is well-nigh universally known and is used very freely.

Thus the rule of exogamy, far from being uniform and wholesale in its application, works differently with regard to marriage and to sexual intercourse ; is allowed certain latitudes by public opinion and permits of evasions of the supernatural sanctions. All this had to be stated in detail to give a clear idea of the mechanism of exogamy.

There is also an interesting difference in stringency according to the clans in which it happens. Of the four totemic divisions, the Malasi have the reputation of being the most persistent exogamy breakers and committers of incest. All the incestuous marriages on record have happened within this clan ; and I was told that this was not an accident but that only the Malasi and no other clan will tolerate such marriages. The myth of incest, which will be described in the next chapter, is associated with the Malasi, and so also is the magic of love and the magic to frustrate incest disease.

Far more stringently are the rules of exogamy obeyed when the two people concerned belong, not only to the same clan, but to the same sub-clan (*dala*). Such people are called real kinsmen (*veyola mokita*, or simply *veyola*) in contradistinction to *kakaveyola*. Between such people a much greater secrecy is observed when incest is committed ; there is no jauntiness or covert boasting, and marriage is impossible.

A still higher degree of stringency obtains when we come to kinship traceable in actual genealogy. Incest with a mother's sister's daughter is a real crime, and it may lead to consequences as serious as suicide. A case of suicide described elsewhere illustrates the manner in which a man guilty of such incest might have to inflict punishment upon himself.[1] Incest with the own sister is, as we know already, a dreadful crime to the natives. Yet even here it would not be correct to assume an absolutely smooth and secure working of tribal law, because cases of breach of the rule occur in reality as well

---

[1] Cf. *Crime and Custom*, pp. 77 and 78, and below, ch. xiv, sec. 3.

as in folk-lore. But of this we shall have to speak presently.

Thus the uniformity of the rules and the simplicity of the sanctions by which they are enforced is shown to be a surface phenomenon, below which run the complex currents and undercurrents which form the true course of tribal life. On the surface we have one word, *suvasova*, one clan kinship, one punishment, one sense of right and wrong In reality we have the distinction between marriage and mere intercourse, between clan and sub-clan (*kakaveyola* and *veyola*), between genealogical kinship and mere community of sub-clan, between the own sister and the classificatory sisters. We have also to distinguish between direct enforcement by public opinion and by supernatural sanctions, neither of which work in a simple or infallible manner. Any attempt to understand this complex state of affairs leads us to the fundamental factor in social organization, that is, kinship, and this again cannot be properly understood without a knowledge of family life, and the constitution of the family.

6

THE SUPREME TABOO

All the sociological divisions, local communities, clans, sub-clans, and classificatory kinship groups of the Trobrianders are rooted in the family. Only by studying the formation of the earliest bonds between parent and child, by following the gradual growth and development of these, and their ever-widening extension into bonds of local grouping and clanship, can we grasp the kinship system of the natives.

The fundamental principles of mother-right had to be stated at the beginning of this book, since without a knowledge of it and of the relationship between father and child no description can be given of any native custom. We know therefore that, according to tribal law, kinship, the identity of blood and body, runs only in mother line. We also know that father and child are related, in the eyes of the native, merely by a system of obligations and reciprocal duties, but that this does not exclude a strong bond of an emotional nature between them. It will be necessary for us at this juncture to become acquainted with an outline of native kinship terminology, though full statement on the subject will have to be deferred to a future publication.[1]

TABLE OF RELATIONSHIP TERMS

A. *Kinship Terms*

1. Tabu(gu).—Grandparent, grandchild ; father's sister, father's sister's daughter.
2. Ina(gu).—Mother, mother's sister ; mother's clanswoman.
3. Tama(gu).—Father, father's brother ; father's clansman ; father's sister's son.
4. Kada(gu).—Mother's brother and, reciprocally, sister's son and sister's daughter.
5. Lu(gu)ta.—Sister (man speaking), brother (woman speaking); woman of same clan and generation (man speaking), man of same clan and generation (woman speaking).
6. Tuwa(gu).—Elder brother (man speaking), elder sister (woman speaking) ; clansman of same generation but older (man speaking), clanswoman of same generation but older (woman speaking).
7. Bwada(gu).—Younger brother (man speaking), younger sister (woman speaking) ; clansman of same generation but younger (man speaking), clanswoman of same generation but younger (woman speaking).
8. Latu(gu).—Child, male or female.

B. *Marriage Relationships*

9. (Ulo)mwala.—Husband.
10. (Ulo)kwava.—Wife.

C. *Relationships-in-law*

11. Yawa(gu).—Father-in-law, mother-in-law.
12. Lubou(gu).—Wife's brother, sister's husband.
13. Iva(gu)ta.—Husband's sister, brother's wife.
14. Tuwa(gu).—Wife's elder sister, husband's elder brother.
15. Bwada(gu).—Wife's younger sister, husband's younger brother.

In the annexed genealogical diagram we find, printed in capital letters, the few words which furnish the key to the whole terminology of kinship and

[1] *Psychology of Kinship* announced to appear in the *International Library of Psychology.*

GENEALOGICAL DIAGRAM OF RELATIONSHIP

I. Terms of Kinship

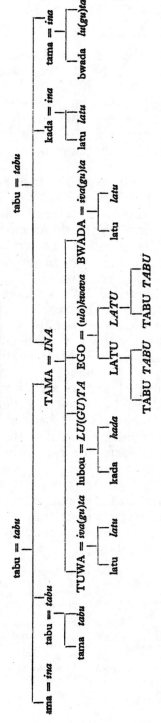

II. Relationships-in-law (Man Speaking)

III. Relationships-in-Law (Woman Speaking)

form the foundation both of the sociological system
within the native culture and of its linguistic
expression.   These are the words used to
designate the inmates of the household, the words
which convey the dominant interests and emotions
of childhood.   They denote those relationships
which are the starting point of all the social bonds of
later life.

Take, to begin with, the word *inagu*, my mother,
which is the first to be uttered by a child in the
Trobriands as everywhere else.[1]   The term correlated to it is *latugu*, by which the mother
designates her own child.   These are the two terms
of the mother-to-child relationship on which the
whole system of native kinship organization rests.
(In our diagram, Ego is addressed by his mother,
latugu, and, later, he in turn uses this word to his
own offspring as indicated there.)   Apart from the
intense emotional interest taken by the mother in
her child, and the response of the infant to the
maternal organism—both these elements being
physiological and universal in all human societies—
the relation in the Trobriands is sociologically
defined by a number of ritual observances, beginning
with pregnancy and leading the woman into those
various duties and taboos of early maternity which
isolate mother and child into a small group of two,
intimately bound up in each other (see ch. viii).
The father, *tama*, not regarded as of the same bodily
substance, stands, nevertheless, in a close emotional,
legal, and economic relation to the child (see
ch. vii).   On the pls. 90 and 91 we see typical

[1] In the genealogical Diagram the terms are given, without possessive
pronouns ; in the Table with the affixed particle of the first person
(*gu*).   This particle is usually suffixed to the end of the root (*inagu*,
" my mother," *tamagu*, " my father," etc.), but it is infixed in two terms
lu-gu-ta and *iva-gu-ta*.   The second person is designated by the particle
m or *mu* ; *tamam*, " thy father," *lumuta*, " thy sister " ; the third pers.
sing. by the particle *la*, and so on.   In actual speech the root is never used
alone.   The abstract meaning is conveyed by using the word with the
third person singular suffix.   *Inala* means " mother " as well as " his
mother ".   All male terms are in roman types ; the female in italic.
Terms for the nearest family relationship are printed in capitals.

illustrations of maternal and paternal attitudes expressing tenderness and pride.

When the child grows up, it gains a gradual independence. But in certain respects this progress is slower and lasts longer in Melanesia than among ourselves. Weaning takes place at a later stage, and the child is surrounded by the tender cares of the mother and father, constantly carried and watched over, until it passes to freedom and independence almost at a single stride. We know already (see ch. iii) that children suffer very little interference from their parents in the matter of sexual freedom, and that in this respect the interests of the child are naturally directed away from home and find an easy outlet among his playmates of the same age.

The removal of a child out of his family is due to yet another factor, which becomes increasingly prominent and which will colour the future sexual life of the individual. This is the supreme taboo of the Trobriander; the prohibition of any erotic or even of any tender dealings between brother and sister. This taboo is the prototype of all that is ethically wrong and horrible to the native. It is the first moral rule seriously impressed in the individual's life, and the only one which is enforced to the full by all the machinery of social and moral sanctions. It is so deeply engrained in the structure of native tradition that every individual is kept permanently alive to it.

The relation between brother and sister is denoted by the term *luguta* (No. 5 of our table). This term means " sister " when uttered by a male, and " brother " when spoken by a female. In its wider meaning it designates a person of the opposite sex and of the forbidden class, that is, of the same sub-clan or clan as Ego. In its widest and metaphorical sense it is used for any tabooed person or thing. As a metaphor the word " sister " (*luguta*) is frequently used in magical formulæ when such things as a blight or a disease are to be exorcized.

The term *luguta* is used only with regard to the tabooed relationship, since children of the same parents and of the same sex use different kinship designations (*tuwagu*, *bwadagu*) to describe each other ; *tuwagu* meaning " my elder brother " (man speaking) and " my elder sister " (woman speaking) ; and *bwadagu* " my younger brother " (man speaking) and " my younger sister " (woman speaking).

Round the word *luguta* a new order of ideas and moral rules begins to grow up at an early stage of the individual's life history. The child, accustomed to little or no interference with most of its whims or wishes, receives a real shock when suddenly it is roughly handled, seriously reprimanded and punished whenever it makes any friendly, affectionate, or even playful advances to the other small being constantly about in the same household. Above all, the child experiences an emotional shock when it becomes aware of the expression of horror and anguish on the faces of its elders when they correct it. This emotional contagion, this perception of moral reactions in the social environment is perhaps the most powerful factor in a native community by which norms and values are imposed on an individual's character.

The circumstantial arrangements and set customs which preclude any possibility of intimate contact between brother and sister are also, of course, very important. Brother and sister are definitely forbidden to take part at the same time in any childish sexual games, or even in any form of play. And this is not only a rule laid down by elders, but it is also a convention rigorously observed by the children themselves.

We know already (see ch. iii) that when a boy grows up and when there is a sister of his living in the parental house, he has to sleep in the bachelors' hut (*bukumatula*). In her love affairs, the girl must most rigorously avoid any possibility of being seen by the brother. When, on certain occasions, brother and sister have to appear in the same company—when they travel in the same canoe, for instance, or participate in a domestic meeting—a rigidity of behaviour and a sobriety in conversation falls upon all those present. No cheerful company, no festive entertainment, therefore, is allowed to include brother and sister, since their simultaneous presence would throw a blight on pleasure and would chill gaiety.

Although, in a matrilineal society, the brother is the guardian of his sister, although she has to bend down when he approaches, to obey his commands and to regard him as the head of the family, he never has any concern in his sister's love affairs, nor in her prospective marriage. After she is married, however, he becomes the head of her family in more than a metaphorical sense. He is called by his sister's children *kadagu* (my maternal uncle), and as such exercises great influence, especially over the boys.[1]

The careful avoidance by a man of any knowledge about his sister's amorous prospects is, I am certain, not only an ideal but also a fact. I was over and over again assured that no man has the slightest inkling as to whom his sister is going to marry, although this is the common knowledge of everyone else. And I know that nothing remotely touching upon the subject would be uttered within earshot of him. I was told that if a man came by chance upon his sister and her sweetheart while they were making love, all three would have to commit *lo'u* (suicide by jumping from a coco-nut palm). This is obviously an exaggeration which expresses the ideal and not the reality : if such a mishap occurred the brother would most likely pretend to himself, and to them, that he had seen nothing, and would discreetly disappear. But I know that considerable care is taken to preclude any such possibility, and no one would

[1] Compare the analysis of this relation in *Sex and Repression*, pt. ii, chs. vi and ix ; *Crime and Custom*, pt. ii, ch. iii ; and in this book, ch. i, sec. 1.

dream of mentioning the subject in the presence of the brother.

Brother and sister thus grow up in a strange sort of domestic proximity : in close contact, and yet without any personal or intimate communication; near to each other in space, near by rules of kinship and common interest ; and yet, as regards personality, always hidden and mysterious. They must not even look at each other, they must never exchange any light remarks, never share their feelings and ideas. And as age advances and the other sex becomes more and more associated with love-making, the brother and sister taboo becomes increasingly stringent. Thus, to repeat, the sister remains for her brother the centre of all that is sexually forbidden—its very symbol ; the prototype of all unlawful sexual tendencies within the same generation and the foundation of prohibited degrees of kinship and relationship, though the taboo loses force as its application is extended.

The nearest female of the previous generation, the mother, is also surrounded by a taboo, which is coloured, however, by a somewhat different emotional reaction. Incest with her is regarded with real horror, but both the mechanism by which this taboo is brought home and the way in which it is regarded are essentially distinct from the brother-sister taboo. The mother stands in a close bodily relation to her child in its earliest years, and from this position she recedes, though only gradually, as he grows up. As we know, weaning takes place late, and children, both male and female, are allowed to cuddle in their mother's arms and to embrace her whenever they like.

When a small boy begins his playful sexual approaches to small girls, this does not in any way disturb his relationship to the mother, nor has he to keep any special secrecy on the subject. He does not, by preference, discuss these matters with his parents, but there is no taboo against his doing so.

When he is older and carries on more serious intrigues, he might, in certain circumstances, even be allowed to sleep with his sweetheart in his parents' house. Thus the relation to the mother and the sexual relation are kept distinct and allowed to run side by side. The ideas and feelings centering round sex on the one hand, and maternal tenderness on the other, are differentiated naturally and easily, without being separated by a rigid taboo.

Again, since normal erotic impulses find an easy outlet, tenderness towards the mother and bodily attachment to her are naturally drained of their stronger sensuous elements. Incestuous inclinations towards the mother are regarded as highly reprehensible, as unnatural and immoral, but there is not the same feeling of horror and fear as towards brother and sister incest. When speaking with the natives of maternal incest, the inquirer finds neither the rigid suspense nor the emotional reactions which are always evoked by any allusion to brother and sister relations. They would discuss the possibility without being shocked, but it was clear that they regarded incest with the mother as almost impossible. I would not affirm that such incest has never occurred, but certainly I have obtained no concrete data, and the very fact that no case survives in memory or in tradition shows that the natives take relatively little interest in it.[1]

The maternal grandmother and her grandson are also sexually forbidden to each other, but there is no horror about this relationship, such incest appearing as a merely ridiculous possibility. As we know, sexual intercourse with an old woman is regarded as something indecorous, ludicrous, and unæsthetic; and this is the light in which any suggestion of grandson-grandmother incest is looked

---

[1] For a comparison of the two attitudes towards incest with the mother and the sister, respectively, and for the correlation of this phenomenon with the matrilineal system of kinship and with the natives' treatment of infantile sexuality, see the writer's *Sex and Repression*.

upon. But such a lapse from good morals and manners does not loom largely in fantasies, folk-lore or tribal morals. These two call each other by the reciprocal term *tabugu*, which also has the wider meaning of " grandparent ", " grandchild ", and wider yet, " ancestor," " descendant."

So far we have discussed individual kinship in the female line and within the household : between mother and child, brother and sister, and, going beyond the household, the relation with the grand-mother. I have intentionally and carefully distinguished this from so-called classificatory kin-ship ties ; for the mixing up of the individual and the " classificatory " relation, kept apart by the natives in law, custom, and idea, has been a most misleading and dangerous cause of error in anthropology, vitiating both observation and theory on social organization and kinship. Looking back to our diagram, and carrying the genealogy beyond the family circle, we can see that certain terms from within the circle are repeated outside it. In the life history of the individual most people who come into contact with the growing child are, in one way or another, partially assimilated or compared to the child's primary relatives within the household and the terms used for parents, brothers, and sisters are gradually extended. The first person from the larger world to enter into the circle of kinsmen is the mother's sister, who, although she is called by the same term as the own mother, *inagu*, is very definitely distinguished from her. The word *inagu* extended to the mother's sister is, from the outset, given an entirely different meaning—some-thing like " second mother " or " subsidiary mother ". When the mother's sister is a member of the same village community, she is a very frequent visitor within the household ; she replaces the mother in certain functions or at certain times, she tends the child, and shows it a considerable amount of devotion. The child is taught by its elders to extend the term *inagu* to her, and this extension is made natural and plausible to the child by the considerable similarity between its relations to mother and mother's sister.

But there can be no doubt that the new use of the word remains always what it is, an extension and a metaphor. In its second sense *inagu* is used with a different feeling-tone; and there are circumlocutions, grammatical usages, and lexicographical indices which differentiate the secondary from the primary meaning. Only to a linguistically untrained European observer, especially if he is not conversant with the native language, can the word *inagu* (2) (mother's sister) appear identical with *inagu* (1) (own mother). On this point any intelligent native, if properly questioned, could correct the ethnographer's error.

The same gradual extension, and corresponding change in emotional content, takes place with regard to other terms, and the word *luguta*, used to the mother's sister's daughter, conveys to the boy only an attentuated and diluted idea of sisterhood. The own sister remains a prototype of the new relation, and the taboo observed towards the own sister has also to be kept with regard to the secondary sister, but the distinction between the two taboos and the two relations is well marked. The real sister lives in the same house; for her the boy, as her future guardian, feels a direct responsibility; she remains the object on which the first and only serious prohibition has been brought home to him. The secondary sister lives in another house or even village; there are no duties or responsibilities towards her and the prohibition with regard to her is a weakened extension of the primary taboo. Thus the own sister and the first maternal cousin appear in an entirely different light, not only as regards the degree, but as regards the fundamental quality of the relation. Incest with the first maternal cousin is regarded as wrong, but not horrible; as daring and

443

dangerous, but not abominable. The early feeling for this distinction becomes, later on, crystallized in the doctrine of tribal law. The man knows and recognises that *luguta* (1) is a person to whom he owes a great many duties, whom he has partly to support after her marriage and with regard to whom he has to observe the supreme taboo. *Luguta* (2) has no specific claims on him, he is not her real guardian nor head of her household after marriage, and the sexual taboo does not operate with anything like the same stringency.

When we pass from the " secondary " relations, denoted by the terms *inagu* (2) and *luguta* (2) to more distant relatives, the intimacy of the bond and the stringency of the taboo falls off rapidly. Taking the relation of *luguta* as an example : if a boy and girl can be traced to a common great-grandmother in the mother line, they are *luguta*. But the taboo would be much weaker. Beyond this it would be difficult even to index the term, as the relationship ceases to be traceable by pedigree. It would be just that of real kinship within the same sub-clan : *luguta, veyogu mokita—dalemasi taytanidesi* (" sister mine, kinswoman mine truly—sub-clan our identical ").

When we go beyond the sub-clan to the clan (*kumila*), the relation becomes less intimate once more and the taboo less stringent : *luguta wala, kakaveyogu—kama kumila taytanidesi* (" just my sister, my pseudo-kinswoman—mine and her clan identical "). This defines the word *luguta* in its fully extended, that is truly classificatory sense. It means, as we know already, one of those women with whom sex intercourse is legally forbidden, but with whom it may be indulged. The widest meaning of the word *luguta* is thus profoundly different from *luguta* (1), the carrier of the supreme taboo.

Thus, starting from the individual relationships within the household and following the kinship extensions in the life history of the individual, we have arrived at the same results as in our

PLATE 65

KAYDEBU DANCE

The circular dance with the carved shield on the baku of Omarakana. Note the plain, though picturesque, headdress of cockatoo feathers. [Cb. X, 1; cb. II, 2]

PLATE 66

A Melanesian Beauty
[*Ch. X,* 1]

PLATE 67

A Type not Admired by the Natives
[*Ch. X, 1*]

PLATE 68

ETHNOGRAPHER WITH A MAN IN A WIG

The Ethnographer talking to Togugu'a, a sorcerer of some repute and a good informant, who is wearing a full wig and holding a large lime gourd and spatula. From this photograph a critical reader can assess the truth of the statement discussed in section 4 (native comparison between European and Melanesian features). [Ch. X, 2 and 4]

PLATE 69

THE LEAF AND THE DRESS

*Man and woman, each holding the palm leaf from which their
respective garments are made. [See also pl. 9; ch. X, 4; ch. I, 4]*

PLATE 70

LOUSING
[*Ch.* X, 9]

PLATE 71

CEREMONIAL DISTRIBUTION OF FOOD

[*Ch. XI*, 2]

PLATE 72

AFTER THE DISTRIBUTION

Women collecting food. The four houses in the front row are store-houses ; behind are living huts, built entirely on the ground. [Ch. XI, 2]

PLATE 73

REHEARSAL OF A *KASAWAGA* DANCE
[*Ch. XI, 2; II, 2*]

PLATE 74

THE CROWD ASSEMBLED OUTSIDE THE VILLAGE FOR BEAUTY MAGIC

[*Ch. XI,* 3]

PLATE 75

THE MAGIC OF MOTHER OF PEARL
[*Ch. XI* 4]

PLATE 76

MAGICAL FACE PAINTING

[*Ch. XI, 4; also ch. X, 3*]

PLATE 77

THE RITUAL PLACING OF THE *VANA*
[*Ch. XI*, 4]

PLATE 78

THE LAST TOUCH TO THE DANCERS' TOILET
[*Ch. XI*, 4]

PLATE 79

READY FOR THE FINAL DANCE
[*Ch. XI, 5 ; also ch. II, 2*]

PLATE 80

WOMEN IN THE WATER COLLECTING SHELLS

[*Cb. XII, 4*]

PLATE 81

HEAD POOL OF THE TIDAL CREEK OF KWABULO
[*Ch. XII, 4*]

PLATE 82

THE INUVAYLA'U DANCE
[Ch. XII, 4]

PLATE 83

USIKELA BANANAS IN KAULAGU
[*Ch. XII*, 4]

PLATE 84

ACCUMULATION OF FOOD FOR A FEAST

Yams are heaped up on the ground and fill the pwata'i (prism-shaped wooden receptacle) : coco-nuts, sugar cane, bananas and bunches of areca nut are displayed on top—the whole producing on the native a strong impression of beauty, power, and importance. This is done at the milamala (annual return of the spirits) as well as at mortuary and other distributions (sagali). [Ch. XIII, 1]

PLATE 85

CROWD COLLECTED ON A BEACH TO ADMIRE A LARGE CATCH

A few of the people are the fishermen, others are there to receive the fish and carry it away ; the majority are spectators fascinated by the success of the fishing expedition and by the accumulation of food. [Ch. XIII, 1]

PLATE 86

A SMALL GROUP EATING TARO
[*Ch. XIII*, 1; *also ch. XI*, 2]

PLATE 87

TYPICAL LAGOON VILLAGE
[*Ch. XIII*, 1]

PLATE 88

TOKEDA—THE BELT OF JUNGLE ADJOINING A GARDEN

The strong fence protecting the crops from bush-pig and wallaby is shown; to the left a stile and a woman crossing it, carrying a load of firewood. [Cb. XIII, 4]

PLATE 89

ANCESTRAL EMERGENCE SPOT IN A SMALL VILLAGE ON THE ISLAND OF VAKUTA
[*Ch. XIII*, 5]

PLATE 90

MOTHER AND CHILD
[*Ch. XIII, 6 ; cb. VIII,* 1 *and* 4]

PLATE 91

FATHER AND CHILD
[Ch. XIII, 6]

PLATE 92

TWO PRETTY GIRLS—ONE DISFIGURED BY MOURNING
[*Ch. VI, 3; ch. X, 2*]

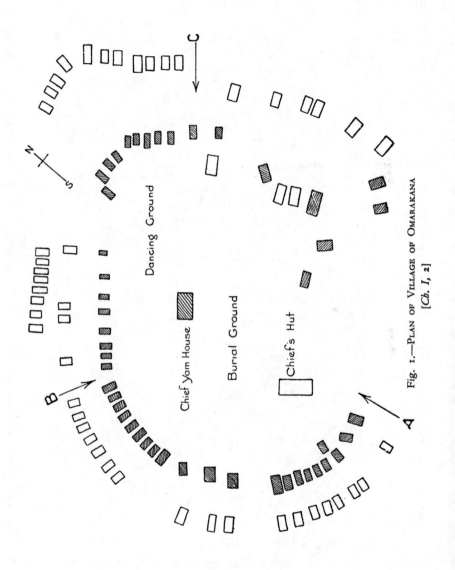

N

S

C

B

A

Dancing Ground

Chief Yam House

Burial Ground

Chief's Hut

Fig. 1.—Plan of Village of Omarakana

[*Ch. I, 2*]

FIG. 2. THE TROBRIAND ISLANDS

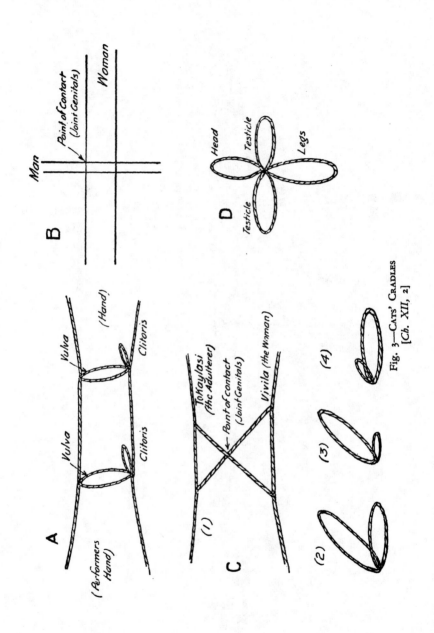

A

(Performer's Hand)

Vulva

Vulva

Clitoris

Clitoris

(Hand)

B

Man

Point of Contact
(Joint Genitals)

Woman

C

ToKaylasi
(The Adulterer)

Point of Contact
(Joint Genitals)

Vivila (the Woman)

(1)

(2)

(3)

(4)

D

Head

Testicle

Testicle

Legs

Fig. 3—CATS' CRADLES [Ch. XII, 2]

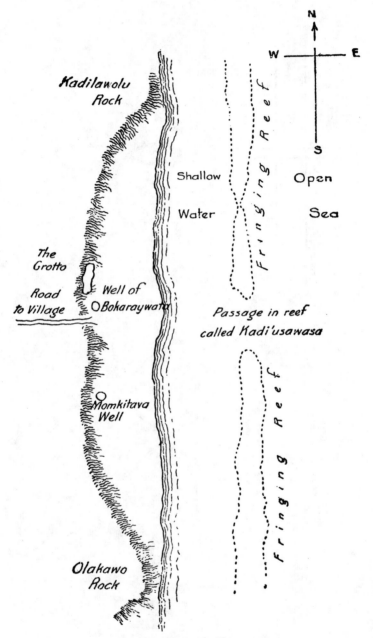

Fig. 4.—The Beach of Kumilabwaga
[Ch. XIV, 1]

discussion of clanship and the general prohibitions of exogamy and incest. The word *luguta* is one term of a dichotomy separating women into " forbidden " and " lawful ".

The other term *tabugu* (" lawful woman ") also originates within the family and is extended thence. To follow this process we must turn to the other side of the pedigree and examine the paternal relations.

The most important person on the father's side is obviously the father himself. Here we meet the second fundamental fact in household morality : though the father is not a kinsman of his children, sexual intercourse between father and daughter, though it occurs, is not only illegal and improper, but it is viewed with definite moral repugnance. Marriage between father and daughter is not allowed nor even imaginable to the native.

Perhaps the most important case on record of the violation of this taboo is that of Kumatala, of the sub-clan next in rank to the Tabalu (the Mwauri of the Lukuba clan), who is headman of the village of Liluta. He is known to live with his beautiful eldest daughter Bodogupo'u. Another recorded case is that of the famous sorcerer Piribomatu, also of very high rank, who " comes to " or " approaches ", as the natives put it, his daughter Bokaylola. It is consistent with native theory that, morally, the natives do not distinguish between a man's real daughter and his stepdaughter, and have no special term for the latter relationship. For since his relation to the child is determined through the mother and since incest is prohibited because of her, it is equally wrong to have intercourse with any of her offspring, whether of the present or of a previous marriage.

Thus Budiya, headman of Kabululo, married a widow who had a daughter named Bodulela :

Matauna imwoyki Bodulela, sene gaga bayse,
This man comes to Bodulela, very bad this,

boge	*latula*	*minana.*	*Isuvi*	*wabwala,*
already	child his	this female.	He enters	in house,

minana	*boge*	*iliku*	*dabela*
this (female)	already	undoes	skirt her ;

ikanupwagega,		*igise*	*matauna*
she reclines with legs apart,		he sees	this (male)

wila—	*ikaya.*
cunnus—	he copulates.

This means : The man happened to enter the hut when his step-daughter had taken off her fibre petticoat for the night and was lying, perhaps already half asleep, in a tempting position. Stirred by this, Budiya succumbed and committed the reprehensible act.

In this version, the cause of incest is ascribed to an untoward accident, but other accounts maintain that Budiya had long desired his step-daughter, that she refused him, and that he seduced her by love magic. Love magic also is said to have been used by Gumabudi, head man of Yalumugwa, who used to cohabit regularly with his real daughter. The latter, Bulubwaloga, we have already met, for she was the wife of Gilayviyaka, one of the sons of the paramount chief, and she left her husband after he had committed adultery with one of his father's wives.

As we have said, the reasons given for the moral reprehensibility of intercourse between father and daughter are all connected with his marriage to the mother and his position in the household. *Sene gaga pela boge iva'i inala, boge iyousi vilakuria*—" very bad, because already he married her mother. Already he caught hold of the first marriage present " (see ch. iv, sec. 3). Again, a man should not sleep with his daughter, since it was his duty to be tender to her when she was a child, to take her in his arms. *Gala tamasisi deli latuda, pela tamala iyobwayli, ikopo'i*—" We do not sleep with children ours (daughters), because her father (the father) fondles, takes into his arms." Or the natives point out that as the father has control of his daughter's marriage and love affairs, he must not sleep with her.

The cases of father and daughter incest just mentioned were univerally known, but they were spoken of with great discretion and never before the people concerned. Should a man guilty of such a crime be publicly told about it, he would have to commit suicide by jumping from a tree, say the natives.

It must be clearly understood that, although father to daughter incest is regarded as bad, it is not described by the word *suvasova* (clan exogamy or incest), nor does any disease follow upon it ; and, as we know, the whole ideology underlying this taboo is different from that of *suvasova*.

The anomalous extension of the word for father (*tama*) to the father's sister's son is important, for it demonstrates the influence which language has upon customs and ideas. Marriage and intercourse with the male paternal first cousin is not strictly forbidden, but it is regarded somewhat askance. It is perhaps least censured among the Malasi of Kiriwina ; and natives from other districts, who lose no opportunity of slandering their neighbours when a difference in custom allows of it, speak derisively of the people of Kiriwina " who marry their fathers and sleep with them ". An ethnographer, ignorant of language and superficially acquainted with native customs and ideas, might speak about the natives' " horror of marriage and intercourse with a father in the classificatory sense " ; and thus imply that they do not distinguish between *father* as " mother's husband " and *father* as " father's sister's son ". Such a statement would be quite incorrect.

A man is not allowed to have intercourse with his daughter because she is his wife's nearest kinswoman ; therefore we might expect to find that the wife's other near female kindred are also tabooed.

This is actually the case. A strong taboo is placed on a wife's sisters, whom, strangely enough, the man calls by the same two names (according to age) which he applies to his elder and younger brothers and which a woman uses to her elder and younger sisters : *tuwagu* and *bwadagu*. Thus here a man uses towards persons of the opposite sex names which indicate identity of sex. Analogously a woman addresses these same two terms to her husband's elder and younger brothers, with whom sexual intercourse is forbidden. There are a few recorded cases of this rule's transgression, the most notorious being that of Manimuwa and Dakiya already quoted (ch. vi, sec, 1). Here, again, although the word *suvasova* is not applied to the taboo, the natives feel strongly against intercourse with a wife's sister, who, after marriage, becomes to him somewhat like his own sister. A man must also abstain from intercourse with his wife's mother, but otherwise no taboo of avoidance exists.

By careful inquiry of several informants and by direct observation, I have compiled the following table of sex taboos in order of stringency. It is meant rather to facilitate a survey of the whole subject than to establish any rigid gradations.

1. By far the most stringent is the prohibition on brother-sister incest ; it is the core of the *suvasova* taboo, and is of very rare occurrence either in reality or legend.

2. Incest with the mother is regarded as unnatural and unthinkable ; there are no cases on record ; it is an important form of *suvasova* ; it is not spoken of with the same abhorrence as brother-sister incest.

3. Sexual intercourse with the own daughter is not called *suvasova* ; it is not sanctioned by supernatural penalties ; it is felt to be extremely bad ; there are several cases on record.

4. Intercourse with the mother's sister's daughter is a form of *suvasova* ; it is of rare occurrence ; it

6] THE SUPREME TABOO

is regarded as very bad and always kept secret ; on discovery it is severely penalized.

5. Intercourse with the wife's sister is not a form of *suvasova*, but it is considered bad ; marriage, whether in the form of polygamy or with a deceased wife's sister, is strongly disapproved of, but it does occur, while intrigues are not infrequent.

6. Intercourse with the mother-in-law or with the brother's wife is not proper, though it is not *suvasova*, and it probably occurs but infrequently.

7. Intercourse with the " classificatory " *luguta* (my sister) is *suvasova* : it is prohibited by legal doctrine and sanctioned by supernatural penalties ; it is, however, frequently practised, and is, so to speak, at a premium.

An interesting commentary upon such gradations is contained in the following statement : *latugu tatougu—sene agu mwasila ; tuwagu, bwadagu— ulo kwava tuwala, bwadala—agu mwasila. Tabuda, kadada, latuda o payomili gala tamwasila ;* which may be freely translated : " My child truly mine— very much my shame ; ' elder brother,' ' younger brother ' (as I call them)—that is my wife's elder sister, her younger sister—my shame. Grand-children, maternal nieces, children—all these in the classificatory sense, we are not ashamed of." Here we have certain gradations recognized and expressed by the natives, and it is characteristic that, in such a volunteered statement, my informant would not mention the classificatory sister. That would not have been quite proper. Another commentary is contained in the fact that, whereas a man would swear at his mother, *kwoy inam* " have intercourse with thy mother " (*sic*), or might invite her to have intercourse with her father (*kwoy tamam*), he would never swear at his sister, and he would never swear at his daughter. Yet, as I have no doubt that incest between mother and son is far rarer than that between father and daughter, I have put it in the second and not in the third place.

One important relationship still remains, that

called *tabugu*, father's sister, or father's sister's daughter, which has already been mentioned as the opposite category correlated with that of *luguta*, sister (man speaking). The father's sister is the prototype of the lawful, and even sexually recommended woman ; that is, in the theory of native tradition, for, in reality, it is her daughter that really plays this part.

To the father's sister exactly the opposite attitude with regard to sexual behaviour is sanctioned and approved, to that which must be adopted towards the sister. Sexual intercourse with the father's own sister is emphatically right and proper. " It is very well when the boy copulates with his father's sister." The natives are never tired of repeating this moral maxim, and they use, in this context, the coarse term *kayta*, instead of the polite circumlocution *masisi deli* (sleep together), or *mwoyki* (come to, visit). Her presence always carries with it the suggestion of licence, of indecent jokes and improper stories. In bawdy ditties, the refrain : *deli sidayase, deli tabumayase* (with our companions, with our paternal aunts) is of frequent occurrence. The paternal aunt and the sister must never be in the same company, since the first relaxes the bonds of propriety and the second constrains them.

Sexual intercourse, however, between a man and his paternal aunt, is important theoretically, symbolically and verbally rather than in actual life. She represents to him the class of lawful women and sexual freedom in general. She might be used to advise or even to procure for him ; with herself, however, sexual intercourse is not frequently practised. She belongs to a previous generation, and, as a rule, what remains of her sexual endowment is not attractive. But whenever she and her nephews desire it, they are allowed to sleep together, preserving only a certain decorum when she is married. Marriage with the paternal aunt, though permissible and even desirable, seems never to occur : it was impossible for me to find a single instance of it among living people or in historical tradition.

The real practical substitute for his paternal aunt, the boy finds in her daughter. The two are regarded by tradition as specially suited for intercourse and for marriage. They are often engaged to each other by infant betrothal (see ch. iv, sec. 4). The natives will say that the paternal cross-cousin should be the first person, if age allows, with whom a boy should copulate.

The term, however, soon becomes extended to other girls belonging to the same sub-clan and clan. Finally by an extension which goes beyond the usual limits of classificatory terminology, it becomes synonymous with " all women not of the same clan as the sister ". It should be realized that the ordinary extensions of classificatory terminology go only to the limits of the clan. The widest sense in which the word for mother is used embraces all the women of the mother's clan. But the word *tabugu*, in its meaning of " lawful woman ", extends over three clans, and embraces roughly three-quarters of female humanity, in contrast to the one-quarter which are forbidden. But this subject — the intricacies of the kinship system and of the kinship nomenclature—leads us beyond the limits of the present inquiry, and will have to be deferred to the future publication already mentioned.

The keynote to sexual morality and sexual freedom lies, as we have found, in the opposition between the two classes designated by *luguta* and *tabugu* (" sister " and " paternal cross-cousin ") respectively. The taboo against incest between brother and sister is the most important and most dramatic feature of the Trobriand social organization ; the more so because of a singular rift in traditional doctrine, a dogmatic inconsistency, which makes love and the magic of love derive from brother and sister incest. To the account of this important myth we shall now proceed in the last chapter.

CHAPTER XIV

A Savage Myth of Incest

The so-called savage has always been a plaything to civilized man—in practice a convenient instrument of exploitation, in theory a provider of sensational thrills. Savagery has been, for the reading public of the last three centuries, a reservoir of unexpected possibilities in human nature; and the savage has had to adorn this or that *a priori* hypothesis by becoming cruel or noble, licentious or chaste, cannibalistic or humane according to what suited the observer or the theory.

As a matter of fact, the savage with whom we became acquainted in Melanesia does not conform to any picture in black and white, in deep shadow or vivid light. His life is socially hedged round on all sides, his morality more or less on a level with that of the average European—that is if the customs of the latter were as frankly described as those of the Trobriander. The institutions which allow of some prenuptial intercourse and even favour it, show little to suggest any previous conditions of unbridled promiscuity or of an institution such as " group-marriage ", so difficult to conceive in terms of any known social facts.

Such forms of licence as we find in the Trobriands fit so well into the scheme of individual marriage, the family, the clan, and the local group—and they fulfil certain functions so adequately that there remains nothing serious or incomprehensible to explain away by reference to some hypothetical earlier stage. They exist to-day because they work well side by side with marriage and family; nay, for the benefit of marriage and family; and there is no need to assume any other causes for their past than those which maintain them at present. They existed probably always for the same reason—in a slightly different form, no doubt, but built on the same fundamental pattern. This, at least, is my theoretical attitude towards these facts.

It is as important to bear in mind, however, that the limitations, taboos, and moral rules are by no means absolutely rigid, slavishly obeyed or automatic in their action. As we have seen again and again the rules of sex are followed only in an approximate manner, leaving a generous margin for infringements; and the forces which make for law and order show a great deal of elasticity. Thus the savage, measured by standards of æsthetics, morality, and manners, displays the same human frailties, imperfections, and strivings as a member of any civilised community. He does not lend himself either to the straightforward descriptive shocker, or to use as a clue for a detective story on the sexual past of the promiscuous pithecanthropus. In fact, as I see him, he will in no way lend himself to quench our thirst for reconstructive sexual sensationalism.

Nevertheless, the story of Trobriand sexual life does not lack altogether certain dramatic elements; certain contrasts and contradictions which might almost excite hopes of finding something really " inexplicable ", something which might justify plunging into frank hypotheses, into phantastic visions of past evolution or cultural history. Perhaps the most dramatic element in the tradition of the natives is the myth about brother and sister incest, associated with the power of the magic of love.

As we know, among all rules and taboos there is one which has a really strong hold over native imagination and moral sense; and yet this unmentionable crime is the subject of one of their sacred stories and the basis of love magic, and thus is directed, so to speak, into the full current of tribal life. Here, at first sight, is an almost incredible inconsistency in belief and in moral tradition, one which might allow us to brand the natives as deprived of moral sense, or prove them to be in the " prelogical stage of mental development " ; or else might be used to demonstrate the survival of marriage between brother and sister, or the co-existence of two cultural strata, one in which brother and sister unions are approved and the other in which they are tabooed. Unfortunately, the better we learn to understand the facts about the myth of incest and its cultural context, the less sensational, incredible, and immoral appear this and similar contradictions in custom and tradition ; the less do they clamour for explanation in hypotheses about the " savage soul ", pithecanthropi or "Kulturkreise"; and we find ourselves able instead to account for them in terms of contemporary and observable fact. But I have indulged long enough in reflections of a theoretical, not to say philosophic and moral nature ; and now I must return to my humbler and soberer task of faithful and dispassionate chronicler.

I

THE SOURCES OF LOVE MAGIC

Love, the power of attraction, the mysterious charm that comes forth from a woman to a man or from a man to a woman and produces the obsession of a single desire, is, as we know, attributed by the natives to one main source : the magic of love.

In the Trobriands, most important systems of magic are founded on myth. The origin of man's power over rain and wind ; of his ability to control the fertility of the soil and the movements of fish ; of the sorcerer's destructive or healing powers— all these are traced back to certain primeval occurrences which, to the natives, account for man's capacity to wield magic. Myth does not furnish an explanation in terms of logical or empirical causality. It moves in a special order of reality peculiar to dogmatic thought, and it contains rather a warrant of magical efficiency, a charter of its secret and traditional nature than an intellectual answer to the scientific *why*. The facts narrated in myth and the ideas which underly it, colour and influence native belief and behaviour. The events of a remote past are re-lived in actual experience.[1] This is especially important in the myth we are discussing, since its basic idea is that magic is so powerful that it can even break down the barrier of the strongest moral taboo. This influence of the past over the present is so strong that the myth generates its own replicas and is often used to excuse and explain certain otherwise inexcusable breaches of tribal law.

We have already spoken about the several systems of love magic, and pointed out that the two most important ones are associated with two local centres, Iwa and Kumilabwaga, which are united by a myth of the origin of their magic.

This is the story of the myth as I obtained it from informants of Kumilabwaga, the locality where the tragic events took place.[2]

I shall first give the narrative in a free but faithful translation, and then give the commentary as received from my informant. The numbers will allow the reader to compare this rendering with the native text, and with the word for word translation, which together form the substance of the next section.

---

[1] A fuller analysis of this functional view of myth will be found in the writer's *Myth in Primitive Psychology*, in *Argonauts of the Western Pacific*, ch. xii ; and in *Sex and Repression*, pt. ii.

[2] In another place, *Sex and Repression*, I have published a condensed and somewhat simplified version of the myth which, as I find, suffered slightly in the process. The version here given, with its full native text and two English translations, must be regarded as the full and correct statement.

The Myth

(1) The source (of love and magic) is Kumilabwaga. (2) A woman there brought forth two children, a girl and a boy. (3) The mother came (and settled down) to cut her fibre skirt; the boy cooked magical herbs (for the magic of love). (4) He cooked aromatic leaves in coco-nut oil. (5) He hung the vessel with the fluid (on a batten of the roof near the door) and went away to bathe. (6) The sister arrived from her firewood breaking expedition; she put down the firewood; she asked the mother: " Fetch me some water, which my brother has put in the house." (7) The mother answered: " You go and fetch it yourself, my legs are burdened with the board on which I cut the skirt."

(8) The girl entered the hut, she saw the water-bottles lying there; with her head she brushed against the vessel with the magic fluid; the coco-nut oil dripped; it trickled into her hair; she passed her hands over it, wiped it off, and smelt it. (9) Then the power of magic struck her, it entered her inside, it turned her mind. (10) She went and fetched the water, she brought it back and put it down. (11) She asked her mother: " And what about my brother? (Where has the man gone ?)"—The mother gave voice: " O my children, they have become mad! He has gone to the open seashore."

(12) The girl ran out, she sped towards the eastern shore, to the open sea. (13) She came to where the road abuts on the sea beach. There she untied her fibre skirt and flung it down. (14) She ran along the beach naked; she ran to the Bokaraywata beach (the place where the Kumilabwaga people usually bathe, and where they beach their canoes). (15) She came upon her brother there—he bathed in the Kadi'usawasa passage in the fringing reef. (16) She saw him bathing, she entered the water and went towards him, she gave him chase. (17) She chased him towards the rock of Kadilawolu. There he turned and ran back. (18) She chased him back and he went to the Olakawo rock. There he turned round and came back running. (19) He came back and went again to the Kadi'usawasa passage (i.e. where he was bathing first). There she caught him, there they lay down in the shallow water.

(20) They lay there (and copulated), then they went ashore and they copulated again. They climbed the slope, they went to the grotto of Bokaraywata, there they lay down again and copulated. (21) They remained there together and slept. (22) They did not eat, they did not drink—this is the reason why they died (because of shame, because of remorse).

(23) That night a man of Iwa had a dream. He dreamt the dream of their *sulumwoya* (the mint plant which they used in their love magic). (24) " O my dream ! Two people, brother and sister are together ; I see in my mind ; they lie by each other in the grotto of Bokaraywata." (25) He paddled over the sea arm of Galeya ; he paddled to Kitava, and moored his canoe— he searched all over—but nothing was to be found. (26) He paddled over the sea arm of Da'uya, he came to Kumilabwaga, he paddled towards the shore, he landed. He saw a bird, a frigate-bird with its companions— they soared.

(27) He went and climbed the slope ; he went and saw them dead. (28) And lo ! a mint flower had sprouted through their breasts. He sat by their prostrate bodies, then he went along the shore. (29) He looked for the road, he searched and found it, he went to the village. (30) He entered the village—there was the mother sitting and cutting her fibre skirt. He spoke : " Do you know what has happened by the sea ? " " My children went there and copulated and shame overcame them." (31) He spoke and said : " Come, recite the magic, so that I may hear it." (32) She recited, she went on reciting, he listened, he heard till he had learnt it completely. He learnt it right through to the end. (33) He came again, and asked : " What is the magical song of the coco-nut oil ? " (34) He inquired, that man from Iwa. " Come now tell me the song of the coco-nut oil."

(35) She recited it to the end. Then he said : " Remain here, I shall go. Part of the magic, the opening part, let it remain here. The eye of the magic, the finishing part, I shall take, and let it be called Kayro'iwa." (36) He went off, he came to the grotto, to the *sulumwoya* plant which sprouted and grew out of their breasts. (37) He broke off a sprig of the herb, he put it into his canoe, he sailed, he brought it to

Kitava. (38) He went ashore in Kitava and rested there. He then sailed and landed in Iwa.

(39) These are his words (which he spoke in Iwa) : " I have brought here the point of the magic, its eye (the sharpest, that is, the most efficient part of the magic). Let us call it the Kayro'iwa. The foundation, or the lower part, (the less important part) the Kaylakawa remains in Kumilabwaga." (Henceforth the words of the speaker refer not to Iwa, but to Kumilabwaga. This is obviously an inconsistency, because in the myth he is speaking in Iwa. This probably was due to the faulty recital of the myth.) (40) The water of this magic is Bokaraywata ; its sea passage Kadi'usawasa. There (on the beach) stands its *silasila* bush, there stands its *givagavela* bush. (41) If people from the lagoon villages would come to bathe (in the waterhole or in the sea passage), then the bushes would bleed. (42) This water is taboo to them—the youth of our village only should come and bathe in it. (43) But a fish caught in these waters is taboo to them (the young people of our village). When such a fish is caught in the nets, they should cut off its tail, then the old people might eat it. (44) Of a bunch of coco-nuts washed on the beach, they (the young people) must not eat a single one—it is a taboo. Only old men and old women may eat them.

(45) When they come and bathe in the Bokaraywata and then return to the beach, they make a hole in the sand and say some magic. (46) Later on in their sleep they dream of the fish. They dream that the fish spring (out of the sea) and come into that pool. (47) Nose to nose the fish swim. If there is only one fish they would throw it out into the sea. (48) When there are two, one female, one male, the youth would wash in this water. Going to the village, he would get hold of a woman and sleep with her. (49) He would go on sleeping with her and make arrangements with her family so that they might marry. This is the happy end, they would live together and make their gardens.

(50) If an outsider would come here for the sake of the magic, he would bring a magical payment in the form of a valuable. (51) He would bring it and give it to you, you might give him the charm : (52) the spells of the *ñika'i* leaves, of the betel pod, of the washing charm, of the smoking charm, of the stroking charm ; you might

give him also the charm of the obsidian blade, of the
coco-nut, of the *silasila*, of the *buresi* leaves, of the
coco-nut husk fibre, of the *gimgwam* leaves, of the *yototu*
leaves, of the comb—and for all this, they ought to pay
the substantial payment of *laga*.

(53) For this is the erotic payment of your magic.
Then let them return home, and eat pigs, yams, ripe
betel-nut, yellow betel-nut, red bananas, sugar cane.
(54) For they have brought you valuables, food,
betel-nut as a present. (55) For you are the masters
of this magic, and you may distribute it. You
remain here, they may carry it away ; and you, the
owners, remain here, for you are the foundation of this
magic.

*   *   *   *

This myth really accounts, not for the origin of
love magic, but for its transfer from Kitava to Iwa.
Its most important cultural function, however, is
that, being believed, it establishes a valid precedent
for the efficiency of love magic ; it proves that the
spells and rites of Iwa and of Kumilabwaga are so
powerful that they can even break down the terrible
barriers which separate brother and sister and
persuade them to commit incest.

Let us now retrace the narrative and insert a
few comments upon certain obscure points. The
additions to the text obtained from the narrator
are indicated by numbers referring to the subsequent
native text.

With reference to the relative age of the two
children, my informant said : (56) " The man was
the eldest child, and the woman followed." The
family belonged to the Malasi clan, which, as we
know already, is reputed to have a special propensity
for breaking exogamous and incestuous prohibitions.
To quote my native commentator : (57) " See, the
Malasi marry their kinsfolk. There was one man in
Wawela, a man by the name of Bigayuwo, who
married Nabwayera (a kinswoman of his) ; one
man in Vakuta ; one man in Kitava, by name of

Pwaygasi, who married Bosilasila." These names, which I have heard only from this informant, might be added to the other case previously recorded (ch. xii, sec. 4), in which a Malasi man married a Malasi woman.

Returning to the myth, it is clear that the natives take it for granted that the Malasi of Kumilabwaga knew the magic already. As a matter of fact, most magic is imagined to have existed from the beginning of time, and to have been brought by each sub-clan from underground. The story of the accidental smelling of the charmed oil receives dramatic piquancy from the part played by the mother. Had she gone into the house herself and brought water to her daughter, the tragedy would never have occurred. She, the very source of the matrilineal kinship bond, she from whose womb the two children sprang, she is also the involuntary cause of the tragedy. It is interesting to note that here, as in most mythological and legendary incidents, the man remains passive and the woman is the aggressor. We find analogies to this in the stories about Kaytalugi, in the behaviour of the women during the Yausa, and in the reception given by female spirits to newcomers in the next world. Eve also gives the apple to Adam, and Isolde holds out the drink to Tristan.

The description of the actual fall is given in clear but somewhat sober terms. To the natives, however, who know well the beautiful setting of open sea, steep white coral cliffs festooned with tropical foliage, and the dark, mysterious grotto hidden among old overhanging trees, this part of the narrative means more than is contained in the mere words. The myth speaks to them in terms of a familiar landscape and of many love experiences which have taken place in just such surroundings.

The narrative lacks, as usual, any explicit allusion to the psychology of the actors. I was able to obtain the following commentary: (58) " The man saw her : she had no skirt on ; he was frightened, he ran : the woman chased him. (59) But then the desire was born inside him ; it upset his mind, and they copulated." And again : (61) " Already his passion was kindled inside ; he desired her with his whole body ; (62) they copulated ; they caressed, they erotically scratched each other." Thus when the man found himself pursued, he succumbed to passion and then he felt the pangs of love as strongly as did his sister.

The description of the pursuit and fall will be more easily understood with the help of the sketch (Fig. 4), in which the main topographical features of the beach are shown. The brother bathes in the narrow canoe passage facing the centre of the beach. On seeing his sister approach naked, he makes for the shore and then runs along the water-line from one of the enclosing rocks to the other. After the fall, they move to the grotto, and there remain until their sad and romantic death. On this map are also indicated the two wells of which we shall hear presently.

After the two have copulated, they remain, consumed by passion, and yet bowed down with shame, until death ends their love and brings them freedom. (63) " They did not eat anything, they did not drink at all, since they had no desire. Shame has come over them, because they have committed incest, brother with sister." The motive of love and death is juxtaposed here, crudely and clumsily, and yet as dramatically as native language and imagination permit. The picture of the two enlaced in death with the symbol of love, the aromatic mint, springing from their bodies is full of primitive beauty.

With the death of the lovers the real drama comes to an end, and what follows has only a dogmatic and didactic connection with the first act. But the somewhat pedantic account of the adventures and doings of the man from Iwa—above all, of how he learnt the magic and how he laid down the rules for its practice, is of great sociological interest, because the pragmatic value of myth and its normative importance for native belief and behaviour are largely contained therein.

Who the man of Iwa was, whether of the same clan as the brother and sister, whether their friend or a magician, none of my informants could say : and unfortunately I was not able to discuss the matter with anyone from the island of Iwa itself.

Why the frigate-birds enter into the myth also remains somewhat mysterious, for they are not associated with the Malasi clan or with love-making. I was told : (64) " They go where they smell human beings." With regard to the somewhat cryptic insistence (verse 33) of the Iwa man to obtain the spell or charm (called in the text *wosi*, " song," and not by the usual word *yopa*, " spell "), I was told by my informant that there is a magic of coco-nut oil somewhat different from the one performed while the oil is being boiled out of the coco-nut. This spell is not indispensable to the system of love magic, and it must not be confused with that chanted over the aromatic herbs boiled in the already made coco-nut oil. This spell will be found in the next section, in verses 65 and 66. I have already indicated in the narrative that the last verses of the myth (from 40 on) should be taken as addressed to the community of Kumilabwaga and not to that of Iwa ; and that this inconsistency was probably due to my narrator's clumsy way of telling the tale. He was perfectly well aware, when questioned, that the details as to what people in Kumilabwaga should do were of no great importance on the distant island of Iwa. But he was not prepared to change his narrative in any way.

It may be noted that, in these days, Iwa is far more famous for love magic than the parent community, and that the myth still tries to claim certain ancient rites of the magic for Kumilabwaga, to which it belongs. In the last paragraph we have incidentally a description of certain elements essential in this magic ; we learn that it is associated in a mystic and mythological manner with the passage in the fringing reef, with the sea-water of the beach and with the wells upon it. In fact, bathing in the surf on that shore improves the personal appearance. (69) " In the reef passage of Kadi'usawasa, we, the male and female youth of Kumilabwaga, bathe and our countenances clear up and become beautiful." A similar effect is produced by bathing in the two wells of brackish water which lie at the foot of the cliffs, under the grotto of Bokaraywata. But here there is a division of sexes. (70) " Bokaraywata is the man's water ; the woman's water is called Momkitava. (71) Should we (boys) drink of that (that is, the woman's water) our hair would become grey." In fact, if either sex bathe in the other's pool or drink the water, their looks will be impaired.

The story of the two small. fish (verses 46–48) is not quite clear, and the comment which I received from my informant was practically a repetition of his original statement, and does not make it any more intelligible (see below, verses 72 and 73 in the native text).

An interesting point in the last few verses of the myth is the insistence on the economic side of the transaction in love magic. It is a further example of the natives' interest in repayment and reciprocity. It must be noted, however, that it has more than a merely economic importance ; it symbolizes also the prestige of the community as masters in magic, and is rather a tribute to their importance, than a mere reward for services rendered. A careful comparison of the free rendering with the word for word translation given below the native text will show that certain commentaries have been implicitly introduced into the former. I cannot enter into a justification of every one of such implicit comments, for this would lead to too elaborate linguistic discussion.

2

THE ORIGINAL TEXT OF THE MYTH

(1) *U'ula*   *wala*   *Kumilabwaga.*   (2)
Base   just   Kumilabwaga.

Le'une   *latula,*   *tayta*   *vivila,*   *tayta*
She quicken with child,   one   woman,   one

ta'u.   (3)   *Imwa,*   *itata'i*   *doba*
man.   She come,   she cut   fibre skirt

inasi ;   *isulusulu ka'i*   *matauna.*   (4)
mother their ;   he cook   leaves   this man.

Isulubuyala   *makwoyne*   *kwoywaga.*
He cook coco-nut oil   this   kwoywaga leaves.

(5) *Isouya,*   *ila*   *matauna*   *ikakaya.*   (6)
     He hang,   he go   this man   he bathe.

Imaga   *luleta,*   *iwota*   *ka'i,*
She come however   sister his,   she break   wood,

itaya,   *inasi*   *ilukwo* :
she dumps,   mother their   she tell :

" *Kuwoki*   *kala*   *sopi*   *luguta.*"
" Thou bring there   his   water   brother mine."

(7) *Ikaybiga* :   " *Kuwoki,*   *wala boge*
     She speak :   " Thou bring there,   just   already

ikanaki kaydawaga   *kaykegu.*"
it lie at trimming board   leg mine."

(8) *Isuvi*   *minana vivila,*   *ikanamwo*
     She come out   this   woman,   it lie here

sopi ;   *iwori*   *kulula,*   *ibusi*   *bulami,*
water ;   it flick   hair her,   it drop   coco-nut oil,

ibwika   *kulula,*   *ivagi*   *yamala,*   *iwaysa,*
it drop on   hair her,   she do   arm her,   she wipe,

isukwani.   (9) *Boge*   *iwoye,*   *boge*   *layla*
she smell.   Already   it strike,   already   it went

olopoula,   *ivagi*   *nanola.*   (10)   *Ila*
in inside her,   it do   mind her.   She go

ikasopi,   *imaye,*   *iseyeli.*   (11)
she get water,   she bring,   she put down.

Ikatupwo'i inala :   " *Mtage   luguta ?* "
She ask   mother her : " Indeed brother mine ? "
Kawalaga :   " *O latugwa*   *boge*
Speech her :   " O children mine   already
inagowasi !   Boge   layla   waluma."
they are mad !   Already he went in open sea."
(12) *Ivabusi,   ilokeya   waluma.*   (13)
    She come out, she go to   in open sea.

Ivabusi   okadu'u'ula,   ilikwo   dabela,
She come out end of road, she untie fibre skirt her,
iseyemwo.   (14) Ivayayri   namwadu,
she put down it.   She follow the shore naked,
ila   Bokaraywata. (15) Iloki   luleta,
she go to Bokaraywata.   She go to brother her,
ikakaya   Kadi'usawasa.   (16)   Ikikakaya,
he bathe   Kadi'usawasa.   He bathe,
ivabusi,   layla,   ibokavili. (17) Ibokavili,
she come out, he went,   she chase.   She chase,
ila'o   o Kadilawolu papapa ;   itoyewo,
she make go   to Kadilawolu rock ;   he reverse,
ila.   (18) Ibokavili,   ila   Olakawo,
he go.   She chase,   he go to Olakawo,
itoyewo,   ikaymala.   (19) Ikaymala,
he reverse,   he bring back.   He bring back,
ila o Kadi'usawasa, iyousi,   ikanarise
he go in Kadi'usawasa, she take hold, they lie down
wala obwarita. (20) Ikanukwenusi, ikammaynagwasi,
just in sea.   They lie,   they go to shore,
ivino'asi   imwoynasi,   ilousi   Bokaraywata
they finish   they climb,   they go to Bokaraywata
o   dubwadebula ikenusi.   (21) Ikanukwenusi,
in grotto   they lie.   They remain lying,
imasisisi. (22) *Gala ikamkwamsi, gala imomomsi,*
they sleep.   No   they eat,   no   they drink,
u'ula   ikarigasi.
reason they die.

(23) *Aybogi*   *kirisalaga*   *iloki*
     Night time   magical effect   it approach

guma'Iwa ;   *imimi*   *kirisala*   *kasi*
inhabitant of Iwa ;   he dream   magical effect   their

sulumwoya.   (24)   "*O!*   *gumimi,*   *tayyu*
mint plant.   "O!   my dream,   two people

tomwota,   *kasitayyu*   *luleta,*   *nanogu*
humans,   they two together   sister his,   mind mine

odubwadebula   *Bokaraywata*   *ikenusi.*"   (25)
in grotto   Bokaraywata   they lie."

Iwola   *Galeya, i'ulawola* ; *Kitava,*   *ikota*
He paddle Galeya, he paddle; on Kitava, he anchor

waga,   *ine'i,*   *inenei*   —*gala.*
canoe,   he search,   he go on searching   —no.

(26)   *Iwola*   *Da'uya,*   *ima*
     He paddle   Da'uya,   he come here

Kumilabwaga,   *i'ulawola,*   *italaguwa,*
Kumilabwaga,   he paddle on,   he disembark,

iginaga   *mauna,* *dauta*   *deli*
he see however bird,   frigate-bird   together with

sala   *ikokwoylubayse.*
comrades his   they soar.

(27)   *Imwa,*   *imwoyna,*   *ila,*   *igise,*
     He come here,   he climb,   he go,   he see,

ikatuvili,   *igise,*   *boge*   *ikarigeyavisi.*   (28)
he overturn,   he see,   already   they die.

U! *laysusinaga*   *sulumwoya*   *ovatikosi* ;
Lo! he sprouted however mint-plant in chest theirs ;

isisu,   *ikanukwenusi,*   *ivayariga.*   (29)
he sit,   they lie,   he skirt shore however.

Inene'i   *keda,* *ine'i*   *ibani,*   *ikammaynagwa*
He search road, he search he find,   he go to

o   *valu.*   (30) *Ikasobusi,*   *minana*   *isisu*
in village.   He drop out,   this woman   she sit

itata'i doba ;   *ikaybiga* : " *Avaka okwadewo ?* "
she cut fibre skirt ; he speak : " What in sea-shore ? "

" *Latugwa   aylosi,   ikaytasi,   ivagi*
" Children mine   they went,   they copulate, he do

kasi   mwasila."   (31) *Ilivala,   ikaybiga :*
their   shame.''   He say,   he speak :

" *Kuma,   kukwa'u   megwa, alaga.*"
" Thou come here,   thou recite   magic,   I hear.''

(32) *Ikawo,   ikikawo,   ilaga,   isisawo,*
      She recites,   she re-recites, he hear,   he learn,

ivina'u,   isawo ;   isisawo,   ivinaku,
he finish,   he learn ;   he learn thoroughly,   he finish,

imwo,   imuri,   kaysisula. (33) *Imimuri,*
he come here,   he shift,   seat his.   He shift then,

igise   iwokwo,   ikaybiga :   " *Kuneta*
he see   it finish,   he speak :   " Coco-nut cream

kakariwosila ? "   (34) *Ikatupowi,   ilivala,*
magical song his ? "   He ask,   he say,

matauna   guma'Iwa :   " *Wosila*
this man   inhabitant of Iwa :   " Song his

kuma   kulivala ! "
thou come here   thou say ! "

(35) *Ilivala   boge   ivinakwo,   ikaybiga :*
      She say   already   she finish,   he speak :

" *Bukusisu,   balaga ;*   *kayu'ula*
" Thou might sit,   I might go however ;   magic herb
                                                                    base

Kayla-kawa   bukuseyemwo,
magic herb of Kawa   thou might put here,

matala   bala'o   *Kayro'iwa.*"
eye his   I might carry   magic herb of Iwa.''

(36) *Ivabusi,   iwoki*   *makayna*
      He drop out,   he approach there   this

sulumwoya,   boge   laysusina,   itoto
mint-plant,   already   he sprout,   he stand

ovitakosi,   ku'igunigu.   (37)
in chest their,   mint plant (special variety).

Ikituni,   idigika   waga,   iwola,   ila'o
He break off,   he load at canoe,   he paddle,   he carry

Kitava. (38) *I'ulawola,*   *italaguwa*   *Kitava,*
Kitava.   He paddle on, he disembark Kitava,
iwaywosi ; *iulawola,*   *italaguwa*   *Iwa.*
he rest ;   he paddle, he disembark Iwa.

  (39) *Kawala* :   " *Matala* *Kayro'iwa*
      Speech his : " Eye his magical herb of Iwa
lamaye   *u'ula*   *Kayla-kawa*
I brought here,   base   magic herb of Kawa
ikanawo   *Kumilabwaga.*   (40) *Sopila*
he lie there   Kumilabwaga.   Water his
Bokaraywata, *karikedala* *Kadi'usawasa* ; *silasila*
Bokaraywata,   passage his Kadi'usawasa ; silasila
                                            plant
itomwo,   *givagavela*   *itomwo.*
it stand here,   givagavela plant   it stand here.
(41) *Kidama*   *taytala* *bimayse*   *odumdom,*
    Supposing one man they might come in lagoon,
ikakayasi, *boge*   *bibuyavi.*   (42) *Bomala*
they bathe, already he might bleed.   Taboo his
sisopi—   *bimayse*   *gudi'ova'u,*
their water—   they might come,   new boys,
bikikakayasi.   (43) *Kidama*   *bikola*
they might bathe.   Supposing he might entangle
yena, gala bikamsi ;   *ikola,*   *ikatunisi*
fish, no   they might eat ; he entangle, they nick
yeyuna, *bikamsi*   *numwaya,*   *tomwaya.*
tail,   they might eat   old woman,   old man.
(44) *Luya*   *ikatupisawo*   *uwatala,*
    Coco-nut   he wash up by sea one pair,
bikamsi   *kwaytanidesi* *bomala,*   *gala*
they might eat one only   taboo his,   no
bikamsi ;   *numwaya, tomwaya bikamsi.*
they might eat ; old women, old men they might eat.
  (45) *Sopila*   *Bokaraywata* *kidama*
      Water his   Bokaraywata supposing
bimayse   *ikakayasi,*   *bilousi*
they might come here they bathe, they might go

orokaywoyne ; iyenisi, imegwasi. (46)
up above ; they scoop out, they charm.

Igauga bimimisi yena ;
Later on however they might dream fish ;

imimimisi, ipelasi ; bilousi,
they dream indeed, they jump ; they might go,

ikanawoyse makwoyna sopi. (47) *Kabulula*
they lie there this water. Nose

natana, kabulula naywela, bikakayasi.
one, nose second, they might bathe.

Kidamaga natanidesi bilisasayse,
Supposing however one only they might fling out,

bila obwarita. (48) *Kidama nayyu,*
he might go in sea. Supposing two,

tayta vivila, tayta ta'u, bikakaysi,
one woman, one man, they might bathe,

aywayse ovalu, vivila biyousise,
they go in village, woman they might grasp

bimasisisi. (49) *Imasisisi, ibubulise,*
they might sleep. They sleep, they stir up,

vayva'i ; iva'isi, boge aywokwo
relations-in-law ; they marry, already it was over

bisimwoyse, ibagulasi.
they might remain, they garden.

(50) *Imaga taytala gudiva'u,*
He come here however one new boy,

kalubuwami, vaygu'a. (51)
magical payment your, objects of high value.

Imayayse, iseyemwasi vaygu'a
They bring here, they lay down here vaygu'a

bukuyopwo'isiga. (52) *Isika'i,*
you might charm however. Isika'i leaves,

kasina, kaykakaya, ripuripu
kasina leaves, kaykakaya leaves, ripuripu leaves,

kaywori bukumegwasi, memetu
kaywori leaves you might charm, obsidian blade

bukumegwasi,   *luya*   *bukumegwasi,*
you might charm,   coco-nut   you might charm,
silasila   *bukumegwasi,*   *buresi*
silasila leaves   you might charm,   buresi leaves
bukumegwasi,   *kwoysanu*
you might · charm,   coco-nut husk fibre
bukumegwasi,   *gimgwam*   *bukumegwasi,*
you might charm, gimgwam leaves you might charm,
yototu   *bukumegwasi,*   *sinata bukumegwasi,*
yototu leaves you might charm, comb you might
bilagwayse.   [charm,
they should pay.

(53) *Vayla*   *mimegwa*   *sebuwala* ;
      For   your magic   payment for magic ;
bilousi   *ikamsi*   *kasi*   *bulukwa,*   *kasi,*
they might go   they eat   their   pig,   their food,
kasi lalava,   *kasi*   *samaku,*   *kasi*
their ripe betel-nuts, their yellow betel-nuts, their
kayla'usi,   *kasi*   *toutetila,*   *kasi*
ripe bananas,   their   ripe sugar cane,   their
woderi—   *bikamsi.*   (54) *Bogwaga*
yam (variety)—   they eat.   Already however
aymayase   *vaygu'a,*   *kaulo,*   *bu'a—*
they brought   vaygu'a,   yam food,   areca-nut—
lukukwamsi.   (55) *Tolimegwa*   *yokwami,*
you eat.   Masters of magic   you,
mtage   *bukusakayse,*   *kusimwoyse,*
indeed   you might give,   you sit here,
bilawoysaga—   *bukusimwoysaga,*
they might carry however—   you might sit here how-
tolimegwa   *yokwami—*   *u'ula.*   [ever,
masters of magic   yourselves—   base.

The Informant's Commentary

I obtained the following elaborations of the
narrative. The number of the sentence referred to
is given at the beginning of each commentary.

See 2. Commenting on the relative ages of the two children :—

(56) *Kuluta   ta'u,   isekeli   vivila.*
    Eldest child man, she follow woman.

Their names are not known. They belonged to the Malasi clan.

(57) *Kugis,   Malasi   ivayva'isi*
    Thou see,   Malasi.   they marry
vesiya :   *taytala   Wawela,*
maternal kinswomen theirs . one man   Wawela,
Bigayuwo—   *Nabwayera ;*   [wife)
Bigayuwo (name of man)—   Nabwayera (name of his
tayta   Vakuta ;   *tayta   Kitava,*
one man   Vakuta ;   one man   Kitava,
Pwaygasi—   *Bosilasila*   [wife).
Pwaygasi (name of man)—   Bosilasila (name of his

See 16.—The behaviour of brother and sister immediately preceding the consummation of incest is thus explained :—

(58) *Ta'u   igisi :   gala   dabela,   ikokola,*
    Man   he see : no   fibre skirt hers,   he fear,
isakauli ; minana vivila   ibokavili.   (59) *Iga'u,*
he run ;   this   woman she chase.   Later on,
boge   itubwo   lopoula   matauna,   ikaytasi.
already   it upset   inside his   this man,   they copulate.

See 14–21.—The diagram (Fig. 4, p. 461) showing the topography will make the account of the pursuit clearer.

See 19.

(60) *Ikanarise   wala   obwarita.*
    They lie down   just   in sea.

Questioned about the meaning of this expression, the informant affirmed that they first committed the act of incest in the water. In going over the story he described the passion in more detail.

(61) *Boge   kala   la'iya   ivagi olopoula,*
    Already   his   passion   it do in inside his,

magila   kumaydona   wowola.   (62)   *Boge*
desire his   all   body his.   Already

ikaytasi,   ikininise,
they copulate,   they scratch lightly,

ikimalise.
they erotically scratch.

See 22.—Explaining why the two lovers remained without food and drink and so died, my informant says :—

(63) *Gala sitana   ikamkwamsi, imomomsi,   pela*
     No   one bit   they eat,   they drink, for

gala magisi,   boge   ivagi simwasila,   pela
no   desire theirs,   already it do their shame, for

luleta   ikaytasi.
brother her sister his they copulate.

See 26.—Explaining the behaviour of the frigate-birds :—

(64) *Ikokwoylubayse— ilousi,   isukonisi   mayna*
     They soar—   they go, they smell odour

tomwota.
humans.

See 33.—This, the spell or chant, designated *wosi* (song) and not *megwa* or *yopa* (spell) is sung whilst they boil coco-nut oil for love magic. It runs :

(65) *Mekaru   karuwagu ;   mevira,*
     Gall bladder,   gall bladder mine ; woman,

viregu   meboma,   bomatu.
woman mine ; North-west wind, North-west wind.

(66) *Ipela   karuwagu   mevira,*
     He change place gall bladder mine   woman,

viregu ;   meboma,   bomatu,
woman mine ;   North-west wind, North-west wind,

medara, dara.
languor, languor.

The rite is not performed in a strong wind :

(67) *Kidama   sene   bipeulo*
     Supposing very much it might be strong

yagila,   gala   tavagi   megwa—   tage
wind,   no   we   magic—   so that not
biyuvisa'u.   (68) *Iga'u   niwayluwa,*
he might blow away.   Later on calm weather,
batavagi   ola'odila,   tamiga'i
we might do   in bush,   we might charm
kwoywaga   ka'ukwa'u.   Kwayavi,   bibogi
kwoywaga plant   morning.   Evening,   at night
boge   tasayki   vivila.
already   we give   woman.

See 40.—The water in the Kadi'usawasa reef-
passage has some magical properties, as bathing in
it improves the looks.

(69) *Okarikeda   Kàdi'usawasa gwadi   yakida*
In passage of Kadi'usawasa child   ourselves
takakaya   bitarise   migida.
we bathe he might beautify   face ours.

About the brackish wells we are told :—

(70) *Ta'ula   lasopi   Bokaraywata ;   vivila*
Man his   water of   Bokaraywata ;   woman
Momkitava. (71) *Kidama   tamomsi   bayse sopi,*
Momkitava.   Supposing we drink this   water,
boge   takasouso'u.
already we become grey-headed.

In general, if persons of either sex bathe in the
other's well, their looks would become impaired.

The *silsila* and *givagavela* plants, mentioned in
the text (verse 40), grow near the wells.

In olden days people from other villages, even
from the neighbouring villages on the lagoon
(Sinaketa and others) were not allowed to bathe
in these waters.

See 46.—Questioned about the fish, my informant
says :

(72) *Imiga'ise,   imimise   yena   nayiyu*
They charm,   they dream   fish   two

naketoki   sikum   nayyu
small animals   sikum (name of fish)   two
kabulula kabulula. (73) Natanidesi, talisala
nose to   nose.   Only one,   we fling away
bila   obwarita,   gala takakaya.
he might go in the sea, no   we bathe.

See 49.—This verse means that such magic would
lead not only to love but to matrimony :—

(74) Bilivala   veyola
     He might speak   maternal kinsman his
vivila : kawala :   " Kuwokeya   kuva'isi,
woman ; speech his : " Thou bring there you marry,
ummwala   boge."
thy husband already."

3

CASES OF ACTUAL INCEST

Let us now pass from legend to reality, and see
how events of the present day tally with their
prototypes in the dim past. It has already tran-
spired that, in spite of the seemingly absolute
taboo, in spite of a real and overwhelming abhorrence
felt by the natives, cases of brother and sister incest
do yet actually occur. Nor are they an innovation
due to European contact—an influence for which
the natives blame so many changes in custom.
Far back, before white men appeared in the island,
such lapses from tribal morality happened and
are remembered and quoted to-day, with names and
details.

One of the previous paramount chiefs, Purayasi,
was known to have lived with his sister ; and another
one, Numakala, is also strongly suspected by history
of this felony. They, of course, belonged to the
Malasi clan ; and there can be no doubt that with
them, as with so many other dynasties and famous
rulers, the feeling of power, of being above the

law, served as a shield from the usual penalties. And, as historical figures, they and their doings would not so easily lapse into oblivion as in the case of commoners. I was told by my informants that, in olden times, discovery of incest would invariably have meant death for both culprits, self-inflicted in the usual form of suicide. This would at least have been the case when commoners were concerned. But, say the natives, with the influx of missionaries and government officials all custom has deteriorated, and even the worst crime can be brazened out.

That a man may still pay the supreme penalty for breach of the incest taboo, has been proved to me by the following instance which came directly under my observation. I had not been in Omarakana more than a couple of weeks when one morning, in July, 1915, I was casually told by my interpreter and only informant (at that time I still worked in pidgin English) that, in the neighbouring village of Wakayluwa, a boy named Kima'i had fallen off a tree and killed himself—by accident. I was also informed that somehow, again by accident, another boy had received a severe wound. The coincidence seemed to me strange at the time, but unable to speak the language and thus gain the full confidence of the natives, I was still groping in the dark ; and being much occupied with the customs of mourning and burial, then new to me, I gave up all attempt at getting to the bottom of the tragedy.

Later on, I strongly suspected that the falling off the tree was a case of suicide by *lo'u*, but the natives remained reticent on the subject. For there is nothing more difficult for an ethnographer than to find out the ins and outs of really important and tragic events of recent date, which, if they came under the notice of the local resident magistrate, might lead to court proceedings, imprisonments and other serious disturbances of tribal life. And in this case, as I learned afterwards, there was some political element involved, since Kima'i was a relative of Moliasi, the traditional enemy of the paramount chief, and the incident had revived the historical tension between the ruler of Kiriwina and that of Tilataula.[1]

It was only during my last visit to the Trobriands, when almost three years had elapsed since the tragedy, that I found out the bare outline of the case. Kima'i had an intrigue with his mother's sister's daughter. This was no secret, but, though the villagers generally disapproved, it was only by the initiative of the girl's betrothed that matters were brought to a head. After several attempts to separate them, his rival insulted Kima'i in public, telling aloud, or rather shouting across the village, the plain fact that he was a breaker of the incest taboo, and mentioning the name of the girl with whom the incest was committed. This, as we know, is the most aggravated form of the insult, and it produced the desired effect. Kima'i committed suicide. The youth who brought about this was, in fact, wounded by the kinsmen of Kima'i; hence the strange coincidence of the two casualties occurring at the same time. The girl is now married and lives happily with her husband. She can be seen on plate 92 made from a photograph taken during mortuary proceedings, at which she wears no mourning (black paint and shaven hair) since she was a real kinswoman of the deceased (see above, ch. vi, sec. 2). The whole occurrence gave me some insight into the legal ideas of the natives, but with this subject I have dealt elsewhere.[2] Here it is mainly the sexual aspect which interests us and to this we will return.

For not all the cases of incest—even in its more

---

[1] For an account of the political conditions among the Trobriand natives, cf. Seligman's *Melanesians* and the present writer's *Argonauts of the Western Pacific*, ch. ii, sec. v, and *Myth*, ch. ii.
[2] *Crime and Custom*, pp. 77 sq.

reprehensible form—lead to the same tragic issue.
There is no doubt that, at present, several couples
are under strong suspicion of being guilty of the
most heinous form of *suvasova*, that is, of incestuous
intercourse between brother and sister. One case
given to me in detail is that of a pretty girl,
Bokaylola, who is said to allow her albino brother to
" visit " her. I had a feeling from the way in which my
informant spoke about it that the concurrence of two
immoralities somehow mitigated both. It is felt
that, since an albino has no chance whatever of
a woman and since he is not really a man, incest
with him is not so offensive.

By far the most instructive and clear case of
brother and sister incest, is the notorious liaison
between two Malasi people of the village of
Okopukopu.

Mokadayu was still very much alive when I
visited the Archipelago, and he gave me the
impression of a man of unusual ability and intelligence. Endowed with a beautiful voice and famous
as a singer, he also for a time exercised the lucrative
profession of a spiritistic medium. In this he
arrived independently at some of the great achievements in which our modern spiritism excels ;
such as the production of ectoplasm and phenomena
of materialisation (usually of worthless objects) ;
but his speciality was rather dematerialization
(invariably of valuable objects). He would conjure
up an arm and a hand—belonging presumably
to his " control "—and this was always ready to
foreclose on valuables, food, betel-nut, or tobacco,
which, no doubt, were transported to the spirit
world. Obeying the universal law of occult
phenomena, Mokadayu's " controls " and other
spirit friends would operate only in the dark.
The famous hand from the other world could
only be dimly seen, clutching at every piece of
worldly goods within its reach.

There are arrogant and inconsiderate sceptics,

however, even in the Trobriands and, one day, a young chief from the north caught hold of the hand and dragged out Mokadayu himself from the shelf where he lay concealed behind a mat. After this, unbelievers tried to belittle and even to denounce spiritism, but the faithful still brought gifts and payments to Mokadayu.

On the whole, however, he found it better to devote himself to love and music, for in the Trobriands, as with us, a tenor or baritone is sure of success with women. As the natives put it: " The throat is a long passage like the *wila* (cunnus) and the two attract each other. A man who has a beautiful voice will like women very much and they will like him." Mokadayu, indeed, used to sleep with the chief's wives, for he preferred married women, who are at a premium in the Trobriands. Finally, after having tasted, no doubt, the minor degrees of *suvasova* (clan incest), he came to what was to be the most dramatic exploit of his life.

His sister, Inuvediri, was one of the most beautiful girls in the village. Naturally she had many lovers ; but a strange change came over her, and she seemed disinclined to sleep with her lemans. The young men of the village were dropped one after another. They put their heads together and decided to find out what had happened to their mistress, suspecting that she must have acquired a new and paramount lover, who was satisfying all her desires. One night they noticed that brother and sister had withdrawn to the parental house. Their suspicions were confirmed : they saw a terrible thing : brother and sister making love to each other. A serious scandal followed ; for the news spread all over the village and brother and sister were made aware that everybody knew of their mutual crime. The story goes that the two lived in incest for some months after this discovery, so passionately were they enamoured of one another, but Mokadayu had finally to leave the community. The girl married a man from another village. I was told that, in olden days, both would unquestionably have committed suicide.

Such is the story of Mokadayu and his sister. Together with other facts previously described, it shows dramatically how inadequate is the postulate of "slavish subservience to custom". It also shows that the opposite view—that native principles are a sham and a fake—would equally be misleading. The fact is that the natives, while professing tribal taboos and moral principles, have also to obey their natural passions and inclinations, and that their practice is the compromise between rule and impulse, a compromise common to all humanity.

The myth of incest, at first sight mysterious and incomprehensible, loses a great deal of its strangeness when we have found that it reflects certain tendencies which can be seen manifested in real life. The temptation to incest evidently does exist in the mind of the natives, though by a powerful taboo it is prevented from finding ready expression.

It is interesting to note how the myth is used to justify the cases of real incest which happen nowadays. For instance, a clansman of Mokadayu tried to explain and to extenuate the latter's crime against tribal morality as follows. He told how Mokadayu had prepared coco-nut oil impregnated with love magic in order to induce an amorous response in another girl; how Inuvediri, entering the house, inadvertently spilt some of the fluid and became intoxicated by the magic; how she discarded her fibre skirt and lay naked on the bedstead, longingly awaiting the brother. How, on entering the hut, and seeing her nakedness—perhaps also feeling the influence of magic on himself—he became inflamed with passion. This paraphrase, or rather copy, of the myth was definitely put to me as a defence of the criminal; it was intended to show that it was fatality rather than fault which had brought about the abominable act. The myth was thus used as a paradigm by which actuality was explained, in order to make the deed more comprehensible and acceptable to the natives. The psychology manifested in this use of the myth makes the function of the myth itself clearer to the sociologist.

Far from being incompatible with the powerful incidence of the taboo, the temptation to incest is probably strengthened by it through the irresistible fascination which forbidden fruit always had, has, and will have for the human being. How far psycho-analysis can help us to solve this problem and where it merely confuses the issues, I have tried to discuss in a previous work.[1] Here I would like only to repeat that, by correlating the Myth of Incest with the realities of life, by placing it side by side with typical dreams of the natives, with their obscene language, and with their attitude towards taboo in general, we find a satisfactory explanation of its apparent strangeness in terms of fact and not of hypothesis.

[1] *Sex and Repression.*

THE END

INDEX

INDEX

Bad language—swearing, 321, 376, 406–9, 449 ; children's, 46

Bagido'u, 84 ; his expulsion of Namwana Guya'u, 11 ; his wife's desertion, 123–4, 317 ; his friendship with Yobukwa'u, 397 ; cited 87

Baku, see Village—Central place

Baldness, 245

Baloma, see Spirits.

" Baloma : The Spirits of the Dead in the Trobriand Islands " cited, 7 *n.,* 211 *n.,* 329 *n.,* 361 *n.,* 364 *n.*

Bam, 141 ; *vatula bam,* 193–5

Banana leaves : for dress, 22–3, 256 ; used in magic, 431 ; seeds as necklaces, 257

Barter of fish and vegetables, 22, 78

Bathing games, 209 (*and see* Sea-water)

Ba'u string figure, 336–7

Ba'u village, 350 ; endogamous district of, 385, 421

Bawdiness, *see* Ribaldry

Beauty and personal charm :
  Ideal of, 241–3, 246, 248–50 ; in detail, 250–5
  Interest in, intense, 291
  Magic of, *see under* Magic
  Taboos regarding, 244
  To'uluwa's formula of, 260

Bellamy, Dr., 196 *and n.*

Belly, desire and affection associated with, 141, 144

Belts : making of, 22 ; wearing of, 256, 257

Bestiality : native contempt for, 395–6, 399 ; case of, 399–400

Betel-nut : for chewing, 106, 282–3 ; for lip-painting, 228–9 ; gifts of, 259

Beyawa, 364–5

Bigayuwo, 459

Bilamapu, 285

Biting, erotic, 279, 286–8, 400

Bi'u (tug-of-war game), 207–8, 214–15

Black-grease-smearing (*koulo*), 99, 246, 250, 374

Blackening of teeth, 225, 252, 259

Blood (*buyavi*) : in menstruation, 144 ; in pregnancy, 149, 160

Bodogupo'u, 445

Bodulela, 74, 265, 277, 445–6

Bogonela, 101

Bokaraywata grotto, 457, 458, 461, 463

Bokaylola, 445, 477

Bokuyoba, 116, 117, 170

Bolobesa, 102, 122

Bolutukwa (Mitigis), 155–6

Bomala, 388–90 (*and see* Taboos)

Bomawise, 118

Bomidabobu, 116

Bomiyototo, 116

Bones as relics, 132–3 ; their final rest, 134

Bo'usari, 123

Bowels, 143, 144

Boyowa Island, 7, 146 (*and see names of villages*)

Boys (*see also* Bachelors' house) :
  Amorous opportunities for, 212 (*and see Ulatile*)
  Boasting of, 277
  Excursions of, with girls, 209, 274–6, 282–3
  Fornication of, with old women, 248, 289
  Friendships of, 396–7
  Games for, 206–7
  Group formed by, 54–5
  Love magic as practised by, 307 ff.
  Orgiastic licence of, 217–18
  Removal of, from home, 438
  Sexual intrigues of, 54 ; their freedom, 56–7 ; the personal preference element, 54, 57, 63

Breasts : native words to describe, 254 ; love-magic associated with, 212

Brother of a woman :
  Guardianship functions of, 15, 24, 30, 72, 110, 171, 439
  Likeness to his sister denied, suggestion an insult, 175, 410
  Original, from underground, 155
  Taboo between sister and, *see under* Taboos

Brother's wife, taboo regarding, 449

Bubunela, 390 (*and see* Convention)

Bubwayayta, 363

Budiya, Headman of Kabululo, 74, 265, 445–6

Bugwabwaga, 148

Bukumatula, *see* Bachelors' house

Bulaviyaka, 61 (*and see* Dwelling-houses)

Bulubwalata, see Sorcery

Bulubwaloga, 118–19, 267, 446

Bulukwa, see Pigs

Bulukwau'ukwa, 100

Burayama, 397

Buresi leaves, 459

482

INDEX

Burials, central space formerly used for, 8, 131 (*and see* Mortuary Ritual)

Bush, the : children's amours in, 48, 56 ; confinements in, 195 ; assignations in, 223

Bush-pigs, 162 ; taboo on, 162 ; mating of, with village pigs, 162–3 ; associated with garden taboo, 415

Butia flower, 255, 301 ; *kayasa*, 215–16

Butura, see Renown

Buwa, 269

Buyavi, see Blood

Bwadela village, 147 *n.*, 232, 236

Bwaga village, 232

Bwala nakaka'u, 54, 61

Bwaulo, 128, 379

Bwaylagesi, 364

Bwayma, see Yam-houses

Bwaytalu village, 352 ; endogamous district of, 385, 420–1

Bwaytuva (white bird), 181–2

Bwoyna, meaning of term, 390–2

Canoe-building : a man's work, 22 ; magic connected with, 35, 36, 41

Canoes, ownership of, 21, 29 ; miniature, contest with, 34, 215

Carving, 22

Cat's-cradles (*ninukula*), 336 and *n.*–339

Ceremonial enterprises, financing of, 69

Ceremonial exchange, *see Kula*

Change of air, curative use of, 199

Chiefs (*see also* To'uluwa *and other names*) :
　Decorous speech in presence of, 402
　Dwelling-house of (*lisiga*), 8, 61 ; its platform, 28
　Festivities, etc., financed by, 69, 111
　Hereditary service to, 9
　Polygamy the privilege of, 9, 29, 69 ; its economic necessity, 110 ff. ; the *kaymapula*, 112 ; for the heir-apparent, 114
　Precedence in household of, 116
　Privileges of, besides polygamy, 111 ; taboos regarding, 385
　Respect paid to, 28 *and n.*², 111, 402
　Social demands on, 69, 111–13

Sons of : their rank, 116 ; their deputizing functions, 81–2, 84

Tributary districts of, 111–12

Villages placed under taboo during absence of, 98–9

Wealth of, derived through marriage, 111–12

Wives of (*giyovila*) : their gifts from relatives, 107 ; three classes of, 114–16 ; choice of, 116 ; head of, 116 ; substitute (*kaymapula*), 112, 114 ; taboo on, 385 ; prostitution of, in Sinaketa, 272

Yam-houses of, 373

Chieftainship :
　Heir-apparent : friction between chief's son and, 13, 83, 87 ; substitute-wife provided for, on death of chief's wife, 114
　Rank associated with, 26
　Women barred from, 29

Childbirth : father's function at, 171 (*and see* Confinement) ; virgin birth of Tudava, 155, 359

Children (*see also* Infants) :
　Boys : early removed from mother and sisters, 47, 53, 438 ; age for beginning sexual life, 49 ; amorous pastimes, 50 ; also separate from girls, 50
　Cleanliness taught to, 376
　Custom, their deference to, 46
　Development of, 437
　Divorce, in cases of, 125
　Father in relation to, *see under* Father
　Girls : accompanying their fathers, 46–7 ; age for sexual indulgence, 48–9 ; also separate from boys, 50
　Illegitimate, 17, 165 ; their rarity, 166–7 ; no preventive means employed, 167–8 ; suggested explanation, 168
　Independence of, 44–6, 437 ; the child community, 45, 54 ; its two groups, 50
　Longing for, 69
　Mother in relation to, *see under* Mother
　Origin of, 146 ff., 152 (*and see* Infants)
　Parental discipline non-existent, 45

INDEX

Dokonikan, 244, 340

Dreams:
Erotic, 330–2
Freud's theory of, 325
Incestuous, 331–2, 334
Magic in relation to, 330–4, 340–1; the spell in love magic, 309
Ordinary, natives' attitude to, 326, 332–3
Pregnancy foretold in, 148, 179, 328
Prophetic, 328, 333
Standardized, 326, 332

Dress:
Festive, 32, 33, 42; semi-festive, at harvest presentations, 105
Men's: the pubic leaf: its form, 256; its material, 255–6; its making, 22; its wearing, 53, 256; its significance, 232; its removal, on fishing expeditions, 46, 380; with lover, 280, 282–3; in lechery, 413; its renewal, 210; taboo regarding, 380; ditty concerning, 204, 205; men's festive attire, 42; women's skirts assumed for a dance, 33
Modesty in, 370, 379–80, 403
Requirements in, 379
Women's: under and upper skirts of grass or leaf-fibre, 18, 20, 42, 256–7; making of, 22–3; the magic for, 37; age for assuming skirt, 48; care at adolescence, 53; renewal of, at harvest festivities, 210; display of, 228; worn by men at a dance, 33; longer sometimes worn, 145, 256; widows', on release from mourning, 135; pregnancy robes, 179–84, 189; maternity cap, 198; discarding of skirts—at night, 142, 280, 282–3; after childbirth, 197; in the *yausa*, 233; taboo regarding skirts, 380

Drums: male ownership of, 21; breaking the taboo on, 32–3

Drunkenness, natives' attitude to, 381

Dual influence of paternal love and matrilineal principle, importance and effects of,
6, 172; tension and friction resulting, 10 ff., 13; domestic aspect of, 18; cross-cousin marriage a reconciling compromise, 81, 83, 88 (*and see under* Marriage); economic aspect of, 110

Dudubile Kautala, 99–100

Dwelling-houses:
Building of, men's and women's work in, 22; help in, 108; gifts requiting this help, 78
Children's sexual pastimes not carried on in, 48, 56
Decorations denoting rank, 27
Interiors and furnishing of, 18
Ownership of, 15, 21
Privacy impossible in, 46
Situation of, 8

Dyeing, 23

Ear-rings, 251, 257

Ears: ideal beauty of, 251; piercing and adornment of, 251–2

Eating: enjoyment of, 372–3; manners associated with, 372–3; privacy preferred, 295, 372

Economic Journal: "Primitive Economics of the Trobriand Islanders" cited, 113 *n.*, 210 *n.*, 214 *n.*

Elopement, 73

Embracing, hugging (*kopo'i*): of infants, 15, 17, 166, 171; of adults, 144

Endogamy, *see* Marriage—Endogamous

Engaged couples: infidelities of, 59; advertisement by, of forthcoming marriage, 59, 66, 71; meals never taken in common by, 64; consent of girl's family, importance of, 73–6

Entertainments, sexual indulgence associated with, 43, 56, 57, 59

Equality of status of men and women, 15, 24, 34, 42

Erotic interest, focus of, 249

Erotic phase of life, sociological importance of, 1

Ethnographical work, methods of, 238–40, 423 ff.

Euphemisms, 376

European physiognomy not admired by the natives, 258

Excrement, insults associated with, 376, 410

486

INDEX

INDEX

497

INDEX

Please remember that this is a library book,
and that it belongs only temporarily to each
person who uses it. Be considerate. Do
not write in this, or any, library book.

DATE DUE

FE 20 '04			
GAYLORD			PRINTED IN U.S.A.